The Victory Lab

★　★　★　★　★　★　★

ALSO BY SASHA ISSENBERG

The Sushi Economy

The Victory Lab

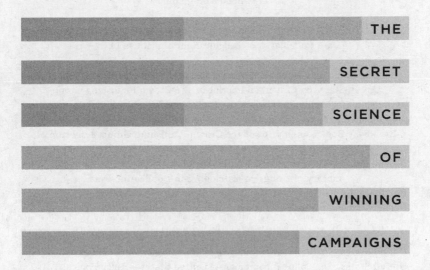

THE
SECRET
SCIENCE
OF
WINNING
CAMPAIGNS

Sasha Issenberg

B \ D \ W \ Y

BROADWAY BOOKS

New York

Library of Congress Cataloging-in-Publication Data
Issenberg, Sasha.
  The victory lab: the secret science of winning campaigns/Sasha Issenberg.
    p. cm.
  1. Internet in political campaigns—United States.   2. Political campaigns—
United States.   3. Political campaigns—Technological innovations—
United States.   4. Political campaigns—United States—Psychological
aspects.   I. Title.

JK2281.I77 2012
324.70973—dc23   2012023774

ISBN 978-0-307-95480-0
eBook ISBN 978-0-307-95481-7

PRINTED IN THE UNITED STATES OF AMERICA

Book design by Jaclyn Reyes
Cover design by Christopher Brand and James Bamford
Cover photograph: selimaksan
Author photograph: David Fields

To my parents,
Bella Brodzki and Henry Issenberg,
for everything

Contents

PROLOGUE — How to win an election without anyone knowing — 1

1 — BLINDED BY POLITICAL SCIENCE — 15

2 — A GAME OF MARGINS — 36

3 — THE NEW HAVEN EXPERIMENTS — 70

4 — THE TWO PERCENT SOLUTION — 87

5 — "YOU MEAN YOU DON'T DO THIS IN POLITICS?" — 107

6 — GEEKS VERSUS THE GURUS — 143

7 — WHEN SHAME PAYS A HOUSE CALL — 181

8 — SHOWDOWN AT THE OASIS — 213

9 — MODELS AND THE MATRIX — 243

10 — THE SOUL OF A NEW MACHINE — 272

EPILOGUE — Pushing the envelope — 302

AFTERWORD — The sovereignty of numbers — 323

POSTSCRIPT — 351

ACKNOWLEDGMENTS — 371

NOTES — 377

INDEX — 393

The Victory Lab

★ ★ ★ ★ ★ ★ ★

PROLOGUE

HOW TO WIN AN ELECTION
WITHOUT ANYONE KNOWING

The ads aired by the two candidates in the 2010 Colorado U.S. Senate race told the story of the ideological war that defined that midterm election. Michael Bennet, a freshman Democrat appointed to replace a man who had become one of Barack Obama's cabinet secretaries, was deeply in hock to a liberal White House. Tea Party Republican challenger Ken Buck was—or so went the punditry and Bennet's attacks—too conservative for the moderate, suburbanizing state.

Meanwhile, one million letters being delivered to Democratic-leaning Coloradoans in the last days of the race made no mention of either candidate, their allegiances, or the issues that separated them. They lacked any allusion to the ideological split riving the nation or reference to the policy consequences of a change in party control of the Senate. The folded pieces of laser-printed white paper were designed to be ugly, with a return address referring to a sender whose name voters were unlikely to recognize. The sender thanked the recipient by first name for having voted in 2008, and then said she looked forward to being able to express such gratitude again after the coming elections. The letter, dispassionate in tone and startlingly personal in content, might have inspired most recipients to dispatch it to a trash can with no strong feeling other than being oddly unsettled by its arrival.

It was not only in Colorado where communications in the last days before the 2010 elections seemed out of whack with such a feral season in American politics. Across the country on the Sunday night before the election, millions of Democrats received an e-mail from Obama's seemingly dormant campaign apparatus, Organizing for America, with a gently worded reminder that they had "made a commitment to vote in this election" and that "the time has come to make good on that commitment. Think about when you'll cast your vote and how you'll get there."

The voters who received either the Colorado letter or the Organizing for America message had likely never encountered anything like them before. At a moment when many candidates, admen, pundits, and organizers thought that the way to get their allies to the polls was to implore them through television ads to consider the election's high stakes and respond in kind, these tactics, designed to go undetected by media coverage, aimed to push buttons that many voters didn't even know they had. The people who had scripted the messages and carefully selected their recipients aimed to exploit eternal human vulnerabilities—such as the desire to fit in or not to be seen as a liar—in order to turn layabouts into voters.

The man who had sent the million letters in white envelopes did the quick math after the Colorado election from his post thousands of miles away. Hal Malchow was a middle-aged Mississippian who had spent his life conniving new ways to win elections, except for a brief detour into securities law that ended when he realized that writing the contracts to guard against complex financial schemes was less fun than trying to hatch them. Now he was playing a different angle, and calculated that the psychological influence he had exerted through his letters would improve turnout among recipients by 2.5 percent. That would mean that his language had created 25,000 new voters, most of them carefully selected to be likely votes for the incumbent. Bennet had lagged Buck for much of the year and had never approached the 50 percent threshold that many experts say is necessary in pre-election polls for an incumbent to expect victory. There was further evidence of a gap in partisan enthusiasms: at the time the polls opened, 74,000 fewer Democrats had returned their early-vote ballots than Republicans. But on election day, something was pushing Bennet even with Buck, and by the time Malchow turned in for the night the two candidates were separated by only hundreds of votes.

The next morning, he awoke to good news from the west. Bennet had pulled ahead of Buck, and was on his way to winning the race by 15,000 votes. His victory would help to keep the Senate in Democratic control. Malchow was having fun.

* * * * *

COLORADO WAS ONE of the rare sources of cheer for Democrats in an otherwise disastrous set of midterm elections in 2010. Party wise men were eager to mine grand lessons from the Rockies; if only they could figure out what made Colorado resist a national conservative wave, they could use Bennet's strategy as a model for Obama's reelection two years later. "The Bennet thing was pretty instructive," Obama's chief strategist, David Axelrod, told the *National Journal* in a postmortem. "The contrast he drew with Buck was very meaningful."

The people who explain politics for a living—the politicians themselves, their advisers, the media who cover them—love to reach tidy conclusions like this one. Elections are decided by charismatic personalities, strategic maneuvers, the power of rhetoric, the zeitgeist of the political moment. The explainers cloak themselves in loose-fitting theories because they offer a narrative comfort, unlike the more honest acknowledgment that elections hinge on the motivations of millions of individual human beings and their messy, illogical, often unknowable psychologies.

In fact, Bennet could have won the Senate seat because of major demographic changes and ideological fault lines around delicate cultural issues, or because of a single letter that exerted a subtle dose of peer pressure on its recipients—or hundreds of other factors big and small that played a part in changing people's minds or getting them to vote.

The political craft thrives on that ambiguity. It allows just about anyone involved to take credit for good results or attribute blame for poor ones, confident of never being proven wrong. After a positive result on election night, everything a winning campaign did looks brilliant. When a campaign loses, consultants usually blame the candidate or the moment—and there rarely seem to be professional consequences for those who had set the strategy or tactics. Longevity, as well as the aura of wisdom that comes from it, is a political operative's most valued trait.

Over a generation, helping Americans choose their leaders has grown into a $6-billion-per-year industry. But the new profession hums along on a mixture of tradition and inertia, unable to learn from its successes or its failures. The tools available to campaign operatives can do little to explain what makes someone vote—and few of the people toiling inside campaign war rooms seem disturbed by this gap in their knowledge. "It's probably the only industry in the world where there's no market research," says Dave Carney, the top strategist on the launch of Texas governor Rick Perry's presidential campaign. "Most things are done with only one check," says Steve Rosenthal, a Democratic consultant who works closely on campaigns with many of the left's top interest groups. "People's guts."

The unheralded arrival of the gently threatening letters in Colorado mailboxes marked the maturation of a tactical revolution against that kind of gut politics. The first stirrings had come a decade earlier, in the wake of the 2000 presidential vote, which shifted on election night from a contest between electoral strategists to a tussle among lawyers. What seemed at the time to be a low-stakes election would have a major effect on the way campaigns were waged. The narrow, almost accidental quality of George W.

Bush's victory—decided by 537 votes in Florida, or really just one on the Supreme Court—provoked a reexamination of where votes come from.

Seemingly small boosts of two or three percentage points quickly became indispensable components of a victory formula, and the intellectual hierarchy of thinking about campaigns changed accordingly. Turnout, the unsexy practice of mobilizing known supporters to vote, could no longer be dismissed by campaign leadership as little more than a logistically demanding civics project to be handled by junior staff or volunteers. Campaigns could not obsess only over changing minds through mass media. "Many strategists had been believers that 'big things are all that matter in campaigns'—the big events, the big TV spots, the debates, the convention and the VP pick," says Adrian Gray, who worked in the Bush White House and on both of Bush's campaigns. "After 2000, for the first time a lot of people who shared that sentiment started to believe that there is a lot that can be done on the margins."

The result has been an ongoing, still unsettled battle between the two parties for analytical supremacy, a fight that Bush data analyst Alex Gage likens to an "information arms race." A new era of statistical accountability has been introduced to a trade governed largely by anecdote and lore. Each side has its own sobriquets for the intellectual rebels—Karl Rove boasted of his "propellerheads" and Rick Perry's campaign of its "eggheads," while those on the left were happy to call themselves "geeks." They have made their cases in the PowerPoint palimpsest that inevitably arrives when an industry quickly learns to appreciate its own data. Suddenly, the crucial divide within the consulting class is not between Democrats and Republicans, or the establishment and outsiders, but between these new empiricists and the old guard.

The latter can be found in both parties, and it was a constellation of new-guard academics and political consultants on the left who had mastered the psychological tool used in the Colorado mailer. Six years before, one of them had first had the idea of ominously reminding citizens that whether or not they vote is a matter of public record. In the next few elections, the language and presentation had been refined through serendipitous collaboration unusual in politics, flowing effortlessly between operatives and academic researchers who previously had neither the opportunity nor inclination to work together. Functioning in a growing laboratory culture, they had jerry-rigged a research-and-design function onto an industry that long resisted it. And by the summer of 2010, they had perfected the politics of shame. It was only a matter of time before a desperate campaign, or interest group, would summon the audacity to deploy it.

★　★　★　★　★

TWO DAYS AFTER the 2010 election, while Colorado election officials were still counting ballots, Hal Malchow sat in his office in Washington, D.C., pleased to see Bennet on his way to victory. A sign hanging on the wall neatly summarized the self-satisfaction Malchow felt at moments like these: *All progress in the world depends on the unreasonable man.* He had spent more than three years obsessing over the technique he had used in his mailers. He had pored over the scholarly research that supported the use of what psychologists called social pressure, and he had finally persuaded the liberal group Women's Voices Women's Vote to overcome its fear of a backlash and send out letters to Colorado households likely to support Bennet but requiring an extra push to get to the polls.

The research had begun five years earlier. In 2005, a Michigan political consultant named Mark Grebner—whose glasses, stringy parted hair, eccentric polymathy, and relentless tinkering earned him comparisons to Ben Franklin—had written to two Yale political science professors who he knew were interested in finding new ways to motivate people to vote. The next year, they collaborated on an experiment in Michigan in which they sent voters a copy of their own public vote histories, along with their neighbors', and a threat to deliver an updated set after the election. It was marvelously effective, increasing turnout among those who received it by

20 percent. But no candidate or group wanted to be associated with a tactic that looked a lot like bullying—and a bit like blackmail.

How to muffle such a potent weapon so that it could be used in the course of regular campaigns became an obsession of the Analyst Institute, a consortium quietly founded in 2006 by liberal groups looking to coordinate their increasingly ambitious research agendas. The Analyst Institute was a hybrid of classic Washington traits: the intellectual ambition of a think tank, the legal privacy of a for-profit consulting firm, and the hush-hush sensibility of a secret society. But its culture derived from the laboratory. The Analyst Institute was founded on a faith in the randomized-control experiment, which had migrated in the middle of the twentieth century from agriculture to medicine as a unique instrument for isolating the effects of individual fertilizers and vaccines. Social scientists later adopted field experiments, transforming research in everything from credit-card marketing to developing-world economics. Around 2000, such experiments found their way into politics, with voters as their unwitting guinea pigs. Over a decade these "prescription drug trials for democracy," in the words of Rock the Vote president Heather Smith, have upended much of what the political world thought it knew about how voters' minds work, and dramatically changed the way that campaigns approach, cajole, and manipulate them.

The Analyst Institute's founding director, a psychologist named Todd Rogers, always liked to remind people that these behavioral science interventions couldn't alter a race's fundamental dynamics. No technique could do that; a good candidate or a bad economy would still set the conditions of an election. But experimental insights could decide close races—by nudging turnout up two points here, six points there—and none has proven as powerful and promising as Grebner's social-pressure breakthrough.

It took three years of trial and error by academics and operatives, including Malchow, until he settled on softer, more friendly language—thanking people for having voted in the past as opposed to threatening them if they didn't in the future—that delivered impressive results in a randomized experiment. During a test conducted during New Jersey's

2009 gubernatorial elections, such a letter had increased turnout among voters who received it by 2.5 percent. Through other tests, Malchow had found that many political messages were most effective when delivered in understated white typed envelopes, as opposed to multicolor glossy mailers, and so he packaged the Colorado social-pressure letters in a way he hoped would resemble an urgent notice from the taxman. "People want information, they don't want advertising," Malchow said. "When they see our fingerprints on this stuff, they believe it less."

The fact that Americans were tiring of political communication was, in many ways, a testament to the success of a profession Malchow had done much to develop. His métier was the direct-mail piece, the postbox-stuffing brochure so often dismissed as junk mail. That form, and Malchow's career, had emerged in the long mid-1980s shadow of television and relegated Malchow to a second-class status in the consulting world's star system. Direct mail is a staple of the category of campaign activity known as "voter contact," distinguished—as compared with media advertising—by its ability to hit a preselected individual with precision. This is the way most voters interact directly with campaigns: the phone calls that interrupt dinner, the knock on the door from a young canvasser, leaflets stuffing the mailbox as election day approaches, personalized text-message blasts. Even as these voter-contact activities often go ignored by the people who write about politics, campaigns continue to spend money on these tactics, and lavishly—as much as a half-billion dollars per presidential campaign season.

Political mail has been perhaps the least glamorous of all the voter-contact tools. At a young age, however, Malchow was drawn to the fact that brochures, unlike broadcast ads or rally coverage on the nightly news, could be unexpectedly personal. Working with mail gave him a distinctive perspective on the electorate—which he saw as an array of individuals rather than a puzzle of blocs and zones—and the ambition to measure the effect of his work on a similar scale. As a result, Malchow had ended up playing a key role in the two most radical innovations in political communication: the use of field experiments to measure cause and effect, and the so-called microtargeting that allows campaigns to confidently address individual voters instead of the broader public.

But even as Malchow found a growing circle of allies in academia and liberal interest groups, partisan campaigns remained skeptical of ideas that would radically disrupt the way they thought about how votes are won. For years, when Malchow couldn't convince campaigns to use the microtargeting techniques he said would help them locate otherwise unidentifiable pockets of persuadable voters, he paid for them himself, at a total loss of around eight hundred thousand dollars. The challenge of innovation came to excite him more than the predictable terms of partisan conflict. In fact, Malchow's giddiness—perceptible as his eyes open wide behind his glasses, and his words break into a gallop—emerged most readily not when he was plotting how to win a specific race for a candidate but when he was figuring out a way to run all campaigns more intelligently.

Even amid the low points of 2009 and 2010 for Democrats, Malchow was heartened to see that the party's few successful campaigns were ones that had some of the most creative analytics on their side. In Nevada, Senator Harry Reid's pollster, Mark Mellman, tested the campaign's messages through a continuous cycle of randomized online experiments, allowing him to see which people were actually moved by specific arguments, not only those who told a survey taker that they might be. In the same race, one independent group backing Reid used data on how neighborhoods voted on ballot initiatives (which show voter opinions on controversial issues like marijuana, taxes, and eminent domain) to define the political ideology of election precincts with a nuance impossible to gauge in partisan vote totals. Along Lake Tahoe, which has become home to wealthy California refugees, Reid's allies defined pockets of rich libertarians they thought were winnable. So they downplayed Reid's statewide message portraying Republican challenger Sharron Angle as an antigovernment extremist intent on dismantling Social Security—a stance the Tahoe targets could in fact find appealing—and instead played up her conservative views on social issues. Reid won the state by five points, boosted by expanded margins in upscale redoubts like lakefront Incline Village.

Data-driven methods were carrying the day in parts of the political process where Malchow hadn't even imagined they would have a use. When Al Franken's lawyers began the 2008 Minnesota U.S. Senate recount by pondering which of ten thousand challenged absentee ballots they should work to have counted, they brought one of the campaign's microtargeting experts into the strategy sessions. Andy Bechhoefer ran each of the disputed voters through the campaign's database, which used a complex mix of personal and demographic information, along with polling, to give each voter a score of 1 to 100, predicting his or her likelihood of supporting Franken over his opponent, Norm Coleman. Armed with these scores, Bechhoefer was able not only to point lawyers to the unopened envelopes most likely to yield Franken votes but also to identify which of the secretary of state's categories for excluding votes had put them in a rejected pile. With that knowledge, Franken's attorneys drafted expansive legal arguments that covered entire categories of problems instead of merely contesting individual ballots in a piecemeal fashion.

Bechhoefer recounted this experience to one of the regular lunch sessions hosted by the Analyst Institute, each detail in the scheme transfixing Malchow. Step by step, Bechhoefer illustrated how lawyers were primed to defend absentee ballots that had been challenged for change-of-address discrepancies (which leaned Democratic) while hoping that those with witness-signature problems (tilting Republican) remained uncounted. At times, Franken's lawyers watched their adversary challenge ballots they knew were almost certain to be votes for Coleman, only because the Republicans had not used such sophisticated methods to model them. Over an eight-month recount, Franken gradually turned a 477-vote deficit on election day into a 312-vote lead when Coleman's last court challenge was exhausted in the summer of 2009, giving Democrats their sixtieth senator. "Everybody in the Analyst Institute was grinning ear to ear—what a triumph," says Malchow. "I was like a Cheshire cat. I thought this was the coolest thing I ever heard."

* * * * *

THE POLITICAL BOOKSHELF is filled with works that have heralded epochal change: 1972 had *The New Style in Election Campaigns,* while 1981 brought *The New Kingmakers,* which profiled the first generation of political consultants. Every time a fresh communication technology has become available, those who practice politics have been quick to announce that elections would be remade in its image. "A campaign rally is three people around a television set," Democratic media consultant Bob Shrum, who made his money from TV ads, boasted in 1986. A decade and a half later, Dick Morris predicted that television-focused media consultants like Shrum were about to be eclipsed by an emerging cadre who communicated online. "The current crop are like silent film stars—their skills will no longer be valuable in the Internet era," Morris told the *Washington Post* in 2000. "They're good at condensation, at the 30-second spot. The new environment of the Internet calls for elaboration, for expansiveness."

Neither consultant's prediction has been entirely right, ignoring less flashy but more influential shifts in how campaigns win votes. The scientific revolution in American electoral politics has relied on lots of technology, particularly to assemble and sift through large databases, but its most lasting impact may be a resurgence in lo-fi tactics. The genius alchemists behind microtargeting spend their days deciding where candidates should send postcards. A gubernatorial campaign in Texas conducted meticulous experiments to learn which was a more worthwhile use of its time and budget: sending the candidate to meet with a newspaper editorial board or to a barbecue restaurant filled with one hundred supporters. Within the headquarters of a presidential campaign widely heralded as the most technologically advanced in history, some strategists think their most impressive accomplishment wasn't their iPhone app but the time when a staffer figured out how to buy ads on a bus whose route he was certain was used by voters the campaign was trying to reach.

By 2012, it has become impossible to correctly interpret campaign strategy without understanding the revolution in tactics. Some of the early decisions that shaped how the presidential race would be run were built on technical innovations invisible to the outside world. Texas governor Rick Perry considered withdrawing from select primary-season debates in part because the social scientists he had invited to run large-scale randomizedcontrol experiments in an earlier race concluded that the candidate could have his biggest impact not through media appearances but through localized travel to targeted states. (In retrospect, no social scientist could have calculated how atrocious a debater Perry turned out to be.) Former Massachusetts governor Mitt Romney, who a decade earlier had been the first candidate in the country to use microtargeting formulas, knew he could hold back on committing resources to identify voters in Iowa because he had algorithms that would instantly tell him how every caucus-goer would be likely to vote even before they had made up their minds. And in Chicago, Barack Obama's aides looking to expand the playing field against their Republican opponent thought they might be able to use psychological tricks— which had significantly reduced the cost of registering new voters—to remake the electorate in certain states in a way that could permanently confuse red and blue.

Electoral politics has quietly entered the twenty-first century by undoing its greatest excesses of the late twentieth. Just as architects have atoned for the vainglories of their field's high-modernist period by pummeling its concrete superblocks and putting sleeping porches and Main Street–style shopping strips in their place, some electioneers are starting to conclude that political campaigns lost something when they became warped by broadcast waves. The campaign world's most sophisticated new thinking about who votes and why, informed by an intuitive understanding of the political brain, has naturally turned attention to the individual as the fundamental unit of our politics. The revolutionaries are taking a politics distended by television's long reach and restoring it to a human scale—even delivering, at times, a perfectly disarming touch of intimacy.

Our campaigns have not grown more humanistic because our candidates are more benevolent or their policy concerns more salient. In fact, over the last decade, public confidence in institutions—big business, the church, media, government—has declined dramatically. The political conversation has privileged the nasty and trivial. Yet during that period, election seasons have awakened with a new culture of volunteer activity. This cannot be credited to a politics inspiring people to hand over their time but rather to campaigns, newly alert to the irreplaceable value of a human touch, seeking it out. Finally campaigns are learning to quantify the ineffable—the value of a neighbor's knock, of a stranger's call, the delicate condition of being undecided—and isolate the moment where a behavior can be changed, or a heart won. Campaigns have started treating voters like people again.

1

BLINDED BY POLITICAL SCIENCE

On February 27, 1919, a radio and buzzer operator at Camp Hancock near Augusta, Georgia, took to a typewriter and composed a message to his superiors requesting a discharge. Sergeant First Class Harold Foote Gosnell was just six months into his military service. He had entered the army the previous fall, answering a draft notice just days after earning his bachelor's degree from his home-town campus, the University of Rochester. As soon as he earned a license as a radio operator, commercial second grade, which required him to type twenty words a minute, he wrote military officials with the news. Eager to be shipped out, he bragged that he had also mastered the flag-signaling languages known as wigwag and semaphore. But by the time Gosnell was called to report for duty with the 47th Service Company at Hancock in mid-September, there wasn't much war left on the calendar for him. Six months later, as the duties for a signal officer were receding, the obliga-tions of a widow's son came to the fore. In February, Gosnell's mother

wrote him from upstate New York to report that she had been sent to the
Clifton Springs Sanitarium on account of her heart trouble. "Doctor says
it's valvular and muscular. Sometimes I can hardly get my breath and sometimes my heart pains me," she wrote. "So that I think you ought to come
home as soon as possible if you want to see me."

Gosnell, twenty-two, was granted an honorable discharge, and left for
his mother's bedside. He had never planned on staying long in the military,
anyway. From Hancock he had applied to graduate schools to study the
new field of political science, but knew he couldn't afford to attend any
of them unless he received some financial support. Gosnell came from a
working-class family and inherited its puritan temperament. One grandfa-
ther had been a Civil War veteran, and Harold's father (who died when he
was four) a vehement prohibitionist who joined the Republicans because
they were "the party of the drys" and railed against the Rochester Cham-
ber of Commerce dinner as "an annual drunk."

Eight-year-old Harold had been captivated by the 1904 presidential
election, which pitted two New Yorkers against one another. Gosnell was
drawn to the swashbuckling profile of the Republican incumbent, Theodore Roosevelt, over Democrat Alton Parker, chief judge of the state's appeals court, and learned to hum the party's campaign ditty: *Farewell, Judge
Parker/Farewell to you/Teddy's in the White House/And he'll stay there too.* In
high school, he was a serious student and prolific artist, contributing hand-
drawn covers with images of columns and coliseums for his high school's
Latin-language magazine, *Vox Populi*. When it became time to focus his
attention, Gosnell knew he wanted to study how votes were won, and few
places were as ripe for examination as Chicago.

In 1919, Chicago was already the country's second-largest municipal-
ity—a lakefront skyline casting an ever-expanding shadow over a farrago
of stockyards, bungalows, and rail lines unspooling across the Midwest—
and had the lively political scene that a capital of monopolists and mobsters
would deserve. "In spite of the city's bad reputation for graft, bootlegging,
gangster killings, election frauds, racketeering, and street violence," Gos-

nell would later write, "buildings went up, superhighways were built, and the functions of an urban metropolis somehow were performed."

That fall, Gosnell arrived in Hyde Park, where stone quadrangles had been planted to give the University of Chicago the dignified air of England's legacy institutions. The university had opened its doors in 1892, one the first schools to do so with the declared goal of welcoming graduate students in search of Ph.D.s, still new to American academia and a matter of scant emphasis at prestigious old colleges like Harvard, Yale, and Columbia. Chicago had the architecture of an old place, which made the young school feel as far from the bustle of the Loop as Oxford did from London. Along the Midway, where the World's Columbian Exposition of 1893 had unveiled Chicago as the model modern city, the school's Harper Memorial Library had recently been erected as a medieval castle. Its crown studded with crenellated turrets, the building seemed to reflect a time-honored model of academic research. Those who studied society had typically done so from the comfort of a carrel, relying on historical documents to bolster their theories of how people live.

But at Chicago, tradition stopped at aesthetics. Through their work, young social scientists were constantly scheming to pull the university deeper into the scrum of the industrial metropolis just a cable-car ride away. "You have been told to choose problems wherever you can find musty stacks of routine records based on trivial schedules prepared by tired bureaucrats and filled out by reluctant applicants for aid or fussy do-gooders or indifferent clerks," sociologist Robert E. Park warned his graduate students. Instead, he said, they should "sit in the lounges of the luxury hotels and on the doorsteps of the flophouses," to observe their subjects in real time. "Gentlemen, go get the seat of your pants dirty in real research." A shelf of the books produced by Park's protégés throughout the 1920s and 1930s gave shape to the idea of a "Chicago school" of scholarship, but they could be mistaken, at quick glance, for a rack of dime-store novels: *The Gang, The Hobo, The Gold Coast and the Slum, The Taxi-Dance Hall, Hotel Life, Vice in Chicago.*

Gosnell, a small man who preferred his glasses round and his hair in a slick, parted wad, was dispirited to find little such adventurism in his department. Political science had few graduate students, and Gosnell had trouble finding friends among his peers. He had little affection for the department's chair, Harry Pratt Judson, who also happened to be the university's president and governed his department by terse memos on presidential stationery. With a background in constitutional law and diplomatic history, Judson had helped to establish one of the country's first departments devoted to "political science," an assertively modern name designed to set the new study of statecraft apart from the historically minded discipline once known as political economy.

But Gosnell felt his department was atrophying under Judson's leadership. Like many of the early tribunes of the new discipline, Judson had little interest in actually bringing scientistic authority to bear on politics. "I do not like the term political science," outgoing Princeton president and New Jersey governor-elect Woodrow Wilson had said at the 1910 conference of the recently established American Political Science Association. Human relationships, Wilson told the gathering at a St. Louis hotel, "are not in any proper sense the subject matter of science. They are the stuff of insight and sympathy and spiritual comprehension." The previous year, Wilson's predecessor as the association's president had drawn a related, if less mystical, distinction. "We are limited by the impossibility of experiment," said Harvard president Abbott Lawrence Lowell. "Politics is an observational, not an experimental science."

In 1923, Judson finally relinquished his chairmanship, fanning Gosnell's hopes that his department could at last modernize. The selection of Judson's replacement may have looked like a default choice: Charles E. Merriam was the department's only full-time professor. But he was also a giant in Chicago life. A native Iowan, Merriam had studied at Columbia, whose president Seth Low had stepped down from his office after winning the 1901 election to be the second mayor of the newly consolidated New York City. Merriam watched Low's campaign closely and saw him as a model for the engaged public intellectual. Upon arriving in Chicago, Merriam quickly began lending his expertise to policymakers, blessing the initiatives of the modernizing metropolis with a scholar's kiss. In 1905, he was asked by the City Club of Chicago to research municipal revenues. Three years later, after business leaders recruited architect Daniel Burnham to draw up a city plan, the mayor appointed Merriam to the Chicago Harbor Commission with a charge to implement a new waterfront agenda.

The idea that academic experts could tutor politicians reflected a popular Progressive era attitude, and Merriam became something of a utility man to reformers intent on fixing the broken city. He was elected to the city council in 1909 as a Republican and immediately agitated for the creation of a Commission to Investigate City Expenditures. The Merriam Commission uncovered graft and corruption involving party machines, winning its namesake few friends among his council colleagues but encouraging business leaders to view him as the kind of man they would like to see in charge. In 1911, Merriam ran for mayor, proudly publishing the names of his campaign contributors even though no law required him to. He won the Republican primary by antagonizing party bosses who never warmed to their nominee, but he narrowly lost the general election.

Still, the professor-turned-politician found himself energized by this new world. For Merriam, city government was also something of a refuge from academic politics, with slightly grander stakes. In 1919, he again sought the mayoralty, challenging William Hale "Big Bill" Thompson, a charmingly corrupt incumbent able to easily dismiss Merriam in the Republican primary. He returned to the university embittered by his decade at city hall, caught between two party machines and what he saw as the institutionalized perfidy of both, raising questions and fixing resentments that would inspire Merriam's research agenda for the rest of his life.

To the extent that scholars believed they could explain why elections turned out the way they did, it was because they thought they understood how parties worked. Those who studied politics tended to study institutions, such as courts and legislatures, and the institutions of campaigns were political parties. Parties were an unmistakably important force in nineteenth-century politics, which Merriam knew intimately: by keeping the Union intact, the Republican Party had earned his father's undying fealty, which he passed down to his son. During the 1896 election, Charles and his brother teased their father for being so reliant on Republican Party doctrine that they joked he had to go to the train depot in their small Iowa town and wait for the newspapers to arrive before he could be sure of what he believed. When Charles got to Chicago, he saw that in big cities, parties—with their clearly delineated hierarchies of county chairmen and precinct officers interlocked with neighborhood ethnic communities—were not merely organizations that told voters what to think but also delivery devices for the patronage spoils that won their loyalty.

But thanks in part to the efforts of reformers like Merriam, parties were weakening their hold on the political process. In 1907, Oregon became the first state to have its senators directly elected by citizens, instead of by state legislatures that often just rubber-stamped the picks of party bosses. In 1908, Chicago implemented primary elections for city offices, replacing party nominating conventions. Merriam was quick to realize that these primaries heralded an important shift in the culture of politics, as voters could no longer rely on party leaders to pick their standard-bearers. As a reformer, Merriam was encouraged by this, and as an academic he thought the shift of power to the citizenry made elections ripe for serious study. He sent a questionnaire to the burgeoning band of political scientists nationwide to get their opinions on what the actual effects of this more democratic system would be. "Does the direct primary bring out a larger vote than the convention system?" was one of Merriam's nine queries.

The political scientists had little insight to offer Merriam. Because they had been so intent on unlocking the dynamics of institutions, they had largely ignored voters themselves. There was no governing theory of where people got their information and how they processed it, or the relative role that parties, issues, and candidate profiles played in their minds as they weighed their choices before election day. In fact, political science could do little to explain why people voted at all when the law did not require it. But to a first-year graduate student drawn to the rough-and-tumble of urban politics, nothing impressed like a professor looking for answers to these questions, and demonstrating equal fluency in scholarly footnotes and ward-by-ward returns. "Naturally, I took every course that Merriam had to offer," Harold Gosnell later wrote.

The same forces that had foiled Merriam's political ambitions were the ones that most fascinated Gosnell. He wrote his thesis on Thomas Platt, the New York senator whose machinations during sessions known as "Platt's Sunday School Class" at the Fifth Avenue Hotel made him for a generation the dominant force in the state's Republican politics. Gosnell said his goal was to mine "the social background, the personal qualities, and the technique of a typical state political boss." That meant looking past the dynamics of institutions and into the motives of the individuals who drove them, and it meant reaching into psychology for tools foreign to political science. "What was there, first in Platt's personality, in his general behavior, that led men to think that he could 'do things'?" Gosnell wrote. The University of Chicago Press was interested in publishing *Boss Platt and His New York Machine* but unwilling to finance it, so Gosnell arranged a discount rate through his nephew's brother's publishing firm and paid to have it printed himself.

Gosnell received his Ph.D. in 1922, and Merriam approached him shortly after to offer a post as an instructor. Merriam was already deep into his efforts to rebuild the department from its decay under Judson; he had made clear he would not run again for political office and now hoped to use the university as his sole perch for improving local politics and government. He established a Social Science Research Council, with the goal of producing scholarship across disciplines—economics and sociology, in addition to political science—that would finally conjoin the university's work with the life of the city. "I accepted the offer with alacrity," Gosnell later recalled.

Gosnell affectionately called Merriam "the Chief" and the two men shared an intimate love of urban politics, but a methodological gap was opening up between them. Gosnell had taken graduate courses in statistics and mathematics and was eager to apply numbers to the political questions that interested him. "While Charles E. Merriam gave lip service to quantitative, psychological, and empirical research he was essentially a philosopher dealing with ideas and an activist dealing with programs," Gosnell wrote. "While he liked to see others strive to be scientific, he personally was a philosopher high in the clouds spinning out ideas, not bothered by the mundane search for facts."

In the spring of 1923, Merriam approached Gosnell with an idea for a joint research project that would merge the older man's activist agenda with the younger's interest in modern research methods. Chicago voters had just booted Big Bill Thompson for a Democratic judge named William E. Dever in a mayoral election that seemed to dominate citywide attention. Indeed, the conversation in political circles focused on the fact that turnout was surprisingly high. But Merriam, fueled by intellectual curiosity and residual bitterness over his own loss to Thompson, turned his attention to those who never cast a ballot. During his own campaigns, Merriam had worked on expanding the electorate by recruiting new voters, especially among new immigrant arrivals who had yet to fall under the machine's spell. Now the city had about 1.4 million adults, but only 900,000 were on the electoral rolls; among them, 723,000 cast a vote for either Thompson or Dever. It galled Merriam, as it had during his own campaigns, that barely half of the city's eligible voters had been involved in picking their leader; the apathy of the rest helped keep the machines in power. He suggested to Gosnell that they investigate the reasons the nearly 700,000 nonvoters had for opting out—and what might be done to lure them into the process.

Gosnell prepared a survey to ask them, relying on U.S. Census data to guide him in each of the city's fifty wards toward a representative mix of respondents. Gosnell and Merriam decided to use a hybrid survey, which would have multiple-choice questions but leave room for free answers, an approach they believed should yield a healthy batch of data but also qualitative responses with richer texture. All interviews would be done face-to-face at people's homes, so Gosnell had to train graduate students to navigate the city's racially and ethnically complex neighborhoods, where he worried they might not find a warm welcome for outside researchers asking nosy questions. Gosnell dispatched a Swedish-speaking student to a heavily Swedish neighborhood, and hired a Polish interpreter elsewhere. (Of the sixteen doors the professor knocked on himself as part of the project, one happened to belong to writer Ben Hecht.) The researchers' forms were then coded, and the data moved onto punch cards so they could be tallied by machine. The university did not have the proper equipment, so Gosnell went to city hall and found a clerk in the comptroller's office willing to run the cards on his own time for one dollar an hour. When Gosnell looked over the six thousand answers his students had gathered, he was pleased by one particular sign of their diligence. Those assigned to the city's so-called Black Belt, where Gosnell had feared that the response rate would founder, had been so aggressive that African-Americans now overwhelmed the sample. Gosnell removed some of them to maintain the delicate demographic equilibrium essential to the project's credibility.

Gosnell's findings, with edits by Merriam, were assembled under both men's names in *Non-Voting: Causes and Methods of Control.* Published by the University of Chicago Press in August 1924, the book—released just months before a presidential election—received national attention for trying to explain the fact that women's suffrage had not dramatically increased voter participation. (Gosnell found twice as many women as men who didn't vote.) But Gosnell's conclusions, that "general indifference" led people to stay home, made less of an impact than his technique. It was the first major political science study to rely on random sampling in a way that broke down the sample by different demographic attributes.

"If scientific methods seem hitherto to have found too little favor with American politicians, political scientists must admit that they themselves are largely to blame," Harvard professor A. N. Holcombe wrote in a short but enthusiastic article in the *American Political Science Review.* "But on the basis of this first experiment at Chicago it ought to be possible," Holcombe suggested, to draw conclusions about elections "with all the assurance of a chemist proving the quality of a new paint-remover or a biologist testing a germicide."

Gosnell was already thinking in those terms. He had begun meeting with social psychologists who recommended tools that would allow him to find out what, if anything, could change nonvoters' behavior. The psychologists explained the rudiments of a field experiment: Gosnell could introduce what they called "controlled stimuli," in this case reminders of a coming election, and then measure their effect. By setting up a control group, whose members did not receive the treatment, and comparing their vote performance against the rest, Gosnell would be able to measure whether various appeals could turn people into voters.

This was the scientific method at work, and despite their title no political scientist appeared to have ever tried such an approach. Gosnell had observed nonvoters and had theories about their behavior based on why they said they did not participate. Now he became convinced that only a randomized-control experiment would allow him to see if anything could change that. This ambitious agenda was making Gosnell's research a lot more expensive than the typical office work practiced by traditional politics scholars. The 1923 poll had cost five thousand dollars. Even in Judson's absence, getting the administration of Robert Maynard Hutchins, one of his successors, to back research forays into the messy world of urban politics was not easy at a school Hutchins was elevating into a global citadel of canonical study. "We were hopeful that democracy could be made to work," Gosnell wrote. "But President Hutchins thought otherwise. All worthwhile ideas were to be found in the Great Books. Social science research in a metropolis was trivial."

But the Chief had his own sources of money and so started shaking the trees for his protégé, approaching his former campaign donors and business leaders. The most lucrative avenue was the Rockefeller family, whom Merriam reached through Dr. Beardsley Ruml, a psychologist, PR man, and Macy's department store official who as a Roosevelt administration official later helped design the country's first withholding system for federal income taxes. Gosnell was dazzled by Ruml, privately sketching caricatures showing the "financial genius as bargain basement statue of Buddha," able to bring Rockefeller cash into Merriam's account to support further research.

Gosnell conceived his experiment as a two-stage study: the first would measure whether citizens who were not registered could be pressured to sign up, and the second would test what could be done to get already registered voters to turn out at a higher rate. Gosnell identified six thousand adult citizens scattered across twelve Chicago zones, and arbitrarily divided them into two groups, checking to ensure that they looked demographically similar. One group would be his treatment sample and the other his control. "The study was aimed to give an answer to the question whether the non-voter is such by a deliberate act of will or whether he is a non-voter from ignorance but not a deficiency of public spirit or alienation," Gosnell later wrote.

In the fall of 1924, Gosnell sent postcards emphasizing the importance of registering to vote before the presidential election that November. (In addition to English, Gosnell drafted versions in Polish, Czech, and Italian.) The postcards had their intended effect: people who received them were nine percentage points more likely to register. Then Gosnell prepared another set of two postcards for the 1,700 voters who were unmoved by the first appeal, one with another nonpartisan message about the urgency of registration and the other with a cartoon picturing nonvoters as "slackers who fail their country when needed," according to the caption. Both pushed people to register at a higher rate than the original control group. In the end, 75 percent of those who received at least one of Gosnell's cards ended up registering, while only 65 percent of nonrecipients did. He had put about three hundred new voters on the city's rolls who wouldn't have been there otherwise.

The next February, Chicago would elect aldermen, as the fifty members of its city council were known, and Gosnell set his sights on the nearly

2,200 new voters who had registered after receiving one of his notices. (Most, he knew, would have registered without his intervention.) Gosnell drew up another cartoon, this time depicting "the honest but apathetic citizen as the friend of the corrupt politician." Again Gosnell left his mark on the election: 57 percent of those who got the cartoon turned out to vote for alderman, compared with 48 percent of those who didn't.

Gosnell did his calculations by hand, and as he looked more closely at these numbers, he realized that his mailings were most persuasive among new residents, who Gosnell concluded had few other sources of information on how to vote, and in districts where party organization was weakest. In demographic terms, they had the most impact on "the native-born colored women and the women born in Italy," wrote Gosnell. The reason, he found, was that the League of Women Voters was directing most of its attention toward native-born white women and little toward minorities. Gosnell's conclusions were obvious—mobilization efforts can have the biggest impact in places where little else is pushing voters to the polls— but no one had ever before quantified them.

It was likely the first field experiment ever conducted in the social sciences outside psychology, and it was well received when published in book form, as *Getting Out the Vote*, in 1927. Political scientist George Catlin wrote that Gosnell's study "has the high merit of being precisely a scientific social experiment." This time Gosnell's innovation jumped from scholarly journals into the news pages. "This study is not only a model of careful method in a virgin area of political exploration," Phillips Bradley wrote in a *New York Herald Tribune* review, "but offers some pretty plain evidence that what has here been done privately in the case of a few thousand voters should become a regular part of our official election procedure."

But Gosnell never ran another experiment. In the 1930s, he turned his attention to pioneering studies in black politics and machine organizations, goaded on by Merriam's continued bitterness about the forces he believed had unfairly denied him his place at city hall. "Perhaps Mencken is right," Gosnell consoled his mentor. "The people usually vote for crooks."

Despite the enthusiasm that greeted Gosnell's method for studying campaigns, no one tried to copy him, replicate his study, or build upon it. After printing Gosnell's article, the *American Political Science Review* did not publish another finding from a randomized field experiment for a half century. During that time, political science grew into a major discipline obsessed with studying voters and elections, but to do so it returned to the library and stayed off the street.

★ ★ ★ ★ ★

THE FEW EFFORTS by political scientists to revive Gosnell's experimental technique proved evanescent. In 1954, University of Michigan professor Samuel Eldersveld used new statistical methods to dispatch mail, phone calls, and in-person canvassing visits across eight hundred Ann Arbor residents according to a random-assignment procedure, and then measured their relative effectiveness on turnout. Eldersveld's experiment had more impact on local politics—three years later, he succeeded where Merriam had failed and was elected mayor of the college town—than on the academy. Afterward, entire decades would pass without a single randomized field study about political behavior being published in a scholarly journal.

Political scientists didn't take to experiments in part because they knew that they would never control the laboratory. The party machines that dominated most American political activity lacked the self-examining impulse, and were unlikely to welcome ivory-tower visitors into their clubhouses. Meanwhile, campaign finance laws and the universities' nonprofit tax status made it hard for them to do anything on their own that, even inadvertently, advanced the interests of a specific party or candidate.

Political scientists instead happily flapped about in deep pools of new data generated by a postwar revolution in research methods. The ubiquity of household telephones made large-scale survey-taking possible, and increased computing power permitted complex statistical regressions.

Specialists in the new field of polling developed protocols for assembling interview samples that would reflect the broader population, and for scripting survey questions to make sure they elicited meaningful responses. Everyone started doing polls, but quality was inconsistent. In 1948, most pollsters flubbed their electoral predictions—leading to the *Chicago Tribune*'s morning-after "Dewey Defeats Truman" front page—because they stopped talking to voters in the race's closing weeks, therefore failing to pick up on a late movement toward the incumbent.

One of the pollsters who did not make that error was Angus Campbell, a social psychologist who had spent the war years in a research office of the Department of Agriculture, modeling how consumers would react to the conflict's end so that policymakers could anticipate what they were likely to do with their war bonds. In 1946, Campbell and several colleagues decamped to Ann Arbor, where the University of Michigan built a new Survey Research Center around them. After the 1948 election, Campbell ran a post-election survey to make better sense of Truman's comeback. As 1952 approached, Campbell mapped an ambitious plan to track the attitudes and opinions of the electorate, unfurling a series of lengthy questionnaires that would be used to interview voters nationwide throughout the election season.

Standards were changing rapidly, and it was no longer acceptable for a professor to publish a credible paper on public opinion that used data gathered by his own students, as Gosnell had in 1923. In the late 1950s, Gosnell, then working as a State Department analyst, approached pollster Clyde Hart to propose a reprise of his Chicago voting studies and suggested he might be able to raise ten thousand dollars to fund it. "He looked at me as if to say, 'Where have you been, Rip Van Winkle?'" Gosnell recounted to a gathering of pollsters to which he had been invited by an old friend, Elmo Roper, who had been a pioneer of national surveys during Franklin Delano Roosevelt's bid for a second term.

"Don't you remember Elmo's famous comment after the 1948 election?" Gosnell went on. "This was a priceless comment about the price of

polling. What were the lessons learned from that slight discrepancy between the polls and the election results in that Dewey-Truman contest?
Was it that last minute change in calculating the turnout? No, none of
these things. Elmo put it in a nutshell. The 1948 polls showed that polling
is a complicated business. It is going to cost customers more."

The costs did not dissuade Campbell, who was looking to develop the
first systematic effort to explain how presidential elections were decided.
His 1952 survey came with a $100,000 price tag, covering interviews with
1,900 subjects and asking 224 different questions. The project, which later
became the American National Election Studies, grew into the definitive
data resource in political science: a massive biannual polling project that
was expensive to collect but created a permanent repository of data on
who voted and what they said about why, all with a consistency that made
it easy to track changes through a campaign and from one year to the next.
Campbell's questionnaire took an expansive view of its subject, with questions about not only the election under way but practical matters of political
behavior ("did your coworkers' opinions influence you?") and philosophical
approaches to citizenship ("should one vote if his party can't win?").

The responses guided Campbell toward nothing less than an all-
encompassing theory of how elections are decided. Along with colleagues
Philip Converse, Warren Miller, and Donald Stokes, Campbell concluded
that a person's partisan identification was the strongest predictor of
how they would vote in national elections, even better than asking them
where they stood on any particular issue. Parties were glorified social
clubs, pulling people in because of class, regional, or religious ties and
keeping them for the long term—with a sort of thoughtless choice resembling the inertia that led people to take the same jobs as their relatives.
Individuals rarely switched parties over the course of a lifetime. Campbell
and his colleagues described individual voting decisions with the image
of a funnel: citizens' social and psychological loyalties narrow them into
a party, which usually guides them toward a candidate.

For all that, though, there were short-term disruptions that pushed voters toward a candidate of the other party. After all, the same voters who had decisively elected Franklin D. Roosevelt four times swung broadly behind a Republican, Dwight Eisenhower, less than a decade later. Voters were attached to parties, but those bonds were generally breakable, the Michigan scholars argued, and sometimes a candidate comes along who is so appealing that his personal attributes overwhelm partisan loyalties. Converse liked to compare it to a big wind sweeping through a field of wheat, which leaves every stalk leaning in the same direction, although bending some more sharply than others.

In 1960, Campbell and his colleagues introduced this metaphor in the book *The American Voter*, the first universal, data-intensive study of electoral behavior, but the argument would prove poorly suited for its era. American politics convulsed in the late 1960s and 1970s, following the passage of the Civil Rights Act, and a partisan-driven model seemed tragically anachronistic. Within two decades, the South had become the base of Republican presidential coalitions even as most of its residents remained Democrats, and political scientists began to thrash about for a new way to explain the American voter. It became popular to say that people deserved more credit for the political choices they made. "The perverse and unorthodox argument of this little book is that voters are not fools," V. O. Key Jr. wrote to start his 1966 treatise, *The Responsible Electorate*, which argued that many voters were "switchers," rationally alternating between parties each election to find the candidate closest to them on the issues.

After Richard Nixon's reelection in 1972, Michigan's Warren Miller desperately rewrote the *American Voter* theory to keep up with changing times. The survey data for that year had shown, for the first time in the two decades of the national election studies, that party influence over how voters chose among presidential candidates had diminished markedly. The "issueless" fifties, as they put it, had been followed by a decade in which the country was politically riven on fractious matters of war and peace, identity and liberty, that crossed the old party lines. Voters ditched their social clubs for the candidate who stood closest to them on policy. The Michiganders explained this by pointing to a way the electorate had fundamentally changed: Americans were better educated than before, and went to their polling places with a more enlightened interest in affairs of state. "Voters with a college education are better informed politically," they wrote, and "therefore, more likely to make a vote decision on the basis of policy preferences than are less well-educated individuals."

Such academic theories were barely acknowledged by those who worked in politics, and when they were it was often with skepticism. In fact, those on both sides of the Nixon reelection battle scoffed at the *American Voter* team's reading of the landslide. The president's pollsters, Bob Teeter and Fred Steeper, disputed the idea that "the 1972 patterns portend great ideological battles for future presidential elections," as they wrote, "and that the political parties must change their issueless ways in order to cope with an increasingly polarized electorate." Relying on their polls for Nixon, Teeter and Steeper delivered a new theory for what had prompted so many Democrats to unmoor from their party and dock with Nixon. They suggested that swing voters were no longer voting on issues, such as Vietnam or the economy. They may not have even had strong ideas of the right and wrong positions on the issues. Now they were giving their votes to the candidate who seemed best able to "handle" those challenges. Nixon, like Eisenhower, had established himself as a more credible leader on the issues of the day. This "candidate-induced issue voting," as Teeter and Steeper called it, had as much to do with the candidates as the issues.

They found an unlikely ally in Samuel Popkin, a University of California, San Diego, political scientist who served as a campaign adviser to the man Nixon had defeated, George McGovern. In 1972, Popkin had been a Harvard statistics professor when three of his undergraduate students, including Pat Caddell, sold the South Dakota senator his first poll for five hundred dollars. Soon Caddell was the chief strategist for the Democratic nominee's campaign and enlisted Popkin, who was only thirty then but still nearly a decade older than his excitable protégé, to join the recently minted Cambridge Survey Research trio as an in-house wise man and extra hand with the numbers.

After the campaign, Popkin aggregated all the polling data and tried to answer the same question the Michigan scholars had tackled: why had McGovern lost to Nixon by more than twenty points? McGovern's early polls suggested the race should be competitive. But as it went on, Nixon's lead widened, and the issues alone couldn't explain such a gap. Even those who agreed with the dovish, liberal McGovern on his top foreign and domestic priorities were drifting away. In September, McGovern led Nixon among voters who considered Vietnam the most crucial issue, believed that the United States should withdraw immediately, and supported a guaranteed family income, by a margin of 52 to 38. By the end of the campaign, McGovern had lost them all. His internal polls showed him trailing even among those who thought the military budget should be drastically reduced. McGovern hadn't lost voters because he was out of sync with them on issues, Popkin argued, but because they thought he wouldn't be able to do anything about those policies. They watched McGovern during the campaign and concluded he was incompetent.

Popkin thought voters were much savvier than the Michigan studies had initially cast them, but that even those with college diplomas could never gather all the information necessary to weigh the entire set of costs and benefits attached to each issue or candidate. They weren't making a buying decision, because they wouldn't get the product they eventually chose. Instead, thought Popkin, it made more sense to think of them as investors, who knew whatever information they gathered to inform their decision making would require time and effort. So when it came time to choose a candidate, they relied on shortcuts. They interpreted symbols and looked for cues where they could find them, and then extrapolated. In one of Popkin's favorite examples, when voters saw Gerald Ford fail to shuck a tamale before biting into it, they interpreted it as a sign that he did not understand issues facing Latinos. (Popkin had worked as a campaign adviser to Jimmy Carter in 1976.) Popkin called this "gut reasoning."

Election scholars had ignored large swaths of modern psychology, which was increasingly identifying ways in which people were neither so-cially preprogrammed toward certain attitudes nor walking calculators able to make perfectly rational choices. In other academic disciplines those theories of human behavior had long fallen from vogue, replaced by a less elegant one. In the 1970s, two Israeli psychologists, Amos Tversky and Daniel Kahneman, began to document the ways that people were incapa-ble of deciding rationally, and in fact kept making the same mistakes over and over again. Around 1980, a young economist named Richard Thaler began translating these insights to the way people handled money, and it became readily apparent that people weren't as rational as economists imagined them to be. When forced to make decisions, people lacked a steady set of preferences. What they had instead were unconscious biases that made them bad at assessing situations and accurately judging costs and benefits.

But even a decade later, this basic insight people are flawed, if well-intentioned, beings—had barely penetrated the political science depart-ment. "The science half of political science is to some extent a bit of a misnomer," says Thaler, who in 1995 began teaching at the University of Chicago, just blocks from where Gosnell and Merriam had designed their field experiment to study voter behavior seven decades earlier. "At least no one has been quite ready to agree on what the science part of it is."

In his 1991 book *The Reasoning Voter,* Popkin introduced a theory of voter activity equally informed by behavioral psychology and his own ex-periences within presidential campaigns. "These contests are commonly criticized as tawdry and pointless affairs, full of dirty politics, dirty tricks, and mudslinging, which ought to be cleaned up, if not eliminated from the system. In their use of sanitary metaphors, however, many of these critiques confuse judgments of American culture with aesthetic criticisms of American politicians," Popkin wrote. "They do not look closely at how voters respond to what they learn from campaigns, and they do not look closely at the people they wish to sanitize. If campaigns are vulgar, it is because Americans are vulgar."

This was a theory of the electorate that could make political professionals, increasingly under attack as overpaid Svengalis of spin, feel good about what they did for a living. In December 1991, Popkin wrote an op-ed for the *Washington Post* whose headline blared "We Need Loud, Mean Campaigns." Paul Begala, a Democratic consultant, clipped Popkin's article from the paper and handed it to his partner, James Carville. Carville and Begala, who had recently joined Bill Clinton's campaign as lead strategists, were both loud, occasionally mean, and always unrepentant about the clangorous tone of the campaigns they ran. Popkin's essay offered affirmation. Carville called Popkin to request a copy of *The Reasoning Voter*. Not long after, Popkin joined the campaign as an adviser. "He's one of us," says Begala. "He gets it."

Popkin spent much of 1992 collecting polls and past election results to build simulations of electoral-college scenarios that could get Clinton to the necessary 270 votes. The results informed key strategic decisions: which states would get offices and staff, visits from the candidate and his family, and a precious share of the campaign's budget for paid campaign communication with voters. "It's an important decision in any war," says Popkin. "Who's going to pick the theater of operation?"

But as those strategic choices atomized into a series of tactical options, Popkin was amazed at how little he actually felt he knew. For two centuries Americans had been electing presidents, and for half of one century specialized scholars had been trying to rigorously study that process. Yet they had accumulated little information useful in deciding how to spend campaign dollars. As one of the few political scientists with access to a presidential campaign's war room, Popkin had his feet in the worlds of people who practice politics and the people who study it, and neither field impressed him with its ability to judge what actually won votes. Popkin thought campaigns had learned to be smart about how they picked their theaters of conflict, but once assigned to one, a general had only his instinct to rely upon in deciding whether to battle in the air (buying TV and radio ads) or on the ground (the hand-to-hand mobilization known as field).

"It's the all-time question of every defense department in the world: army versus air force. What is the ultimate value in any war of a soldier versus a bomber?" asks Popkin. "You can target a state, and everyone could say 'the swing voters are in Peoria' and '*Oprah* costs this many dollars.'" But that information alone was of little use. "No one has any idea of the value of the ad versus a phone call from a friend," he goes on. "If you have a dollar to spend, do you spend it on an ad or do you spend it on a phone call? And if you only have money to spend on ads, do you give one person fifty ads or two people twenty-five? Nobody knows."

2

A GAME OF MARGINS

Harold Malchow's first campaign activity was hanging a Nixon sign in the window of his Gulfport, Mississippi, school bus as it trundled to Christ Episcopal Day School in the fall of 1960, his show of support for the Republican competing with classmates' Kennedy signs for the attention of passersby. Nine-year-old Hal had inherited Republicanism from his mother, a college professor who specialized in econometrics. She was so forceful in her views that it took forty years for Hal to learn that his father—a civil engineer who worked on roads and sewer systems along the Gulf Coast and avoided politics—voted for Lyndon Johnson. By eighth grade, Hal was busy going door-to-door for the Republican ticket and nailing Goldwater signs to telephone poles. On a long bus ride to Pennsylvania for the National Boy Scout Jamboree that year, while other boys lost themselves in comic books Hal read *U.S. News & World Report* for election coverage.

But coming of age in the 1960s radicalized Malchow, at least by Mississippi standards. His ninth-grade class was among the first in the state to desegregate, and Malchow signed on with the Mississippi Freedom Democratic Party, spun off in 1964 to protest the racism of the state's Democratic leadership. At Millsaps College, a liberal-arts school in Jackson, Malchow wrote lefty editorials for the weekly student newspaper and helped to organize small antiwar rallies. "We thought maybe if we could do these things in Mississippi, people would notice," he says. In 1972, Malchow was a Democratic poll watcher at the Madison County Courthouse, less concerned with bolstering George McGovern's hopeless candidacy than looking out for the seven black candidates running for the local election commission. Pretty soon, thoughts Malchow had had of teaching political science faded, replaced by a new goal: running campaigns himself. "The real world was exciting," he says.

At twenty-three, Malchow was invited by one of his former professors to participate in a newly formed seminar series called the Institute of Politics. The Ford Foundation had sponsored the project to train promising young Mississippians in how to "improve the quality of practical politics in Mississippi." Malchow cringed a little when he saw this mandate—"Everyone looks at Mississippi and says 'What a pathetic state.'" But he exulted when he saw the institute's list of guest speakers. Each was identified as a political consultant, a term that didn't exist when Malchow began reading about elections as a child, but in a decade had become a common descriptor for the men—and it would take a while for a woman to enter their ranks—who made their money trying to win them.

For several months, Malchow spent his weekends in a Millsaps classroom marveling at a procession of consultants who talked about their careers and the distinct roles they played in the modern electioneering enterprise. Bob Squier had happily abandoned public television when Lyndon Johnson invited him to the White House and asked him to serve as his television adviser; Squier's camera work quickly defined the aesthetics of the thirty-second advertisement, which became the common currency of late-twentieth-century politics. Peter Hart launched his polling firm in

1971, one of the first generation of opinion researchers to put social science survey-taking to work for campaigns. Memphis advertising executive Deloss Walker had begun advising southern Democrats on their media strategy and eventually played the new role of the general consultant, hired by candidates to manage the increasingly varied retinue of specialists that campaigns kept on contract.

Yet even as these new sages talked about tracking and shaping public opinion in a mass-media age, the speaker who most captured Malchow's attention was the one who practiced the oldest art. Matt Reese's specialty had been long described as "organization." It manifested itself in "voter contact," the category of campaign activity that, unlike broadcast and newspaper ads, was defined by its ability to hit a single individual with precision. Reese was a gigantic West Virginian whose voice boomed through the Jackson classroom, his hands gesturing wildly as he spoke. This choreography seemed appropriate, because Reese practiced politics at its most tactile—democracy as it looked from the mailbox, the doorstep, or the distant end of a telephone line. "He had all these schemes," Malchow recalls, marveling at the terms Reese had invented: Go Days, Blitz Days, Block Captain Kits. Reese's practically minded lexicon represented an earthbound counterpart to the narrative of politics in a mass-media era, the lofty contest of ideas and broadcast messages dueling to win over the American people. Instead, Reese's priorities revolved around whose opinions had already been won—counting their votes, sifting between supporters and opponents to turn out the right ones, leave the others behind, and isolate the select few whose minds were still up for grabs.

Reese had been John F. Kennedy's only full-time employee in West Virginia before the Massachusetts senator showed up to contest the state's primary in 1960. Kennedy's team of high-powered volunteer advisers arrived clutching what they called "the O'Brien Manual." The bound sixty-four-page book had been compiled by Kennedy retainer Lawrence O'Brien, whose successes in Boston politics had informed a best-practices volume for campaigns. Reese's job was to translate the O'Brien Manual from Charlestown to Charleston, taking lessons first divined in neighborhoods packed tight with three-decker houses and interpreting them for farflung hollers where letters traveled by rural delivery and telephone calls over party lines. Reese worked to get the Democratic party apparatus on Kennedy's side, assembling chairmen in thirty-nine of the state's fifty-five counties, and under each of them a volunteer hierarchy. Kennedy's win in that primary is often remembered as a triumph for American pluralism—a Catholic showing he could carry a heavily Protestant state. More quietly, it also validated a new technical approach to the nuts and bolts of politics.

Over the next two decades, as television ads came to dominate campaign communication, Reese refined the far less glamorous art of turning out voters. He effectively rewrote the O'Brien Manual in a succession of field plans, organizational charts, and checklists. Reese compared the way he found voters to his method for picking fruit: "You go where the cherries is." In the early days of a campaign, Reese wouldn't spend much time worrying about the known strongholds for one side or the other—the precincts where his candidate, or others like him, had run well before or had an established partisan or demographic edge. Instead Reese's attention would go to the areas that were likely to deliver more muddled results on election day.

There he would start looking for cherries. He would ask around for a phone bank, or in the worst cases build one anew; it could sometimes take months to get a room properly wired with phone lines. (The phone banks had to be local because interstate calls were at this time still prohibitively expensive.) Reese would hope to find an available voting roll maintained by a local board of elections or party boss, but usually there wasn't one. So he would hand a phone book to his volunteers or paid callers with instructions to start dialing names one by one, to ask if the respondents were registered and which candidate they supported. For Reese, only two types of voters mattered. "I wish God gave green noses to undecided voters, because between now and election eve, I'd work only the green noses. I wish God gave purple ears to nonvoters for my candidate on election eve, because on election day I'd work only the purple voters," Reese often explained. "The ones we go after are nonvoters who are for us and the undecided voters."

As head of the Democratic National Committee's voter-registration division during Lyndon Johnson's 1964 campaign, Reese added as many as four million likely new Democrats to the rolls. ("If the 1964 election had not been a landslide, everyone in the country would have heard of him," wrote David Lee Rosenbloom in his book *The Election Men*.) Reese moved in and out of governing, landing jobs as an administrative assistant on Capitol Hill and a Small Business Administration functionary, but he always drifted back to the cherry orchard. In 1966, he opened Matt Reese Associates. It was one of the country's first full-time political consultancies, and so far ahead of the curve that it would be years before the term itself existed. Reese and wealthy, self-funding candidates were drawn to one another. He offered them "organization on demand," an instant stand-in for the party structures—with their permanent hierarchies of county chairs, ward bosses, precinct committeemen, and block captains—that had been undercut by twentieth-century reforms and the rise of independent media. "Consultants have become possible because of the decline of the political parties," Reese later explained to an interviewer, "and the consultant has made the parties even more irrelevant."

* * * * *

REESE MAY HAVE PROFESSIONALIZED the practice of getting the vote out, but he did not invent it. In January 1840, after returning from the state convention of the Illinois Whig Party, state representative Abraham Lincoln wrote to the party's county committeemen, urging them to aid "the overthrow of the corrupt powers that now control our beloved country." To bring Whig voters to the polls that November on behalf of the party's presidential nominee, William Henry Harrison, Lincoln instructed each committee to divide its county into districts and appoint a subcommittee for each. "Make a perfect list of all the voters in their respective districts, and to ascertain with certainty for whom they will vote. If they meet with men who are doubtful as to the man they will support, such voters should be designated in separate lines, with the name of the man they will probably support. It will be the duty of said subcommittee to keep a constant watch on the doubtful voters, and from time to time have them talked to by those in whom they have the most confidence, and also to place in their hands such documents as will enlighten and influence them."

That Lincoln quote eventually found its way into countless sets of canvassing instructions and photocopied party-organizing manuals, affixing a noble patrimony on some of the most arduous work in politics. But the eternal applicability of the future president's instructions was also a reminder of how little had changed in the ways campaigns rustled up votes in the century since Lincoln's death. In 1924, a national party convention was first broadcast live by radio. In the 1940s, a president retained a pollster to have his own personal accounts of public opinion. In the 1950s, candidates hired Madison Avenue agencies to draft their TV ads. But when it came to finding voters and bringing them to the polls, it was still 1840.

In 1964, as Reese was modernizing the DNC's election operations, a twenty-nine-year-old aspiring marketing professor named Vince Barabba took some time off from graduate school at the University of California, Los Angeles, to work as a regional field director on Nelson Rockefeller's campaign against Barry Goldwater in the California primary. Charged with organizing volunteers and setting up campaign events from Burbank to Pasadena, Barabba thought there had to be a better way to predict which voters would be favorable to his candidate without knocking on each of their doors. There was already a little information about each voter publicly available from the local board of elections—usually name, age, how long they had been registered, and the elections in which they had participated—and election officials released results down to the precinct, often equivalent to a single set of voting machines or boxes of ballots. But electoral boundaries had to be redrawn every ten years and when voters moved they took their vote histories with them.

In most parts of the country, established political machines kept track of maps and election returns, or more likely relied on old hands to recall which terrain was enemy turf and which was favorable to their cause. But California had weak parties and little institutional knowledge. Past votes there offered little guidance to present conditions, since the population changed so quickly with new arrivals whose partisan loyalties were fluid. "Things were changing so quickly out there, and there never was an entrenched political organization," says Barabba. "It had a more open approach to politics."

Barabba imagined it should be possible to augment the precinct-level political histories with demographic profiles of voters derived from U.S. Census data about race, ethnicity, age, and family type. It was good for a Republican candidate to know that a neighborhood had broken in favor of his party in the last four statewide elections, Barabba thought, but that information became all the more useful if coupled with the insight that its bungalows were packed with married white retirees. Barabba went back to UCLA and proposed such an analysis as his dissertation for a business degree, but professors rejected it because it did not pursue a "new theoretical approach." So he quit school and reached out to an old boss, Stu Spencer, who had directed Rockefeller's California campaign. Together they started a business called Datamatics, and took Ronald Reagan's 1966 gubernatorial campaign as one of their first clients.

Barabba was fascinated by the work of two California sociologists who had developed a model they called Social Area Analysis to profile the socioeconomic character of the state's urban neighborhoods. Based on 1960 Census data, they categorized tracts along two axes, one reflecting class and the other family composition. Barabba wanted to map these onto precincts, where he could merge them with political information. He hired a programmer to write a computer script and rented time at a local insurance company's IBM 1401 when the computer wasn't in use. Late at night, the two would feed it punch cards that merged these two levels of data to create what Datamatics marketed as the Precinct Index Priority System

(PIPS). In 1965, Barabba's numbers helped two candidates get elected to the Los Angeles City Council, and Datamatics looked for new clients.

The next year, Barabba was summoned to Flint, Michigan, to meet a Harvard Business School student with big plans. Don Riegle had worked at IBM as an analyst before heading to Cambridge and was now intent on returning to his hometown to run for Congress there as a Republican. Barabba met Riegle in the lobby of the Durant Hotel, in a downtown still vibrant with General Motors' Buick City, and detailed how PIPS worked. The district was a traditionally Democratic one, and Flint's rich union tradition usually scared off Republicans. "There were enough Republicans to get you close, but if you got every Republican out there you could never win," says Barabba. "So you had to get swing voters."

Barabba thought Riegle's campaign would be a perfect test case for a demographically driven approach to political organizing. The scale of the challenge was clear: the first poll, commissioned in May, showed incumbent John C. Mackie leading Riegle, 63 percent to 26 percent. Riegle's advisers believed that their candidate, a smart young moderate technocrat, was the campaign's greatest asset and that the rising specter of inflation was a boon to any challenger. Barabba and Spencer had bought thirty minutes of television time on a Sunday afternoon in an effort to have him directly address local elites. At one point during the broadcast, Riegle dramatically took a cleaver to a piece of steak and threw one-third of it onto the trash—a demonstration, he said, of what inflation did to workers' buying power.

The performance helped establish Riegle as a serious challenger, and Barabba knew if he could get his candidate in front of the right voters he would be able to pick up support. Polling showed that, despite their historically Democratic allegiances, union members would be persuadable by Riegle's appeals. Barabba put his Precinct Index Priority System to work finding neighborhoods whose demographics reflected a more conservative profile even if they were not traditionally thought hospitable to Republicans—the white, working-class union members who would later become known as Reagan Democrats. "Everyone had classified union workers all the same," says Barabba. Now he was going to try to capitalize on that mistake.

In September, the gap stood at 20 points, with Mackie still comfortably at 51 percent. Barabba doled out the candidate's time in the places where PIPS told him it would be most valuable. The Riegle for Congress Volunteer Committee canvassed the most promising areas by phone to identify individual voters, while the candidate went to knock on doors in the precincts where Barabba thought his physical presence could have the biggest influence. On election night, Barabba was at the Biltmore Hotel in Los Angeles, at what became Ronald Reagan's victory party in his first run for office. Around the same time that Reagan was declared California's governor, Barabba got a telephone call from Michigan. It was Riegle reporting that he had beaten Mackie by eight points. The man who emerged from the Biltmore would become the greatest broadcast performer ever in American politics, but Barabba believed that what happened on the streets of Flint ought to resonate as widely. "At that point we were in an era of mass communication, and everybody thought that that would be the way to go," says Barabba. "We kept questioning that."

Barabba's success with Riegle, and four other congressional candidates for whom Datamatics played less significant strategic roles in 1966, caught the eye of the American Medical Association, whose political action committee had emerged during the 1960s as one of the business world's leading political players. Imagining itself as a counterweight to the campaign clout of organized labor, AMPAC participated in congressional races nationwide, almost always to boost Republicans. "The guys who were heading the PAC at the AMA were disappointed at how much money was spent on political campaigns. They wanted to make sure that when the doctors got involved, their money was spent wisely," says Barabba. During Barry Goldwater Jr.'s 1969 congressional campaign, Barabba's analysis enabled the AMA to target telegrams emphasizing different issues by precinct in the Los Angeles area district. "We thought we could do a better job by focusing on smaller areas." But after Watergate, as campaign finance laws curtailed the ability of outside groups to spend freely on behalf of campaigns, the AMA struggled to sustain its influence on elections.

Across Washington, one of the AMA's nemeses confronted a similar identity crisis and headed in an altogether different direction. The National Committee for an Effective Congress had been founded in 1948 by Eleanor Roosevelt as a backer of liberal congressional campaigns nationwide. Its financial primacy may have been threatened by post-Watergate reforms, but NCEC was intent on remaining a central player in stacking Capitol Hill with allies. What if instead of merely giving money to campaigns, committee strategists wondered, they developed common resources that Democratic candidates and party committees could use to plot strategies and tactics for districts nationwide?

Political operatives have long thought of winning a vote as a three-step process. First a voter needs to be registered. Then comes "persuasion": the challenge of emerging as the preferred choice among two or more candidates. Finally, once a person has been registered and persuaded, the campaign has to convert that support into a vote: mobilizing him or her to the polls through get-out-the-vote operations, often known simply as GOTV, that can include a battery of last-minute reminders by phone or mail or election day visits offering a ride to the polls.

Every voter is different and has varying degrees of openness to a candidate's arguments or a need to be pushed to the polls. Campaigns use canvassers (either volunteers or paid workers) to touch these voters one by one, through a phone call or a doorstep visit, and gauge their support and likelihood of voting. Canvassers are typically given a script—do you expect to vote? which candidate do you support? do you think you could change your mind?—and then charged with plotting responses on a five-point scale: a 1 is a certain supporter, 5 a firm backer of the opposition. But in the 1970s few campaigns had the time or resources to tailor a distinctive strategy for following up with each of them. As a result, operatives often had little choice but to blanket an entire category of people with arguments they thought would be persuasive—or, in the scramble of election day, to blindly pull them out of their homes and to the polls. As a result, the parties conducted direct contact almost exclusively on turf they deemed safe.

Improving their knowledge of each patch of turf was of special value to Democrats. The party's strongholds, usually in cities, tended to be packed full of precincts that turned out for the party in such overwhelming numbers that Republicans reflexively accused their opposition of vote fraud when they saw the lopsided election returns. (There has indeed been vote fraud, but also many precincts that Democrats legitimately carry with 95 percent of the vote.) Meanwhile, Republicans were spread more widely, between cities, suburbs, and rural areas and taking on a slightly different cast in each. There were few precincts anywhere in the country that consistently voted 70 percent Republican.

These differences in political geography shaped the way each party practiced politics. Democratic ward leaders in Chicago and Boston and Philadelphia rarely employed the vote-counting rigor and discipline that Lincoln advised. They would rely on TV and radio ads blanketing the city to do the work of persuasion, air cover for a ruthless ground war below. Party bosses would take areas known to be more than 65 percent Democratic and flood them with manpower on election day, hitting the door of every voter they could find without bothering to check their party identification or candidate preference. Operatives had different terms for this get-out-the-vote practice, but each reflected a relative lack of nuance. In Philadelphia they dubbed it "knock and drag"; in the black counties of rural Virginia it was "hauling and calling." Both represented a fast-food strategy, identifying reliable margins and counting on volume for victory.

Because of these tactics, pinpointing the difference between 70 percent support in a precinct and 60 percent was very valuable to Democrats. In large swaths of the country that job was getting more difficult. What mattered wasn't just how people registered but the way districts voted, and the partisan realignment that began during the civil rights era confused the map. Through the end of the twentieth century, Dixie was filled with registered Democrats, but—at least when it came to presidential contests at the top of the ticket—few Democratic voters. (Alabama voted for only one Democratic presidential candidate after 1964, but its state legislature didn't go Republican until 2010.) Working-class whites in Milwaukee and Cleveland may, too, be self-identified Democrats and even union members but increasingly they were open to voting for Richard Nixon and, later, Reagan. Flushing out a precinct's worth of votes on historically Democratic turf could mean producing margins for the other side.

As part of its post-Watergate reinvention, the National Committee for an Effective Congress decided in 1974 that it would take on the challenge of mapping political geography so Democratic candidates could intelligently target every precinct in the country. Nearly all the data necessary to accomplish that was publicly available but prohibitively fragmented. Some states maintained voter files—which usually listed an individual's name, age, and gender—but assembling precinct vote data was a laborious process. NCEC hired teams of researchers whose days were spent calling county election boards for past vote returns and maps that showed where precinct lines were drawn. It would all arrive on paper and need to be inputted manually to computers. Then analysts added neighborhood-level Census data to enliven the portrait of residents, by categories like race, ethnicity, and household type. (In states covered under the 1964 Civil Rights Act, officials were required to keep individual racial markers in their voter file. Ethnic name dictionaries helped flag those likely to be Jewish, Hispanic, or Asian.) Of course, NCEC analysts knew that every ten years, districts at all levels would be redrawn to match new Census figures—and many precinct lines would change even more frequently—so they had to not only keep tallies of votes but also translate them over time to align with changing boundaries.

NCEC analysts boiled this stew of data down to three key formulas they could apply to any precinct in the country. The first was a Democratic-performance index, an estimate of how an average Democratic candidate would fare on the ballot. It was a useful indicator of which party controlled the turf: anything over 50 percent was a Democrat-friendly area, while beyond 65 percent represented the party's base. Then NCEC calculated a "persuasion percent," which took the measure of how much an area swung between parties due to crossover votes. (Some people thought it made more sense as a "volatility index," measuring how much voters were willing to swing between the parties.) A persuasion percent of 30 indicated an area where a campaign could expect nearly a third of voters to be open to appeals from both sides, like a Denver suburb where partisan identity is weak and voters hopscotch between Democrats and Republicans as they make their way down a ballot. A persuasion percent of zero reflected a place where party loyalties are firm and voting patterns predictable regardless of which candidate is on the ballot—whether that means Democrats win with 70 percent of the vote each year or always lose with 30 percent, or whether races come down to a 50–50 split. A third formula, the "GOTV percent," measured the volatility of turnout: how much did the number of people who actually voted shift from year to year?

When combined, these calculations made it possible for Democratic electoral strategists to meticulously separate their voter contact resources between persuasion and turnout and spread them around to areas where each could have the most impact. By the mid-1980s, NCEC had become a crucial utility in Democratic politics, contracted by the DNC and other party organs to crunch precinct-level election data for them. In essence, NCEC had determined the odds that a given voter in any precinct in America had Reese's green nose or purple ears. A campaign no longer needed the resources to count every single person; it could just play the averages.

*   *   *   *   *

AFTER COMPLETING HIS TERM at the Institute of Politics, Hal Malchow was more certain than ever that he wanted to make a career out of winning votes. He approached elections with the same self-discipline that led him to devour thick volumes of American history in continuous stretches and to eat his meals by clearing out one ingredient from his plate at a time:

all the fried okra before moving on to collard greens, all the potato before touching his steak. Malchow had a mustache and bushy hair, and spoke in a voice that began as a thick southern treacle but accelerated into a staccato yawp as he got excited. "Hal has strong core values and beliefs, but it was the love of the game that most enthralled him," says Hank Klibanoff, a journalist who with Malchow shared a Jackson house that became a way station for itinerant political operatives coming to work on Mississippi campaigns. "Loving the game meant mastering the mechanics of the game."

Even an understanding of the latest voter contact strategies failed to make Mississippi politics a friendly place for a reform-minded liberal. Malchow's candidates always seemed to lose. After managing several such races, never winning more than 40 percent of the vote, Malchow grew dispirited and decided to become a lawyer, which he thought would at least help him earn enough money to stay involved in politics through other channels. He enrolled at the University of the Pacific, but was rarely engaged by his law-school studies. Then, in his third year, Malchow took a mandatory corporations class. The gamesmanship between the people who wrote the byzantine rules and regulations governing companies and the people who set out to elude them mesmerized Malchow in much the same way that Reese's electioneering machinations had. "All of a sudden you have all these cases where people have these wild, creative financial schemes," he says. "And I'm a creative person, so I'm looking at this thinking, 'That's fun! I can do that.'"

Upon graduation, Malchow became a securities lawyer at one of the leading firms in Jackson, a job that consisted largely of writing the fine print for life insurance programs administered by local auto dealers. Malchow found this, and just about everything related to the practical application of the law, to be tediously unimaginative. He kept an eye on politics by faithfully reading the weekly edition of the *Washington Post* and distracted himself by drawing *Loophole,* a cartoon strip about the fictional Simon Legree School of Law, which was syndicated in forty student newspapers and had begun when Malchow had found himself similarly bored in law-school classes and started caricaturing his professors and their teaching styles.

In early 1982, Malchow found a more socially productive distraction. Blocks from Malchow's law office, the state's governor, a progressive named William Winter, was hard at work trying to modernize the country's most backward education system through compulsory-attendance laws and the introduction of public kindergarten classes. When legislators blocked Winter's reforms, Malchow—along with much of the state's business community—was disgusted. "It was the rabble who was opposed to this," he says. "But the rabble in Mississippi, especially at this time, was a healthy majority." Malchow gathered a few friends with the goal of knocking off some of the old bulls in the state legislature.

The group, which called itself Mississippi First, found office space in a Jackson house where it shared a phone line with what seemed like the entirety of the state's liberal community, including the American Civil Liberties Union and the Mississippi Gay Alliance. Malchow and his volunteer allies approached each of the state's living former governors, who had little in common politically other than an enduring hatred of the legislature, and convinced three of them to share the rosters of donors they had kept on index cards. It was the first time anyone had ever assembled a thirty-thousand-person political mailing list in Mississippi, and Malchow began plotting how to shake down its names for his new cause. He hired people to type up the names and addresses, and raised enough money to buy an Apple II computer, which ran on floppy disks with such little storage that it took 110 of the disks to keep track of donors spread across Mississippi's eighty-two counties.

Malchow had heard of Richard Viguerie, who had built a financial foundation for the Reagan Revolution in the late 1970s by collecting mailing lists of right-wing groups and conservative magazines and bombarding them with contribution requests. Malchow had also heard of Morris Dees, an Alabamian who played a similar role on the left, and probably even had some of Dees's handiwork filed away in his office. Malchow had kept the fund-raising letters he received—one sent for Sargent Shriver's 1976 presidential campaign, another for Jimmy Carter's reelection—all of which he assumed had come to him because his name was on the *Washington Post*'s national subscriber list.

After watching his candidates fail to raise the funds they needed to run their campaigns, Malchow was enthralled by the letters. "I thought it was fascinating: you could send letters out and get money back," he says. "This seemed like a pretty cool concept to me." He took the letters and tried to ape their style—language so excitable that recipients would be moved to immediately open their checkbooks in response—as he raised the alarm about Mississippi's perpetually obstinate legislature. "It's time to fight back," Malchow wrote. One night, he invited twenty volunteers to help stuff his new four-page letter and a return mailer into envelopes, before affixing labels that emerged from a dot-matrix printer tethered to the computer where Malchow kept his list of names. By the end of the evening, only 1,200 envelopes had been stuffed. It took Malchow a month to complete all 30,000, and only then because someone informed him that professional mail shops had machines to fold and stuff envelopes. The first day that Malchow checked the post office box that Mississippi First had rented, he found ten letters. Nine could be described as hate mail, with copious use of "communist" and "nigger-lover."

Ultimately, though, the group got six hundred contributions from the letter, a 2 percent response rate that Malchow later realized was considered a solid return in the direct-mail world. The group cashed the checks and began dispersing the money to legislative challengers it supported. One day, the group's president, Brad Pigott, entered a meeting waving a copy of *The New Kingmakers,* a just-published book profiling the era's influential political consultants, including Viguerie and Dees. "Look at this," Pigott said. "Viguerie says you're supposed to mail them again!" The book described Viguerie's practice of alternating between tapping a prospecting list—a collection of new names with typically a low response rate—and his house list of previous donors who usually constituted a movement's true believers.

Now, following Viguerie's example, Malchow wrote to his six hundred again, this time with an even more dire appeal for money. The house list responded as Viguerie believed it would: Malchow got a 15 percent response rate. In the end, Mississippi First collected $100,000, about half of its total budget, through Malchow's letters, and helped to defeat six committee chairmen each with more than two decades in the legislature. Even before the election in 1982, the legislature acquiesced to Governor Winter's progressive agenda, approving his education bill as well as political reforms that had not even been on the Mississippi First agenda. "No one in the world had ever sent thirty thousand people a piece of mail talking about what a bunch of ignorant degenerates the legislature was, and it freaked them out so much they passed everything in the next session," Malchow says. More than that, the victory convinced Malchow of the unique power of political mail to galvanize activists behind a cause.

The next year, Malchow traveled to Nashville to meet with a young congressman named Al Gore, who was looking to follow his father into the Senate. Gore liked Malchow but wondered how he would justify to his donors the decision to hire a campaign manager who had lost all three of his races. "Al, you tell 'em that everybody in the state says you think you have this campaign wrapped up and in the bag," Malchow said, "and that you hired the best and hungriest son of a bitch in America."

After Gore's win, Malchow moved to Washington in search of his next client. He was afraid he would become pigeonholed, and he was eager to find a race in a state like Illinois or Pennsylvania where he could show he was more than just a southern operative. Malchow printed up business cards and made the rounds pitching candidates as they came through Washington in search of a campaign manager, but never clicked with any of them. In 1985, he was living in a basement efficiency apartment, overdrawn on his credit cards and down to twenty-five dollars in his bank account, beginning to worry that he had been rash in leaving the South. Then Malchow got a call from Tim Wirth's embryonic Senate campaign in Colorado, offering a three-thousand-dollar-per-month contract to do the campaign's fund-raising letters. He forgot about the campaign manager jobs and promoted himself instead as a consultant who knew how to raise money through the mail. He signed up five Senate and gubernatorial campaigns nationwide over the next year.

The field of consulting was booming, with more and more specialists offering their services to campaigns. The term *political consultant* was coined by Joseph Napolitan, who designed his first television ad in 1957 for a mayoral candidate in his native Springfield, Massachusetts, and oversaw much of the strategy for Hubert Humphrey's presidential campaign eleven years later. In 1969, Napolitan convened the first meeting of the American Association of Political Consultants, taking a field whose most notable practitioners had been PR men and Madison Avenue agencies dabbling in politics and giving it an economic identity and professional code. By 1972, Napolitan was already defending his neologism. "To me, a political consultant is *a specialist in political communication,*" he wrote in his 1972 book, *The Election Game and How to Win It*. "That's all there is to it, and I don't think it's anything very macabre or Machiavellian."

Direct mail was one of the political industry's first clearly defined specialties. Fund-raising had taken off amid the campaign finance reforms implemented after Watergate, which placed the first limits on individual contributions. No longer could large donors write unlimited checks to campaigns: gifts were capped at one thousand dollars per person. All of a sudden, campaigns had to build a base of donors before they could even begin plotting how they would assemble a coalition of voters. While some campaigns and political committees relied in part on telemarketing, the most lucrative way to raise money was through poison-pen letters rousing donors to fear an opponent and dash off a check for protection.

The maturity of the direct-mail sector, and the introduction in the 1970s of discounts for presorted bulk shipments for nonprofit purposes, opened up a conduit for candidates to approach voters with customized messages. Campaigns had long dropped off leaflets and handbills on doorsteps, but they had never trusted the postal service to handle them. In

1982, candidates spent $100 million on direct mail, according to an estimate at the time, with Republicans taking the lead in crafting messages too specific to have worked on television or radio. In New York, wealthy gubernatorial candidate Lewis Lehrman ran a $1 million mail program that split the state's independents into two groups—upstaters in Republican-leaning districts, and downstaters in areas that skewed Democratic—and gave a specific pitch to each. Catholics and Jews received different letters, the latter of whom were told "Lew Lehrman speaks our language." Republican congressman Stan Parris broke his Northern Virginia district into fifty-three different categories, and sent a total of 1.3 million letters—nearly ten for each person who ended up casting a ballot. Lawyers, teachers, and policemen, their names culled from lists maintained by professional associations, got appeals targeted to their interests. Voters in Alexandria learned that Parris had won federal money for the Woodrow Wilson Bridge, while those in Mount Vernon were warned that Democrats were planning to place a prison nearby.

Malchow looked on with admiration as some of his Democratic peers developed a new genre of persuasion mail known as "the California style." Their brochures were colorful and irreverent, eager to win a laugh if that's what it took to get a voter to pay attention to a political message. "No one had ever seen mail like that," says Malchow. With the California-style innovators as his models, Malchow in 1989 launched a new firm, the November Group, that would specialize in persuasion—helping to define the mail vendor for the first time as a central figure in a campaign's operations. "Those who succeed will need the eyes of an artist, the words of a poet, and the elegant equations of a mathematician," he later said, with only a bit of cheek. "Of all the professions in all parts of the universe, there is only one place where all these skills reside together."

For inspiration, Malchow often looked past his fellow political consultants and toward commercial marketers, who had made the mail-order catalog business into a dominant force in American retailing. Their ability to manage and manipulate databases was built on algorithmic breakthroughs that allowed marketers to get more out of their statistics. Malchow, however, had failed trigonometry his senior year in high school and managed to get through college without ever taking a math course. "I just wasn't interested," he says.

But he was drawn to the challenge of continual self-improvement, so in the early 1990s he started taking night classes in topics like statistics and pre-calculus at George Washington University and traveling up to New York for multiday seminars put on by the Direct Marketing Association, a trade group that catered to commercial vendors rather than political firms. There Malchow was introduced to CHAID, a statistical technique designed to locate relationships among a large number of potentially intersecting variables at once. (It stands for Chi-Square Automatic Interaction Detector.) It was notable for its simplicity to users. CHAID software on a desktop computer was arranged as a decision tree: click on a population of men and it will sprout a series of branches showing their views broken down by race, each of which can be clicked to subdivide those groupings by income—all the way until the smallest sliver of the electorate can be revealed.

Few Democrats thrived in the contentious aftermath of the 1994 Republican takeover of Congress as much as Malchow, who had won the Democratic National Committee's contract for fund-raising mail. "Nothing is better for direct mail than this sort of discord," says Malchow, who eagerly cited Newt Gingrich's latest outrage in his letters. So many rank-and-file Democrats had become energized by Gingrich's agenda that Malchow thought he could dramatically expand his pool of fund-raising targets. At the time, there were about 2 million established liberal donors who would reliably write checks to campaigns and lefty causes like the ACLU and the Sierra Club. But there were 40 million committed Democratic voters, and Malchow thought it might be time to start soliciting them, too.

Malchow had pushed himself to master CHAID, taking his statistics textbook on vacation and reading it on the beach, to his wife's complaints. Now he thought he had the perfect application for it in politics: he would use CHAID to break down the party's ranks of existing donors to isolate traits they had in common geographically—using donors' nine-digit ZIP codes to group Census data in twenty-five categories like education, income, race—and then assemble those into a "model" of what a potential Democratic donor ought to look like. In the end, Malchow could never quite master the computer models, but he became fixated on the idea that CHAID could be used to find not only people worth begging for cash but also those whose votes were up for grabs, too. "I'm hungry to do this," Malchow recalls thinking. "Looking for the first chance."

★ ★ ★ ★ ★

RON WYDEN WAS a former college basketball player with an idiosyncratic streak on health policy. Gordon Smith was the former CEO of his family's frozen food business and—despite his Mormon faith—had a liberal instinct on social matters. But within days of winning Oregon's Democratic and Republican primaries, respectively, in December 1995, these two thoughtful men reduced each other to partisan caricature. Smith dismissed his Democratic opponent as a "tax-and-spend liberal," while Wyden accused the Republican of "extremism." It was the most generic version of a mid-1990s election imaginable, a proxy battle in the Washington war between Bill Clinton and Newt Gingrich over the size and role of government.

Wyden and Smith were joined in this conflict only through unusual circumstances. Three months earlier, Senator Bob Packwood had resigned from the seat he had occupied for nearly three decades, shortly after the Senate Ethics Committee voted to expel him over charges of sexual harassment. Since 1969, no one but Packwood and Mark Hatfield had represented Oregon in the U.S. Senate, and the two moderate Republicans had used their longevity to build the state's clout in Washington and check their party's rightward movement. Their permanence had also made it difficult for other Oregon politicians of either party to rise, so when Packwood stepped aside it offered a rare opening. Wyden, an eight-term congressman, and Smith, who had served in the state senate for only three years but was already the body's president, rushed into the race.

The special election was scheduled for January 30, 1996, effectively inaugurating a campaign year that would culminate in Clinton's reelection effort that November. But the Oregon race would be controlled by a distinctive set of factors. Because the campaign would bridge the holidays, when it is ever harder to recruit volunteers and reach voters at home, the campaigns had to expect that Oregonians would check out of politics for one of the race's final weeks. There would not be time for the patient introduction usually necessary for a first-time statewide candidate: the biographical television ads, the policy speeches that allow a candidate to knit policy positions into a coherent ideological worldview. The calendar offered little chance for candidates to visit with voters individually or parry with local journalists and editorial boards that could help filter the politicians' backgrounds into rich portraits of the two men. In addition, because of a change in Oregon law, the primary and general elections would be the first ever conducted entirely by mail ballots anywhere in the United States, and no one knew what that would mean for voter turnout. It was nearly impossible for strategists to forecast how many votes were likely to be cast and where they would come from, crucial information for allocating scarce campaign resources.

In December, Wyden had just emerged from a hard-hearted primary against a fellow congressman, Peter DeFazio. The fault lines among Democrats were delicate—the populist DeFazio had attacked Wyden as a "corporate Congressman"—but there was scarce time for patient coalition building or diligent canvassing to discern exactly where they ran through the electorate. The six-point primary victory was best interpreted with a map: Wyden carried the Portland metro area that housed his congressional district but lost southwestern Oregon, where DeFazio's district hugged the Pacific coastline, by more than 2 to 1. Wyden's strategists hoped that portraying Smith as a doctrinaire right-winger would help them consolidate

Democratic support, but they were also aware that independents, who made up nearly one-quarter of the state's voters, might not respond as readily to such partisan messages. "The fundamental strategic challenge was how to break out of that trench warfare, just big bombs back and forth," says Mark Mellman, who presided over one of Washington's top Democratic opinion research firms and had consulted on Wyden's campaigns for years.

Mellman's polls were great at showing where the campaign stood, and in their ability to run a sequence of questions that gave a deeper under-standing of what people knew and what they believed, where there was room to give them new information and change their views. Pollsters loved to use their queries to identify the conflicted public mind: Did voters like the incumbent personally but show disappointment in his work on a particular issue? If so, should a challenger focus on that specific policy difference in-stead of a broader leadership critique? Then the pollster could break down the numbers into demographic blocs, showing how opinions differed by gender, race, party, age, or region of the state. Going back into the field with the same methods each week would allow the pollsters to see which type of voters were moving, and start to make educated guesses about why.

Hal Malchow had worked with Mellman since Al Gore's first Senate race, in 1984, when Malchow served as campaign manager and Mellman conducted polls from the New Haven, Connecticut, apartment where he had lived while finishing his graduate studies at Yale. Malchow thought highly of Mellman's statistical acumen, strategic perspective, and will-ingness to experiment with new methods made possible by changes in technology. But in his capacity as Wyden's direct-mail consultant, Mal-chow found that Mellman's insights on the race had limited utility. Each of Malchow's brochures was destined for a specific mailbox, so he was less interested in understanding the nuances of public attitudes than he was in identifying which individual voters held which views. He wanted to send per-suasion mail to people whose minds were not yet made up but who looked like they could be swayed by pro-Wyden appeals. Paying for persuasion mail to one of Wyden's firm supporters would be a waste, while sending it to one of Smith's risked inflaming the opposition with a reminder of an election that could otherwise be easily ignored. For Malchow's purposes, knowing that 20 percent of seniors or suburban blacks were undecided was not terribly helpful. A mail program that aimed at voting blocs defined in such crude terms would ensure that 80 percent of the printing and postage costs went to waste.

More and more types of individual data were showing up on Malchow's computers, and he thought he could use them to cut the electorate into much finer slices. In 1990, the U.S. Census Bureau started releasing information on individual city blocks, which typically include eight hundred households, in three dozen demographic categories—and each was attached to a nine-digit ZIP code. While a pollster could break down a six-hundred-person survey into key constituencies, as he subdivided those into the smaller categories they called crosstabs (for "crosstabulation") they lost their statistical power. Once you started looking at what, for instance, young, college-educated Republican women thought of your candidate, the margin of error on the poll numbers rose to double digits, which made it effectively worthless. Malchow wanted to invert the quality of the data: more information on the people, less on their views. Instead of contacting a small sample with a long battery of questions, he wondered, why couldn't the campaign ask just one or two questions each of a lot of people?

Campaigns were already making calls to identify potential supporters: one of the first places a field organizer would stick an eager volunteer was a phone bank, with a list of voters and a few simple scripted questions written to discern whether the person on the other end had picked a candidate and how strong his or her support was. This effort helped campaigns decide which voters needed to be badgered in the run-up to election day, and which ones would be a priority to rouse to the polls in the closing get-out-the-vote operations. While some strategists asked for daily summaries of phone bank interviews as a rough indicator of where voters stood, the calls were far from random—lists usually started with party registrants because it made little sense to waste time identifying the other side's loyalists—and had no statistical worth as representative of public opinion. But Malchow didn't care where the body politic was headed; he wanted to pull out its parts and dissect them so he could see how every cell inside pulsed differently and assign each a slightly different prescription.

With CHAID, Malchow could get beyond the limits of precinct targets and aim for actual people. If it was possible to address mail to an individual, why were campaigns still profiling them based on the neighborhood in which they lived? He would need a large-scale poll, as much as twenty times bigger than the standard opinion survey conducted by media organizations to identify a front-runner or a campaign pollster to measure the dynamics of a race. In this case, Malchow thought it would take about ten thousand phone calls to get the detail he wanted, costing about a dollar each from a professional call center. But it would not require a sophisticated polling operation, which would have been far more expensive. With just a handful of questions there would be little worry about the order in which they were asked—which with opinion polls can bias the results—and since the responses wouldn't be assembled to assess public opinion, there was less of a need for a representative sample.

In Wyden's campaign, Malchow knew he had found the perfect opportunity to experiment. He was not, however, well positioned to propose a radical departure from traditional campaign tactics. Malchow was already deep in battle with Amy Chapman, Wyden's campaign manager, and the only reason he thought he had succeeded in holding on to the contract was that Chapman's brother worked at his firm. There was no way that Chapman would write a check for a ten-thousand-dollar poll on top of the existing budget for voter lists and mail, so Malchow decided he would pay for it himself.

The Wyden campaign reached 9,051 voters and asked them three questions to identify whom they supported and how committed they were. The first surprise was one that should have been picked up by a standard poll, although the massive sample meant Malchow could put great confidence in the finding: the 30 percent of voters undecided about their choice were not necessarily clumped in the ideological middle. While 32 percent of independents said they hadn't settled on a candidate, 30 percent of Republicans and 28 percent of Democrats hadn't, either.

It was the last group that most interested Malchow. There was no reason to spend forty cents to print and send another piece of persuasion mail to the 72 percent of Democrats who were already with Wyden. But if Malchow could pick out those 28 percent, one by one, and speak to only their mailboxes, he could make better use of his resources and communicate with them more often. CHAID revealed a chunk of them were Democrats who lived in the Eugene media market, several hours south of Portland. This was logical: the area was home to Peter DeFazio, the man Wyden had just beaten in a contentious primary.

Another group of Democrats in the 28 percent were those who lived in neighborhoods with the lowest education levels, an indication that they could be the type of so-called low-information voters who do not follow politics closely and tune in to races just before election day, if at all. According to Malchow's poll, more than one in three of the voters in this group were undecided: not only were these Democrats still making up their minds, but the numbers showed that they presented a more target-rich environment than the general category of independents. One hundred leaflets sent to this group would reach more actually undecided voters than merely pulling the names of registered independents.

Then Malchow looked at the 32 percent of undecided independents and started sprouting branches off the tree to see if he could find clusters that would be more fruitful. When he clicked on independents to break down by age, he got three more boxes: 18- to 44-year-olds, 45 to 64, and seniors. The youngest group was 37 percent undecided, compared with 26 percent and 34 percent of the older ones, respectively, so Malchow clicked on that category. When he divided those young voters by the education level of their Census blocks, he saw a meaningful split: those in neighborhoods with the fewest graduate degrees were undecided at a much higher

rate—42 percent to 33 percent—than those in the more educated neighborhoods. Malchow broke down that group by family size, and hit gold:
those in neighborhoods with the most children were undecided at a rate of
58 percent. He thought these young independents in neighborhoods with
lots of kids but few graduate degrees resembled a politically familiar bloc:
the culturally conservative, working-class voters now known as Reagan
Democrats. Only 67 of the original 9,051 people surveyed fit the category,
but Malchow's file of all Oregon voters revealed a much larger pool of
targets likely to share a frame of mind: around 8,000 likely voters. Malchow expected they would be nearly twice as likely to be undecided as
other Oregon independents. A dollar of Wyden's campaign budget would
go twice as far with them.

Malchow returned to the areas with the most graduate degrees, and
looked at what the Census data told him about their ethnic and racial mix.
He found that these neighborhoods were clustered in Portland and had
large Asian populations. Malchow called Wyden's campaign to find out
why this group, not the typical profile of a low-information voter, might
be holding back from supporting the Democrat. For those who knew the
city's streets, the answer was obvious. Portland was receiving a stream
of new Asian immigrants and it made perfect sense that those new to Oregon were still learning about the candidates and the issues. Chapman, the
campaign manager, couldn't even see Mellman's crosstabs, because the
computer files were so big that every time he tried to send anything more
than the top-line horse-race number he crashed the campaign's e-mail.
But even if she had been able to open the file, the polls barely included
enough Asian-Americans to show meaningful crosstabs for them as a
single group—certainly not enough to see the granular pattern now un-
folding on Malchow's screen.

Malchow lumped together thousands of these new targets—four clusters of independents that were a combined 46 percent undecided, along
with the Eugene area working-class Democrats—and proposed to Chapman that the campaign send them the most mail making the case for

Wyden, while abandoning outreach to those whose support had already been won or lost. Like many young Democratic operatives of the era, Chapman had come of age treating NCEC percentage scores as the essential guide for targeting voters. "They were the gold standard in this business for so long," says Gail Stoltz, the Democratic Senatorial Campaign Committee's political director. Malchow's way of viewing the electorate, as a congeries of people rather than a patchwork of precincts, was anathema. Chapman decided not to change the campaign's voter contact program, and stuck to the more traditional methods of hunting voters. Thanks to Wyden's deft handling of the novel vote-by-mail process and tactical miscues by Smith, the Democrat won on January 30, 1996, by 18,220 votes, among the closest statewide elections in Oregon history.

Malchow couldn't take credit for the victory, but he knew the narrow margin could help make the case that finding small pockets of votes should matter. He emerged from Oregon convinced both that his new statistical technique could change the way campaigns looked for supporters and that it would be a monumental challenge to get political decision makers to adopt it. "There were people who couldn't get their head around CHAID," says Jill Alper, who was then national coordinated-campaign director of the DNC. "It was unthinkable that you wouldn't communicate with everyone."

*　*　*　*　*

NOT LONG AFTER the Wyden race, Malchow went to see Mark Penn, then Bill Clinton's pollster and the White House's leading strategist, with an unusual proposal. Malchow wanted the Democratic National Committee, with whom his firm had a seven-figure election-year contract, to impose experimental controls on the millions of pieces of get-out-the-vote mail it sent out. It was a peculiar moment in the cutthroat political profession: a consultant coming to his biggest client and asking, in essence, to have his work audited.

Malchow knew he was already becoming something of a gadfly, always agitating for a new way of doing things. Malchow's employees tired of their boss's constant tinkering. "At times it made it difficult to work for him because there wasn't a lot of stability," says Christopher Mann, who later served as vice president of Malchow's firm. "We didn't do things the same way twice because he would always want to try something new. It was hard to get into a routine with that." This was an unusual character critique to level at a political consultant, since if anything they were known for holding on to such hardened styles—a favored tactical gambit, checklists verging on superstitions—that they were often accused of marketing one-size-fits-all strategies to customers.

Malchow was creative by nature, but a decade in direct mail had made him an obsessive believer in trial and error. The fund-raising cycle was by its nature a constant feedback loop. At each stage there were simple ways to test which messages and typefaces worked, and who should receive them: consultants would send out slightly different letters to multiple groups of recipients, and then identify which brought in the most money. The successful ones would become the standard, until it was time to tweak again. Malchow was fond of the game—deciding when to tap the house list to fund a prospecting effort, and then refining the pitch itself through each new cycle of mail—but he also loved the way it crescendoed to a pristine finality in an industry of messy uncertainties. It was easy for Malchow to measure the relative effectiveness of every paper and envelope that left his office: the one that brings in the most money is best.

But nothing else done within campaigns came with the same built-in accountability. Malchow felt that, through CHAID, campaigns had gained the capability to do something radical: speak to voters in small, refined batches instead of the broad swaths that broadcast television or radio markets represented. Yet there was no mechanism to measure whether they were actually generating votes. "We send a big postcard with Martin Luther King to African-Americans, but we don't know whether it worked," he complained to Penn.

In 1992, Malchow had made the same pitch for experimental controls to DNC officials. They were skeptical, dwelling on the possibility that the one essential component of a controlled experiment—removing a randomized sample from, in this case, urgent appeals to vote—could jeopardize Clinton's strategy to win over voters. "What if we pulled ten thousand people into our control group and the election is decided by two hundred votes?" Paul Tully, the party's political director, asked Malchow. His luck wasn't much better four years later with Penn, who made clear he had little interest in testing the campaign's voter contact programs. "I didn't think he was invested in fighting the battle he would have had to fight to really do this. He would have had to go to all the players and say we're going to do something different this time," Malchow reflects. "If they roll their eyes, it's not good business to battle over it. There's only so much you can lobby people for something that they're not interested in."

Malchow felt the same way as he bounced around Washington conference rooms promoting his other agenda. In each new conference room, he would reveal a PowerPoint presentation that described his CHAID method and how he had tried to put it to use in Oregon. Some of the campaign operatives, party officials, and consultants who saw Malchow's slides were intrigued, but none was sold. He came to realize that his foe was not only inertia, but also an institution that had developed a monopoly on the left's campaign data. The National Committee for an Effective Congress scores that had thwarted Malchow's efforts in Oregon existed for every precinct in the country, and a generation of Democratic operatives had been taught to treat the hundred-point figures with reverence. It was NCEC scores that made politics modern, the place where the guts of ward heelers were pushed aside by the statistical rigor of the computing era. Malchow's proposal to throw out these talismanic scores, built from actual vote totals, and instead use polling to conjecture how an individual might vote looked—to nearly everyone in the Democratic campaign establishment—like alchemy.

Upending the party's culture of precinct targeting with individual-level modeling would require what Malchow called a "battle royal" with

Mark Gersh, a brilliant but headstrong New Jerseyan who had worked on Capitol Hill before joining NCEC in 1978. Gersh built the committee into an indispensable player in Democratic campaigns, personally emerging as such an unrivaled expert in political geography that Gersh assumed a lucrative sideline helping broadcast networks call winners and losers on election night. When Malchow heard about a conference being planned in Las Vegas for Democrats rethinking get-out-the-vote strategies after the 1998 elections, he called friends to wrangle an invitation—but was told Gersh would never let him near it. "You get this model, and it's hard for anyone to rearrange the model," says Malchow. "All the parties at the table have a financial interest in the model."

The development of the political consulting profession meant that campaign conference calls were filled with an ever-increasing number of specialists all fighting to expand their slice of a limited pie. For the phone vendor, more phone calls were a natural solution; for the media consultant, a bigger ad buy would always do the trick. Everyone had an interest in promoting their own tool and whatever theory of the electorate helped to make a case for their tactics. They usually got paid for each piece of mail or phone call they put out, or a percentage of each ad buy they placed. But it was never a fair fight. It didn't hurt that the television was the one place where a candidate, retiring to his hotel room at the end of a long day on the trail, could actually spot his investment.

As he shopped his newfangled targeting system, Malchow was selling an investment that would either be invisible to candidates or seem redundant to them. After all, the significant cost in targeting was for a large-sample survey that overlapped with what pollsters were already being paid to do—and the best he could promise is that it would rearrange the campaign's existing mail strategy. When Malchow explained CHAID targeting to pollsters, he realized that they not only played little role in planning a campaign's mail program but often considered themselves rivals to it. Even though they served dramatically different functions for a candidate, pollsters and mail vendors fought for a share of the same budget.

What interest did a pollster ever have in making the mail program a more efficient investment?

Malchow found few takers even when he began offering his targeting service at cost, charging campaigns only the five thousand dollars in call center fees. "Everything he said made perfect logical sense to me. But he had a hard time selling it to other people—getting them to change the old tools they were using and people were comfortable with them. And a lot of people didn't understand what Hal was saying," says Anil Mammen, who worked for Malchow at the time. "Convincing people to ignore people they would otherwise mail or contact people they would otherwise ignore is a major hurdle. You're making an argument that's counterintuitive and your evidence is something they haven't seen before."

If you wanted to build a business designed to resist learning from itself, Malchow was discovering, it would look pretty much like the American electoral campaign. Candidates, who effectively serve as chairmen of their corporate boards, tend to come in two types: those who have won their last race and think they have cracked the code, or those who have never done it before and understand little about the increasingly specialized work done by campaign professionals. "Their job is to run government," says Mellman. "They certainly aren't immersing themselves in the tactics and techniques of campaigning, and nor should they."

Meanwhile, the candidate sits atop an evanescent multimillion-dollar business that has only one goal: market share on a single Tuesday. Election outcomes end up being treated as their own measure of political success, even though everyone involved knows that the final tally is shaped by factors both bigger and smaller than the acumen of any particular person involved. As soon as the votes were counted in Oregon, Wyden's campaign, and its late tactical shift from attacks on Smith to positive issue-based ads, was memorialized in triumphant terms. Smith's is recalled for having squandered a financial lead and structural advantages. Yet the result was decided by only eighteen thousand votes, such a marginal difference that a labor conflict distracting one of Wyden's union allies could have inverted the result. (Smith was elected to the Senate later that year to succeed Hatfield, and served two terms before losing his seat to Democrat Jeff Merkley in 2008.)

"There's only winning and losing," says Malchow. "You could run the best campaign for a loser against a huge headwind and against a whole lot of odds come close—and you're still a loser. If you do something different, everyone will point at the thing you did different and say that's why you lost. So if you're the campaign manager you don't do anything different. If you follow the rule book strictly they can't blame anything on you."

The paper trail that might illuminate what actually happened—the binders filled with polling data, the hard drives filled with databases accounting for every direct contact made with a voter—usually ends up in the nearest Dumpster. Often no one even convenes a postmortem among the staff operatives, consultants, and candidate to talk about what went wrong and why. "There's a real penalty for having a nickel left in the bank," says Laura Quinn, a deputy chief of staff to Vice President Al Gore. "So if you have any money left over for post-election analysis you must have done something wrong—that's the theory."

And then everyone goes on to the next campaign. Malchow never worked for Wyden again.

In January 1999, Malchow was summoned to the Eisenhower Executive Office Building to meet with the brain trust for Gore's nascent presidential campaign. Malchow's PowerPoint peregrinations had brought him a fair bit of notice, if little new business, among Democratic operatives. Now he was being invited to make the biggest pitch of all: trying to sell a front-running presidential candidate on the value of an altogether new system for targeting a national voter contact program. Malchow had some credibility in Gore's world, thanks to his successful management of the Tennesseean's first race for Senate fifteen years earlier. Back then, Gore didn't flinch at Malchow's proposal to invest in three computer terminals for the Nashville headquarters and hire a computer programmer to develop software to manage the candidate's schedule and track donations. From that experience, Malchow considered Gore one of the smartest people he had ever met, if ultimately less suited to politics than other intellectual pursuits. ("In some senses, I think he ended up in the place where he was least talented," Malchow says. "His confidence in his political judgment was never as high as his confidence in a wide range of other interests. This is why he was often overly cautious in his campaign strategies.")

The two had had little interaction in the intervening years, but Malchow's impressions of his old boss were confirmed as soon as Gore arrived for the presentation. Gore announced that he had just come from a meeting in his West Wing office with physicist Stephen Hawking, with whom the vice president enjoyed discussing such arcana as how cosmology supercomputers could measure previously imperceptible antigravitational forces. *Manna from heaven,* Malchow thought. "That's great," he told Gore. "Because I am here to talk about putting some science into this campaign."

Malchow described his CHAID technique, and he thought he saw Gore react approvingly. But when Malchow tried to follow up afterward with the campaign manager, Craig Smith, he never heard back. A simultaneous effort to convince the DNC to impose experimental controls on its mail program—what had become a quadrennial quest for Malchow—came up empty, too. Malchow became convinced that the political profession could never muster the skepticism to examine its own practices. The revolution would have to find its momentum elsewhere.

3

THE NEW HAVEN EXPERIMENTS

Don Green was still new to the Yale political science department when he began to suspect that his chosen discipline was intellectually bankrupt. In the 1950s, political scientists had started talking like economists, describing politicians and citizens as rational beings who acted to maximize their self-interest. Voters were believed to peruse a ballot the same way they examined a store shelf, calculating the benefits each product had presented and checking the box next to the one offering the best value. "Voters and consumers are essentially the same people," the economist Gordon Tullock wrote in his 1976 book *The Vote Motive*. "Mr. Smith buys and votes; he is the same man in the supermarket and in the voting booth." By the time Green began teaching in 1989, such thinking was pervasive among his peers. They saw politics as a marketplace where people and institutions compete for scarce power and resources with the clear, consistent judgment of accountants.

This detached view of human behavior was particularly galling to

Green, who was trained as a political theorist but found his greatest joy amid sophisticated board games. Growing up in Southern California, Green had played Civil War and World War II games with his brothers, a diversion he partly credits for his later interest in politics and history. When he first arrived at Yale, Green bonded with students and colleagues through games, which filled the interstices between classes and office hours, with a single competitive session often stretched over weeks. In the late 1990s, Green was playing at his colonial home in New Haven with his seven-year-old son and five-year-old daughter, using the plastic construction toy K'nex to build a lattice-like structure. The kids imagined spiderlike monsters moving from one square to the next. Green started to visualize from this a new board game, in which Erector-set-like limbs could be grafted onto basic checkers-style coins and every piece would become dynamic. Tinkering in his spare time, Green created a deceptively simple two-player game on a two-dimensional grid. At each turn, a participant could move one of his or her starting pieces or add a limb that would increase its power by allowing it to move in a new direction. "When you're playing chess, you play the hand you're dealt, where here you build your own pieces," says Green. "Imagine a game of chess where all the pieces start out as pawns." To bring his game to market, Green needed a prototype, so he taught himself woodworking and built a studio in his basement—the first time in his life, he realized, that he had done anything truly physical. Within a year, a Pennsylvania company had agreed to produce Octi—in which each turn required a player to make a choice between moving and building, all while trying to anticipate the opponent's response. Green described it as "an abstract idea of a game about mobilization."

Watching people play Octi only illustrated what Green already believed about their behavior. Even in a board game, human beings were incapable of logically assessing all of their options and making the optimal decision each time. Yet rational-choice scholars thought this is what people did every time they participated in politics—and what frustrated Green most was that these claims were purely speculative. The rational-choicers had built entire theoretical models to explain how institutions from Congress to the military were supposed to function. The more closely the rational-choice model was applied to the way politics actually worked, the less it seemed able to explain. In 1994, along with his colleague Ian Shapiro, Green coauthored a book titled *Pathologies of Rational Choice Theory,* in which he argued that the ascendant movement in political science rested on a series of assumptions that had not been adequately demonstrated through any real-world research. "There was reason to think the whole thing might be a house of cards," says Green.

When political scientists did try to explain real-world events, Green didn't think the results were much better. The principal tool of so-called observational research was correlation, a statistical method for seeking out connections between sets of data. Academics relied on a declaration of "statistical significance" to explain just about everything, yet demonstrating a correlation rarely illuminated much. For instance, one element that defined twentieth-century politics was the fact that people who lived in urban areas voted overwhelmingly Democratic. Were cities pulling their inhabitants to the left, or were liberal people drawn to cities? Or was there some other explanation altogether for the pattern? Perhaps most frustrating of all to Green and a junior colleague, Alan Gerber, was the inability of their discipline to even justify the individual decision to vote at all. Casting a ballot is the basic act of political behavior in a democracy, and yet political science offered little reason to explain why people would bother when there was no legal requirement. After all, considering the economic logic favored by rational-choicers, voting carried a known set of costs (the time and inconvenience of registering, learning about the candidates and going to the polling station) and little in the way of benefits (a tiny probability that an individual's vote would affect government policies). "There was good reason to think no one should vote," Green says.

Political scientists had toyed with this question for a generation, and by 1998 the most sophisticated thinking relied on the proposition that, as election day approached, voters calculated the likelihood they might be the pivotal vote deciding the race. In other words, before changing her plans to stop at a local firehouse on a rainy Tuesday in November, a harried working mother paused to assess the likelihood that she would cast the tie-breaking vote in a race with thousands, or even millions, of other citizens each making his or her own simultaneous calculations. "Is that how a typical voter thinks when he's casting his ballot?" Gerber asked.

If we can't explain what makes people vote, he and Green thought, let's see if we can affect their calculus behind doing so. To bolster their claim that basic political theories were unproven in the real world, Green and Gerber decided to do something political scientists were not supposed to. They would conduct an experiment.

* * * * *

IN THE LATE SUMMER of 1998, Green and Gerber sat in adjacent, wood-paneled offices at Yale's Institution for Social and Policy Studies, sheltered in a Richardsonian Romanesque building that was once a clubhouse for the secret society Wolf's Head, and scoured all they could find of the experimental tradition in political science. As an undergraduate at Yale, Gerber had learned how field experiments had been taken up by policymakers, notably those developing Lyndon B. Johnson's Great Society, to test the effects of new social programs. Perhaps the most famous were a series of experiments coordinated in 1968 by the White House to test the viability of a so-called negative income tax. The experiment, designed by a graduate student at the Massachusetts Institute of Technology, would randomize households below the poverty line to receive bonus payments and then measure their levels of employment afterward. The target was a major behavioral riddle that vexed the welfare state—how could the government give aid without undercutting the motivation to work?—and an empirical approach to solving it proved popular across the ideological divide. Running the federal Office of Economic Opportunity for the two years in which it oversaw the experiments were its director, Donald Rumsfeld, and his assistant, Dick Cheney. "In the deep recesses of my mind was the notion that some kind of large-scale experimentation was a thing that social scientists at one point or another did," says Gerber.

But that interest had never really pervaded the study of elections. Gerber and Green were surprised to find that the use of field experiments had begun, and effectively ended, with the publication of Harold Gosnell's *Getting Out the Vote* in 1927, and they were eager about the possibilities that opened up for them. "There are very few things in academia that are more exciting," says Green, "than doing things that either haven't been done before or haven't been done in a very long time." So he and Gerber began to read more generally about the origins of field experiments in other areas. The term hinted at the history: the earliest randomized trials grew out of searches for fertilizer compounds conducted by nineteenth-century researchers for the nascent chemical industry.

Each season, scientists at the Rothamsted Agricultural Experimentation Station in England would take a blend of compounds such as phosphate and nitrogen salts, alter the ratio of the chemicals, and sprinkle it over plots of rye, wheat, and potato planted in the clay soil of the estate north of London. One year's plant growth would be compared with the next, and the difference was recorded as an index of fertility for each chemical mixture. When the pipe-smoking mathematician R. A. Fisher arrived in 1919 and examined ninety years of experiments, he realized that the weather probably had had more to do with the variations in growth than the chemical blend. Even though Rothamsted researchers tried to discount for the volume of rain in a given season, there were many other things that varied unpredictably and even imperceptibly from year to year, like soil quality or sun or insect activity. Fisher redrew the experiment so that different chemical ratios could be compared with one another simultaneously. He split existing plots into many small slivers and then randomly assigned them different types and doses of fertilizer that could be dispensed at the same time. The size and proximity of the plots ensured that, beyond the varying fertilizer treatments, they would all experience the same external factors.

Not far from Fisher, a young economist named Austin Bradford Hill was growing similarly impatient with the limits of statistics to account for cause and effect in health care. In 1923, for example, Hill received a grant from Britain's Medical Research Council that sent him to the rural parts of Essex, east of London, to investigate why the area suffered uncommonly high mortality rates among young adults. Hill returned from Essex with an explanation that had little to do with the quality of medical care: the healthiest members of that generation quickly left the country to live in towns and cities. The whole British medical system was built on similarly misleading statistics, and Hill worried that the faulty inferences drawn from them put people's health at risk. Hill joined the Medical Research Council's scientific staff and began writing articles in the *Lancet* explaining to doctors in straightforward language what concepts like mean, median, and mode meant.

But even as he worked to educate the medical community about how to use the statistics it had—most from the rolls of life and death maintained by national registrars—Hill knew the quality of the numbers themselves was a potentially bigger problem. In medicine, "chance was regarded as an enemy of knowledge rather than an ally," writes historian Harry M. Marks. When clinicians ran controlled experiments, they looked to find two patients as similar as possible in every measurable respect, treat them differently, and attribute the outcome to the care they received. But Hill thought that this matching process—or alternating treatments on patients in the order they were admitted to a hospital—would always let uncontrolled variables leak in. "It is obvious that no statistician can be aware of all the factors that are, or may be, relevant," he wrote.

In 1943, a New Jersey chemist isolated streptomycin, an antibiotic that put up a promising fight against tuberculosis, and the pharmaceutical manufacturer Merck began producing it in large volumes. After the war ended, several companies in the United Kingdom, where the disease killed twenty-five thousand residents annually, made plans to introduce their own streptomycin. Meanwhile, a Mayo Clinic tuberculosis researcher traveled to London and Oxford to trumpet findings from his successful laboratory experiments on guinea pigs. The Medical Research Council received fifty kilograms of streptomycin and was quickly overwhelmed by requests from tuberculosis patients for some of the miracle cure. For Hill, who had become honorary director of the council's statistical research unit, the medicine shortage offered a promising opportunity to try a new type of experiment.

There was only a distant precedent for the idea of randomly splitting patients into separate groups and measuring the varying effects of treatments on each. The seventeenth-century Flemish physician and chemist Jan Baptista van Helmont had defended his technique by daring academic rivals to "take out of the hospitals, out of the camps, or from elsewhere, 200 or 500 poor People that have Fevers, Pleurisies, etc. Let us divide them into halfes, let us cast lots, that one half of them may fall to my share, and the other to yours . . . we shall see how many funerals both of us shall have." Into the twentieth century, however, such controlled testing came to be seen as ethically dodgy, since it meant consciously denying the best known care to those who wanted it. But because there wasn't enough streptomycin for everyone who requested it, the council had no choice but to leave people untreated. A decision to pass over some people randomly, Hill realized, offered an opportunity to improve the statistical quality of an important clinical experiment—and would also be a fairer method of distributing potentially lifesaving medicine.

Hill set out to translate Fisher's technique from the farm to the hospital. Each of the 107 tuberculosis patients in Hill's study was randomly assigned a number that put him in one of two treatment groups. The "S" cases were to receive two grams of streptomycin daily, spread over four doses, along with bed rest. The "C" cases were assigned only bed rest. Even once admitted to the hospital, a patient never learned which treatment he or she had been assigned.

After one year, Hill's investigators reviewed the health of the whole sample: a majority of the patients assigned streptomycin, 56 percent, had improved their condition over the course of their hospitalization, compared with 31 percent of the control sample. Over the same period, 22 percent of the S cases had died, compared with 46 percent of the C cases. Since Hill had randomized the treatment, there was only one way to explain the result: the new medicine worked. British companies began manufacturing streptomycin, which became an essential tool in the doctor's bags of those fighting tuberculosis, since most of the others were scalpels to cut a hole in the patient's chest and an air pump to collapse the infected lungs.

In an era in which wonder drugs emerged from labs worldwide, such blind randomized-control experiments quickly became the dominant tool for demonstrating that a new treatment worked and delivered no mitigating side effects. When, a few years later, Jonas Salk isolated a vaccine for polio, a successful large-scale randomized experiment—involving 1.8 million children—was a natural way to test it. In 1962, the Food and Drug Administration changed its standards to require "adequate and well-controlled investigations," and not merely clinical judgment, before approving a drug for wide use.

Gerber and Green believed they could bring this approach into politics. They wanted to explain electoral behavior with the same degree of authority that doctors now had in describing therapeutic care. Instead of patients, they would randomize individual households to separate the factors that affected voter participation. Most of the money in major campaigns was spent on television and radio, and it was impossible to treat one voter differently from a neighbor when broadcast waves covered a whole region. But individualized forms of contact—a canvasser's knock on the door, a pamphlet arriving in the mail, live or recorded phone calls— could be easily isolated.

Gerber was three years younger than Green, a political scientist by curiosity more than training. Gerber had arrived at Yale from MIT, where he earned a graduate degree in economics just as the school was becoming known as a center for cutting-edge research employing novel tools to examine subjects outside the typical bounds of economic study. Gerber and a classmate, Steve Levitt, kept being drawn to political questions, like whether the winner's fund-raising advantage could explain the outcome of congressional elections. (Levitt later won a John Clark Bates Medal and cowrote the bestselling book *Freakonomics*, exploring subjects such as the hierarchy of drug gangs and the ethics of sumo wrestlers.)

In his dissertation, Gerber used economic techniques to answer the type of question usually left to political scientists or historians: what happened when the United States adopted the secret ballot in the 1880s? That moment, when Americans went from picking their candidates aloud in crowded pubs to making their selections in curtained solitude, was key in forming the country's modern political culture, but it had never been analyzed in that way. "Until you read about the adoption of the secret ballot it would never occur to you that the secret ballot would need to be adopted," says Gerber. He wanted to know whether the shift had had an impact on how many Americans turned out on election day, how incentives might have changed when voting was converted from a public act to a private one. "At the most general level it seems pretty obvious that the payoffs for voting are social and psychological, not instrumental," says Gerber. "It seems very hard to imagine people figuring out the idea of the payoff for voting being literally your odds of being the pivotal vote."

The world of elections was not an academic abstraction to Gerber, who had spent just enough time around political campaigns to be interested when Green suggested putting their methods to the test. The stories that stuck with him from his own campaign experiences were ones that revealed a deep crisis of knowledge among those who practiced politics for a living. In 1987, not long after graduating from Yale, a twenty-three-year-old Gerber went to work as the New Hampshire scheduling director on Paul Simon's presidential campaign, responsible for managing the Illinois senator's itinerary in the first primary state. One day, he fielded a call from Simon's top Illinois-based consultant, a former journalist named David Axelrod, who was working on a batch of radio ads attacking one of Simon's midwestern rivals, Missouri congressman Dick Gephardt. "He even supported the neutron bomb," one of Axelrod's scripts read.

"For reasons not entirely clear to me, he asked the scheduler," recalls Gerber, referring to himself, " 'How do you think that'll play in New Hampshire?' "

"I'm not sure people in New Hampshire will know what the neutron bomb is," Gerber told Axelrod.

After he started teaching at Yale in 1993, Gerber interned for a summer in the Washington office of Democratic pollster Mark Mellman to get a different perspective on the way campaigns worked. One of the firm's polls itemized a list of qualities and asked voters if they would be more likely to support a candidate who shared that trait—including, to Gerber's amusement, "doesn't listen too much to polls."

Just as Green was coming to question his discipline, some political scientists had begun to conclude that the whole political-consulting profession was a farce. With nearly a half century of rich electoral data and ever-better measurements of national conditions, researchers had thought that they could explain presidential outcomes with a basic set of facts—primarily which party held power and how the economy fared while they did. Ads, debates, candidate speeches, and election organizing were mere spectacle at the margins of a predetermined outcome. The debate was summarized by an unusually succinct question: *Do campaigns matter?*

The more time Gerber spent within Mellman's polling operation, the more he appreciated that political scientists themselves lacked the tools to ever arrive at a convincing answer. Much of what academics thought they knew came from exit polls and post-election surveys like the University of Michigan's national election studies. Pollsters would ask people whether or not they voted, if they were contacted by a campaign before the election, then look for a correlation between the two. Gerber saw flaws in this method. He assumed that the people who answered polls were more likely to be those reachable by campaigns. Logic suggested also that respondents highly attuned to politics were more likely than others to remember when they were contacted by campaigns. Campaigns decide which voters to contact in the first place based on their own calculations of who is more likely to vote. "If you put this all together, you get a causal explanation of who knows what?" says Gerber. "These are technical issues, but until they are resolved you have no good answer to the question you are trying to understand."

* * * * *

SHORTLY BEFORE ELECTION DAY in 1998, Don Green and Alan Gerber walked through the streets of New Haven trying to monitor the dozens of students they had dispatched across the city, keeping an eye on approaching rain clouds and fretting that when they arrived there wouldn't be enough umbrellas to keep everyone dry. They had recruited off Yale bulletin boards, promising the generous pay of twenty dollars per hour, and assigned students into pairs according to buddy-system precepts. Where possible, Gerber and Green tried to hire local residents to serve as Sherpas in unfamiliar city neighborhoods. They checked in with their employees often and called everybody back in from the field at dusk. "We tried not to take chances," says Green. The students were knocking on doors to encourage people to vote in an upcoming election; that Green referred to this as "dangerous work" was evidence of just how detached, and sheltered, political science had grown from the world it supposedly studied.

Gerber and Green had designed a field experiment to measure what effects, if any, the most fundamental campaign methods could have on an election's outcome. They had selected three basic modes of voter contact—an oversized postcard arriving by mail, a scripted ring from a far-off call center employee, and a doorstep visit from a canvasser—and within each a series of different appeals to participate on November 3. One message pointed to an idea of civic duty, with an image of Iwo Jima, under the slogan "They fought . . . so we could have something to vote for." Another raised themes of community solidarity: "When people from our neighborhood don't vote we give politicians the right to ignore us." The last emphasized the prospect of a close election, illustrated with a "Dewey Defeats

Truman" headline. "Will yours be the deciding vote?" the postcard version asked. Various combinations of mode, message, and number of contacts were randomly deployed across thirty thousand New Haven voters scattered among twenty-nine of the city's thirty wards. (To "get away from students," as they later put it, the Yale professors removed the ward including the university from their study.) A control group would go without any contact. Afterward Gerber and Green would check the electoral rolls maintained by the town clerk to measure the influence of each type of contact on voter turnout.

Despite the national furor over the looming impeachment of Bill Clinton, there was little suspense about the outcomes of the top statewide races in Connecticut that fall. The state's popular Republican governor, John Rowland, and its longtime Democratic senator, Chris Dodd, were both going to be comfortably reelected. But the experiment made no reference to the particulars of that year's ballot, largely because Gerber and Green had chosen to partner with nonprofit groups prohibited by the tax code from taking a side in elections. That summer the two professors had presented their plan—which amounted, in essence, to creating their own political action committee for the sake of the experiment—to the local League of Women Voters chapter, which agreed to attach its name to the project. Then Gerber and Green found a Connecticut foundation willing to put up nearly fifty thousand dollars for the operation in the hopes that it would yield new strategies for increasing civic engagement after a generation of falling participation nationwide.

In that regard, the timing of Gerber and Green's gambit was fortuitous; everybody wanted to understand why Americans seemed to be retreating from public life. Three years earlier, Harvard professor Robert Putnam had emerged as the most visible political scientist in the country on the basis of a journal article titled "Bowling Alone: America's Declining Social Capital." (It would later become the basis for a bestselling book.) Putnam looked at declining membership figures in nonpolitical community organizations—from bowling leagues to Elks Lodges and the League of Women Voters, whose ranks had shrunk nearly in half nationwide since the late 1960s—to argue that a distinctively American civil society had dissolved into a fizz of solitary entertainments and self-interest. Putnam mostly kept clear of electoral politics in his article, but the same pattern was apparent there, too: between 1960 and 1988, voter turnout rates in presidential campaign years fell by 12 percentage points. A director of the University of Michigan's National Election Studies at the time, Steven Rosenstone, dove into decades' worth of survey data in search of explanation. In a 1993 book resulting from that effort, Rosenstone and John Mark Hansen had spread responsibility widely. The electorate had expanded (with the constitutional change of the voting age to eighteen) while individual voters grew disengaged (they were less attached to candidates and parties, and had lost confidence in their electoral power). But much of the blame, according to Rosenstone and Hansen, belonged to politicians themselves for losing touch with voters as they embraced new media. Party organizations that had once mobilized votes by speaking directly with their constituents had receded into the background, replaced by candidate campaigns that chose to blare their messages over the airwaves.

In early 1999, Gerber and Green waited restlessly for local election authorities to update New Haven's individual voter histories to reflect who had cast a ballot in November. They were in an unusual situation for a pair of political scientists: they did not know what they would be arguing, if anything at all, when it came time to publish the results. But they already had a hunch. In the days before the election, Gerber and Green were able to patch into the North Dakota call center they had hired to dial voters, and they were amazed by how perfunctory the exchanges were. The caller often sounded like he or she was rushing through the script to get to the end before the recipient hung up. (Most political call centers are paid based on the number of "completes" they fulfill.) Even when the caller successfully reached the end of her script, the academics listening in heard little that made them think the voter was being engaged by the appeal, or even listening. "There's no way this can work," Gerber told Green as they eavesdropped on one call.

He was right. When the results of the experiment came in, the phone calls showed no influence in getting people to vote. The direct-mail program increased turnout a modest but appreciable 0.6 percentage points for each postcard sent. (The experiment sent up to three pieces per household.) But the real revelation was in the group of voters successfully visited by one of the student teams: they turned out at a rate 8.7 percentage points higher than the control sample, an impact larger than the margin in most competitive elections. When Gerber and Green reread Rosenstone and Hansen, they began to question whether the authors had fully accounted for the historic drop in turnout during the late twentieth century. Maybe the issue wasn't just that Americans were being mobilized by campaigns any less, but that even the new forms of individual contact lacked a personal touch. A message that may have once been spoken at the doorstep would now come facelessly by phone or mail. The professionalization of such consulting services, and the growth in campaign budgets to employ them, meant that it was often easier to find paid workers to deliver a message than it would be to recruit and manage volunteers.

Other academic research had shown that in-person appeals were particularly effective in encouraging other "prosocial" behaviors, like recycling newspapers or donating blood. How to get people to undertake activities that offered no individual-level benefits but helped the community as a whole was a conundrum that theorists called the problem of "collective action," and it sat at the center of most rational-choice explorations of why people vote (or don't). In their experiments, Gerber and Green concluded, the costs and benefits of voting had not been appreciably altered by the volunteers' visit, but it had certainly changed whatever internal calculus people used when deciding whether to go to the polls. "There's nothing about that which should make you more likely to vote," says Green. "It was a collective-action problem before I showed up, and it's a collective-action problem after I showed up." But now his experiment was pointing to a potential solution: maybe one way you could get people to vote was simply to have other people ask them to.

The Yale researchers began turning their findings into an article with an understated title, "The Effects of Canvassing, Telephone Calls, and Direct Mail on Voter Turnout: A Field Experiment," that reflected the modest pragmatism of their accomplishment. What had started as a pilot study to settle internecine disputes within their discipline turned out not to yield any bold theoretical insights. Instead, Gerber and Green had stumbled into almost embarrassingly practical but valuable lessons in street-level politics. They sent their paper to the *American Political Science Review,* the discipline's most prestigious venue and the same one where Gosnell had published his work seventy-five years earlier. The paper was rejected. "In short, its findings are entirely confirmatory of previous work. The paper does not offer any new theory about voter behavior," an anonymous peer reviewer wrote. "That said, I think the study is useful, and I wish the authors luck in getting it published elsewhere."

Gerber and Green successfully appealed the decision and in September 2000 their study appeared in the journal, but then only under the secondary designation of "research note." But the fusty peer review standards did not much concern the campaign professionals whose methods were under examination, and who welcomed the Gerber-Green study with the same mixture of dread and flattery that washing machine dealers likely felt when the inaugural *Consumer Reports* came out. Political operatives had been trained to view political scientists with skepticism, even hostility. They saw academics as intellectual snobs with no practical experience, conjuring abstract models on college campuses far removed from the chaos and urgency of real campaigns. "Those smart guys speak that smart language. They collect smart theories to properly arrange their smart facts. Then they publish smart papers to make sure people know they are real smart," says Tom Lindenfeld, a former Democratic National

Committee campaign director and one of the party's leading field tacticians. "The rest of us just know what works."

The Gerber-Green experiments, though, were hard to overlook. The findings assailed many of the consulting class's business models and provoked a minor civil war within it. Direct-mail vendors happily used the Gerber-Green findings to suggest that candidates would be wasting their money on phone calls. "It created a furor because what it effectively was saying was that a lot of the expenditures weren't getting you bang for the buck," says Ken Smukler, a Pennsylvania-based consultant.

As word of the New Haven findings circulated, battered photocopies of the article passed from one hand to the next like social science samizdat. "A lot of what gets done on campaigns gets done on the basis of anecdotal evidence, which often comes down to who is a better storyteller. Who tells a better story about what works and what doesn't work?" says Christopher Mann, a former executive director of the New Mexico Democratic Party. "It might be that their phone script made a difference—or it might be that one was Alabama and one was Arkansas and they were fundamentally different races."

Gerber and Green had identified the first tool that was able to satisfyingly disentangle cause and effect and demonstrate what actually won votes. "It became really obvious to me very quickly that my quibbles about what had been going on in campaigns were being addressed with field experiments," says Mann. The next year he applied to graduate school at Yale so that he could study with Gerber and Green, who were eager to have someone with Mann's political experience as they plotted new field trials. "They had a very clear sense that what they had done to that point was just scratching the surface," says Mann. "They had an idea that there was an audience for this stuff among campaign folk. But they needed to understand how to ask the questions that mattered to campaigns and not just academia."

In the fall of 2000, Gerber and Green were invited to speak to the

Carnegie Corporation, one of many civic-minded institutions that had added dwindling voter turnout to their list of concerns over the course of the 1990s. Because the tax code allowed nonprofit organizations to run registration and turnout drives as long as they did not push a particular candidate, organizing "historically disenfranchised" communities (as Carnegie described them) became a backdoor approach to ginning up Democratic votes outside the campaign finance laws that applied to candidates, parties, and political action committees. Major liberal donors got into the GOTV game: Project Vote organized urban areas, Rock the Vote targeted the young, the NAACP National Voter Fund focused on African-Americans. "You were seeing much more energy devoted to turnout," says Thomas Mann, a Brookings Institution scholar who hosted an event with Gerber and Green in a Capitol Hill committee room at the time. "They were putting resources into it, and didn't have a very good way of measuring the effectiveness of it."

When Gerber and Green stepped into a conference room at Carnegie, they unwittingly stumbled into an epic battle for resources within lefty interest groups. Ground-level field organizers had been losing their share of budgets to broadcast ads and commercial-style marketing campaigns, for what the organizers believed was no reason other than that mass-media platforms looked sexier. The Gerber-Green study demonstrating that door-knocking delivered results was the redemptive evidence for which they had long waited, salvation with footnotes. "Someone off to my right whispered, 'This is like the Beatles,'" Green recalls of the Carnegie visit, the air particularly electric for a think-tank session. "It was only beginning to dawn on me why we were heroic figures."

4

THE TWO PERCENT SOLUTION

I n the early afternoon of November 7, 2000, Karl Rove began to panic. The first wave of national exit polls had been released at midday, and as the numbers arrived at Governor George W. Bush's headquarters in Austin, Texas, they foretold catastrophe. Rove, the campaign's chief strategist, was worried. He summoned his regional political directors one by one into his office to ask what they were hearing from each of their states.

Matthew Dowd, who oversaw Bush's polling operation, was not as shocked as Rove. Dowd had prepared for a tough election day. Typically campaigns cease their polling on the Thursday prior to a vote, just before voters become hard to reach on their home phones over the weekend. Even then, there is little room for strategic adjustments; a campaign manager who learns on Friday that the dynamics of a race have shifted has few tools left to use. It is usually impossible to find a block of advertising time still for sale, and the closing spots have already been cut and delivered to stations. At best, the manager can reroute the candidate's weekend itinerary, order a final burst of new robocalls, or try to shuffle GOTV resources. But the headlines would force Dowd to break from standard practice. On Thursday, Dowd learned that a Maine television station had unearthed a driving-under-the-influence charge that had been lodged by local authorities against Bush twenty-four years earlier. Unbeknownst to Rove, Dowd ordered up two more nights of polling in three crucial states.

What had been a slight advantage for Bush at the end of the previous week disappeared. In Michigan, Bush had trailed Al Gore by one to two percentage points on Friday; when Dowd awoke to new numbers on Tuesday his candidate lagged by five points. Bush's three-point lead in Florida on Friday was gone; the state had become dead even. Maine moved from a toss-up to out of Bush's reach. As Dowd looked closely into the polls, he saw why margins had closed: social conservatives, who had always been a bit skeptical of Bush, had lost enthusiasm for him after the drunk-driving revelation.

As election day wore on, the updates Rove was getting from the regional political directors grew more dire. From around the country came increasingly fearsome reports of Democratic field operations outmatching their Republican counterparts. "We found out there were state parties that lacked sufficient volunteers to get the job done," says Rove. "We recognized we were having a problem. It just became a bigger problem than we had anticipated because of the impact of the DUI."

When the polls started to close on the East Coast, the consequences of this tactical gap grew evident to Dowd. The county-by-county returns in battleground states delivered the dénouement in a narrative that had been foreshadowed by the weekend polls. While Bush had suffered slightly depressed turnout among voters who should be the Republican base, Democrats—though never particularly enthused about Gore's candidacy—still showed up in force. Even before the first planes of lawyers set off from Austin to Florida, a consensus developed at Bush's headquarters that Democrats had turned the election into an effective tie because of their mobilizing prowess.

A few Republican strategists were prepared for this. Some had even quietly suspected that the opposition's surprising strength in the 1998 congressional elections could be attributed to what appeared to be a newly toned turnout muscle of Democrats and their labor allies. But Republicans readily accepted this disparity as a fact of life, just as Democrats cursed their opponents' advantage in financing their campaigns. Now the outcome of a presidential election hung perilously in the balance as a result. "That was a little bit of a shock to the Republican system," says Curt Anderson, a longtime Republican consultant who worked on Bush's campaign. "They were better equipped to communicate with their voters and get them to the polls. We'd been doing the same thing over and over again for twenty years."

* * * * *

OVER THOSE DECADES, the Democrats started to approach field operations with a new seriousness. The reason had a lot to do with Paul Tully, a chain-smoking former Yale offensive lineman who had made his name in Democratic circles organizing the Iowa caucuses for Ted Kennedy in 1980. Four years later he strategized Walter Mondale's path to the party's nomination, and he became a mentor to dozens of young operatives who were inspired by the way that he brought a quantitative rigor to Matt Reese–era advances in electioneering. "Paul was always poring over numbers and looking for an interesting hook," says Doc Sweitzer, who was Tully's partner in a Philadelphia-based consulting firm in the early 1980s. "So many consultants aren't good at this because they never took a math class. That made him different from guys who come from the political-hack side."

Tully was one of Ron Brown's first hires when Brown became the Democratic National Committee's chairman in early 1989. Democrats had suffered three straight presidential losses and were seen as hopelessly divided. Compared with the regimented Republicans, the Democratic Party of the 1980s resembled a loose alliance of identity-based groups and organized labor—too undisciplined and varied ideologically to rally around broad, thematic election-year messages. Brown, who was close to Kennedy and had worked on Jesse Jackson's campaign in 1988, thought that only the DNC could rise above the party's fractiousness. He relegated the ethnic and racial caucuses, imagining the committee as the permanent presidential campaign organization. (Tully made clear he didn't think the DNC's agenda included electing Democrats to Congress, a branch of government to which he referred collectively as "the midgets.") Committee operatives, he decided, would spend the four-year cycle between votes compiling binders stuffed with opposition research and state-specific strategy plans, ready for handoff to whichever candidate Democrats nominated at their 1992 convention. The fact that Brown had hired Tully as his political director—and Tully had accepted the job, which many thought beneath him—was an immediate signal to the Washington political community of Brown's seriousness.

"Up until that point many people had thought of the DNC as a party in some European sense," said Mark Steitz, who had worked with Brown on Jackson's campaign and joined the committee as its research director. "He made clear to us that every day our job was to come in and figure out what we could do to win the presidential election in 1992. Anything else—improving the image of the Democratic party, making the coalition of people in the Democratic party happy with one another—we could spend time on, but only if it was in the purpose of electing a president in 1992."

Late in the day, Tully would often stop at the National Committee for an Effective Congress's office on the other side of the National Mall, and lose himself in the maps and files overnight. When he returned to the DNC in late morning, he would spend hours on the phone with people around the country, gathering information on what was happening in their states. "I'm in the information business!" he would pip, by way of explanation. Precinct-level data was getting richer and richer, and when Tully was dispatched to Little Rock, Arkansas, in 1992 to coordinate Bill Clinton's campaign he had a new trove of numbers at his disposal. After its 1990 count, the U.S. Census for the first time introduced data on block groups—previously tabulated only for cities—for every county nationwide. That gave analysts a granular unit, around four thousand people, for measuring education and income, often complementary measurements of socioeconomic status. Fresh Census numbers matter, especially in dynamic areas like the Sun Belt, where populations churned so much that data became stale by the end of a ten-year cycle. An early user of computers for campaign work, Tully was obsessed with finding new sources of information—especially economic data that could pinpoint political terrain that had become more competitive during a recession—helpful to a Clinton war room working to discern where its voters were.

Six weeks before election day, the forty-eight-year-old Tully, whose perpetual energy had been sustained by voluminous amounts of coffee, cigarettes, and pizza, died of a heart attack in his Little Rock hotel room. "He had worked for four years on this—he had every map, every target, he probably knew the name of every swing voter in the country," Clinton strategist James Carville told the *New York Times* for its obituary. On election night, the laminated necklace credentials granting access to the campaign's boiler room said "270 for Tully," a reference to the number of electoral votes necessary to win the presidency. (Clinton ultimately won 370.) "The Republicans' orientation towards data at the time had been more advanced," says Celinda Lake, a Clinton pollster. "Tully was the first person who really tried to drive innovation on data on the Democratic side."

Tully had left the DNC a new apparatus designed to specialize in turnout. The national and state parties, legislative campaign committees, and statewide and congressional candidates were all required to chip into a single fund that would run unified GOTV operations for the entire Democratic ticket. These so-called coordinated campaigns handled all of the voter contacts and IDs (and the heavy election-day machinery of phone banks and vans) so that instead of duplicating the same contacts Democrats could widen their universe of targets. As Bill Clinton antagonized liberal interest groups in his first term with his support of welfare reform and the North American Free Trade Agreement, party leaders saw a well-organized turnout operation as key to rousing the "base vote," referring largely to urban minorities, before his 1996 reelection. Party efforts were boosted by a new "Labor '96" program, led by the AFL-CIO and its affiliated unions, which made a conscious effort to reassert themselves in Democratic politics by turning out voters directly rather than merely writing checks to favored candidates.

A sense was settling in that the parties simply approached election day differently. Democrats, whose voters tended to be packed into dense settings where door-to-door contact was highly efficient, equipped their canvassers with clipboards and maps outlining friendly precincts that targeters at the National Committee for an Effective Congress had flagged for "blind pulls," indiscriminately yanking voters from their home. Republicans imperiously ran voter contact operations from afar, their typically better-funded campaigns blasting messages over television and relying on a well-networked coalition of satellite groups—gun owners, churches, farm bureaus—to talk to their members through voter guides. One side practiced politics as though it were a series of Great War infantry battles, the other as though directing the Kosovo air war from a command center hundreds of miles away, disinclined to muddy a single boot on the ground.

The efforts Tully had inspired were solidified in legend only one election later. The most revered Democratic operative of 2000 was not Gore speechwriter and strategist Bob Shrum or campaign manager Donna Brazile, but Michael Whouley, an elusive Bostonian whose job description was often given as "field general." His cult extended from the party's most junior field organizers to the political reporters to whom he refused to grant interviews all the way to Gore himself, who fanned his aide's aura of mystery. Newspaper profiles were filled with accounts of his tricks, notably the rush-hour traffic jam Whouley had been accused of instigating on the day of the New Hampshire primary to keep supporters of Gore's primary rival, Bill Bradley, from the polls. The Whouley mythology courted a component of the party's often smug self-conception: Democrats won their elections through hard work and street smarts. It was, in essence, a labor theory of value in politics, favorably contrasted with the top-down capital-intensive efforts of the right. "It's just a cultural difference," says Tom Bonier of NCEC, who spent the fall of 2000 working on Democratic campaign efforts in Michigan. "They just don't do this the way we do."

Bush may have carried the election, but Democrats had won the ground game. Republicans had shown themselves highly disciplined about every part of politics but the voting. Next time, many Republican strategists worried, they might not be so lucky, or able to count on lawyers and judges to carry them through. Now they had one of their own in the White House, and if they wanted to keep him there they had four years to catch up in the crucial game of turning out votes.

* * * * *

EVEN BEFORE GEORGE W. BUSH moved into the White House, Matthew Dowd installed himself in an office at the Republican National Committee in Washington. He had spent the previous two decades working exclusively on Democratic campaigns, and even though he had been detailed to the RNC by George W. Bush's closest adviser, Karl Rove, the party's Capitol Hill headquarters still felt a bit like enemy territory. Dowd was an Austinite whose entry into Republican politics had come on local terms: not as the result of any ideological shift but from a confidence in the charismatic power of Bush. Dowd had been assured that his tour of duty at the RNC would be a brief one, offering him a chance to resettle in Austin before being called up for Bush's reelection. "Dowd was in the enviable position of being on the outside with a lot of time to think about stuff," says Sara Taylor, who became a regional political director at the White House. "He was the guy sitting in the room with no dirt on his hands."

While the Bush campaign leadership litigated the outcome of the 2000 election, Dowd looked ahead to 2004. He saw a country more riven than ever before along partisan lines. The phenomenon of ticket-splitting was effectively dead. In 1984, one-quarter of voters had cast a ballot that included both Democrats and Republicans; in 2000, only 7 percent had. The next campaign would be a "motivation election," as Dowd put it in the first strategy memo of Bush's reelection. Swing voters had entranced presidential strategists for a generation, Dowd thought, but those mercurial centrists were shrinking in number. A new premium should be placed on finding and mobilizing those who already identified with Republicans. It would be easier to grow Bush's market share by expanding his base than by chasing new votes in the middle.

Bush's reelection campaign was about to inherit two of the most valuable advantages in American politics: an incumbent president's unchallenged control of a national party committee and the ability to raise hundreds of millions of dollars. At the White House, an exultant Rove envisioned using the four-year term to plot a partisan realignment of the electorate just as his hero, Mark Hanna, had engineered one on behalf of William McKinley a century earlier. Rove believed Bush's "compassionate conservatism," with its focus on education and immigration reform, could sand off the hard edges of post-Reagan Republicanism and create a long-lasting home within the party for Latinos and moderate suburbanites, two of the country's fastest-growing demographics.

Dowd had an agenda that was at once more historically modest and practically ambitious. His long, ovaloid head was perennially racked with worry, a condition that friends attributed to having been raised as one of eleven children in a Michigan Catholic family. Rove dubbed him "our dour Irishman," and now Dowd's almost primal sense of fatalism focused on the political moment. Perhaps the president's leadership will trigger a permanent shift, thought Dowd, but it would be foolish to plan on it. In fact, Dowd's analysis glumly foretold an indefinite era of ideological deadlock. "We would go into the election assuming it would be as close as 2000," says Dowd. "What are things we could do differently that might affect a point or two?"

The RNC's chief of staff, Jack Oliver, enlisted his deputy, Blaise Hazelwood, to help assemble an "Election Day Operations Task Force" to investigate an answer. Hazelwood, a twenty-nine-year-old veteran of presidential, statewide, and legislative campaigns, was known as one of the most disciplined and discreet operatives at party headquarters. Hazelwood had started working for the party in 1994, just out of college. After November, she was supposed to be laid off as part of a routine downsizing between elections. But when Curt Anderson, the party's political director, would arrive at headquarters at 6 a.m., he would find the coffee made and Hazelwood hard at work. "She was on the list to be fired but she would not let herself be fired," says Anderson. "What I found is you can't ever fire her." Hazelwood had long, dark, wavy hair and a tentative manner on the few occasions she spoke to large crowds, as though nervous that saying too much could lead her to give away valuable secrets. But her obsessive attention to detail, and her perpetual willingness to work eighteen-hour days without complaint, made her a perfect candidate for a project Dowd realized would require epic feats of organization and indefatigability.

They named the project the 72-Hour Task Force, a reference to the closing three days of a campaign during which Dowd believed Republicans were being repeatedly outmuscled by Democrats in the quest to make sure supporters voted. By happenstance the task force's first full meeting, in mid-March, took place in room 2000 of the party headquarters. The reminder of the previous November had its uses, Dowd thought. Many of the party's most influential consultants had worked on Bush's presidential campaign, and Dowd worried they were insufficiently chastened by the outcome. Bush had lost the popular vote nationwide by half a million votes, had carried six states by a margin of five percentage points or fewer, and his election had been secured only by thirty-six days of epic litigation and petty political maneuvering in Florida. "We basically got through on the skin of our teeth," Dowd said.

The materials spread out before select members of the RNC, congresspeople, and other party grandees who attended were meant as a sobering tonic after months of intoxicating triumphalism. Hazelwood had asked the RNC's research department to scour newspapers for accounts of what liberal allies had done on Gore's behalf the previous fall. Their six-page compendium—bearing the headline "What the Bad Guys Did?"—documented the way Democrats had learned to mobilize like an infantry, from the forty field staffers that the NAACP dispatched to battleground states to a Service Employees International Union phone bank with thirty-six lines, computer-assisted dialing, and the ability to make one thousand calls an hour, all within the trailer of a purple eighteen-wheel truck that volunteers called "Barney." What most awed Republicans was the turnout strategy from Hillary Clinton's successful run for Senate the previous year. A copy of the document found its way into Hazelwood's hands, and she studied its careful assignment of activity by paid and volunteer staff, plotted over a six-month period down to the block level. "We were obsessed with her plan," Hazelwood says.

Hazelwood was astonished at how different this looked from the way that Republicans prepared for election day. Reagan's new right showed the movement's core to be an assemblage of enthusiastic constituencies—religious true believers, free-market enthusiasts, military loyalists committed to a hawkish foreign policy. Even though conservatives scorned Democrats as beholden to unions and other identity organizations, Republican strategists started thinking about their party as a coalition of distinct interest groups, all invited to march in lockstep at election time. In the late 1970s, Richard Viguerie, the direct-mail fund-raising innovator, had acquired lists from ideologically sympathetic institutions—religious book clubs, righty magazines, and gun clubs—and mailed their members on behalf of conservative causes, with dire warnings about the liberal threat. In the 1980s, thanks in large part to Viguerie's success cultivating small donors, the Republican National Committee had built up a permanent financial advantage over the Democrats. Party leaders made heavy investments in burnishing the party's brand through television ads and pushing issues over talk radio. Yet when it came to directly getting their voters to the polls, Republican strategists hewed largely to Viguerie's approach of sub-franchising the work to coalition allies, trusting outside groups to know their followers.

In 2000, Hazelwood had served as the RNC's coalitions director, over-seeing three dozen networks, including sportsmen and Hispanics. Mean-while, the Bush campaign focused on seven major coalitions, including agriculture and social conservatives. The campaign collected membership directories from the farm bureaus and megachurches whose ranks were packed with active Republicans, and then developed a strategy for com-municating with each set of voters on the issues they could be expected to care about (agriculture subsidies, prayer in school). But the coalitions rarely had significant manpower of their own to offer, and certainly not on the scale of what Democrats got from labor unions, so when Republicans wanted to put out pre-election reminders by phone they had to use paid call centers. When it came to their party's turnout strategy, Republicans would chuckle that GOTV stood for "Get on Tele Vision"—a joke about the lack of an available workforce and the diffusion of their supporters. "When Democrats walk a precinct they're going to hit more votes than we are. It's just the nature of it," says Adrian Gray, who worked as a regional political director for Bush in 2000 before joining the White House staff. "We had to take geography out of the equation."

One of the biggest problems, as Dowd laid it out in room 2000, was the voters Republicans took most for granted. Christian conservatives were the Republican counterpart of the Democrats' labor base, but task force members griped that they lacked the "intensity of organization at the grassroots level" that the unions had. Dowd presented exit poll data showing that after Republicans took back Congress in 1994, the share of voters who identified with the religious right slipped. (One of Dowd's slides showed that while unions and religious conservatives each repre-sented about 20 percent of the voting-age population, 26 percent of those who voted in 2000 were union members and only 14 percent were reli-gious conservatives.) If capturing both houses of Congress diminished the conservative base's appetite for power, task force members wondered, what messages could mobilize it when the movement was represented in all three branches of government, as it was now?

Dowd was interested in a debate over issue message and strategy, but he thought there were more basic matters to address. How could Republicans tailor narrow messages to their base if they did not know, in individual terms, who the members of their base were? And how would they deliver those messages if the party had no protocols for voter contact? Republicans, he decided, had to figure out what made people vote. "I had heard enough of these stories, but where's the fucking data? Everybody always bullshits all the time about *Oh, this won the campaign!*" says Dowd. "We just knew that a systematic approach was the only way we could really judge it, and rate differences as opposed to stories, anecdotes."

Dowd had quit graduate school at the University of Texas in the 1980s to work on campaigns, but the former political science student prided himself on paying more fealty to academic research than did many of his consulting peers. At the end of 2000, as Dowd tried to catch up on reading that had piled up during the campaign thrum, he came across the article in *American Political Science Review* in which Don Green and Alan Gerber recounted their New Haven experiment. The findings that in-person contact worked better than mail and phones confirmed Dowd's instincts. The article also convinced him that the academics' randomized-trial method was one the party could adopt to run its own experiments and develop a new set of best practices for turnout. "One of the incentives for doing tests was to change the culture of allocating resources," says Hazelwood. "To convince our campaign managers and general consultants to take money out of their media buys and put it into the ground, we needed real results and real tests."

Dowd knew a serious experimental regime would threaten many of the party's longtime consultants and vendors, especially media specialists whose overfed campaign budgets had starved Republican field operations. He didn't much care. "Having come from the Democratic side, I wasn't aware of all these people," he says. "I didn't have a stake in it." But Hazelwood, who had worked in Republican campaigns her whole career and was married to one of their leading direct-mail vendors, did. It would be her job to insulate the party's culture from the jolt Dowd was about to deliver. To reduce the likelihood of internecine conflicts that could follow among consultants whose interests were newly pitted against one another, Hazelwood decided it would be important that their research agenda look like a party-wide effort, at once centralized and collaborative. Hazelwood's e-mailed invitations to meetings of the 72-Hour Task Force did not need to spell out a warning that the 2004 campaign budget would be shaped by the task force's decisions, and that it was better for any consultant to be inside the room than outside it. "It was Karl Rove's baby and they wanted to be part of that," says Hazelwood.

Every week or two throughout the spring of 2001, around forty Republican consultants, summoned by Hazelwood's e-mail, would arrive in Washington, traveling from across the country at their own expense. The group slowly compiled a list with dozens of possible research queries, many skeptically addressing "things we all thought we knew," according to Hazelwood, and others with questions no one had ever thought to ask. They would test the value of a message sent by phone as opposed to mail, obviously, but what about two phone calls versus one, or two phone calls versus two mailed brochures? Did a piece of mail followed by a phone call have a different impact than the opposite sequence? Did it matter whether the caller or door-knocker was a volunteer or a paid contractor? What could the party do to increase new registrations and take advantage of opportunities to cast an absentee ballot or participate in early-vote programs being introduced in several states?

Unlike Dowd, who had worked in media and polling, Hazelwood saw a particular value in the experiments beyond the findings themselves. Because Republicans lacked the tradition of in-person canvassing that ran deep in Democratic culture, Hazelwood worried that field organizers would have trouble convincing volunteers to take on unfamiliar, and often charmless, duties. A scientific study with measurable effects could help show field-workers that their tasks were crucial to the broader effort. "They were crying out for this data, all of the time asking: 'Why are we doing this?'" she says, recalling her interactions with grassroots activists she tried to enlist in 2000 as part of her coalitions work. The next time those questions came up, "we could say: 'I know it sucks in Florida walking in the summer, but look at these tests—it improved turnout.'"

Hazelwood mapped out a rough schedule for the next three and a half years. She wanted to complete the tests quickly so that Republicans could start to rebuild their electioneering operation in 2002, when one-third of Senate seats and a majority of the nation's governorships would be in play, and perfect them in time for 2004. For those seeking to shift the balance of power in the United States, 2001 offered a meager roster of elections. But for those seeking to learn how campaigns work, it amounted to fertile experimental terrain.

* * * * *

THE FIRST WEEK of October 2001, eight RNC staffers drove from headquarters seventy miles to the northwest of Washington, D.C., and came to a halt, as though looking to settle just beyond the periphery of the capital's influence. They had journeyed through dense inner-ring Virginia suburbs, and then past the blossom of office parks and new housing developments that marked the quickly emerging communities demographers like to call "exurbs" and that White House strategists saw as friendly turf nationwide for Bush's moderate, family-oriented conservatism. The caravan settled in Winchester, the redbrick seat of bucolic Frederick County, in the Shenandoah valley. The RNC staffers found an empty storefront between a local Republican headquarters and an Irish pub and began to turn it into a field office in a place where the national party had never before had a direct presence.

As in much of rural Virginia, Republicans had taken Frederick County's votes for granted ever since they broke for Richard Nixon in 1968. With its network of politically involved churches and active gun culture, there was little chance of the area going blue. But it was also a place where the Republicans' laissez-faire approach to base turnout may have limited their vote totals at the expense of statewide candidates. A few months earlier, Hazelwood had approached Timmy Teepell, who had succeeded her as coalitions director, to propose that he design and oversee the most ambitious experiment on the task force's docket. Hazelwood had prepared to make a large investment to test how a new approach to coalition organizing could benefit Republican performance. What would happen if the RNC overwhelmed one of its strongholds with both paid contact and volunteer operations?

Virginia had one of the few gubernatorial elections on the calendar, a race whose stakes would matter to social conservatives. For comparison, Teepell selected two counties whose size and demographics were similar, and where coalition allies had a large footprint: Frederick, in the northwest corner of the state, and Roanoke, to its south. (In 2000, Bush had carried both counties with more than 60 percent of the vote.) In one, the RNC would try to maximize its presence; in the other, they would stay away and let the state party proceed with its normal efforts on behalf of its gubernatorial nominee, who was Attorney General Mark Earley, and down-ballot candidates. "Frederick was closer to my home, so we used that as the test and Roanoke as the control," says Teepell, who commuted to Washington from suburban Loudoun County. "I had three kids and wanted to sleep in my own bed."

Teepell's eight-person team, comprising the RNC's entire coalitions department, arrived in Winchester in time to spend the last five weeks cultivating the conservative base there. Teepell was given the standard binder of research that the party had prepared on Democratic gubernatorial nominee Mark Warner, a former telecom entrepreneur who in an earlier Senate race had built a statewide reputation as a probusiness moderate with the potential to win crossover votes. The material that polls showed was most likely to provoke social conservatives was an unearthed clip from a Warner speech to a Democratic convention seven years earlier when Warner, the party chairman, attacked the state's conservative activists as extreme. In Frederick County, Warner's quote became grist for four targeted mail pieces ("Mark Warner described the views of people of faith and homeschoolers as 'threatening' to America"), four paid phone calls, and two ads on local Christian radio stations.

Because he came out of the world of coalitions organizing, Teepell tended to think of politics not as an activity conducted in well-bounded geographic spaces but as one that pulsed through networks of people linked by common interests. Teepell had his team make a list of the local communities he called "social precincts," and when it became time to recruit volunteers he had his staff fan out to gun shops and church events. "You may have a neighborhood that tends to vote a certain way," he says. "You can also have a homeschool cooperative who think similarly about the same issues, but because they are across the region you can talk to them when they come together." Teepell arrived in Frederick with a particular interest in marshaling those homeschool families, many of them Christian conservatives opting out of secular schools. His own political career had begun as a homeschooled fifteen-year-old going door-to-door for Republican candidates in his native Baton Rouge, Louisiana. Now he looked at families like his—who tend to be exceptionally well networked because parents organize extracurricular-style activities to bring homeschooled children together—as an ideal volunteer constituency. A coalition-based volunteer strategy, more broadly, was based on a similar logic: finding people who are used to being active together and assigning them a new political mission.

As his staffers recruited new volunteers and oversaw phone bank shifts and printed out walk lists for them, Teepell obsessively tracked their work to report back to Washington. Over the course of the month, volunteers spent a combined 407 hours at the door identifying voters and 459 hours persuading them there, leaving behind doorhangers with a picture of a crawling baby under the slogan "Protect Virginia's Values." From a phone bank, volunteers added 305 hours on IDs and 314 on persuasion. On election day, 75 volunteers were assigned to rouse voters at their doorstep while 53 did it by phone.

Warner beat Earley statewide, in one of two governor's races the Republicans lost that night. But there was a glimmer of good news for those monitoring results in the RNC's political department. Earley ran five points stronger in Frederick than he did in Roanoke, four points of which their later analysis credited specifically to the coalition exercises they had run to motivate social conservatives. "That was like, 'Oh my God!'" says Hazelwood. "That was pretty shocking to me, that we could increase turnout that much."

In Hazelwood's mind, 2 percentage points had been something of a benchmark for turnout improvements. Any intervention that exceeded that was promising and worthy of future attention; one that fell short probably was not worth the trouble. The numbers from Frederick suggested Hazelwood had been dramatically underestimating the influence a rigorous campaign could have. When RNC pollsters called social conservatives in the two counties, those in Frederick were 16 percent more likely to say they had been contacted about Earley's campaign, which suggested that not only had the additional resources and manpower expanded the party's reach but also that the quality of volunteer interaction had been high enough to make an impression.

By the end of 2001, Hazelwood had overseen fifty experiments and had developed a formidable body of knowledge about what worked in voter contact. In South Carolina, calls from volunteers had turned out voters at a rate five points higher than paid call centers. Sending new Republican registrants in suburban Philadelphia a piece of literature with local polling place information increased their turnout by six points. Dispatching "ground troops" to flush voters to the polls on the Monday and Tuesday of the election improved Republican turnout by an average of three points. Assigning a full-time precinct worker, as the party did in both Pennsylvania and Virginia, added three. At one time, such margins might have been shrugged off as negligible. "One good thing about the closeness of the last presidential election is that it erases the need to convince people how important two percent can be," Hazelwood, recently promoted to RNC political director, told the party's winter meeting in Austin the next January.

Hazelwood devoted a considerable share of her PowerPoint presentation at that gathering to explaining the Frederick County coalition test, as an example of what Republicans could do when they flooded an area already home to a developed network of coalition allies. "We aren't here to tell you about your state, but rather to give you an idea of what can be accomplished within a target group if you really make a commitment to do it," she said to the gathering of party officials at an Austin hotel ballroom.

Another set of experiments offered lessons that might prove more portable to other parts of the country where Republicans lacked an existing infrastructure. In two precincts in different states, a new-style targeting of phone and mail messages had increased Republican vote share by almost exactly the same amount: a 3.6-point gain by Earley in the Virginia governor's race, and 3.4 points for congressional candidate Joe Wilson in South Carolina. In these cases, the targeting was based on the standard individual-level data available on the party's national voter file, which mostly designated voters by straightforward demographic categories. Richer data, Hazelwood explained to her crowd, would only make the targeting sharper. "Knowing where a voter lives, how old they are, what gender they are, and all those things are very important. But nothing is as important as understanding what they really care about," she said. "To accomplish this, we need better information on more voters. This can be done, but it will take a team effort and a lot of people willing to give some time."

Hazelwood concluded her presentation by encouraging state and county party officials to schedule a daylong turnout seminar in which the RNC staff would train local activists to better use volunteer door-knocking, paid phone banks, and coalition lists to identify individual voters for the

2002 midterm elections. Already Hazelwood had hosted four regional meetings that included party leaders from forty-seven states. "The other three states have been kicked out of the party," she joked.

Dowd was sitting on a panel to discuss the findings. Though he kept it to himself at the time, he had recently learned of a method that promised to render entirely moot the arduous and costly process that Hazelwood had just outlined. This new tool would offer a powerful boost to whichever party first mastered it: a way to divine what issues every single voter in America cared about without having to track them down and ask them individually.

*   *   *   *   *

A FEW MONTHS EARLIER, Matthew Dowd had wandered the long, colonnaded porch of the Grand Hotel on Michigan's Mackinac Island, aware that the political terrain he had so delicately mapped with 2004 in mind was already shifting beneath his feet. It was one week after Al Qaeda's assault on New York and Washington. Immediately after the attacks, staffers at RNC headquarters had been instructed not to place any phone calls or send e-mails outside the building, for fear they would be seen as playing politics at a time of national tragedy. Pundits speculated that partisanship could be indefinitely pushed aside in favor of a greater sense of national purpose. But the point of the Mackinac Republican Leadership Conference was partisanship, and the island's autumnal camouflage offered a low-profile refuge for swing state operatives whose competitiveness had not been dulled by the terrorist attacks.

Alex Gage arrived on the island with his mind fully on 2004. That summer, Gage, a longtime Republican pollster based near Detroit, had attended one of Hazelwood's many presentations of the 72-Hour Task Force's work. Two of the eight items on her "Prescription for Victory" checklist particularly drew his attention. One was the need for "sharper targeting" of messages by phone and mail; the other was "voter identification," where Hazelwood said Republicans demanded more efficient methods. Gage decided to treat these "almost like a Harvard Business School problem," as he put it. When he traveled a few months later to northern Michigan, he was eager to tell Dowd that he might have figured out a way to meet both challenges at once.

5

"YOU MEAN YOU DON'T DO THIS IN POLITICS?"

In a consulting industry filled with hucksters, Alexander Gage was an awkward salesman. He fidgeted constantly and his sentences shared a tendency to trail off before reaching their destinations. But his discomfiting manner belied a career building political relationships. He spent much of his childhood near Washington, the son of a lobbyist representing E. & J. Gallo Wineries, but by Gage's teenage years his father had moved the family to Detroit to oversee the vintner's regional interests. At Christmas, Gage was given the job of driving cases of wine to the houses of Michigan legislators as holiday gifts. He went to a small college in northern Michigan in search of a hockey career; when the time came to give up on that, Gage transferred to the University of Michigan and studied politics. Desperate for work after graduation, he took a job cleaning rooms at the University Motel in Ann Arbor. One day, he read a newspaper reference to a poll conducted by a Detroit firm named Market Opinion Research. Gage looked up the company in the Yellow Pages, sent his résumé, and after months of his follow-up calls was hired as a part-time intern in the summer of 1974.

To the political world, Market Opinion Research was known as the home of Bob Teeter, a young Republican operative who had little training in statistics but had stumbled into polling when it was still, in his words, "a kind of black art." Teeter was barely out of college when in 1964 he traveled to San Francisco with his father, a small-town Michigan mayor serving as a delegate for favorite-son presidential contender George Romney, and marveled at the spectacle of a national party convention. That year, while working as a teaching assistant and football coach at Adrian College, Teeter spent his summer vacation as an advance man on Romney's reelection campaign. From there he was hired to manage a southern Michigan congressional campaign, and toyed with rudimentary precinct analysis so he could target prerecorded supportive phone calls from Romney to unaligned voters. In 1967, a twenty-seven-year-old Teeter joined Market Opinion Research and set out to recruit a roster of political clients; by 1970, his analysis had helped to elect a series of midwestern governors.

Polling was the fastest-growing consulting specialty of its day. The academic survey-taking on which the American National Election Studies had been based was slow, and typically occurred after the fact. To the extent that campaigns used polls through the 1960s it was for what pollsters called "benchmarking": to take stock, usually at the beginning of an election season, of where voters stood—what issues they cared about, their attitudes toward the economy, what they thought of politicians in the news. By the end of the decade, polling grew more nimble, allowing candidates to use short-term, small-scale surveys to inform tactical decisions as a campaign proceeded.

By 1971, Teeter was so celebrated for his ability to translate survey data into practical strategic advice that Richard Nixon pushed aside his pollster and hired the young Michigander for his reelection campaign, which went on to spend more than $1 million on surveys. Teeter decided he had to get serious about statistical research, and to do that he hired

Fred Steeper, then a twenty-nine-year-old graduate student at the University of Michigan who had worked at its Institute for Social Research during the 1968 election study. Steeper's academic credentials impressed Teeter, who wanted to style Market Opinion Research as more analytically rigorous than its peers. Each poll the firm would return to a candidate would include a complete report, sometimes as long as one hundred pages, even when a candidate or campaign officials made clear they had neither the time nor interest in more than a five-page summary. Market Opinion Research's name occasionally appeared on articles in political science journals challenging academics' voting models with data from private surveys. Although Teeter and Steeper shared authorship of the journal articles, there was no question how the firm divided its labor. Steeper wrote the scholarly material while Teeter brought in the clients and translated the survey results into strategic advice, which usually required repositioning conservative candidates so they could appeal to centrist ticket-splitters. One client, Illinois governor James Thompson, called Teeter the "Midwestern barometer."

Gage's first job at Market Opinion Research mostly amounted to grunt work, but the ambitious young man—with intense blue eyes, broad cheeks, and the parted, slicked-back hair of an early Hitchcock protagonist—thrilled at how it put him at the center of the action. "I had the best of both worlds. I got to follow a brilliant tactician from the back of the room," he said. "And I got to work with the best pure researcher in the business." But less than a year after joining Market Opinion Research, Gage was laid off. It was a cyclical business, following the double-time rhythms of the political calendar. Encouraged by the academic orientation of the firm's leaders, Gage went back to school for his master's degree. Then, in the fall of 1975, he was summoned by Steeper to help with the polling for Gerald Ford's presidential campaign. Gage was rehired as a twelve-thousand-dollar-per-year assistant analyst, effectively an apprenticeship to Steeper. Gage would gather the raw data collected by the firm's Detroit phone room and wait for Steeper to come over to his desk to weight the samples, or watch as Steeper proofread his survey questions. Then Gage would run the numbers to the departments responsible for coding or entering the collected data onto mainframe computers.

This infrastructure necessary for what was known as "survey research" kept newcomers out of the business. Throughout the 1970s, there were three major Republican polling firms, who divided the country by region, an arrangement enforced by gentlemen's agreements and basic economics. Lance Tarrance of Houston dominated the South; Richard Wirthlin, who had worked on Ronald Reagan's campaigns for governor, owned California; and Teeter the Midwest and the Northeast. Even as the high cost of long-distance calling made it expensive for any of the three to expand outside their home regions, the lack of competition allowed them to take on ambitious projects.

Gage, who rose to be a vice president of Market Opinion Research, presided over a culture of innovation. In the mid-1970s, the firm perfected the method of rolling nightly samples that became known as "tracking polls," which for the first time empowered a campaign to measure daily changes in a candidate's standing and how fast it was rising or falling. Later Gage worked with an Oregon manufacturer to develop handheld "perception analyzers," which allowed researchers to monitor a viewer's instantaneous response to words and images by turning a dial to reflect support or disapproval. These so-called dial sessions became the dominant tool for campaigns trying to understand how particular phrases or ideas from speeches and debates resonated with voters. "They weren't a polling firm," says Mike Murphy, a Michigan media consultant who worked with Market Opinion Research. "They were a research firm that used polling."

By the mid-1980s, as the personal computer supplanted the mainframe and the expense of phone calls dropped, polling became just another political consulting service. Falling costs grew the customer base to nearly everyone in politics: even state legislative candidates would routinely commission a poll to help them prepare campaign strategy. Amid the boom, academic training no longer amounted to much. Many of the top Republican polling firms were filled with former operatives who lacked statistical expertise but had an instinct for political strategy and a Rolodex full of potential clients. Polling was a growth industry, and it offered Beltway types an easier lifestyle. Unlike field work—which usually required settling down in a single district for weeks or months—a pollster could stay in his or her office in suburban Virginia, lining up dozens of campaigns each election season and corporate or lobbying clients to occupy the off years.

In 1986, Market Opinion Research did nearly $10 million in business and was one of the thirty largest research companies of any kind in the country. The firm was preparing to serve as lead polling consultant to the presidential campaign of George H. W. Bush, whom Teeter had befriended when Bush was chairman of the Republican National Committee. But even as Teeter's firm sat atop the political world, it became harder to sustain the ambitious agenda or culture of scholarly inquiry and technical entrepreneurship that gave Market Opinion Research its early character. "Profit and loss in a polling firm is basically a function of volume—how many interviews you do," says Will Feltus, who worked alongside Gage at the firm. "Research is not a profit center."

Even Bush's victory could not ensure Market Opinion Research's future. Teeter had signed a contract to sell the company after the campaign and cash out of the business, and his employees scrambled to stick together after a new owner swept them out. In 1989, Gage, Steeper, and three other members of senior management formed their own firm, Market Strategies. Political clients may have given the firm its prestige—Steeper was the chief pollster for Bush's reelection, with Teeter serving as the campaign's chairman—but the business was increasingly coming from other sectors. For Market Strategies' first two years, politics and policy delivered half of the firm's revenue; a decade later, that figure had fallen to one-quarter. Polling in the political world had become a static enterprise; innovations in using data to measure and track personal opinions were all taking place in commercial research.

Gage still enjoyed the scrum of politics, keeping ties to Michigan's

Republican circles and dabbling in election season punditry for Detroit television stations. "He was always thinking about the practical problems facing a campaign," says Steeper. But by the late 1990s, Gage's portfolio had become stocked with corporate clients like the American Forest and Paper Association, and the work he most wanted to do looked like a distraction from Market Strategies' core business. "Gage wanted to come up with these one-off projects that sometimes were profitable and sometimes were not at all profitable," says Brent Seaborn, who started as an intern in the firm's atrophying Washington office. "He's always trying to think of the new idea, which for Market Strategies was a difficult position to be in, because Market Strategies wanted you to fill out a spec sheet, conduct a poll, present the results, and cash the check. They were a very big company and they had a very good routine."

The engines of the firm's growth were customer satisfaction and relationship management, interlocking concepts winning fans in the corporate world. Relationships between salespeople and customers were once considered an ineffable part of business, where commerce mingles with courtship. But in the 1980s, some companies started to track all of their interactions with individual customers—every purchase made, service call placed, rebate submitted, product returned—and farmed out the volumes of data to outside firms for analysis. Electrical utilities and health-care providers, in particular, would hire Market Strategies to question their customers about their views of the company (often monthly surveys of thousands of respondents) and use the results to determine managers' pay. Along the way they marshaled as much information as they could about the people who used their services and how they responded to different stimuli. "The concept is 'know your customer,'" says Gage. "When you touch him, know how you touched him. Did the touch cause him to do something you want him to do?"

This corporate data-hoarding was creating a major imbalance between the information available to commercial marketers and those in politics. A voter file might have a half-dozen categories of information for each person: gender, age, when they last moved, how often they vote. Consumer databases stockpiled hundreds of them, such as whether they had recently taken a cruise or had registered for a hunting license. When he had started in polling in the 1970s, Gage saw commercial marketers trying to learn from their political peers, who had after all pioneered the study of public opinion. Two decades later he was frustrated to find that the roles had clearly flipped. "Back in the seventies and eighties, there was this view that there were really smart new things in campaigns then being adopted by business," says Gage. "Now all the smart stuff is happening over there."

* * * * *

AS HE STOOD on the porch of Mackinac Island's Grand Hotel in September 2001, Dowd recognized the approaching figure of Gage, who at fifty-one maintained a hockey player's large build even as his white hair thinned into unruly curls sloping off the back of his head. The Michiganders did not know each other well, but they shared a common instinct that campaigns had a lot to learn from consumer research. Dowd's father had worked in marketing for Dodge and had told his son about how automakers used data-mining services to sift through the hundreds of pieces of information on each possible customer. The data miners would profile individual buying practices and then clump people into clusters based on their tastes and habits. When Gage told Dowd he thought it would be possible to target voters the same way, it immediately clicked. Gage was proposing, in essence, the same technique Dowd's father had used, but this time with Bush as the product instead of sedans.

Gage left Mackinac Island with Dowd's enthusiasm ringing in his head. One thing that always depressed political creativity was the uncertainty that anyone would pay for a fresh way of doing things: campaign practices were so hardened, and campaign budgets so predictable, that consultants would rarely invest in new methods until they had seen them successfully demonstrated elsewhere. When he heard the 72-Hour Task

Force declare that one of the major impediments to effectively turning out Republican voters was that the party could not locate them, Gage assumed it was a problem the commercial world had already solved. "They just had bad customer files," Gage says of his party. "They didn't know who their customers were."

That year, the Michigan Republican Party had approached Gage and a longtime collaborator, media consultant Fred Wszolek, with a similar challenge. The 2002 midterm elections loomed, poised to feature a busy ballot with races for all statewide offices, including governor. Even though Michigan was a presidential battleground, Republicans felt they always started from way behind when they had to rely on mobilizing votes from friendly precincts. Voters did not register with a party, so every Michigander was effectively an "independent." In precincts without a clear partisan character, the state party would hire phone banks to identify voters where it could afford to, and rely on coalition partners like the National Rifle Association and Christian Coalition to augment its roster of targets. But in working-class Michigan, this amounted to a fatal math for Republican candidates: there simply weren't enough voters in non-Democratic precincts or on coalition membership rolls to meet a statewide vote goal. "There were 1.2 million people, and we needed two million votes to win," says Michigan Republican Party executive director Michael Meyers. "So we all knew we had a problem of 'how do we get to two million' and the phones weren't going to be able to fill in an eight-hundred-thousand gap."

The flip side of that problem was that the party basically wrote off precincts that voted reliably for Democrats. In sections of populous Macomb County, a historic Democratic edge meant that the state Republican Party gave up directly contacting voters altogether. Gage imagined his job as developing "search-and-rescue" tools, using data to spot sympathetic bodies in a disaster zone and plucking them out to the polls. "We could say, over here on Elm Street in Sterling Heights, Michigan, this person needs a life jacket, and a helicopter comes in and pulls 'em out, takes 'em to the polls," says Gage. "Otherwise he never would have been touched in any way."

Such a tool would have immediate application in races around the country. With Dowd's tentative support, and the RNC's demonstrated seriousness about its 72-Hour initiative, Gage knew that any targeting breakthrough he could make in time for Bush's reelection could prove extremely lucrative, and he started to think of the Michigan project as a "beta test" for the bigger contest two years later. He took the five-million-person state voter file and tried to match it to available consumer data from Acxiom, one of a few large commercial data vendors who maintained profiles of nearly every American. He found that 80 percent of Michigan voters matched up against an Acxiom record, which included hundreds of variables, from marital status to pet ownership. In May 2002, Gage commissioned a massive survey to ground those personal details in the political realities of a campaign year. He randomly selected a "test set" of five thousand households from the Acxiom records and called them with around twenty questions about the 2000 election, Michigan politicians (like outgoing governor John Engler and the various figures plotting to replace him), and issues that played a role in state politics (like abortion and the role of unions). Gage had algorithms find patterns linking personal characteristics with political beliefs so that he could use what he knew about his test set to predict how the other five million voters likely approached politics.

In August 2002, the month of Michigan's primary elections, Gage got a call from Mike Murphy, who had left Michigan to become one of the country's top ad makers. Murphy had been lead strategist on John McCain's 2000 race and was now playing a similar role for Mitt Romney, a former venture capitalist and management consultant running to be governor of Massachusetts. Murphy was familiar with the work Gage was doing in Michigan and thought it could be especially useful for Romney, who could build a winning coalition in the liberal state only by sorting through independents and conservative Democrats to identify what he considered the "subtribes" open to crossing over to back a Republican. He summoned Gage to Romney's headquarters in Cambridge, Massachusetts, nestled between the start-ups that had sprouted from nearby MIT, and suffused with a similar spirit of innovation.

Gage frequently grew restless before giving a presentation, his nervous energy leading him to endlessly tweak his slides—moving images slightly, adjusting the color of text—until the moment he had to show them. There was a particular reason for Gage's nerves as he waited for his meeting with Romney's brain trust to begin. The campaign's ranks were filled with Harvard MBAs and former management consultants, perhaps the world's foremost PowerPoint artisans, and Gage was pitching them a targeting technique yet to be fully implemented anywhere. Gage gave his primer on what he called "super-segmentation," explaining how with the latest technology and data it should be possible to merge new consumer records with traditional political information to develop a rich profile of each individual, and then model them to look for once-hidden patterns that could help predict which voters would make the worthiest targets. Once Gage was done, he looked around the table for questions. Alex Dunn, a former high-tech venture capitalist who had left the business world to serve as Romney's deputy campaign manager, raised his hand. "You mean," Dunn asked Gage, "you don't do this in politics?"

* * * * *

THE PUZZLE GAGE believed he had solved was one that had, largely unbeknownst to him, bedeviled analysts for nearly a half century. To social scientists and campaign operatives, breaking the electorate into clusters represented a holy grail; to outsiders, it was an alternately dazzling and dystopic symbol of modernity as democracy entered the computer era. For the close circle around John F. Kennedy, however, the quest to segment the country was a key part of the secret history—a project formally denied at the time and since forgotten to all but those who engineered it— of how they had won the White House.

In his 1964 novel, *The 480,* Eugene Burdick, a University of California,

Berkeley, political scientist who had edited a collection of essays on voting behavior, unfurled a thriller about an unlikely presidential campaign of an American engineer who stumbles into a South Asian border conflict and emerges a national hero back home. Within weeks, John Thatch is being drafted to run for president by Madison Curver, a dashing young Ivy League–educated lawyer who believes he can use a novel statistical system—which splits the electorate into tiny demographic clusters—to shape the unformed Thatch into the perfect Republican candidate to defeat John F. Kennedy's bid for a second term in 1964. "They went through every poll worth looking at and after a lot of work came up with four hundred and eighty groups which seem to react and vote in the same way," Curver explains to a Republican power broker. "And now they know a lot about each of those groups, so much, in fact, that they can simulate how the group will act before the group has even heard of an issue."

Two years earlier, during the Cuban Missile Crisis, Burdick cowrote *Fail Safe*, about an accidentally triggered nuclear conflict. Four years before that, he had cowritten *The Ugly American*, describing Western diplomats meddling in Southeast Asia. *The 480*, too, was grounded in real-life power games: during his brother's 1960 campaign, which he managed, Robert F. Kennedy had ordered up top secret mathematical simulations of electoral outcomes run on a computer some ominously described as a "people machine." In the discursive preface to his novel, Burdick described the Kennedy project as the catalyst for a new movement that would replace "the underworld of cigar-chewing pot-bellied officials who mysteriously run 'the machine.'"

"The new underworld is made up of innocent and well-intentioned people who work with slide rules and calculating machines and computers which can retain an almost infinite number of bits of information as well as sort, categorize, and reproduce this information at the press of a button," Burdick wrote. "This underworld, made up of psychologists, sociologists, pollsters, social survey experts and statisticians, cares little about issues. That is one reason the candidates keep them invisible."

Even though the academics who had run Kennedy's "people machine" shared some of the details of their operation with Burdick, he may have overstated the reach of their underworld. In 1959, Columbia sociologist William McPhee had begun using IBM 704 computers to predict how population changes would alter the electorate over a four-year presidential cycle. His tool was the simulation, measuring how strings of variables would interact under different conditions, an approach popular with military planners gaming out battles and engineers eager to see the potential effects of repeated stresses on a structure. When MIT political scientist Ithiel de Sola Pool heard of McPhee's research, he thought it could be possible to rewrite the program so that it could simulate the potential impact of tactical decisions as candidates made them. McPhee in effect aimed to design a long-term climatological model; Pool wanted to predict the next day's weather.

Pool, along with McPhee and psychologist Robert Abelson, spent a year compiling sixty-six pre-election polls from the previous decade, which included 130,000 respondents who could each be identified by their race, religion, gender, party, place of residence, and professional and socioeconomic status. With these categories, Pool's team was able to divide the United States into 480 "voter-types." In 1959, they conducted a poll to take the temperature of each voter-type on fifty-two "issue-clusters," to determine if "Eastern, metropolitan, lower-income, white, Catholic, female Democrats" had different attitudes than "Southern, rural, upper-income, white, Protestant, male Independents" toward civil rights, Harry Truman, and which party was best in a crisis. With that framework, Pool believed, the computer could simulate the effect that a change in the issue terrain—a shift in a candidate's position, or a reordering of voter priorities—would have on broader public opinion and even electoral-college math. "The Presidential election of 1960 was the first in which all the technological prerequisites for our project existed: survey archives, readily available tape-using large-memory computers, and previously developed theories of voter decision," wrote Pool, Abelson, and research assistant Samuel Popkin.

McPhee brought the nascent technology to Edward Greenfield, a New

York businessman and leading reform Democrat, who introduced the academics to officials of the Democratic National Committee and a liberal affiliate, the Democratic Advisory Council, which found a group of donors willing to invest thirty-five thousand dollars in the project. Because universities would not allow their professors to mingle scholarly business with political money, they organized as a private company that could make its research available for sale. Greenfield became the president of the Simulmatics Corporation, housed in a dowdy office in a converted town house near the New York Public Library. He enlisted many of the day's most prominent political scientists in advisory roles, including Samuel Eldersveld, the Michigan professor who had run field experiments in his own campaigns for office in Ann Arbor, and Harold Lasswell, a protégé of Charles Merriam's at Chicago.

One of Simulmatics' academic advisers had already had a formative influence on the logic of unpacking the country into "voter-types." Paul Lazarsfeld, a colleague of McPhee's at Columbia, was a Vienna-born sociologist and prominent socialist who had stumbled into the study of elections from his interest in how people made consumer decisions. During the 1930s, as Austria became inhospitable to Jews, Lazarsfeld decided not to return home and resettled at Columbia University and launched an Office of Radio Research. A major project was panel studies that followed households to measure the effects that broadcast advertising had on their shopping habits. In 1940, Americans would be selecting not only dairy items but a president, and Lazarsfeld thought an election would offer a rich venue to study what he called "the psychology of choice." With colleagues Bernard Berelson and Hazel Gaudet, Lazarsfeld went to Sandusky, Ohio, for seven months before the election, interviewing the same six hundred voters each month to track how their views changed with time.

Lazarsfeld and his colleagues had expected to find that voters chose between candidates the way they picked among brands, individually assessing products and their packaging before making a choice shaped by the influence of advertising propaganda. But in the book they published on the study, *The People's Choice: How the Voter Makes Up His Mind in a Presidential Campaign,* Lazarsfeld and his colleagues were surprised that the centralized forces they expected to play a direct role in driving decisions—especially the party organizations, as mediated by television and radio—proved to have a meager impact. Voters arrived at an election season with existing "brand loyalties" to parties, derived from the religious and class context in which they lived and reinforced by the influence of peers. Likening voting to a "group experience," Lazarsfeld was ready to altogether abandon the analogy to consumer choice that had first drawn him to study electoral politics. "For many voters political preferences may better be considered analogous to cultural tastes—in music, literature, recreational activities, dress, ethics, speech, social behavior," he, Berelson, and McPhee later wrote. "Both are characterized more by faith than by conviction and by wishful expectation rather than careful prediction of consequences."

In 1948, the three professors decamped from Columbia to Elmira, New York, with the goal of more properly studying those dynamics. Again they used the method of panel interviews—revisiting the same group of respondents in sequence. As the race between Harry Truman and Thomas Dewey narrowed, the Columbia scholars had Elmira residents explaining their decision making in real time. They saw Democrats who, despite worrying about Truman's international leadership, returned to their home party as its nominee emphasized economic issues that were at the core of the party's appeal. (This, as much as faulty polling, explained Truman's comeback.) In their 1954 book *Voting,* they labeled this a "reactivation" of latent class loyalties, which had been temporarily weakened as Americans were distracted by the early rumbles of the Cold War.

Throughout the 1950s, the so-called Columbia Studies dueled with the Michigan Studies for primacy as a universal model of voter behavior. The midwesterners eventually won out, thanks to the weight of the regular election year polls backing their 1960 release of *The American Voter.* But the Columbia model proved psychologically potent, and Pool saw that the notion of different identities exerting competing forces on the human mind lent itself to the same kind of mathematical study as the engineering simulations that measured how a bridge held up against earthquakes or beneath the daily rumble of trucks. "The lifelong Democrat who is a rich, rural, Protestant is under cross pressure. So is the rich urban Catholic," wrote Pool, Abelson, and Popkin. "The latter's coreligionists in the city mostly press him toward what was the group's traditional Democratic affiliation. His wealthy business colleagues press him to a Republican one." Since their 480 voter-types included all these various identity permutations, the Simulmatics team believed they could measure how each of them would respond if the candidate's choice of issues put new weight on one pressure, such as emphasizing foreign policy over economic concerns.

On August 11, 1960, nearly one month after the Democratic convention concluded in Los Angeles, Robert F. Kennedy ordered a series of reports from Simulmatics. The campaign's leadership was most racked by the question of how to deal with his religion in a country that had never before elected a Catholic. Nixon led in summertime polls, and reports of anti-Catholic activity trickled in with growing frequency to John F. Kennedy's Washington headquarters. Kennedy's advisers knew they had two strong options: they could ignore religious questions altogether or they could address the subject directly and condemn as bigots those who would let Kennedy's faith affect their vote. The latter approach, they knew, would take what had been a subterranean issue in the election—the stuff of flyers and local rumor, but ignored by the Kennedy and Nixon campaigns—and force it to the surface. When trying to assess what that would do to the race's dynamics, none of the campaign strategists had much to go on but instinct.

So Pool ran the numbers for the Democratic National Committee. One of the Simulmatics issue-clusters had compiled respondents' views when asked how they felt about having a Catholic president. (The typical question: "If your party nominated an otherwise well-qualified man for President, but he happened to be a Catholic, would you vote for him?") At this point, he had to rely on a little guesswork of his own. Among his 480 voter-types, Pool identified nine significant subsets he thought worth measuring on the faith question, mixing and matching between three party categories (Republicans, Democrats, and Independents) and three religious ones (Protestant, Catholic, and Other). Two groups, Protestant Democrats and Catholic Republicans, he felt, would face the greatest cross-pressure on the question of a Catholic in the White House. Raising the salience of religion in the election would likely push each group in a different direction. (Other groups would also be affected but to a smaller degree, Pool predicted, such as Catholic Democrats, who would be less likely to defect if Kennedy's faith became an issue, and "Negro and Jewish Republicans," who could be pushed to vote Democratic if the election became a referendum on bigotry.)

After two weeks, Simulmatics returned its report on "the consequences of embitterment of the religious issue" to Robert F. Kennedy, each copy numbered to guard against leaks of a document considered highly sensitive. Inside was a ranking of thirty-two non-southern states in their likelihood of going for Kennedy if he directly addressed the Catholic question. Eleven states, they projected, would move away from Kennedy on religion alone, totaling 122 electoral votes. But the issue could pull six states, including three out of the four largest in the country, into the Democratic column. Together they were worth 132 electoral votes. "Kennedy today has lost the bulk of the votes he would lose if the election campaign were to be embittered by the issue of anti-Catholicism," the Simulmatics report stated. "The simulation shows that there has already been a serious defection from Kennedy by Protestant voters. Under these circumstances, it makes no sense to brush the religious issue under the rug. Kennedy has already suffered the disadvantages of the issue even though it is not embittered now—and without receiving compensating advantages inherent in it." Less than three weeks after his brother received that advice, the Democratic nominee traveled to Houston to talk about his faith before a gathering of ministers. "I believe in an America where religious intolerance will someday end," Kennedy said, "where there is no Catholic vote, no anti-Catholic vote, no bloc voting of any kind."

It was an ironic aspiration for Kennedy, since his campaign's embrace of Simulmatics reflected by far the most serious effort ever to develop a science of bloc voting. Pool did not know if their math had changed the campaign's calculus around the Houston speech, or if any of the three reports that Simulmatics delivered (others concerned Kennedy's image, Nixon's image, and the role of foreign policy as an issue) informed strategic decisions. "They were seen during the campaign by perhaps a dozen to fifteen key decision makers, but they were read intelligently by these talented and literate men," Pool and his colleagues wrote. Even if their analysis had not shaped campaign plans, the returns in November offered some validation for their technique. Pool calculated that Simulmatics' state rankings had an 82 percent correlation with the actual vote.

When the existence of the 480 voter-types was reported after the election, the Simulmatics project was heralded as ushering in a new era of space-age politics, as *Harper's* described it in a story headlined "The People-Machine." "This is the A-bomb of the social sciences," Lasswell said, likening it to the first self-sustaining nuclear chain reaction, conducted by wartime Manhattan Project researchers at an abandoned University of Chicago football stadium. "The breakthrough here is comparable to what happened at Stagg Field." Newspapers and wire services covered the *Harper's* report as news, even as Kennedy's spokesman denied the existence of the Simulmatics reports altogether. "We did not use the machine," press secretary Pierre Salinger lied to UPI.

Even though Burdick wrote affectionately about the scholars looking to bring new rigor to smoke-filled political backrooms, *The 480* was often read as a cautionary tale about the ability of campaigns to be cynically mechanized at the expense of real people. Pool may have been able to disassemble the electorate into microscopic pieces, but the tools for speaking to voters—national advertising, broadcast television, and speeches covered by metropolitan and regional papers—still existed only on a macro scale. Simulmatics had a good idea of knowing what a small-city, Catholic, Democratic, lower-income woman was likely to think of tax policy, but it offered no guidance to a campaign that wanted to locate members of that category and speak to them directly.

New sources of granular data would make that easier. In 1962, the U.S. Postal Service rolled out its Zone Improvement Plan, which split the country into thirty-six thousand zones and assigned each a five-digit code to help post offices automate their procedures. Soon businesses began using these ZIP codes to presort their catalogs and magazines, and as the direct-mail business boomed these numerical anchors became a useful way to root consumer data in place: they were more compact than counties or towns, the closest thing to quantifying neighborhoods. In 1974, computer scientist Jonathan Robbin used research from customer surveys and block-level Census data to compile 535 demographic variables that could be attached to each ZIP code. Those boundaries had been drawn to aid mail delivery, but Robbin's Claritas Cluster System used the arbitrary lines to fence people in by their common lifestyle traits. Robbin's computers assigned each ZIP code to one of forty different clusters, which he gave colorful names, from Furs & Station Wagons ("new money in metropolitan bedroom suburbs") to Norma Rae–Ville ("lower middle-class milltowns and industrial suburbs, primarily in the South"). The profiles became popular with marketers, from Colgate-Palmolive to *Time,* who relied on Robbin's data and vivid social portraiture as a new lens onto America: a way of visualizing their consumers, and then knowing where they lived. Robbin soon became known as the "King of the Zip Codes."

In 1978, he persuaded Matt Reese, the already legendary Democratic voter contact consultant, that his clustering system could be used for politics. That year, Reese was working on behalf of the United Labor Committee of Missouri to beat back a proposed right-to-work referendum in Missouri, an issue that did not fall neatly along partisan lines. Reese hired Democratic pollster Bill Hamilton to survey 1,367 Missouri voters about their political views, and then used the respondents' addresses to identify them with one of Claritas's clusters. Hamilton's polls found eighteen clusters rich with persuadable voters, building a list of 595,000 targets, and identified the most promising arguments for each. Those who lived in areas Claritas had designated as Grain Belt clusters received Reese's "pocketbook argument" (which emphasized that right-to-work laws would also hurt those farmers whose customers belonged to unions) while those in Coalburg & Coaltown clusters saw mail with a "status quo" message (pointing out that neighboring right-to-work states had impoverished economies). "The campaign was so carefully targeted," Hamilton said, "that one resident of Springfield, Missouri, might think that defeating the initiative was the most important thing since the invention of sliced bread. Meanwhile, a few blocks away, someone might not even know the initiative was on the ballot."

Upon defeating the Missouri referendum, Reese credited the clustering method (which had cost three hundred thousand dollars, one-fifth of the labor committee's budget) that he called "the new magic." Reese and Eddie Mahe Jr., a former RNC deputy chairman and leading Republican consultant, joined forces to become bipartisan evangelists for clusters in Washington. The clusters seemed ready-made for a new decade that would, at least in the popular imagination, be remembered for its consumerism. Claritas was selling a map key for decoding the politics of a mobile, postindustrial America where even the middle classes had the means to self-segregate according to their tastes and interests, and people were more likely to identify themselves as consumers than as workers. In director Sidney Lumet's 1986 film *Power,* a mercenary political consultant played by Richard Gere—always shuttling by private jet to prop up Latin American strongmen with media manipulation or lifeless domestic campaigns with disingenuously action-packed TV spots—introduces clusters to his clients. "We've concluded a high favorable is Pools & Patios: suburban, white-collar, married twenty-five- to forty-nine-year-olds," Gere's character tells a New Mexico gubernatorial candidate. "We tailor the mail and phone pitches based on what we know is already bothering them. But the really exciting stuff comes when I work out a simulation model. That's when you tell me what you're thinking of saying and I tell you how they're going to react."

At the same time, the Times Mirror Company was deep in a three-year statistical project to split the electorate into eleven clusters it called "typology groups." While the party identity of the 4,244 Americans whom Gallup surveyed played an important role in defining the clusters, the report issued in September 1987—as both parties wrestled with open primaries to find nominees to succeed Ronald Reagan—radically avoided using the language of an ideological continuum to define any of them. "In 1987, the conventional labels of 'liberal' and 'conservative' are about as relevant as the words 'Whig' and 'Federalist,'" the report's authors declared. "We will divide that electorate into distinct, new constituencies and identify the fundamental outlooks on life and major institutions that animate virtually all American political behavior." Two of the clusters were distinctly Republican (Enterprisers and Moralists), four Democratic (New Dealers, Sixties Democrats, the Partisan Poor, and the Passive Poor), and two leaning in each direction (Upbeats and Disaffecteds towards the Republicans, Seculars and Followers towards the Democrats). Eleven percent of American adults were found to be fully, and seemingly permanently, detached from politics; Times Mirror called them Bystanders.

And yet even as clusters infiltrated pop culture and public opinion research, they never found a steady place in the political arsenal. Reese and Mahe, who had negotiated an exclusive franchise to market Claritas to political customers, struggled to translate the clusters so they would be easier for Washington hands to grasp. "The names of the groups didn't resonate politically," says Mahe. "The descriptions were written with marketing in mind." He and Reese rewrote profiles so they invoked political behaviors, with terms like *conservative* and *swing voter,* and emphasized that the clusters would nonetheless be most useful to campaigns not for visualizing types of voters but for locating them geographically. Still they were unable to sell clustering to any presidential candidates in 1980 or 1984. It was an expensive proposition for a campaign, and only a handful of congressional candidates ever bought it. By the end of the 1980s, Reese and Mahe had let their Claritas franchise expire.

Those who looked closely at the categories of data being used to shape the clusters were shocked to see that they didn't include markers for race or ethnicity as a demographic variable. A two-page summary of Claritas's "Downtown Dixie-Style" cluster recorded that its residents, in working-class neighborhoods of cities such as Fayetteville, North Carolina, and Selma, Alabama, were disproportionately devoted consumers of soul records, malt liquor, and *Jet* (and infrequent overnight campers, *Ms.* readers, or frozen-yogurt eaters), but never emphasized the one attribute they shared above all else: they were overwhelmingly African-American. "I'd have to sit through all these pitches where they'd say 'We know this stuff better than you guys, what we do applies to your work, we know how to do it,'" says Tom Bonier, who as one of the lead analysts for the National Committee for an Effective Congress was invited to observe marketers' presentations to the DNC and the party's campaign committees. "But the big thing they didn't use, which is sensitive in the corporate world but not in the political world: they don't use race in their clusters, because to them it's distasteful whereas in politics it's an accepted fact."

When pollsters tested the clusters, by looking at how members of different groups answered political questions, they realized that they didn't add much to the basic mix of precinct-based targeting and polling to find basic demographic splits. The arbitrary lines around ZIP codes had forced Claritas to effectively compromise when it tried to summarize an area's character, defining it only by its dominant lifestyle traits. What about all the people who didn't match the prevailing consumer sensibility? (One political data expert stumbled upon a glaring example of the risk of treating everyone in a cluster as the same. The areas that Claritas called Pools & Patios included significant populations that looked nothing like the people with whom they shared an address: those who lived in the ZIP code in order to clean their neighbors' pools and patios.) It may be a sensible business decision to put a GapKids in a New Homesteaders neighborhood that is 55 percent childless households, but it would be malpractice for a Republican campaign manager to run a GOTV operation in that same area if it is 55 percent Democratic. "While they may have worked very well for selling Sonys or Toyotas or Mercedeses or Fords, they didn't work very well for the politics. They didn't discriminate that well," says pollster Mark Mellman, who began experimenting with clusters in 1996. "You're stuck with how they divide people for marketing purposes, and those marketing purposes might not overlay with political purposes. The truth is the political purposes from one election to another may vary."

*　*　*　*　*

YET WHEN THE MICHIGAN REPUBLICAN PARTY approached Gage in 2001 about moving beyond precinct targeting, his first instinct, too, was Claritas. He ordered up the profiles and commissioned a poll to survey two hundred people in each of its clusters. Initially, Gage encountered many of the same shortcomings others had faced before him. When he looked more closely at the components of the clusters, however, Gage saw that all the ingredients should be available to him in raw form. Gage could reassemble that raw data into his own clusters, purpose-built for nothing other than politics. Then, he concluded, he could unshackle the clusters from the arbitrary geography of ZIP codes. Gage could put people into the clusters that really suited them—based on their political views and behavior—regardless of where they lived.

Gage and Seaborn traveled to Little Rock to meet with officials at Acxiom, one of only a few data vendors that claimed to have built a file covering the whole American population. In 1969, an Arkansas school bus manufacturer named Charles Ward had decided to start the company as a way to help the Democratic National Committee use computers to manage its fund-raising lists. As Ward's staff got better at gathering personal information, their manila punch cards became valuable to customers outside of politics, such as the American Bible Society, which Ward was pleased to learn was a more reliable client than parties and campaigns. Over the years, the company, which took the Acxiom name in 1988, acquired smaller list vendors and cut deals to bring in data from a variety of businesses about their customers: magazine publishers like Rodale, mail-order retailers like Lands' End, financial institutions like Charles Schwab, pharmaceutical manufacturers like Pfizer, plus hundreds of boutique lists that compiled things as arcane as the types of motors purchased by boat owners. Between 1983 and 2004, with advances in computing, the amount of data Axciom was able to store increased a millionfold, and the company used every byte to fill out one of its personal portraits of an American with a new brushstroke of data. While civil libertarians chafed at companies buying and selling personal consumer information, some of the most valuable details came from government itself. Bureaucratic applications, for gun licenses and construction permits, could say a lot about how much money someone had and how he or she spent it.

With Acxiom's individual dossiers, Gage realized, he could finally design clusters that were unmoored from geography. The Republican National Committee had assembled the country's first national voter file in 1990, and had compiled IDs conducted by local parties and campaigns, information shared by coalition partners, and some so-called enhancements from commercial vendors, such as individual phone numbers. (Because that data would come from a magazine subscription record or completed rebate form, it included many numbers unlisted in the phone book.) No one had ever proposed that the RNC buy a list of pool owners, because it was extremely expensive and no one knew how it could possibly be useful in a political campaign.

If Gage merged Acxiom's personal dossiers with the RNC voter file, he could use that as the base for polling calls, picking names off the file instead of dialing random digits. Then he wouldn't have to waste polling time asking people how much money they made or what job they had—Axciom already had categories that knew the answers to those questions, or at least predicted them based on information it did have. The polling questions could stick generally to political matters, taking in respondents' views of issues and personalities in the news. Gage could come away with nearly one thousand variables for each of his respondents, most of them Acxiom's consumer categories. Gage knew that a lot of those variables would never have any bearing on politics, but it wasn't possible to tell for sure in advance which ones he would need. He would let the computers find out.

In Little Rock, Gage and Seaborn realized that the logic of political targeting was foreign to Acxiom officials. They were used to dealing with corporate clients who knew their intended audience, and so Acxiom could offer them things like a roster of truck owners, or of Kansas City truck owners who also buy religious reading materials. Bewilderingly, though, Acxiom didn't have a way to order a list of truck owners who did not read the Bible—or any other combination based on subtraction as opposed to just addition. Perhaps more important, the company's pricing was struc-tured for commercial customers who wanted to string together a few vari-ables on a limited group of people. Gage would need to cover a whole state's voting-age population, and demanded many more pieces of data on each of them; he needed all the variables so he could isolate the ones that were helpful in predicting political behavior. Gage and Seaborn negoti-ated a deal to get access to all the variables Acxiom had available at a flat rate, and left Little Rock with hundreds of them for every Michigan adult so they could start hunting for patterns that would pull them together into targetable groups.

Because his groupings would not be defined by geography, Gage pre-ferred to call them "segments" instead of clusters. He viewed their creation as something of a passive process. It wouldn't be for political consultants to divine that segments should be formed around socioeconomic status or religious views or participation in party primaries. Algorithms could find the variables that were pulling people together in ways that informed their likelihood of backing Bush's reelection, whatever they may be. The segments would be only as large as they needed to be to ensure that every-body within one of them belonged there equally. And when the campaign wanted to speak to a segment of voters, there would be no doubt on how to find them. Gage could print out a list for a mail vendor or canvasser, with enough information on every single member of a segment to ensure that he or she was only a phone call, postcard, or door knock away.

* * * * *

IN EARLY 2003, Gage returned to Dowd, this time with PowerPoint slides that referred to the method as "MicroTargeting." Gage thought this was an improvement over "super-segmentation" (even if a search of news archives revealed that the new term was used elsewhere to describe a medical technique for removing cancerous tumors). Gage had emerged from the 2002 elections with a mixed record in gubernatorial campaigns, but he thought he had a good story to tell—especially as Dowd began plotting an electoral-college strategy for Bush that emphasized some traditionally Democratic states, like West Virginia, Oregon, and Wisconsin. "We've got to find out who is more likely to be a Republican," says Gage. "We know they're in there, somewhere."

The previous fall, Michigan Republicans lost the governor's mansion but won the attorney general's office for the first time in four decades, while expanding their footprint in both houses of the state legislature. "The down-ticket performance of the party that year was incredible," says Gage, who credits it to an advanced ability to rouse Republican voters living in Democratic strongholds. In Massachusetts, Romney had entered the last week of his campaign for governor lagging Democrat Shannon O'Brien by five points, according to his internal polls. He ultimately beat her by that margin, helped by major gains among the independents and conservative Democrats who had been Gage's targets. Gage had not been given a lot of time to develop a new data-driven strategy for Romney before the September primary. He merely wanted to rank-order the state's nearly two million independents based on their openness to Romney's appeals, so that the campaign could devote its resources to speaking to its friendliest targets first. Gage invented an index he called "consideration,"

a ten-point scale predicting how likely a voter would be to "consider voting for Mitt Romney." At the same time, Gage modeled those voters' issue
priorities to see which ones should be approached with mail and phone
calls emphasizing Romney's tax plan and which ones should get an education pitch.

As he ran his numbers, one variable popped out. Those who ranked
highly on Gage's consideration index were very likely to be premium cable-
TV subscribers. Gage suspected HBO subscriptions were a proxy for other
variables—something that neatly packaged the well-to-do and highly educated suburban independents who would warm to Romney's technocratic
approach—but the reason didn't matter as much as the result. Now instead
of trying to pay or recruit the manpower to canvass more than one million
potential targets by phone and to judge whether they should receive Romney's mail, Gage could just send brochures to everyone shown in Acxiom
files to be a premium-cable subscriber. Meanwhile, the campaign used the
targeting to bring new value to its volunteer operations. Romney, strug-
gling to overcome the almost complete lack of Republican organization in
Massachusetts, was able to assign the campaign's five thousand volunteers
to speak to those persuasion targets who lived within their own neighborhoods. "We felt like it was a pretty powerful way to do outreach in these
communities, because you had someone who was calling from two blocks
away and could talk about the local school," says Dunn.

Dowd found the results from the Michigan and Massachusetts efforts
to be promising enough that he persuaded Bush's White House advisers to
back a trial run of Gage's approach in Pennsylvania, which had a series of
judicial elections in 2003 and would be a key presidential battleground a
year later. Gage again attached Acxiom consumer data to the RNC's voter
records, and commissioned a survey of five thousand voters. Then he used
algorithms to divide the state's electorate into more than twenty-five segments based on concentric patterns in voters' lifestyles and beliefs. Sometimes the Acxiom variables that formed Gage's segments were apparent:
many of the 446,698 "Bible Believers" had shopped at a Christian book-

store, had told a consumer survey that they had religious material in their home, or otherwise resembled those who did. Regardless of how they got into the group, Gage wrote, "despite their higher than average scores on other conservative indicators, social conservative messaging is a must to maximize the vote in this segment." Other segments—like Pennsylvania's 243,517 "Dining Room Debaters," or the 139,586 members of the "Republican Intelligentsia"—were a little less intuitive or self-explanatory. "That's where we saw the data dance a little for us," says Adrian Gray, who became the campaign's voter contact director.

Still, it wasn't clear that Gage's computer models were any more effective than traditional targeting methods. After Pennsylvania's election, the RNC hired Dave Sackett, a pollster for the Tarrance Group, to sample voters and see how accurately the microtargeting had predicted voter behavior. Sackett's memo argued that Gage's microtargeting had actually been less efficient than traditional methods at predicting turnout, but had succeeded at finding friendly Democrats and independents and determining which were likely to be pro-life. "That was the piece that was most radical—with microtargeting we're talking about things that are not necessarily absolutes. You have to trust the statistical inferences in the data set, and that's a bigger leap of faith," says Terry Nelson, the campaign's political director. Because Republicans were used to mailing issue-specific messages to those whose names had been gathered by coalition partners, there was some certainty about why people were on the lists. This was particularly important on cultural and social themes where there was a constant fear of backlash; Gage's segments appeared, in some ways, to be too refined for the Manichean moral conflict waged on the glossy surface of direct mail. "With a segment said to be eighty percent likely to be pro-life, was it really eighty percent likely?" Nelson asks. "If it was sixty percent likely to be pro-life we'd probably target it differently—because you might not want to mail them with these messages because it would turn them off."

Furthermore, the price tag for expanding the technique used in Pennsylvania to the entire battleground nationwide was staggering. Gage estimated it could total $3 million, which would cover the cost of acquiring consumer data from Acxiom and other vendors, the lengthy large-scale surveys to benchmark the electorate, and the statistical analysis that would bring them together. In 2000, the RNC and Bush campaign had spent little of their election-year budgets on data, relying on the party's permanent voter file and the generosity of coalition groups.

Even for a campaign many expected to be the best-funded in history, $3 million was a lot of money, the equivalent of two weeks of very heavy advertising across Pennsylvania. Dowd set out to do something he knew was among the hardest tasks in politics—rewriting a campaign budget to include a line item from a category no one had ever seen before. Dowd had already successfully persuaded Bush's top political advisers, particularly Karl Rove, to invest in a year of voter contact research. Gage's technique, as he saw it, was a natural extension of the 72-Hour Task Force's findings. Now, as Dowd and White House political director Ken Mehlman argued to Rove, the only way to reap the benefits of more efficient field contact was to ruthlessly segment the electorate. "Without the ability to find three people out of ten on a block, we wouldn't have had the resources," says Dowd. "We would have had to knock on all ten doors." Microtargeting, he and Mehlman explained, could effectively automate the sort necessary at the beginning of any voter persuasion operation: separating those already on board from those who will never be, and then sifting through the remainder to identify the best candidates to receive mail and phone calls making the case for Bush. This process, Dowd hoped, would help pay for itself.

In many ways, Rove should have been an ideal consumer for microtargeting. He was an unabashed data nerd who had run nonrandomized experiments in 1994 to measure the impact of his mail and phones in Bush's first gubernatorial campaign. Previous political strategists in the Oval Office had been pollsters, media consultants, or campaign managers; he was the first presidential consigliere to have a background working in voter contact. But Rove's experience in direct mail also made it hard for him to imagine a contact universe built from anything other than the mix of precinct targeting, coalition rolls, and paid IDs that had proved so effective at illuminating a latent conservative coalition in Democratic Texas. Those lists had been built through manual assembly—a few hundred names from here, a couple thousand from there—whereas Gage conjured his through the alchemy of computer algorithms. "Karl was against this originally, because it was new and different," says Dowd. "He's a direct-mail guy and so he thinks he knows that."

Dowd and Mehlman finally won him over. Someone would now have to contend with consultants certain to feel threatened by Gage's technique, especially the phone vendors who each year performed millions of dollars' worth of ID calls that would now be considered superfluous. Coddy Johnson, a Mehlman deputy who had become the campaign's field director, traveled the country to meet with senior state party officials to tell them that their targeting methods, which usually focused on their strongest precincts, were no longer going to be supported by the RNC. "We're not mailing them, we're not going to call 'em, and we're not buying radio in their neighborhoods," Johnson would explain. "Here's how we're going to do it." He brought with him PowerPoint slides of the Pennsylvania microtargeting project, and would flip to a Stay-at-Home Independents segment: families in suburban areas that might not be loyal Republicans or even regular voters but that the algorithms showed would be ripe targets for Bush. "That's who we are targeting," said Johnson. "We're not going after the fifty-year-old man who's voted in every primary and caucus in the last twenty years."

Dowd, the former Democrat, didn't care that his decisions would antagonize local Republican officials and the party's consulting class. "Everybody knew I was going to be bailing quickly, and that I wasn't going to be part of any new regime," says Dowd. "After election day I wasn't hanging around to do a bunch more campaigns." That message would become clear to anyone who walked by Dowd's office at Bush's suburban Virginia headquarters and saw the handwritten sign he affixed to it. "GTT," it read, the same abbreviation for "Gone to Texas" that Tennesseeans—including many who ended up dying at the Alamo—had scrawled on their homes before fleeing the state to escape their debts after the Panic of 1819. When Dowd envisioned the conflict he was triggering with his new political methods, another nineteenth-century analogy came to mind. "It's a business," he says. "You show up with an automobile that runs on gasoline and the horse-and-buggy people go crazy."

*   *   *   *   *

IT WAS CLEAR to anyone closely watching ground-level politics in a battleground state that the Republicans were doing something different in 2004. By the last weekend of the campaign, there were six thousand field-workers walking streets with clipboards (or in some cases primitive handheld digital devices) or manning phone banks. Many of them were in places that had never before seen Republicans hunt for votes, let alone in such a disciplined fashion. When Ryan Johnson, a Bush field organizer responsible for five suburban counties ringing Minneapolis, led canvassers into blue-collar, union-heavy neighborhoods of South St. Paul, he had to reassure them they hadn't made a wrong turn. "It was like, 'Why are we going there?' " he recalls. The same question was asked on one of Bush's visits to the state, when he stopped in Duluth, a Democratic stronghold that rarely made Republican target maps let alone earned a few hours of the president's time. Now, Bush's strategists could count the number of voters they were trying to reach in Duluth, even if they were a minority, in the hopes of tipping the whole state—"real people who support you behind enemy lines," as Nelson put it.

In Washington, deputy party chairwoman Maria Cino had converted the fourth floor of RNC headquarters into a command center for 72-Hour operations, filling conference rooms with staffers responsible for booking flights, hotels, and rental cars for ground troops nationwide. Cino had, in effect, created a travel agency, with five people handling arrangements for Ohio alone. When Democrats talked about enlisting volunteers for field, it often involved union members and college kids. The RNC found its volunteer ranks thick with congressional staffers and lobbyists. "This is not a volunteer effort where you can have everybody staying in people's homes," she says.

They arrived at their destinations to find clear instructions waiting for them. Bush's state directors were judged by the weekly spreadsheets they sent back to headquarters listing the number of phone calls and house visits their volunteers had made, and perhaps more important, how many new ones they had recruited. During the summer, headquarters demanded that each state administer a "Test Drive for W." operation, devoting a day to a full-scale deployment of turnout resources, giving Hazelwood's team a new array of data on which to judge their state-level personnel. Afterward, she spent weeks leaning on state party officials to enlist county leaders, with local field organizers walking the new recruits through PowerPoint presentations titled "You will be the Margin of Victory," which outlined the 72-Hour Task Force's new set of highly regimented best practices. Those identified as turnout targets would typically get three rounds of contact by phone or door knock, the first two in September and October to encourage them to vote early or by mail. Field organizers were able to show the results of experiments demonstrating that, in states permitting it, getting voters to cast a ballot early was more efficient and cost-effective at delivering votes. "They ate it up, and it made them true believers," says KC Jones, the campaign's deputy executive director in Minnesota. "They worked harder. A lot of volunteers, if they feel they're just leaving voice mail after voice mail, they wonder: Am I making any sort of effect on this? Now they knew they were."

But even as those experimental findings were projected onto the crudely spackled walls of field offices across the country, the microtargeting information was closely held. The term itself was rarely spoken beyond the upper echelons of the campaign, or even outside the team assembled to match the new data with the traditional voter contact program of mail and phones. The Michigan gang relocated to Washington to run the numbers operation, with Seaborn and Meyers building the data models. From his new home in South Carolina, Wszolek wrote the pithy segment names and descriptions that Gage felt helped him explain the data to political operatives in a way they could visualize it.

These issue profiles were conceived to make it easy for operatives to intuitively match messages to specific groups of voters. Minnesotans who received federal farm subsidies were almost certain to get a piece of mail arguing that Bush's free-trade position would not damage the state's sugar beet economy as badly as many farmers believed. Moderate Republicans in the Philadelphia suburbs learned about Bush's support for the Clean Skies Initiative, which the campaign presented as a policy of pragmatic environmentalism. "The universes shrank but they did many more pieces," says Kevin Shuvalov, who worked on Bush's mail team. "Once you took all these little clusters and put them together you were basically having an ongoing conversation with the entire universe you have in a state."

There were so many specialized pieces that Ted Jarrett, who coordinated the mail operation at Bush's headquarters, stopped looking at the individual orders he sent to vendors. One day, Jarrett got a call from one of the firms producing a mail piece. Did they really want to print only three hundred copies? It was comically microscopic: city council candidates rarely put in mail orders that small. "If there's one thing I think people don't get about the Bush election in '04, it's this idea that it was a base election and all they were concerned about was the base," says Meyers. "That was in a sense true but they treated the base as anyone who agreed with them strongly on an issue."

Dowd had already made a priority of knowing how to rile up a voter who stood with Bush on only a single issue. As he watched 72-Hour Task Force refine the party's procedures and protocols for reaching their supporters, Dowd had worried that Republicans wouldn't know what to say to them once they had. So he asked Fred Steeper for what the survey taker called a "mobilization poll," focused only on one piece of the electorate.

What issues or themes could Bush use to push loyal Republicans to the ballot box on his behalf?

A decade earlier, the RNC had ordered up from Steeper another poll of Republicans, this one to explain why they seemed to have deserted George H. W. Bush in his loss to Bill Clinton. Traditionally, polls asked people to process politics analytically, but from what Steeper had witnessed on campaigns it seemed that the issues that really drove elections were the ones that pushed voters emotionally. Steeper decided he would just ask them directly "how pissed off they were," as he put it—a hunt for what he thought of as their "anger points." Instead of prompting people to place abortion's importance as an issue on a five- or seven-point scale, or asking whether Bush's position had changed their likelihood of voting for him, Steeper's survey asked "how angry" they were made by the number of abortions that took place annually in the United States.

Steeper's polls convinced him that one popular take on the elder Bush's electoral failure—that Republicans had been fractured over social issues—didn't ring true. After the election, few respondents recalled having been energized by Pat Buchanan's convention speech declaring a "culture war." Yet all of Steeper's questions about unemployment and the economy elicited a strong reaction. Anger points did not need to be only a retrospective tool, he realized; they should help media consultants isolate issues and craft messages around them while a race was still to be won or lost. "The practitioners are always looking for hot buttons!" Steeper says.

When Dowd ordered up the mobilization poll, Steeper thought it was time to hunt for hot buttons. He gathered a sample of people who had identified themselves as Republicans in other surveys done for Bush by Jan van Lohuizen, and felt around for their anger points. Did estate taxes make them angry? What about activist judges, late-term abortions, or trial lawyer fees? Steeper's polls showed that while September 11 had had a temporary effect on Bush's broad popularity—the president's national approval jumped to 86 percent immediately after the attacks—it had an enduring influence on Bush's base. They were emotionally invested in the "war on terror" that Bush had declared: angry about efforts to repeal the PATRIOT Act, pleased about Saddam Hussein's removal. As he drafted questionnaires for the benchmarking surveys on which his microtargeting segments would be built, Gage decided to add a battery of questions, inspired by his old mentor Steeper, that would probe for "anger points." In one of the campaign's endless sequence of conference calls, another Bush adviser asked why the poll didn't investigate voters' emotional responses to the administration's successes. Gage called these "pleasure points," a term that reliably made him snicker even as he was pressured to include such questions in his polls. "How pleased and happy are you that Bush has reformed the education system?" he says, derisively. "It was easier to write anger points."

When funneled into Gage's microtargeting algorithms, anger and pleasure points helped to turn message development on its head, with acceptable language trickling up from voter contact needs instead of sent down from media consultants trying to translate advertising themes for smaller audiences. The pleasure points questions yielded one unlikely pocket of targets for Bush—his No Child Left Behind school reforms had left a mark on Hispanic women in New Mexico—and helped identify issues for others, such as the environmentally minded Pennsylvania moderates. Weak anger points scores also helped exclude voters from contact on sensitive issues. "We realized some people were pro-life but that talking about it put their religion or their morals on their sleeve and were uncomfortable," says Todd Olsen, who inherited Rove's Austin-based firm and worked on the campaign's direct-mail team. Most important, the new measure of intensity allowed those writing direct-mail pieces to calibrate the emotional potency of their language and imagery. "It helped with the body language of message, the nuance," says Chris Mottola, a media consultant on Bush's ad team. "It helped you know how far you can go in terms of rhetoric."

The last weekend of the campaign, a four-page brochure started arriving in mailboxes across the country. By most aesthetic and moral standards of the time, this mailer went too far. The front flap featured a collage of September 12, 2001, front pages of the *Des Moines Register* and *Orlando Sentinel,* newspapers intentionally chosen to represent battleground states, with an image of the World Trade Center in the midst of the previous day's plane attacks. "How can John Kerry lead America in a time of war?" it asked. On the back, in hazy chiaroscuro, was Osama bin Laden, making eye contact with every reader. The head shot may have been the single most familiar facial image in news coverage from 2001 through 2004, but it had never entered the official visual language of the campaign. An informal prohibition on explicit depiction of the September 11 events had been accepted by both sides, and studiously enforced by elite opinion. When Bush had run an ad in March showing the World Trade Center wreckage and a firefighter carrying a body from the site, victims' families hosted press conferences to protest. A draft of the proposed mail piece sat around untouched for months amid a heated debate over its propriety. Many of Bush's advisers argued that such a graphic appeal could force swing voters to recoil from Bush, goaded by a media eager to claim that the White House was preying on a climate of fear it had helped to nurture.

But the microtargeting scores that Gage had built suggested that swing voters were precisely the right audience for the most visceral appeal of Bush's candidacy. The targets would be ones Gage thought of as a persuasion reach: they were very likely to vote, but according to Gage's numbers there was a less than 50 percent chance they would pick Bush. The anger points questions revealed this group of voters to be emotionally sensitive to the war on terror. Bush's mail team knew they were setting off a bomb, but they had placed it so precisely that they could be fairly confident of its blast radius; they had drawn the circle so tightly there would be no downside. "If we lost them it wouldn't be a big deal," says Jarrett, the national director of voter contact. "This was to pull votes from Kerry."

After election day, little was said about the bin Laden mailer or the complex research that had given Bush's mail team the confidence to take on such a touchy subject before an unlikely audience. The popular storyline among Democrats looking to explain Bush's victory credited the campaign's use of quiet communication to rile its base over issues like gay rights. Yet even though Bush allies pushed to get anti-gay-marriage initiatives on the ballot in key states, the campaign rarely found those fruitful topics for direct contact. "That's been the big myth in that campaign: that we drove on the social issues which we really didn't," says Shuvalov. "Because Kerry was not going to challenge us on them."

Gage, whose name had barely appeared in newspapers during the campaign, was profiled by the *Washington Post* in the weeks after the election. The story noted his breakthrough as being able to calculate "Coors beer and bourbon drinkers skewing Republican, brandy and cognac drinkers tilting Democratic." Those who worked on the microtargeting project knew that this detail, even if in parts technically accurate, completely misrepresented their work. They laughed at the fiction that the race had been won and lost through mastery of liquor store transactions. "The Bush campaign people were paranoid. As we talked about this publicly we had to make stuff up," says Wszolek. "We had to give examples that were completely phony. It would drive the Democrats completely loony. We just wanted to keep them from knowing how accessible it is."

6

GEEKS VERSUS THE GURUS

In September 2004, Mike Podhorzer walked two blocks from his office in the AFL-CIO's megalith near Washington's Lafayette Square to John Kerry's headquarters, carrying a laptop loaded with PowerPoint slides whose numbers had troubled him for more than a year. As the deputy political director of the AFL-CIO, which was typically among the largest outside players in national elections, Podhorzer was one of Washington's most eager consumers of polling data, searching for places where the group could invest labor's money and manpower on behalf of favored candidates, who were almost always Democrats. In the summer of 2003, even as the party was far from selecting their nominee—Howard Dean led a desultory pack of contenders—Podhorzer noticed that George W. Bush was entering the campaign season with startling support from AFL households. "Bush was beginning to get more traction with union members than we wanted and than seemed justified," he recalls.

This was not the first time a tough-minded Republican incumbent charmed working-class whites: Richard Nixon and Ronald Reagan had also earned significant shares of the union vote, and each had been re-elected overwhelmingly. Podhorzer knew 2004 would be close, which was all the more reason that the approximately 45 percentage points of the union vote that his polls showed Bush poaching from the Democratic nominee could be crucial. Podhorzer expected to have an election-year budget of $44 million, and—in addition to the usual AFL program of mobilizing union voters already primed to vote for Democrats—he would have to invest in a significant new election-year priority: preventing defections by warning union members about the dangers of a second Bush term.

Podhorzer's polls identified one-quarter of the AFL's 13 million members as swing voters, regularly crossing party lines, but he had little sense of who exactly those holdouts were. The AFL had been relying on standard 1,000-person-sample national polls, which could only measure one or two subsets of the electorate at a time. The number of white men alone among those union swing voters amounted to a voter list roughly the size of Minnesota, an unwieldy and costly universe to approach directly with persuasive messages over the year and a half till election day. To boost the number and value of those demographic subsets, Podhorzer had the AFL's pollsters call twenty thousand union household voters in Ohio and Pennsylvania. "With that much data," says Podhorzer, "your ability to predict who was going to be vulnerable to Bush was a multiple of what it would be with any of the traditional targeting methods."

As 2004 approached, Podhorzer used the information to reshape the AFL's strategy with an eye toward minimizing the Bush vote. "We were taking anyone who would be willing to listen to why Bush was bad for unions and convincing them that Bush was bad for unions, as opposed to concentrating on turning out our most avid Democrats who were just as motivated and angry as Democrats everywhere," says Podhorzer. But that strategy was not shared by the Kerry campaign and many of its allies, who remained almost monomaniacally focused on mobilizing the party's base. In Ohio, that meant aggressively organizing the counties surrounding Cleveland, Columbus, and Cincinnati, with their easily defined liberal precincts and large minority populations. "I felt like that was certainly part of the equation," Podhorzer says. "But it was horribly ignoring voters we could get but weren't even trying."

And so on a day in September, Podhorzer gathered the data and hustled down I Street to visit the Kerry campaign. Because campaign finance laws stipulated that union dues could be spent only on communication with member households, Podhorzer was unable to reach many of the Bush sympathizers who the AFL's polls indicated might be persuaded to vote for the Democrat. To reach its full potential, Podhorzer's "swing voter project" would have to be undertaken by Kerry's campaign—a shift in strategy that he also realized was rather unlikely. "At that point, it was totally unrealistic to think they were going to turn their whole program around because of a couple of PowerPoint slides," he says.

Democrats had entered 2004 with new electoral machinery in their corner. Rocked by their close loss to George W. Bush in 2000 and challenged by new campaign finance laws enacted two years later, nearly a dozen key liberal activist groups—led by the AFL, and encompassing the labor, environmental, and feminist movements—formed the America Votes coalition to coordinate mobilization efforts in key states so they weren't competing to knock on the same doors but could expand their range. (Conservative reporter Byron York would later describe it as part of a "vast left-wing conspiracy.") A separate entity, America Coming Together, was established to administer voter registration and turnout. ACT was legally restricted from coordinating its efforts with the Democratic campaigns it wanted to help, but a division of labor between the two became clear. In Ohio, which Kerry had designated as his one must-win state, field presence belonged almost entirely to ACT, which concentrated its efforts in the thirteen most Democratic counties and ignored the rest of the state.

This was the strategy that concerned Podhorzer, who worried that the approach reflected "an overconfidence in the liberal mind that only a fool would vote for Bush again, so therefore all we had to do was base turnout." He returned to the AFL dispirited by his exchange with the Kerry campaign and his sense that Democrats had chosen to ignore winnable votes in part because the statistical methods used to identify them were not properly understood by campaign decision makers. "At the time," says Podhorzer, "all of this just sounded like alien talk to most people."

So Podhorzer started dialing others who he thought spoke his language. He called some of the AFL's consultants, including Hal Malchow, its mail vendor, and Celinda Lake, one of its pollsters. Others were Podhorzer's peers at other liberal groups. Podhorzer thought they all had two things in common: they shared a scientistic approach to politics, and they all trusted him. "My motivation," Podhorzer told them, "is winning elections, not having trade secrets." In the end he invited about a dozen people to join him for lunch at the AFL's headquarters, which faced down the White House with a southbound stare that reflected either a sense of menace or a patronizing promise of protection, depending on who occupied the Oval Office. The soft-spoken Podhorzer, whose beard and glasses gave him a professorial mien, was barely recognized outside the building, but he knew the return address would give him clout. "I'm not naïve," says Podhorzer. "Convening people to come to the AFL is different from just convening people to come to a generic meeting. So people came."

The group included few of the brand-name consultants whom campaigns liked to unveil in press releases as a way to establish their credibility to donors and media. "It's not the big names on the door," says Maren Hesla, who directed the Women Vote! program at EMILY's List, an independent group that works to elect Democratic women. "It's all the—God love them—geeky guys who don't talk to clients but do the work and write the programs."

Even after Kerry's loss, the group continued meeting about every three weeks, becoming known to its participants as "the geek lunch." Conversation flitted from the obscurely technical to the phenomenological (what does it really mean to say a voter is persuadable?). Just about the only thing they didn't discuss were the day-to-day tactical and messaging questions that so occupied small talk among Washington consultants. Podhorzer began to imagine that the group could be capable of great things: a Manhattan Project for developing electioneering superweapons. At the same time, he knew it would be valuable to establish just how little of that kind of expertise there was within the existing political-industrial complex. Podhorzer assembled a sample of more than fifty party operatives and surveyed them each month for opinions on which of three possible mail pieces would prove most effective. It was, in a way, a version of the "insiders poll" that the *National Journal* had recently launched to document the views of Beltway lobbyists and consultants on political issues of the day, except Podhorzer was less interested in exalting the views of experts than in exposing them as hokum.

The secret ballots in Podhorzer's insiders poll seemed to divide rather consistently: about one-third of the vote each time for each of the three mail pieces. "You came to the conclusion that either one-third of the people were geniuses, or that basically none of them really had a clue," he says. "The same people wouldn't be right from month to month. And that just reinforced my belief that this empirical approach was far better than a guru approach where someone came in and said 'This is the piece you had to send' because of some theory they had about the election or the candidates or about how human beings think."

* * * * *

THE GURUS WERE the celebrated political wise men whose practices had become the industry default, thanks to their success serving up a cocktail of lore and myth, anecdote and inertia, able to so thoroughly intoxicate the candidates who paid their bills. Throughout the 1990s, politics was awash with cautionary tales of a guru culture out of control. When California businessman Al Checchi decided to run for governor in 1998, the wealthy neophyte enlisted two of the Democratic Party's most famous consultants. For his polling, Checchi retained Mark Penn, a gruff, territorial infighter who had successfully battled for control of Bill Clinton's 1996 campaign and had been credited with helping to mastermind Clinton's ultimately easy reelection. Checchi's media consultant, Bob Shrum, was known as an eloquent narrator of lost causes. As a speechwriter for Ted Kennedy he had drafted the candidate's "dream will never die" concession speech in 1980; he later taught himself to make ads, although his firm developed such a knack for picking losers that many in Democratic circles began to joke of a "Shrum curse."

To Checchi, Penn and Shrum were brand names, and once he expressed an interest in hiring them "the gold rush was on," as one campaign aide told the *Washington Post*. Shrum negotiated a contract to produce one hundred television ads, only forty of which ever aired. The remainder flunked shopping mall screenings Penn conducted before voters, one of his signature techniques for testing the effectiveness of ads and mail. When Penn's polls showed that the Shrum ads that had aired were not succeeding in changing voters' minds, the gurus managed to convince Checchi to blame the largely unknown firm that purchased the airtime. Shrum then secured an arrangement whereby his firm would take control of the ad placement, too, earning on each spot a commission that he split with Penn. By the end of the campaign, Checchi's friends were telling him he had been fleeced, spending $40 million of his own money on a losing primary campaign, $2 million going to Penn and Shrum in fees and commissions. But it was Checchi, the candidate, who was laughed out of politics. Shrum went on to be the lead strategist for the campaigns of Al Gore and John Kerry, Penn for Joe Lieberman and Hillary Clinton.

A lot of the political operatives who entered the field in the 1980s and 1990s did so because they envied the wealth and celebrity that flowed to consultants like Penn and Shrum. Podhorzer entered the field because he aspired to outsmart them, and the only counterweight he knew to the tyranny of the gurus was the incisive power of data. As a child in Brookline, Massachusetts, Podhorzer was a baseball fan who obsessed over the board game Strat-o-Matic, through which contestants could replicate entire games based on odds derived from ballplayers' real-life performance. When computers arrived, Podhorzer realized that he could write his own programs testing scenarios in the game, and by the age of twelve he was trekking to local libraries and nearby universities to find time at a Wang terminal. "It at a very early age makes you interested in probabilities and statistical outcomes and so on," says Podhorzer. "It made the value of thinking about the world in analytical terms—and not taking people's old saws at face value—ingrained in my personality. That's the way I've pretty much approached everything in politics."

After graduating from college, Podhorzer went to work for the consumer group Citizen Action, for which he led issue-based campaigns on Capitol Hill. In 1983, when Ronald Reagan announced a proposal to deregulate the natural gas industry, Podhorzer set out to build a bipartisan coalition to beat the White House. But he didn't buy the ads or hire the lobbying team typical for a high-stakes legislative fight. Instead, Podhorzer identified midwestern Republicans in Congress who weren't typical allies on progressive issues but had large concentrations of natural gas users in their districts. Then Podhorzer created lists of the Republican members' supporters and encouraged them to push their representatives to oppose the bill. "We let data inform our pre-strategy," he says. "One of my first impulses is always thinking 'what do we know and how can we make that information work for us?'"

In 1997, Podhorzer was approached by Steve Rosenthal, who had just become the AFL-CIO's political director and was tasked with building the biggest turnout operation in labor's history. Rosenthal had been appointed to his post by the AFL's newly elected president, John Sweeney, who vowed that organized labor would reassert itself as an election day force. Rosenthal's job was to mobilize union households who had been dispirited both by a Clinton term they saw as accommodationist and probusiness and by Republican congressional victories in the 1994 midterms. Sweeney helped to raise $32 million for the campaign called Labor '96, several times more than any other AFL electoral project in years, but Rosenthal quickly despaired that they were unprepared to spend it effectively.

In his first few weeks on the job, Rosenthal traveled the country to sit in on political training sessions that the AFL hosted for local labor officials. At one, Rosenthal perked up when he heard an AFL staff organizer tell her trainees that "union members read their mail on Fridays"—too busy to read it daily, they let it stack up until the end of the week, when they sort through the piles and open the pieces that interest them. So, the organizer went on, an effective mail program was one that targeted its brochures to arrive on Fridays. "I was just completely blown away," says Rosenthal. "I had never heard this before, and I couldn't possibly imagine every union reader had the same habits in reading their mail. I confronted her afterwards, and effectively what she said was 'That's how I do my mail, and I'm sure other people are in the same position I'm in.'"

Rosenthal thought labor's tactics deserved a little more rigor. He had followed Podhorzer's work at Citizen Action and asked his new bosses at AFSCME, the public employees' union in whose political department Podhorzer now worked, if they could lend him out to the new campaign. "I had a very good gut sense of the message—what union members wanted to hear, what they needed to hear," says Rosenthal. "Mike had a very good sense of the mechanics, and thinking outside the box about what needed to be done to move people."

The two men could not have been more different. Rosenthal was a bearish Long Islander with a bushy mustache who made a point of getting out of his Washington office and personally visiting labor's organizing campaigns around the country, raising his own voice to rally a crowd of workers clad in vinyl jackets. (Sweeney, who had been elected as a consensus candidate during a fractious campaign, was a poor communicator and left an outsized public role to his political director.) Podhorzer looked like he would be far more at home in a faculty lounge than a union hall. "He had the lowest profile of anyone in D.C.," says Judith Freeman, who worked in the AFL political department under Podhorzer. "He's just naturally introverted. He didn't spend his time out there in the city telling people how smart he was."

Rosenthal was pleased with the results of Labor '96, which helped to increase labor's share of the total popular vote to 23 percent (from its dismal 13 percent in 1994). But as he drew up plans for a 1998 sequel he wasn't convinced he knew which items in the AFL's variegated budget actually delivered the votes that had helped to return Clinton to the White House. "I looked at it and said there isn't an industry in America that would spend $32 million without spending a significant piece of that budget trying to understand what works and what doesn't," Rosenthal says. "The problem with almost everything the party committees and campaign did is that people rarely take the time to look back." So he and Podhorzer began casting about for ways to measure the effect of their voter contact programs. They organized one program where they paid union members in battleground states one hundred dollars each to collect all the political mail they received—marking each leaflet with the date of arrival before placing it in a pre-addressed envelope to Washington—and even asked some for permission to install cameras in their homes to tape them as they received mail and opened it.

Along the way, the AFL continued to spend hundreds and thousands of dollars each year on polling and focus groups, much of it to gauge what persuaded or motivated voters. But neither of those more traditional methods revealed much. A good poll can present an indication of how the electorate, and significant demographic groups within it, is moving over time, but cannot isolate the effect of any individual message—and certainly not a single mailed leaflet, one of organized labor's favorite tools. Campaign pollsters often tested new messages by first asking voters whom they supported, bombarding them with a set of new facts about a candidate—his views on issues, an aspect of his record, a fact about his personal life—and then repeating the initial question. "You're going to base your whole campaign on who within a minute changes their mind?" asks Democratic strategist Kevin Looper. "There's a good reason campaigns treat people like idiots."

When pollsters wanted a more nuanced look at how voters made assessments, they would convene a focus group. For presidential campaigns, this required identifying a swing state city and inviting around a dozen people, embodying a range of ages, genders, and races roughly representative of the electorate. Their opinions were valued, the invitees were told, and they would be compensated for a few hours of their time with all the sandwiches they could eat. A moderator might show an ad, pass around a brochure, or read a snippet from a possible speech, and then call on people around the table to see what they thought of it. Under the odd conventions of the consulting business, the same public opinion firms that did polling typically did focus groups, so often the person charged with coaxing latent opinions out of strangers was there only because he had shown a deftness with numbers.

Focus groups could give a rich impression of how a collection of voters responded to an individual leaflet, but they would only get the instant reaction of someone being paid one hundred dollars for his or her attention. A focus group could not reveal much about whether a typical voter would even notice the brochure if it showed up in the mail wedged between a birthday card and a water bill. Consultants who sat behind the one-way glass noticed that voters being paid in cash and sandwiches to weigh in on political communication are often overcome by self-consciousness. In focus groups, people say they don't like negative ads, but when the ads come over their airwaves they seem to succeed in worsening voters' impression of their target. "You get this spiral of negativity about an ad. People want to compete with each other to be more cynical," says Mark Mellman, whose firm ran both polls and focus groups. "They're noticing things just to notice them, because you've asked them to fill up the two hours."

Podhorzer was desperate for a method that would cleanly measure cause and effect in the real world, and he found one after encountering James McGreevey. In the summer of 1997, McGreevey, a young state senator and mayor running for governor in New Jersey, came to Washington to introduce himself to political directors of the national unions, a typical stop for statewide candidates seeking support. It did not go well. "He came in and gave what was probably the worst presentation any of us had ever seen by a candidate," Rosenthal recalls. McGreevey's delivery was flat and his themes too general, showing little interest in workers' issues. (For years, Rosenthal and his peers would call it "pulling a McGreevey" when a rookie candidate came to Washington and bombed.) Rosenthal concluded after the meeting that McGreevey's challenge to Republican incumbent Christie Todd Whitman was hopeless, unworthy of the AFL's investment—but a useful ground for research that could help more promising candidates in 1998. Podhorzer designed a test in which he let some of the state's 3,300 union locals continue with their plans to deliver pro-McGreevey mail and phone calls to members while others stayed on the sidelines. Afterward Podhorzer was able to compare turnout by union members across the state and attribute disparities to the different levels of communication by locals. Podhorzer's experimental design (which did not clinically randomize voters) may have failed to meet academic standards, but he was onto the same approach Gerber and Green would refine the next year. Yet after the election, the AFL kept the details of their test secret: Whitman ended up winning by barely twenty-five thousand votes, and Rosenthal worried that his decision to allow locals to sit on their hands could get blamed for failing to put McGreevey over the top. "The running joke," he says, "was that if we had just run the full program to everyone we could have helped bring home a good chunk of those votes."

After the 2002 elections, Rosenthal left the AFL. New campaign finance laws taking effect would dramatically restrict the way candidates and parties could raise money, and Rosenthal intended to launch an independent organization that would assume some of the campaigns' core functions, like registering and turning out voters, under looser fund-raising rules. (Rosenthal's group became America Coming Together.) Podhorzer remained at the AFL, but with a diminishing faith in the traditional infrastructure of political expertise. The debates over which institution would be responsible for turning out voters seemed to ignore the fact that none of them really knew how to do so.

Podhorzer came to believe that his perch at the AFL offered a unique opportunity to reinvent the way campaigns work. Such permanence was a rare trait in the political world. Candidate campaigns were short-horizon projects, rarely interested in developing unproven techniques. The national parties might have looked more durable, but they had turnover, too, and it usually came at the worst time imaginable—in the middle of a presidential election season when the party's nominee was granted effective control of the enterprise. Only institutions like labor unions—and other allies in the Democratic coalition, like the League of Conservation Voters and the women's group EMILY's List—would always have a stake in improving their tactics for the next election. "Until you get into a more rigorous approach, you are essentially left with what we had," says Podhorzer, "which is that everything you did in a winning campaign was a good idea, and everything that you did in a losing campaign was a bad idea."

Podhorzer had read the first Gerber-Green paper when it came out, and he began implementing their conclusions about the relative value of campaign tools. Robocalls, proven ineffective at turnout, were banished from the AFL's GOTV repertoire. Along with Malchow, one of three AFL mail vendors, Podhorzer began regularly speaking to the Yale professors about how to adapt experimental methods to the particular challenges faced by organized labor. "Most of their studies have focused on simply why people vote, not who they vote for, which is of obvious importance to an organization that's involved in politics," Podhorzer says.

In the run-up to the 2004 elections, the AFL would be sending almost monthly mailings to targeted members, and Podhorzer thought randomized-control trials could offer the basis for a "continuous feedback loop." The twenty-thousand-person Ohio survey sample would be converted into a massive focus group, but without any of the respondents knowing they were under examination. Voters would encounter the AFL's messages the way they normally did, fetching them from a mailbox, instead of having them handed by a moderator. Podhorzer could test different messages with small subsets of voters, while leaving a control group untouched. If voters never looked at a piece of mail, or picked it up but never paid attention to it, or read it and seconds later forgot what it said, that was worth measuring. If they studied the brochure but their opinions didn't shift, that was worth measuring, too. Polling across all the groups would make it possible to isolate the specific impact of the mailer and send the most influential ones to a broader array of members.

In November 2003, Podhorzer began three-week cycles, during which he would send out three different mail pieces and compare their effectiveness. Not only did the method allow the AFL to save its resources for the most effective messages; the large-sample polls also gave Podhorzer new insight into those who were really susceptible to having their minds changed. The polls showed him with increased precision what could make voters move away from Bush, and also groups that were resistant to arguments; with the latter, he went back and tested different mailers to see if other language might resonate more strongly. Overall, only between one-third and one-fifth of people in Podhorzer's target universe moved in the way he had expected they would. Many did not show any effect, and some seemed turned off by the mailers. "It was obvious," says Podhorzer, "that we were wasting a lot of our resources communicating with people who would never support us or people who would support us even if we never talked to them."

As the experiment got under way, Podhorzer became increasingly frustrated with how little meaningful information he had about the voters he was trying to reach. The AFL's conventional polling recorded what voters thought of the candidates and what issues were most important to them, but it revealed almost nothing about what information could change their minds. "You had someone answer a survey and say global warming is their most important issue, but sending them a piece saying Al Gore is for fighting global warming is useless," says Podhorzer. "Unless their head's under a rock they know Al Gore is against global warming."

When a pollster asked if someone would be more or less likely to vote for a candidate in favor of shipping jobs overseas—a typical way of auditioning what was then a promising line of attack against Bush—they would often hear from voters across the board that it made them "less likely." But when the AFL sent out a draft leaflet about Bush's free-trade policies, it turned out to have little impact on the autoworkers who received it. The knowledge of factory job loss was "baked in" to their impressions of Bush, as Podhorzer liked to put it: the workers already knew what the union wanted them to think about Republican trade policy. They liked or disliked Bush regardless. But other groups, like construction workers and Republicans, did not know as much. A piece of mail that gave them information turned out to be persuasive in changing their attitudes toward Bush. Experiments allowed Podhorzer to see which voters actually moved, not just those who said they might.

＊　＊　＊　＊　＊

BUSH'S REELECTION, and the fear that the newfound Republican vote-hunting mettle behind it might presage a generation out of power for Democrats, brought new urgency to the left's previously fitful efforts toward innovation. On a cold, rainy afternoon in late November 2004, Laura Quinn called Debra DeShong and asked her to come to the consulting firm Quinn owned. Quinn said she had a Christmas gift for her former Democratic National Committee colleague, but it became quickly evident to DeShong that a wrapped iPod was not the only thing Quinn was eager to share. Quinn's desk was covered with newspaper and magazine clips about how Bush had won, many of them lionizing Karl Rove, whom Bush had described the morning after his victory as "the Architect."

It is common for operatives to spend much of their time trying to figure out what the opposition is up to, but by the end of 2004 Quinn's fixation on Rove had risen to the level of obsession. She kept easily accessible on her computer desktop the video of a 1972 CBS News report in which Dan Rather visits the Committee for the Re-Election of the President to marvel at the latest techniques being used to support Richard Nixon's reelection, including the earliest efforts at data-driven direct-mail fundraising. "If you've ever contributed to the Republican Party or subscribed to a conservative magazine, or purchased Idaho Steaks through the mail or written away for a dry washcloth for your car, chances are your name is on the computer," Rather intones. "And if you haven't been asked to contribute to the Nixon campaign, you will." The correspondent then travels to the basement, where he meets the executive director of the College Republicans, busy plotting Nixon's youth registration efforts. "Young people have got to reach other young people, and that's what we're seeking to do," says a twenty-one-year-old Karl Rove, decorated with glasses, a tie and vest combination, and luxurious sideburns. "It's just so fun," Quinn would say right before pressing play, a rare turn toward girlishness from a woman who regularly impressed colleagues and intimidated rivals with her intense, and occasionally joyless, focus.

Now, while others who had played a role in Kerry's campaign were scattered on tropical beaches trying to put 2004 behind them, Quinn found a sense of purpose in her pile of Rove clips. She marveled at the way he had outfoxed the left at the aspects of campaigning where it had claimed mastery, and she was intent on reverse-engineering his methods from the general descriptions that had appeared in newspapers. Upon arriving at Quinn's office, DeShong was surprised to find her friend unusually chipper. "She was very upset about losing the election, as we all were," DeShong recalls. "But she was so excited that she had figured out what Rove had done."

Looking for "the mark of Rove," as some took to calling it, had become a popular pastime for many Democrats. In June 2002, a Senate staffer crossing Lafayette Square, just across Pennsylvania Avenue from the White House, came across a CD-ROM. Upon examination, the mysterious find revealed unusually compelling contents: two PowerPoint presentations that Rove and White House political director Ken Mehlman had delivered to a Republican gathering at the nearby Hay-Adams hotel. The slides, which contained a forecast of that fall's midterm elections, were given to a Capitol Hill columnist and made news because they revealed a White House more pessimistic about the chances of two Republican Senate candidates than officials let on publicly. But the actual presentations gave away little except suspicions that the accidental loss of the disk was not what it appeared. (During the 2000 campaign, a videotape of Bush's debate-prep sessions had arrived by mail at Gore's headquarters, and allegations of older false-flag operations had followed Rove from Texas to Washington.) Could the famously disciplined Bush operation really be so sloppy? Or were they hoping it would be found?

That winter, another set of PowerPoint slides found its way into Democratic hands. The computer file lacked the concise founding narrative of the Lafayette Square disk, and even the most fevered conspiracist couldn't imagine why Rove would want to see it public. The presentation had been designed by Blaise Hazelwood a year earlier, before the RNC's 2002 winter meeting, with a complete set of findings from the party's 72-Hour experiments. The material alerted Democrats that the Republicans had turned their attention to turnout and had developed an intellectual infrastructure for their field operations that towered over anything the institutions of the left had ever built. "You would have thought this was nuclear code, or a DNA sequence had been cracked," says Tracy Sefl, the DNC's deputy research director.

Hardly any details about Alexander Gage's microtargeting project had made it into the press during the election. Instead, the stories that had come out about the implementation of 72-Hour tactics had been ones Republicans wanted told: about the "multilevel marketing" that was making Bush a ground-level force and helping to empower volunteers. Quinn and her allies suspected that Republicans had sharpened their approach to voter contact, but never knew how. They rigorously collected distinctive pieces of mail—the 2004 brochure sent to New Mexico Spanish speakers with a chart contrasting the positions of Bush and Kerry on abortion and gay marriage, over the slogan "Vote Sus Valores"—and speculated about the methods behind them. After the election, Rove and other advisers revealed what they had been up to, taking what Democrats described as a "victory lap" for the so-called microtargeting methods that made them possible.

Even though no Democrats had used the word *microtargeting,* several party operatives had arrived separately at the same basic insight as Gage. They knew large-scale surveys could isolate the influence of personal characteristics that were combining in ways imperceptible to traditional polls, and how to track back to find specific individuals who fit those categories. In 2001, two former Gore advisers at Boston's Dewey Square Group tried to market a clustering system called Fusion, modeled on products Claritas had developed for the commercial market. The next year, Malchow sold a CHAID program, similar to the one he had used for Ron Wyden in Oregon six years earlier, to Democratic-coordinated campaigns in three states.

But a small group of veterans of the Kerry operation known as the BullsEye felt the greatest frustration as they read the press accounts of Gage's triumph. The BullsEye, which commandeered a small room at headquarters hidden off to the side of the communications war room, was designed to be the tactical hub of Kerry's general election campaign, where a constant pulse of data from battleground states would help redirect the candidate's plane or a communications blast to the areas that needed it most. One of the most important tools at their disposal was a master database that pollster Mark Mellman had built to contain all the interviews conducted by Kerry's retinue of far-flung survey takers throughout the year. Instead of relying merely on a rolling series of state-by-state snapshots, the BullsEye could aggregate tens of thousands of respondents, track each of them back to a record in the voter file, and look for unusual patterns.

Before the Iowa caucuses, Ken Strasma, a former analyst for the National Committee for an Effective Congress, had conducted a ten-thousand-person poll to build a statistical model that could identify likely Kerry supporters for the candidate's voter contact operation to target and turn out for the caucuses. In the general election, Mellman's database would make it possible for Strasma to design similar models for voters nationwide. But there was little interest from the campaign's leadership; Strasma didn't even speak with the campaign manager, Mary Beth Cahill, until well after Kerry's dramatic Iowa victory. "It was just one of the things that wasn't on her radar screen," says Strasma.

Mellman's database yielded important tidbits that helped to shape message strategy, such as the insight that voters who had contributed to disease-related charities were a promising audience for Kerry. As a result, the campaign gave Ron Reagan, the former president's son, a prominent convention speaking slot to argue that Kerry's support for stem-cell research could help cure the Alzheimer's that had crippled Reagan's father. But when it came to talking to voters directly, Kerry's targeters had trouble getting state directors to put aside their precinct-based strategies and use the new individual-level profiles instead. At a weekend-long retreat held in Maryland for Kerry's state-level operatives, only one hour was devoted to introducing and explaining Strasma's new targeting program. "They would fight with me," says Mellman. "The resistance was substantial, because people are used to looking at things in the way they're used to looking at things."

That resistance finally began to crack after the election, as victorious Republicans flaunted their fine-grained knowledge of the electorate. In one particularly potent example, Gage told how his party had turned even shopping patterns into political intelligence, discovering that bourbon drinkers leaned Republican while cognac sniffers were more likely Democrats. "It just scared the shit out of all the Democrats," says Malchow. "The best way to get anyone to do anything on the Democratic side—and I'm sure it's the reverse on the Republican side—is to tell people that the Republicans are doing it. It doesn't matter: the Republicans could be doing something completely stupid, but if you tell the Democrats they get scared and think they should do it. They all think the Republicans are smarter than they are."

Malchow, Strasma, and others started to look closely at some of the consumer variables that journalists loved to highlight in their stories, such as the idea that knowing what type of car someone drives will say something new about how they vote. Even Malchow got scared: "The Republicans learned how to do car ownership!" When he looked more closely, though, he realized that even if Gage had managed to acquire the data and append it to a voter file, it couldn't possibly be a usefully predictive variable for political contact. The car most overrepresented by Republican drivers was the Jaguar: 59 percent of Jag owners were Republicans. (Among Democrats, Subarus were strongest—43 percent of Subaru owners were Democrats.) But Jaguars amounted to only one-half of a percent of the total U.S. auto market, and there were plenty of other ways to identify older, ostentatiously wealthy suburbanites (like their addresses) than mining auto registration records for hints. A lot of the most colorful examples, Malchow concluded, were hype.

As Democrats learned more about the scale of what the Bush campaign had done, they realized that the opposition's edge wasn't about a particularly potent set of consumer files it had acquired but rather the political structure they had built around them. "On the Republican side, the RNC was so much stronger than the DNC was at the time," says Hesla. No Democrat, and certainly not Kerry, had invested as much in individual-level targeting as Bush had, or did so early enough to integrate it fully into the campaign's operations. A *Washington Post* analysis of the $2.2 billion spent on the presidential campaign—split almost evenly between efforts on behalf of Bush and Kerry—concluded that Bush's $3.25-million contract with Gage's firm TargetPoint was among the best money spent that year. The *Post* story pointed to the increase in Bush's turnout in Ohio, and included one quote from an anonymous Democratic operative declaring that the party's targeting power was a full election cycle behind the Republicans'. "They came into Democratic areas with very specific targeted messages to take Democratic voters away from us," Terry McAuliffe told the *Post*.

As she explained these machinations to DeShong, Quinn took out a paper napkin and started diagramming. She drew a line to represent the partisan continuum, from left to right, and then laid upon it a series of bars reflecting targeted messages, annotating as she scribbled furiously. One bar symbolized "terrorism and late-term abortion for older Hispanics," Quinn said, while another of different length was "terrorism and guns for male union members." DeShong sat dumbfounded by the squiggly lines, until Quinn explained her point: Democrats were polling to make messages for broad audiences, while Republicans were modeling to match messages to specific audiences. They were able to do that because they had not only better data than the Democrats to find the voters they wanted, she went on, but also the statistical tools to profile those they couldn't reach and nonetheless predict what views they were likely to have.

"Now we have to do it," Quinn said. "And we have to do it better."

* * * * *

LAURA QUINN WAS something of an accidental technologist: a communications aide always looking for the newest way to get a message out. While working on Capitol Hill in the mid-1990s, she helped build a new television studio for Democratic senators and hired the first full-time Web expert to help members of Congress develop an online presence. In 1999, she moved to the White House to work for Al Gore as he prepared for a presidential campaign. After his loss, newly elected DNC chairman Terry McAuliffe hired Quinn to prepare a report on the party's tech infrastructure.

Quinn was a tall, lithe woman with long gray hair and austere Modigliani features who climbed rock faces for fun, and she prowled the party's salmon-colored, concrete-block headquarters with the same expeditionary spirit. Encountering fleas, mice, and large concentrations of radon along the way, she found an underused television studio and a press office with no database of media contacts. There were telephone lines that had been installed to support long-forgotten election-year call centers and became themselves forgotten; in one case, Quinn discovered that the committee was somehow paying the monthly phone bill of a Florida dentist. Her report to McAuliffe recommended a thorough renovation of the building with an eye to both making it inhabitable and modernizing its technology. "It was really a terrible mess," Quinn says.

The physical decay of the Democratic National Committee was the inevitable result of a cycle of strategic disinvestment. Every four years, the Democratic presidential nominee would inherit command of the structure, installing cronies in top jobs and filling the lower ranks with staff shifted off the campaign payroll. "The Democratic Party strategy had very much been, going into presidential elections, that you just spend everything down to the dirt," says Quinn. "Then the DNC is in debt and everything is broken." The DNC's election-year job was largely to be a fund-raising vehicle for the big-dollar contributions known as "soft money": unrestricted gifts, often from union and corporate sources, that the parties could legally raise but candidates could not.

McAuliffe had risen in national politics as a fund-raiser for Bill Clinton, and together they had helped to expand the Democrats' reach into Hollywood and Wall Street wallets, narrowing the soft-money gap between the parties. But the DNC still lagged significantly in raising so-called hard money, small contributions from everyday people. It was a predicament that Democrats couldn't write off as an inevitable consequence of the opposition's close ties to big business. "How is it that the Republican Party was consistently and substantially outraising the Democratic Party in small-dollar donations?" asked Quinn. "What was allowing them to do it?"

Quinn looked enviously at the RNC headquarters, two blocks away and across a set of railroad tracks. It had always been a more stable, centralized entity than the centrifugal DNC. National Republicans effectively ran their state parties from Washington, even paying the salaries of executive directors. Democratic state chairs, on the other hand, were frequently appointed by the governor or an influential legislator and felt little fealty to national leaders. As she closely examined parties' spending over the previous two decades, Quinn marveled at how the opposition had repeatedly made farsighted investments in new communication technologies. For a generation, conservatives distrustful of the mainstream media had made a priority of finding new channels to directly address their base. In the early 1990s, the RNC had built TV and radio studios so that party figures could call in to sympathetic talk shows. A few years later, Republicans put money in a website and even designated supporters as Internet captains at a time when Democrats had yet to begin taking the online world seriously.

But when he became chairman in early 2001, McAuliffe felt an urgency that had moved few of his predecessors. He was already looking ahead to the ways in which life would change under the campaign finance reform bill known as McCain-Feingold, which vowed to ban soft money and would be enacted the following year. McAuliffe foresaw that the national parties would be forced to reinvent themselves as engines of small-dollar contributions. Ironically, the soft-money parity that McAuliffe had helped to achieve during Clinton's presidency now made the party disproportionately dependent on a mode of giving that would soon become illegal. The DNC had to learn to talk to people.

In April, Quinn returned to McAuliffe with her assessment of the infrastructure, which was filled with reasons for alarm. McAuliffe fixated on one set of statistics: the DNC's list of names—donors and volunteers, mostly—totaled two million, and for many of those Quinn feared the information on file was no longer current. The e-mail list included only seventy thousand people. The party had little capacity to hunt for other loyal Democrats who could be converted into contributors. McAuliffe decided that his goal, as he started to tell people, would be to have "more live e-mails on the file than dead voters."

Quinn's report to McAuliffe had not recommended investing in a unified national voter file. The RNC had begun its own project to do so in the late 1970s, hiring private vendors to collect information on voters in all fifty states, standardize its format, and develop a system that could be continuously updated with new voters, changed addresses, and expanded vote histories. The Constitution leaves responsibility for administering elections to the states, and RNC officials quickly learned what a rough-hewn patchwork of laws and protocols had emerged to simply manage voter registration practices. "I can't overestimate how bad a shape the voter registration files were in in this country when we started," says Eddie

Mahe, the committee's executive director. In New Hampshire, each of the state's 234 townships was responsible for maintaining its own registration records, many times on handwritten rolls stored in officials' homes. In Montana, Republicans had to send someone to gather computer tapes from every courthouse in the state. One Maine town was reputed to keep its voter list on chunks of tree bark.

It took more than a decade for the RNC to complete its national file, and during that time voter data became a high-stakes business for private-sector entrepreneurs. As a junior physics major at Princeton in 1976, John Aristotle Phillips had written a thirty-four-page paper that described how to assemble a plutonium fission bomb, like that which had been unleashed on Japan in World War II, for two thousand dollars. Phillips was approached by a Pakistani operative who tried to buy his paper, which prompted Phillips to both contact the FBI and call a press conference. The bribe had proven Phillips's point, as he later wrote, "that a terrorist, with a background in college physics, a small amount of stolen plutonium and the wherewithal to construct the device, could pose a threat to world peace." After graduating, Phillips ran for Congress in 1980, a Democrat looking to represent Connecticut on an antinuclear platform, but as an outsider he couldn't win access to voter files controlled by local party officials. After two unsuccessful campaigns, Phillips stopped running for office and enlisted his younger brother, Dean, a computer engineer, to develop tools for those who did. In 1983, their Aristotle Industries released Campaign Manager, one of the first pieces of consumer software for candidates, and started assembling voter lists to feed into the program. By 2000, the company had sixty-nine employees and was expanding worldwide. "If the parties were doing a great job then we wouldn't have any data business," says Phillips.

Quinn knew this history and decided that a national database would be too big an undertaking to successfully complete before the 2004 election season arrived. Along with the technological and logistical hurdles, above all there was a political one: a network of state parties ready to thwart any of Washington's efforts to seize one of their most prized commodities.

"There's always been a trust issue between the DNC and state parties," says Ray Buckley, then vice chair of the New Hampshire Democratic Party and a longtime DNC official. "Nobody believed that someone in Washington would not screw them."

In some cases, party officers used the list as a fund-raising device—presidential candidates in Iowa had to pay forty thousand dollars for its list of past caucus participants. In other states, kingmaker state chairs considered the list a plum to be shared with party-endorsed candidates. The Democratic Party of Illinois didn't even own a voter file but relied on one built and personally controlled by the state house speaker, Michael J. Madigan. "The idea that they were never going to give their data to the national party was so ingrained," McAuliffe says. "That was their asset, and they weren't going to give it to me."

But he was ready for the fight. The only path McAuliffe saw to hard-money parity ran through cycles of prospecting new donors, in the mail and online. To accomplish that on the scale he believed crucial, Democrats needed the list of 100 million new names, sortable by party registration or voting behavior, that would fill a national voter file. McAuliffe proposed a deal to the state chairs, that the DNC would effectively borrow their files, help clean them up, add new data like donor information and commercially available phone numbers, and then return them for the state party's use. At the same time, McAuliffe went to Vinod Gupta, a major Democratic fund-raiser and Clinton friend who was the founder and CEO of Info-USA, one of the country's large commercial data vendors. Like many of his rivals, Gupta had been trying for years to find customers in the political world, and offered McAuliffe a good deal for his product. McAuliffe agreed, and as the state files came in, the DNC would send them out to InfoUSA's Omaha servers, where hundreds of pieces of new information were added to each voter's profile. A new interface was built to navigate it all. It was called Demzilla.

The so-called datamart that McAuliffe helped to assemble was riddled with errors, and many state-level campaigns did not even know how to get their software to properly handle the information that was returned to them. But a roster of more than 150 million new targets was a great gift for the DNC's fund-raising operation, just as liberals were getting energized to rally against Bush. At one point, McAuliffe descended to the basement of the headquarters to invite the entire technology department out to dinner at the Palm as a sign of his gratitude. Merely by having built a website that could process new contributions online, they had begun to compete with the finance department as a fund-raising source.

McAuliffe's term was scheduled to end in early 2005, and a wide-open race for the DNC's chairmanship loomed. Quinn knew that whichever candidate succeeded McAuliffe would set new priorities, potentially jeopardizing the datamart's future. Howard Dean in particular worried her. His primary campaign for the presidency in 2004 had been framed as an insurgency against the party's Clinton era leadership, whom Dean pilloried as too centrist and money-obsessed, a caricature that fit McAuliffe perfectly. While Dean's campaign had often proven incompetent at the basics of voter contact, it had pioneered the use of the Web for small-dollar fund-raising and communicating with the party's activist class. Quinn suspected that if Dean won he would bring in his old campaign technology team, several members of whom had started their own firm, Blue State Digital, after his loss to Kerry.

Quinn began to think that the innovation necessary for Democrats to regain their footing would have to take place outside the DNC headquarters. The politics of the moment compelled it, but Quinn saw another benefit. Although party committees could share their lists with state affiliates and candidates, campaign finance laws restricted them from coordinating with outside groups. So while party officials had counted on AFL, ACT, and EMILY's List to assume a growing share of Democratic voter contact work, they couldn't speak to their allies about strategy or divvy up a list of voters to avoid duplicating efforts. It was time, Quinn thought, for the left to built an institution that had no purpose but to warehouse and share voter information. "For a long time, data was something you made valuable by keeping it in a drawer away from everyone else," says Quinn. "Only through the last decades have people realized that data becomes much more powerful when it is combined with other data, and it is free to grow and multiply."

She started plotting with Mark Steitz, a former DNC official who had drifted out of politics for a decade before resurfacing as the philosopher-king of Podhorzer's early geek lunches. Steitz was a garrulous former economist who had followed his boss, Senator Gary Hart, into presidential politics, and had grown frustrated with the idiocies of most political consultants. (Only a handful of them earned Steitz's highest praise: to be called "a serious human.") He usually took the long view of the political developments his peers preferred to assess in news cycles, and would often say things like "the Clinton campaign in 1992 was the full flower of what might be called the neoclassical synthesis of polling, media and field" or, when referring to the state of public opinion polls, "I think what you'll find out is there is more of the doctrine of eternal recurrence rather than Kuhnian scientific revolution against it. You know what I mean?"

Steitz had spent his self-imposed exile from politics in the corporate world. He had overseen communications for the 2004 Athens Olympic Committee and marketing for the Body Shop, the lefty British cosmetics retailer. ("They didn't believe in marketing per se," says Steitz. "So it was an interesting place to work.") When Steitz reinserted himself in the Washington campaign world during the 2004 election season, he found a circle of Democratic operatives eager to develop a culture of learning he had usually found absent from strategy sessions. They shared a spirit of entrepreneurship, inspired by recent events to conjure something altogether new rather than fight over market share in existing campaign budgets. "Losing is a great tonic for internecine bullshit," says Steitz. "We had been beaten badly enough and repetitively enough that lots of people were willing to sit down with one another who previously would not have."

* * * * *

THOSE DEFENDING THE UNPOPULAR VIEW that there is actually not enough money in politics frequently take refuge in the fact that Procter & Gamble each year spends more money advertising soap than Americans do on the quadrennial marketing pageants that choose their presidents. Political operatives have often gazed covetously at their analogues in the corporate suite, with their big budgets and multiyear market research studies, and imagined that on the other side someone stood on the verge of a major breakthrough in understanding human behavior. But the envy runs both ways. "The political business and the corporate business are like movie stars and rock stars," says Alex Lundry, who works with Gage at TargetPoint Consulting. "Everybody wants to be doing what the other side is doing. Every movie star wants to be a rock star, and vice versa."

After a decade in each sphere, Steitz maintained a more realistic view of the two sectors. "I had higher hopes for what the consumer world would do. I kept assuming that the commercial world had everything solved. When you actually got neck-deep, you realized that there are many things they knew that we didn't know, but there are many challenges that were very similar," says Steitz. "Neither is as far ahead of the other as they would hope."

Still, the commercial sphere had produced one piece of data that mesmerized Steitz, and it came from credit-card companies. It was a single predictive variable that allowed its analysts to compare at a glimpse tens of millions of people in behavioral terms. Through the first half of the twentieth century, lenders—from banks issuing mortgages to retailers with store accounts—would hire underwriters to look at individual borrowing histories, compiled by financial institutions and merchant associations, before deciding to issue credit. This was a subjective process, and an arduous one. In 1956, engineer Bill Fair and mathematician Earl Isaac began developing computer programs that could automate this analysis, and two years later started rating would-be borrowers for the St. Louis–based American Investment Company. By using these scores, the bank was able to cut delinquencies by one-quarter, or, depending on the adventurousness of loan officers, increase its lending volume by as much without spiking delinquencies. Fair, Isaac & Company credit scores were the common point of reference enabling a postwar lending boom that included the introduction of mass-market credit cards in the 1960s. Now everyone who wanted to lend money—the small-town credit-union officer, independent landlord, store with a house charge account, or corporate risk officer at Bank of America—could decide whether an individual was worthy of credit. A process that once often took weeks collapsed to minutes.

Fair, Isaac funneled consumer information from a variety of sources (there are now three major credit reporting agencies in the United States) into a shared numerical language. In 1989, the company introduced its FICO score, which assessed every individual on a 300–850-point scale of universal risk. A few years later, Fannie Mae and Freddie Mac started to require FICO scores for home sales, and they quickly became part of a standard mortgage application. As they matured, credit scores went from being merely a hunt for red flags in someone's past to a prediction of their future actions based on patterns in others' behavior.

In April 2005, Quinn and Steitz started a firm to market a credit score for voting. They called their new company Copernicus Analytics, after the sixteenth-century Polish astronomer. "Copernicus took individuals out of the center of the physical universe; we are trying to put them back at the center of the political world," Steitz announced at the time. They looked to the credit industry for an early hire. Ben Yuhas had studied math as an undergraduate and then earned an advanced degree in electrical and computer engineering. He went to work at Bellcore, the research institute opened by the regional phone companies alongside the legendary Bell Labs in northern New Jersey, and in 1995 joined AT&T as it beefed up antifraud efforts around its recently introduced no-fee credit card. Yuhas quickly became a creature of Wilmington, Delaware, America's credit-card company town, changing affiliations as banks consolidated but never having to move.

As a mathematician, he loved the fact that everything the companies did was very neatly measurable, and he looked admiringly at Capital One.

An offshoot of Virginia's Signet Bank, Capital One was the first credit-card company to take analytics seriously. Two consultants, Richard Fairbank and Nigel Morris, had approached fifteen banks in the late 1980s offering "information-based market strategy," and Signet was the only one to say yes. Fairbank and Morris used the large database that Signet had built of its transactions to look for patterns between customer behaviors, their credit scores, and the revenue they generated for Signet. When they saw that the most lucrative customers for Signet were ones who quickly borrowed large sums and slowly but responsibly paid down the balances, Fairbank and Morris proposed the bank introduce a balance-transfer card. (Signet spun off Capital One as a publicly traded company in 1994.)

Capital One became known for its culture of testing, eventually running three hundred different experiments at once, many of them using mailed credit-card offers that could be easily randomized in the way Gerber and Green had with campaign brochures. There were plenty of dependent variables to track: Capital One analysts could account for responses to a particular promotional offer, or examine the rates at which cardholders paid off their bills or went bad altogether. At the same time, credit scores offered a matrix to compare different types of customers. Did lowering fees appeal more to low-risk or high-risk borrowers, and how did different groups adjust their buying patterns when given new terms? "You had this really clear feedback loop, so you could focus on making the math better," says Yuhas. The goal was to convert a once-binary decision about risk (should we issue the card or not?) into a dynamic one (what rates and fees should we charge each of them to maximize our return?).

It was Yuhas's job to apply that math to politics. Ultimately his goal was to locate an algorithm with predictive power for two basic questions: how likely someone was to vote and how likely he or she was to support a certain candidate. An algorithm was, in effect, nothing more than a complex equation in which each variable was given a different weight, with those variables tested in different combinations to see which exerted the most force on the desired outcome (support and turnout) and weighted accordingly.

Yuhas's challenge was to design a model that accounted for which personal variables would play a consistently predictive role in a particular election. (Those variables could change from election to election; in a statewide race between San Francisco's mayor and Los Angeles's, for instance, having an Oakland ZIP code might be a major determinant in predicting a voter's support. In a race between two Angelenos, it might not matter at all.) Credit agencies had learned that household income and age played different roles in determining creditworthiness; Yuhas had to determine what influence they—and hundreds of other variables to which Copernicus had access—had on voting behavior.

In the spring of 2005, Tim Kaine hired Copernicus to put its new algorithm to work in his campaign to be Virginia's governor. Democrats saw the state moving gradually in their direction, but there was something else about Virginia that made it an appealing venue for Quinn and Steitz to put their scoring strategy to the test. Virginia is among the states that do not allow voters to register with a party, which means that the most useful predictor of general-election behavior was not available on the voter file. "We were at a real disadvantage knowing who was a Democrat and who wasn't. We are taking a guess on a lot of people as to whether they'd vote for us," says Mike Henry, Kaine's campaign manager. "There were only two ways to get it: call 'em or go and talk to 'em."

Even the old method of looking at precincts would have been of limited use to Kaine. His strategists thought their candidate, a former Richmond mayor finishing a term as lieutenant governor, was a different kind of Democrat than had run statewide before. Even the map from 2001, when Kaine had first won statewide office as Mark Warner's running mate, offered little guide for those seeking to put together a coalition for Kaine. Any Democrat had to turn out black voters in cities like Richmond and Norfolk, but the question was where white votes would come from in a state that had voted Republican in every presidential campaign since 1964. Warner lived in the Washington suburbs but had used his conservative stance on guns as well as a NASCAR aesthetic to win over rural voters. Kaine's positions on cultural issues—he was a former missionary and civil rights lawyer who opposed capital punishment—made Warner's map impossible. "No one had ever run a race in Virginia that was against the death penalty and had an F from the NRA and we had to overcome these obstacles," says Henry. Where Warner had been carried to victory on a rural-urban coalition, Kaine's advisers looked to the suburbs and exurbs of central and northern Virginia. These included some of the fastest-growing counties in the country, the type of place where Bush had used microtargeting to pick up new votes the year before.

Based on a large-sample poll in the summer of 2005, Copernicus was able to give each voter two different scores derived from Yuhas's algorithms. Each set to a ten-point scale, one predicted the likelihood that an individual would support Kaine, and the other that the voter would go to the polls in November at all. A person with a 7 support score was more likely to back Kaine than anyone with a 6. Steitz prepared a pair of maps to show Kaine's advisers how a new statistical method could effectively change the political geography of a state they thought they understood. One highlighted the counties that would get attention under a traditional precinct-targeting strategy, where large numbers of voters lived in areas regularly delivering 65 percent of their votes for Democrats: about ten counties appeared in the most intense color, and another ten in the next darkest shade. Yet a map that colored counties by the numbers of voters whose Kaine-support scores were in the top 20 percent darkened nearly every county in the state. From the void, a thick column of newly targetable counties emerged, stretching from Washington to Richmond.

Many of the Kaine targets in these counties had scored very high in Yuhas's models for Kaine support, but unusually low for turnout. That was a familiar profile for Democratic organizers: largely minority urban precincts overwhelmingly supported Democrats but lagged behind suburban precincts in turnout. This was much of the reason that the party and its allies had made such a conscious push to invest in GOTV during the 1990s. But some of the other counties that became filled in with Kaine

targets on Steitz's maps were suburban, generally white and fairly afflu-
ent. When Yuhas looked more closely at who the individuals were in these
areas, he found a distinctly different political profile than the poor African-
Americans the party was used to rousing with another round of phone
calls and a flotilla of vans ready to drive them to the polls. These upscale
suburbanites, Yuhas found, lived in reliably Democratic precincts and regularly voted in midterm congressional elections but sat out the state elections held in odd-numbered years. "They were definitely our voters," says
Henry. "If we could turn them out we'd get them." The campaign referred
to them internally as Federal Democrats: their lives revolved around Washington, not Richmond, and their local newspaper and television stations
often paid more attention to Maryland issues than their own. It would take
more than a phone call and a van to push them to the polls. "We needed to
show them why it's important that they vote in a governor's race," says Mo
Elleithee, Kaine's communications director. When Copernicus produced a
list of 250,000 such voters, Kaine's team designed a mail campaign about
transportation spending—traffic was a perennial issue in Northern Virginia, and one that could only be fixed by local governments—and started
sending canvassers to areas they had never gone before. "They almost had
a list of the people by name they needed to win the election," Steitz says.

When Kaine won, largely by making significant inroads into exurbs
that Bush had carried, it was heralded as a harbinger of a Democratic
comeback. Even though their scores had been developed specifically for
Kaine's race, Quinn and Steitz thought that the numbers could help others
running lefty campaigns in Virginia—from a candidate for the state house
of delegates to the League of Conservation Voters—in the same way that
credit scores were useful to anyone looking to make a business decision.
After Bush's reelection, *microtargeting* had become a faddish buzzword,
but it remained inaccessible to most people in politics. Large commercial
data warehouses like InfoUSA, Acxiom, and Experian were all trying to
sell their products to political campaigns, but their products were priced
for corporate clients. Typically they charged hefty rates for every record

pulled from the master file; while presidential reelection committees and national parties could afford such costly data bills, they were out of reach for local campaigns and advocacy groups. "One of the things that pricing model does on the political side is it creates incentives for people to use as little data as possible and as late as possible," says Quinn. "The idea was deliberately to change those incentives, to give people more data sooner, so they could experiment, consistently measure themselves."

Even so, many smaller groups would also not know what to do with such a large array of data when they got it. A single category of raw data had obvious applications for commercial marketers; when Home Depot wanted to know where to put a new store, it made sense to buy a list of people in a given ZIP code who had swimming pools. But political campaigns were less interested in a single consumer variable than in combining many of them with election-specific information, such as polls or phone bank IDs, to find patterns in the two sets. That took a level of expertise and computing power that didn't exist in the average statewide campaign headquarters or union hall.

In April 2006, Quinn and former Clinton White House adviser Harold Ickes folded Copernicus into a new company, Catalist, that would serve what they described as a data "utility" for Democratic campaigns and liberal causes. Ickes, who had helped to found America Coming Together, had returned to many of the same donors who had funded that effort. Placing calls from a hospital bed as he recuperated from a shattered hip incurred in a Vespa accident on Pennsylvania Avenue, Ickes made the case that the left needed a unified data infrastructure if it was ever going to catch up with what Republicans had built to prepare for Bush's reelection. "Two thousand four really got big donors and movers and shakers on the progressive side interested in voter contact. Philosophically they kind of liked it," says Ickes, who won the first $1 million commitment toward his $5 million goal from financier George Soros. "George comes from the European mentality and I think he was very enthusiastic about voter contact, much more than media—he didn't give the back of his hand to media but thought voter contact was something that we ought to, as progressives, get involved in."

Ickes was asking would-be backers like Soros to be investors rather than donors, but in a company that declared its "double bottom line": Catalist would pay attention to revenue but was more interested in keeping its prices down to help partisan and ideological allies win elections. Incorporating as a business would, in an era of restricted campaign finance laws, allow Catalist to operate as a for-profit vendor and not a nonprofit committee (as ACT and others were). They could do business with candidate campaigns, parties, and outside groups like unions all at once, as long as the flat, unlimited-access fees they charged each were considered fair-market value. In the same way that a video archive could legally license the same waving-flag footage to John Kerry and the AFL-CIO's independent-expenditure committee without being accused of coordinating between the two, each group could be a Catalist client. They could buy the same voter files, with the same modeling scores attached.

When clients signed on, Catalist account representatives would ask for old voter IDs compiled from canvassers and phone banks. The best-case scenario was often being introduced to a desk drawer filled with records from past elections that the groups had never synthesized into a permanent file. In Catalist's hands, each individual ID would be another data point that the algorithms could use as they profiled individuals. Catalist's "ballots cast" table—the simple voter-file category of who voted in which election—quickly had well over a billion pieces of data in it alone.

Already, Catalist was operating on an astounding scale. Because many Catalist clients wanted data that could help them target nonvoters in registration drives, the company aspired to have a record for every voting-age adult in the United States, unlike the party's databases, which included only registered voters. The standard statistical-processing software used for those who had done microtargeting on a state-by-state level, or had managed a single union's membership list, couldn't handle much more than ten million records. Catalist was building a file with 200 million—with the exception of the credit-rating agencies, very few other private-sector entities ever needed to look at the whole country at once. "The things happening in the political sphere were approaching the more sophisticated techniques being used" in the corporate world, says Vijay Ravindran, a former Amazon .com software developer who became Catalist's first chief technology officer. Catalist now maintains one-half of a petabyte of data, the equivalent of one thousand hard drives.

In Catalist's early days, as Ickes tried to line up investors and Quinn recruited clients among liberal interest groups, they felt they had to fend off what Ickes describes as "backbiting" from party leaders he suspected of maneuvering behind the scenes to discourage support for Catalist. At the Democratic National Committee, Dean was working to complete the costly national voter file project that McAuliffe had started. Party officials made the case that Catalist would be redundant, but Ickes believed that they simply sensed the threat from a new power base that would sit outside the DNC, part of an inexorable shift in influence from the parties to independent players. "Dean had the aura of being the tech candidate, and knowing everything about technology," says Ickes. "I think the establishment just didn't want something that the establishment couldn't control."

Quinn and Ickes weren't the only Democratic operatives trying to build common political tools that could be shared across the left. Throughout 2004, a Democratic consultant named Rob Stein had traveled the country meeting the wealthiest liberals he could find to show them a series of PowerPoint slides he had prepared. Democrats had long agonized over what they saw as the right's supremacy in developing political soft power: the web of well-funded conservative think tanks and foundations, generating ideas and arguments that flow to voters through sympathetic media channels. Stein's presentation, "The Conservative Message Machine's Money Matrix," validated the existence of what Hillary Clinton in 1998 had called a "vast right-wing conspiracy," only Stein did it with an accountant's authority. He assessed the matrix as a $300 million annual operation, and showed how the right systematically outspent the left in every category of political communication: $170 million to $85 million in think tanks, $35 million to $5 million in legal advocacy groups. Stein had begun his research after the 2002 midterms, but after Kerry's loss his argument burned with new urgency. Beginning in late 2004, Stein persuaded Soros and Peter Lewis—who had each given $20 million to launch America Coming Together and its affiliated Media Fund—to look past short-term organizing and toward long-term institution-building. Soros and Lewis led other liberal donors to band together as the Democracy Alliance, a loose confederation that would direct investment into new projects. The group, and its participants, directed money to keystone institutions of the new new left, including the Center for American Progress, which rapidly emerged as one of Washington's most influential think tanks, and Media Matters for America, a watchdog group that worked, largely in vain, to embarrass the Fox News Channel and Rush Limbaugh.

At the same time, Kerry's defeat also quietly inspired an era of entrepreneurship centered on the hard power of winning votes. The New Organizing Institute was launched in 2005 by young veterans of the Kerry and Dean campaigns to train operatives in online organizing. The Atlas Project established an archive of old strategy plans and polling memos from Democratic campaigns, the type of thing generally lost to trash collectors the morning after the votes are counted. "All of this stuff together is building an infrastructure for Democratic candidates and progressive groups to change the way business is being done," says Steve Rosenthal, the former AFL-CIO political director who helped found the Atlas Project.

Meanwhile, Podhorzer's geek lunches continued, and even though he was not actively recruiting participants the community grew slowly by word of mouth. The biweekly sessions became known as the Analyst Group, and over sandwiches and diet Coke and a big green salad that often went untouched, many of the new attendees ended up revealing the tinkering they had been quietly doing within their organizations. "One of the things about the Analyst Group that's been jaw-dropping is how much people report failure," says Hesla. "It's like AA for geeks: it's this very trusting environment where everyone shares."

By the time the Democrats won back Congress in late 2006, Podhorzer had moved the lunch discussions to the President's Room on the first floor of the AFL's headquarters to accommodate the sixty people regularly showing up for them. The group's reach, in fact, was becoming so broad that it needed a structure to coordinate new research projects and share findings. In 2007, Podhorzer and his circle created the Analyst Institute, designed to operate with the sensibility of a think tank but the privacy of a for-profit consulting firm.

Quinn and Steitz joined the board, and they had an idea that the new entity's destiny had to be interlocked with Catalist, each a political business founded with little interest in profit. Steitz thought back to Nigel Morris, whom Steitz had approached in late 2005 to discuss how American progressives could adopt lessons from the testing culture of Capital One. If the company wanted to stay ahead permanently, Morris said, it could do so only by perennially experimenting—testing everything, and then agglomerating the data in a way that could reveal new insights about each individual in their database over time. Already the company ran nearly fifty thousand experiments yearly, part of a goal to have more "laps around the track" than any competitor, as Morris put it. Steitz began to adopt the metaphor as his own. Catalist and the Analyst Institute were, he thought, the vehicles the left had long needed. "The progressive movement," Steitz wrote in a memo, "needs to increase our laps around the track by orders of magnitude."

Podhorzer became the group's chairman and cast about to hire an executive director who would decide what the left's next round of experiments would be. Gerber and Green recommended one of their protégés, David Nickerson, who was then teaching at Notre Dame and running his own battery of experiments. But Nickerson turned down the job, worried that he would be performing "proprietary science" for activists rather than making his work public in scholarly spaces.

Gerber then suggested Todd Rogers, on whose dissertation committee he had recently served. Rogers had an unusual profile to run a Washington consulting firm: a psychologist who graduated from Harvard Business School after performing research that examined whether the way individuals managed their Netflix queues could illuminate how they felt about a carbon tax to fight global warming. Elsewhere in his dissertation, Rogers had run an experiment that fooled citizens into visualizing themselves going to the polls, and then measured whether they actually did. Another proposed that it might be possible to drive up turnout merely by talking it up as a popular activity.

These were turnout levers that the Analyst Group members had never before thought about pulling. Green said he was struck by Rogers, not yet thirty, as "a throwback to older days in which psychologists were interested in the dynamics of social action." Podhorzer was attached to a more modest historical analogy. The statistical revolution that had fascinated a teenaged Podhorzer had transformed baseball, as many of those who had grown up using numbers to undermine the wisdom of elders now ran their own front offices. In an early job posting after he moved to Washington as the group's director, Rogers wrote, "Some people have described what we are trying to do as '*Moneyball* for progressive politics.'"

7

WHEN SHAME PAYS A HOUSE CALL

n 2002, Todd Rogers opened a manila file folder and let a flurry of newspaper and magazine clips settle on the kitchen table of his Western Massachusetts home. Less than two years earlier, the recent Williams College graduate had turned down opportunities to work at bigger Washington polling firms to join Abacus Associates, whose small office was run by two former academics and where Rogers handled junior tasks like data analysis and writing survey questions. But now he was itching to do something new, as was made clear by the fact that he was opening the folder. When Rogers started at Abacus, he had christened the file, and gradually filled it with news articles: every time he found himself intrigued by something outside his intellectual comfort zone, he would stuff it in the folder. As he spread years of clips on his table, he was trusting them to guide him toward a new career. "Eventually it all made sense. It was all about behavioral science experiments," says Rogers. "Your interests reveal themselves."

The twenty-four-year-old had experienced revelations like this before.

As a teenager living in Philadelphia's western suburbs, Rogers learned just after Thanksgiving of his junior year of high school that he had been diagnosed with non-Hodgkin's lymphoma. He scheduled his trips for chemotherapy around his team's lacrosse schedule, and every two weeks would check in to the oncology ward of a local children's hospital. Most of Rogers's fellow patients were much younger kids, and he kept a distance from them, and from the Happy Meals and video games their presence drew. Rogers further rebelled against the frivolity by proudly refusing to watch television and choosing instead, for the first time in his life, to read for pleasure. The first book he picked was Henry David Thoreau's *Walden,* which led him to other works of American transcendentalism. By the next Thanksgiving, Rogers had beaten cancer, completed his junior year on schedule, played in fourteen of his team's sixteen games, and developed a new sense of the self. "Even when you are healthy again you don't feel normal," says Rogers, who as an adult kept a fit physique and a gleaming shaved head. "You carry some secret differences."

Now Rogers was driving back to Williams, where he had played Division 3 lacrosse and been elected student body co-president. He met with one of his favorite professors, Al Goethals, whose Introduction to Social Psychology class Rogers realized had fertilized his now-blossoming interests. Goethals had introduced his students to behavioral psychology, the burgeoning subdiscipline that took a pessimistic view of the human brain as a flawed instrument for navigating life's most challenging decisions. Rogers had voraciously consumed writings by some of the field's most prominent scholars, including psychologist Robert Cialdini, an expert in the way that consumers were simply unable to make rational choices, and economist Richard Thaler, who explored how that flawed "mental accounting" warped markets involving everything from auctions to savings accounts. As he sat down again with Goethals years later, Rogers expressed the frustration he had with the polling profession, and its inability to bring rich insights to understanding the political brain. "I knew psychology was powerful, and wanted to learn more," he says. Goethals assigned Rogers further reading, and the two started to regularly meet in what amounted to a personal tutorial in the behavioral sciences. Eventually they came to the same conclusion: that Rogers should apply to a graduate school that would allow him to study the psychology of decision making.

When Rogers told Abacus's partners, Janet Grenzke and Mark Watts, that he was planning to leave politics for the academy, neither was surprised. They had seen the curiosity on his face when he asked questions like "how do we know this?" in response to some piece of received wisdom, and his disappointment when he heard their replies. "The answer was," Watts says, "'In our field, in general, we learn as we go along. We have a lot of beliefs that aren't well-tested because no one can afford to test them.'" Both Grenzke and Watts had earned Ph.D.s from political science programs, and yet they both discouraged Rogers from entering one. "Political science as a discipline just isn't asking applied questions," says Watts. "Psychology is getting at this in a better way than political science."

In 2003, Rogers enrolled at Harvard in the social psychology program, but after a semester he became frustrated that professors kept trying to steer him away from studying questions with broad, real-world consequences. Rogers transferred to an integrated psychology program at Harvard Business School and quickly aligned himself with a professor, Max Bazerman, famous for his research on negotiations. Bazerman had helped to shape the field of behavioral science in the 1980s, and like many of his peers with backgrounds in psychology or economics he ended up at a business school, where insights on decision making had immediate, and potentially lucrative, applications.

Bazerman had just published an article in the *Journal of Behavioral Decision Making* titled "What We Want to Do Versus What We Think We Should Do." This "want-should" research, as Bazerman labeled it, examined the conflict in how people struggled with multiple goals: there are things they think they should do (stay on a diet) and those they want to do (order the banana split). Along with five coauthors, Bazerman had designed an experiment in which they tweaked the "dictator" ultimatum game used by game theorists to demonstrate that test subjects who said they would treat their opponent fairly didn't always do so when faced with an immediate game situation where they could punish opposing players.

One day in class, to illustrate this conflict, Bazerman mentioned that he had noticed that some movies his wife had placed in their Netflix queue lingered there seemingly forever, leapfrogged by new additions she pushed to the head of the line. Foreign documentaries might be the things people thought they should see, Bazerman speculated, but romantic comedies and action flicks were always what they wanted to watch. Rogers and a class-mate, Katharine Milkman, thought the movie example could give them the chance to yank the study of want-should conflicts out of artificial lab settings and into the real world. When Milkman persuaded an Australian online video rental company, Quickflix, to share its customer data, they had discovered the type of naturally occurring experiment upon which economists love to stumble. Milkman was fascinated by consumer deci-sion making, but Rogers liked the subject because he thought its lessons would be applicable for understanding how people approach policy ques-tions. He already had global warming in mind: people know they should reduce energy use, but don't want to drive any less. Could policymakers build support for controversial proposals by committing to them well in advance, while people are still thinking about the trade-offs in "should" terms rather than "want"?

Rogers was surprised that applying the sensibility and methods of behavioral psychology to politics remained a largely virgin endeavor, as political scientists looked past the nonconscious mind and psycholo-gists explored other dimensions of human experience. Rogers started to compile an open-ended list of topics he wanted to research, and he found them plentiful and self-evident—many either topics that psychologists had examined in laboratory settings, but never in the field, or that had been demonstrated in situations other than politics. While most of his peers at Harvard saw behavioral psychology as a means to commercial ends, Rog-ers was looking for ways to make people better citizens, and impressed colleagues as an unlikely humanist. "There are people in the experimental world who think that people are silly and we understand the truth," says Mike Norton, a professor who taught and collaborated with Rogers. "He's more interested in how do people respond, how do people work, rather than 'let's change their actions.'"

Rogers struck those around him as combining—in a way unusual among grad students—a restless mind that spotted a lot of potential research avenues with a practical sense for how to quickly head down most of them. Norton saw Rogers's charisma as a motivating tool, noting his "ability to get people excited so they'll work." But Rogers also ran up against the limits of graduate school, especially when his experimental agenda fell outside the standard purview of business school research.

Rogers had become particularly enamored of the work of Cialdini, who began studying sales techniques in the 1980s after he concluded that he was "an easy mark for the pitches of peddlers, fund-raisers, and operators of one sort or another." Cialdini documented how consumers followed bad cues or were drawn to faulty assumptions, and the ways marketers could exploit them. Eventually he turned his powers toward promoting good behavior with cynical mind games. It was Cialdini, for instance, who documented the success of hotels that encouraged guests to reuse their towels by informing them how many guests also did so, rather than by highlighting how disappointingly low recycling rates were or the general importance of environmental concerns.

Rogers proposed to Bazerman that he follow a similar tack to promote voting, another bit of good civic behavior that suffered from low rates of participation. Massachusetts didn't have any elections scheduled in 2003, so Rogers decided to see if he could instead increase voter registration by talking up its popularity. He dispatched several students to Boston bus stations with stacks of registration forms and instructions to approach riders with alternating messages: one emphasizing how many people signed up to vote, the other emphasizing how few did. But the experiment stalled before Rogers could get the necessary scale to draw meaningful conclusions;

his researchers struggled to find enough who weren't already registered to measure the relative effects of the different messages. Rogers tried to save face by referring to the failed experiment as merely a "pilot study," and leapt quickly when a presidential campaign offered to let him test out his theories on its voters.

* * * * *

MOST WEEKENDS IN THE FALL OF 2003, Rogers left Harvard Square in his grandmother's old gray Subaru station wagon and embarked on the hour-long drive from Cambridge to Derry, New Hampshire. As fall became winter, the foliage was drained from yellows and oranges into dour browns, and the roadside palette enhanced by the patriotic tricolor of signs announcing Democratic candidates for president. Rogers would arrive at a suburban office complex housing the presidential campaign of Wesley Clark, a retired four-star general who had entered the race late and was counting on a win in New Hampshire to launch him nationally. Rogers was drawn to Clark as a credible, progressive voice on national security issues, and offered himself to the campaign as a volunteer. Clark's gamble was that he could squeeze enough space for himself between the two flawed candidates fighting for first place: Howard Dean, who had emerged as the candidate of the party's romantics, and John Kerry, who by default had become the choice of its realists.

After a year studying behavioral psychology, Rogers was no longer capable of being a romantic about politics, or for that matter any aspect of human activity. When he would arrive in Manchester, Rogers would either be pointed to a phone or handed a clipboard and local street map. Whether he was making calls or canvassing at doors, Rogers would get a script for interacting with a voter, and he always wondered what Cialdini would have made of it. The scripts would say things like *You can make the difference* or *We need your support*. These phrases had become so deeply enmeshed in the aural tapestry of elections that it was unlikely that anyone actually listened to the words themselves anymore. But Rogers did, and he heard a begging whimper on behalf of a lonely cause. This was the same tone the hotels had used when they beseeched guests not to be part of the problem, before Cialdini came along and showed them experiments that demonstrated people would rather fall in line with something already popular.

The previous spring, Rogers had written a paper for one of Bazerman's classes that applied what Cialdini called "social norms" to voter turnout. Cialdini had found repeatedly that what he described as injunctive norms ("you should not litter") were far less effective at changing behavior than descriptive norms ("few people litter"). Perhaps, as political scientists had always assumed, voting was a different type of activity from reusing one's hotel towels, in which case the calls to civic duty might resonate with their audience. But what if the motivation to vote came from the same place that determined human decision making in other spheres where people had a clear choice, like what to buy or how to spend their time? When Rogers decided to answer the question with the only tool he trusted, he despaired over the difficulty of executing field experiments in politics. "I was just a grad student," Rogers says. "I didn't think I could scare up thirty thousand dollars for an experiment."

So when he started volunteering for Clark in the fall of 2003 and realized that a friend ran the campaign's Derry office, Rogers saw a chance to piggyback an experiment onto the tens of thousands of voter contacts that Clark's volunteers would be doing in the last days before the late-January primary. Rogers had seen only one of the papers by Alan Gerber and Don Green, but he was familiar with the rich tradition of field experiments in psychology and he saw those as models for a large-scale randomized test of different turnout messages. He was introduced to a campaign official, who eventually contacted Rogers with good news: the campaign would let him conduct his experiment in the run-up to the New Hampshire primary.

Rogers plotted an experiment to measure if a Cialdiniesque *voting is popular* spiel would prove more successful at motivating voters to turn out than the usual *we need your support* appeals. He drafted a pair of scripts that reflected different approaches, and developed a plan to randomize the call sheets and walk lists assigned to volunteers, leaving a control group that would get no contact at all. On his weekend trips to New Hampshire, Rogers started making fewer calls on Clark's behalf and instead worked to engender enthusiasm for his experiment among the field staffers who oversaw the canvasses and whose diligence would be necessary to ensure the test's purity.

When the final week of the campaign arrived, Rogers believed everything was in place. But he couldn't actually reach his campaign contact—a dozen e-mails, all unanswered—and Rogers grew increasingly panicked. Eventually the bad news reached Rogers through other channels: his experiment had been killed. The campaign leadership had decided that Clark, who had skipped Iowa to contest New Hampshire, couldn't afford to take voters out of his contact universe before a crucial primary just to maintain the sanctity of Rogers's research, although Rogers never heard it directly from the person he thought was responsible for the decision. "The decision makers never told me," says Rogers. He adjusted to the reality that he would spend the closing days of the campaign as a volunteer knocking on doors and not as a social scientist presiding over a potentially groundbreaking experiment.

That weekend, Rogers had stopped in a supermarket in Derry for some basic shopping. As he rounded the edge of an aisle, he faced the campaign official who had first signed off on his experiment but then dodged his e-mails, thus bringing the project to an ignominious end. Rogers begged for an explanation. Why had the campaign given up on an experiment it once saw as so promising?

"There is no day after the election," the official told him.

Rogers insisted that Clark's operatives in other states would be able to integrate the findings to adjust their GOTV tactics in later primaries. "You'll learn in time for it to be useful in the next primary," Rogers pleaded.

The two argued about the project's fate near an end display. "They just shut it down," Rogers recalls, before wryly noting that Clark's third-place finish in New Hampshire effectively ended his presidential campaign. "Turns out they were right: there was no day after the election."

Rogers returned to Harvard with mixed feelings from his first encounter with politics as a social scientist. If anything, the resistance he had encountered—and the institutionalized lack of curiosity it appeared to reflect—made Rogers all the more interested in studying the frailties of political communication. But he wondered whether he had the fortitude to continue begging campaigns to effectively sponsor his research. "My experience with the Clark campaign prompted me to do experiments on my own," he says.

A colleague recommended that Rogers contact the Yale political scientists who had developed something of a franchise running these kinds of experiments. Rogers wrote to Gerber, and shared with him a copy of the social norms paper he had written the previous spring and his idea for how to structure an experiment to test his thesis in a live campaign. Gerber already had a busy research agenda for 2004, but he and Rogers made plans to take the turnout messages into the field the next year, when a few states would have governor's races. Within weeks they had started to design an experiment testing messages that they could run in the following year's New Jersey gubernatorial election.

Rogers first had to prepare the terrain. That summer, he visited the Democratic National Convention in Boston, and with a clipboard prowled the corridors of the Fleet Center looking for party operatives. He ended up surveying fifty of these "self-identified experts in voter mobilization"—as Rogers later identified them with as much sarcasm as a dissertation would permit—to ask whether they thought it would be more effective to use a message that warned that turnout in a coming election was expected to be high or low. The survey had no statistical power—the sample was too small, and it had not been assembled randomly. But Rogers thought he was on the cusp of undermining a matter of standard political practice, and before he destroyed that conventional wisdom Rogers wanted to enshrine it for the historical record. He was benchmarking the opinion of so-called experts, so that after his study none of them could say: *Duh, that's obvious, we knew that all along.*

Rogers knew that his research path was putting him on a collision course with political professionals he began to describe as "shamans." From his psychological training, Rogers instinctively resisted the idea that the decision to vote was the self-interested choice described by political scientists. Instead he thought of it as "self-expressive social behavior." He didn't visualize the mathematician in the privacy of the voting booth, coolly calculating how to maximize his democratic utility, or the accountant attaching a price to civic engagement. He wondered what happened to that person in the days before and minutes after casting a ballot, about interactions that brought shame or pride or a desperate need to fit in. For Rogers, this seemed like a modest intellectual breakthrough, "just taking a behavioral science understanding of how people conform to the behavior of others and applying it to politics." As a result, Rogers ignored the fine demographic distinctions that consumed many working in politics and instead focused on questions that went deeper into what he considered the universal human condition. Were there things campaigns could say to people that—regardless of their ideology or background—would nudge them to the polls?

* * * * *

MARK GREBNER WAS STUMBLING to a similar conclusion from a different starting point. Since 1974, he had run almost continuously for two-year terms as an Ingham County commissioner, always representing a district containing the Michigan State University campus. Grebner was a familiar college town archetype, an ungainly hybrid of perpetual student and public intellectual, of the local institution but with few credentials to attest to his ties. On the wall of his office two blocks from the campus's edge, there is no diploma to commemorate the eleven years it took Grebner to complete the requirements of a bachelor's degree, a path detoured in large part because he insisted on taking graduate courses instead. A more impressive token is framed just above Grebner's most comfortable chair, which offers a natural opening for any conversation he starts there: a primitive megabit chip, one million bits strung together, the size of an open magazine. When the Michigan State computer lab retired the part, which was rumored to have once cost four hundred thousand dollars, in favor of more compact processors, it was given to Grebner, the way a renovating pub might save a familiar bar stool for a prolific patron. "It's on loan, technically," he says.

Grebner came of age with the technology. "I met computers when I was eighteen," he says, referring to the day in the spring of 1971 when as a college freshman he enrolled in a computer class. He had turned eighteen just in time to take advantage of a constitutional amendment granting him the vote, and as the MSU campus was being radicalized by Vietnam. He volunteered for local Democratic campaigns but grew impatient with their culture of endless deliberation. "Very quickly I looked around and realized that the thing I could do that was the most valuable was not sit in these meetings and argue about what color the campaign lawn signs should be, but was to computerize stuff," says Grebner. Campaign records were kept in file folders, with typed lists of voters or legal pads scrawled with the names of those who had received lawn signs two years earlier. Grebner began buying computer time at the university lab, coding punch cards to feed a mainframe database. Even though he had converted the information into digital form, it was no less bulky: the records of ten thousand voters meant five boxes of computer cards weighing fifteen pounds each. Moving data from the lab to a campaign office required pulling a hand truck across campus. "It was almost closer to threshing wheat," says Grebner, for whom hardship became a teachable lesson he likens to Soviet scientists who developed a knack for improvisation because their labs were often short of glassware and other basic materials. "Most of what I know I picked up when computing was relatively difficult."

One day, frustrated by a message strategy meeting for a state legislative candidate that ended without an agreed-upon message, Grebner walked out and decided he would just write his own literature for the candidate. The three-panel brochure proved memorable only for the fact that Grebner avoided the campaign's internal bureaucracy to get it copied, folded, and into the hands of volunteers to distribute it. "People said, 'But that wasn't approved?'" Grebner recalls. "No, it wasn't. But unlike the other ones, it actually got written."

In 1974, he ran for office the first time, for a part-time seat on the county's commission. At first, Grebner did almost all the canvassing himself, a one-man GOTV operation trundling from dorm to dorm with a list of voters. He would remind the students that election day was approaching, and ask if they planned to vote. They would almost always say yes, and following that, Grebner would usually give them his pitch. After rounds like this, Grebner felt unsatisfied, as though he was not having a meaningful interaction with voters; the yeses seemed mindless, as were the inert nods he saw as he talked up the Democratic ticket. So he started asking people if they were going to vote, and then when they said yes ended the conversation. "Oh, good, thanks," he would say, then mark a check next to their name and move down the corridor. "This leaves the person who you interview with this very unsettled feeling," Grebner says.

Grebner liked that unsettled feeling, and he felt especially good when he saw it reemerge on election night. He had developed a computerized system with punch cards for each of the voters who had self-identified as his supporters and became his GOTV targets. As they showed up at the polls on election day, Grebner would remove their card from the pile, and then at around 6:30 p.m. he would use the remaining cards to track down those who had yet to vote, and hustle to their dorm rooms to pull them out. Grebner showed up at the doors of his targets, and even before he could reintroduce himself he started hearing excuses and justifications. "I changed my mind, you can't tell me what to do," one nonvoter told him. Another declared defiantly he had just gotten back from the polls. "As soon as they see you with the deck of cards, it already bothers them so much that they're telling you," says Grebner. "That is so different from the normal experience of GOTV, so it was clear to me I was onto something." A few years later, Grebner felt that his hunch was vindicated by something of a natural, if unscientific, experiment. He split campus GOTV responsibilities with another campaign but found out after the fact that his partners had failed to follow his peculiar script to abruptly short-circuit the conversation. After the election, Grebner saw that the six precincts he had canvassed significantly outperformed the other five. "We had dedicated the same resources to it. The only thing different that we had done is they screwed up my interview," he says. "I almost thanked them for having done that."

In 1982, Grebner had an epiphany. He was reading the book *Who Votes?* by Raymond Wolfinger and Steven Rosenstone. Their work relies on an unusual data set that few other political scientists had ever fully appreciated. The Census Bureau's Current Population Survey questions a rolling panel of fifty-six thousand households every month to prepare the regular labor market report. But every two years, it adds a battery of post-election questions to the mid-November survey that yields the unemployment figures announced in December. Commerce Department interviewers do not ask people to say how they voted or why, but they do ask if respondents are registered and if they voted in the election that took place earlier that month. Often the number gets reported in the press as a first estimate of nationwide voter participation that year, and it almost always prompts stories about how unusually high turnout had been. Months later, when researchers are able to fully examine updated state voter rolls, the Commerce Department estimate gets revised downward by as much as 10 percentage points. As this pattern became evident, academics who had relied on such self-reported turnout figures (including those working on the University of Michigan's national election studies) began to worry that their numbers were inflated by inaccurate survey samples. So they started matching respondents to the voter rolls. The survey methodologies were right, but as many as 10 percent of its respondents were wrong. They hadn't voted.

"The fascinating thing for me is they conduct this survey ten days after the November election, and already ten percent of the population is lying about having voted!" says Grebner. "They didn't forget, right? If there were a forgetting process it would be gradual. I refuse to believe that people honestly don't remember if they voted ten days earlier. Bullshit! A whole bunch of people lied."

This piqued Grebner's attention, in part because the political science literature had offered a lot of explanations for why people vote—their civic duty, their desire to pick a winner, their calculation that a particular result would serve their self-interest—but no one had proposed an incentive for lying about having turned out. "Hypothesis: Why do people fail to vote? This is the classic answer: *Because they didn't know it was election day! They're too fucking stupid to know it was election day!*" says Grebner. "Crap! If you had done a survey of severely psychotic people, people living under bridges, people with IQs below sixty, and you asked them, 'Is today election day?' I'd bet you eighty percent of the vegetables in this country knew it was election day. If you asked psychopaths, 'Is voting a good thing or a bad thing?' I'd bet eighty percent of the psychopaths in this country— people who've completely rejected all social norms—would be able to tell you the right answer about that social norm," says Grebner. "So reminding people 'It's election day, you should go vote' or telling people 'It's a good thing'—are there people who are unfamiliar with this norm? That norm is universal; the knowledge it's election day is universal." But campaigns kept using the same language to beseech people to vote. "Why do people go out and sing Christmas carols before Christmas?" he asks. "Because they've always done it!"

Grebner went on to build Michigan's first statewide voter file, an arduous task in a state famous for its decentralized registration policies and poor record keeping, and then did the same in Wisconsin. He happily sold the files to Democrats and Republicans. It was a decent business, run out of a second-floor office suite above a pinball parlor, in the back of which Grebner maintained a small apartment he insisted was not his primary residence. ("I don't live here exactly, but I spend the night here," he explains, by way of not explaining all too much.) Having his own voter file also gave

Grebner a new playpen for his extraprofessional curiosities. In the language of statistics, he had six million data points (Michigan voters) and fifty replications (elections available in individual vote histories), and he enjoyed wading through them in different combinations, looking for patterns to who votes and when. "It's like a pig farmer who just naturally has pig shit on his boots," says Grebner. "I just naturally have data clinging to me."

Grebner never stopped thinking about the 10 percent of the electorate that regularly claimed, falsely, to have voted. He would look for their traces in the voter rolls, like a detective always waiting for the one fresh clue that could take a vexing cold case and heat it up again. Grebner certainly understood why some people voted, and he could comprehend some of the reasons why others didn't. But the 10 percent who existed in this liminal space between voting and not voting seemed to offer Grebner a skeleton key to unlock the internal arithmetic of voter behavior that confounded political scientists. In some ways, the liars seemed to have the most finely tuned valuation of the costs and benefits of voting. "Why do people lie? They've discovered it's a secret whether or not you vote! You discover you can get out of voting by lying, and once you discover that why waste half an hour?" asks Grebner. "Fifty percent of Americans say they go to church on Sunday. Go count cars in parking lots. They must all walk to church!" Grebner, whose instinct for blasphemy is so refined that when he wants to describe something unfavorably he reflexively analogizes it to organized religion, pauses as he winds toward a constructive solution to this problem. "If they believed they couldn't get away with it, how would that affect them?" he asks. "How about if we threaten to expose them?"

In the spring of 2004, Grebner picked up the new book *Get Out the Vote!*, a compendium of campaign field experiments by Don Green and Alan Gerber, who had included in their text an open call for new collaborators to contact them. Late on Friday night at the beginning of the July Fourth weekend, Grebner wrote a long e-mail to Green and Gerber to describe an experiment he planned to run in the next month's primary: mailing entire Michigan blocks what he called voting "report cards." Before the primary, everyone would receive a list of the block's residents with blank boxes next to their names, and then after the election he would send another round in which those who vote would get a checkmark. "The question I'm looking at is different from the approaches you have tested: stressing the importance of voting," Grebner wrote. "Instead of appealing to their civic responsibility, I plan to try to work their sense of shame." He told the Yale professors he would be back in touch at year's end, when he would send over the results of his test.

But the academics didn't want to wait that long to hear more about his ballsy experiment, and within days the Michigander was predictably doing most of the talking in a two-hour phone call as Gerber scribbled notes trying to keep up. Grebner explained that before he had even read *Get Out the Vote!* he had tried to run his own field experiment shaming nonvoters but had not collected the results in a form useful for analysis. ("It was a personal project, designed to learn rather than to convince anybody else," Grebner explains later.) Nonetheless he sent the materials he had used to New Haven. "His original mailings were quite a quirky bundle," Green observed. He and Gerber thought Grebner had muffled their potential effectiveness, especially by prominently labeling the letters with the word *experiment.* To ensure that the findings from Grebner's next mailing passed scholarly standards, Gerber and Green proposed that they design the experiment from Yale and contract with Grebner's firm to prepare the list and handle all the mail. To refine the approach, they postponed Grebner's planned August launch and looked ahead to Michigan's 2006 primary, and began familiarizing themselves with the psychological underpinnings of shame. Gerber opened the *Handbook of Social Psychology* to identify what he called the "active ingredients" of social pressure, and drew up different letters that would trigger them separately so that the experiment could compare their effects.

Gerber wrote four letters, each with a reminder of the upcoming August 8 election and the sign-off "DO YOUR CIVIC DUTY—VOTE!" The first message, the least provocative, was designed to gently scold. "Why do so many people fail to vote? We've been talking about this problem for years, but it only seems to get worse," it said. "Your voice starts with your vote." The next was inspired by a legendary industrial study at an Illinois factory called the Hawthorne Works, which found that worker productivity changed when the subjects knew they were under observation. "YOU ARE BEING STUDIED!" the so-called Hawthorne treatment letter warned, noting that the analysis would rely solely on public records to track why people do or do not vote and offering his reassurance: "Anything we learn about your voting or not voting will remain confidential and will not be disclosed to anyone else." (As with all university-funded research, Gerber and Green had to get this experiment approved by the Yale Human Subjects Committee.)

The other two letters were written to jolt nonvoters out of their complacency. One was based on the idea of "norm compliance," a theory associated with Robert Cialdini after he used a littering experiment to demonstrate that people adjust their behaviors to match what they think their peers do. "WHO VOTES IS PUBLIC INFORMATION!" announced the letter addressed to a whole family at a single address, above a chart naming each voter in the household and whether they voted in elections held in August and November 2004. "The chart shows your name from the list of registered voters, showing past votes, as well as an empty box which we will fill in to show whether you vote in the August 8 primary election. We intend to mail you an updated chart when we have that information."

The most incendiary letter included a similar chart, but instead of revealing a recipient's vote history to other members of the household, Grebner found all the registered voters on the block and included theirs. "We're sending this mailing to you and your neighbors to publicize who does and who does not vote," the letter explained. "The chart shows the names of some of your neighbors, showing which have voted in the past. After the August 8 election, we intend to mail an updated chart. You and your neighbors will all know who voted and who did not."

Once the letters had been prepared, Green set up a betting pool for himself, Gerber, Grebner, and Christopher Larimer, a doctoral student they had enlisted to work on the project, to wager on which they thought would have the biggest impact on turnout. They all agreed that the "neighbors" mailing, the most heavy-handed of the bunch, would lead, but they differed slightly on how large the effects would be. The four estimated the neighbors letter would increase turnout by 3 percent, which would put it ahead of the straightforward get-out-the-vote mailers Gerber and Green had tested elsewhere. As a result of that estimate, they set up their experiment with massive samples, totaling eighty thousand across treatment groups, so that if one piece of mail was four times more effective than the next, the numbers would be large enough to calibrate meaningful distinctions. Grebner prepared the letters on laser printers in his office, and as he often did, hired local high school students to sit around an ovaloid table and run the baby-blue sheets through a folding machine.

A few days after he had wheeled the last of the letters to the post office, Grebner learned that he and his collaborators had all dramatically underestimated their ability to alienate voters. Grebner had suspected voters might not take well to the bullying tone of the neighbors letter, and the academics had reason to concur. The behavioral science literature was split between case studies in social pressure, where outside attention performed a suasive role, and of "reactance," in which people respond to overbearing advice not to drink or smoke by doing ever more of it. But tobacco warnings rarely include a phone number for the surgeon general; Grebner had listed his own after the words "For more information," along with his e-mail address and a return PO box, on each of the letters he sent out.

Grebner was never able to calculate how many people took the trouble to complain by phone, because his office answering machine filled so quickly that new callers were unable to leave messages. (When he tried, unscientifically, to match complainants to particular mailings, it looked as though those who got the neighbors letter were angriest.) Then there were the people who found a live line for Practical Political Consulting. One man, who Grebner's office staff said sounded drunk, announced that he was in Bay City and headed to East Lansing to get Grebner. Then he called later to report he was in Saginaw en route, and then in Flint. Grebner knew the geography of his state well enough to become nervous. "Then he called us from Durand and said he had sobered up and he wasn't going to come down, and please tell the police he was sorry that he threatened us," Grebner recalls.

Grebner found more satisfaction when he learned, the day before the election, that Nolan Finley of Livonia, an upscale Detroit suburb, had received one of the twenty thousand neighbors letters. Finley was the editorial-page editor of the conservative *Detroit News,* a favorite antagonist of Michigan Liberal, a group blog that Grebner had helped to launch the previous year. In a signed editorial in the *News,* Finley communicated his outrage at having his personal vote history—which showed his dutiful turnout for general elections every two years but poor participation in primaries—made public to those around him. "It turns out for all of Nolan having written probably a thousand editorials telling people to vote against every millage and vote against these candidates for judge, he actually hadn't voted in a primary himself in twelve years, because he's too fucking lazy," says Grebner, in a voice that does not suggest the dispassionate social science experimenter. "His wife votes in elections, and his kids vote in elections, but Nolan is such a dishonest piece of shit that he hadn't actually voted. Which is as far as I'm concerned a good thing! Nolan gets this thing dropped on him—I don't know if his wife saw it, but it basically says: 'Your husband's a lying asshole! It just says that right there: Your husband is a lying asshole!' "

A few months later, Grebner smiled when he saw that Finley had cast his first primary ballot since 1992. (Finley told the publication *Stateline* that he didn't typically vote in primaries because identifying with one party would compromise him as a journalist.) The state had updated its voter file, with records of which Michiganders turned out in the primary, and Grebner was busy matching them against names of residents of the 180,000 households in the study, which represented nearly 350,000 people. When he calculated turnout percentages for each group, the results were staggering. The control group had voted at 29.7 percent, those who received the "civic duty" message at 31.5 percent, the Hawthorne treatment 32.2 percent, and the "self" mailer that showed other members of their household at 34.5 percent. Among those who received the neighbors letter, 37.8 percent voted—which meant it was roughly three times more effective at increasing turnout than any other piece of mail ever tested. It was several times better to deliver a threatening letter to a nonvoter than to have a neighbor sweetly remind her of the importance of voting in the upcoming election. At one point, Gerber calculated that the neighbors mailing had increased turnout at the enviable price of two dollars per marginal vote, and began to estimate that they could have reached the entire electorate for half a million dollars—and, for instance, swung the outcome of a Republican senate primary. "Alan," Grebner said, "if we had spent five hundred thousand dollars and covered the whole state, you and I would be living with Salman Rushdie."

They agreed that they had isolated the single strongest tool ever recorded for turning nonvoters into voters, but they already knew that it would be unlikely that anyone—a candidate or an independent group—would ever put its name on such a mailer. "How," asked Green, "can you take this static electricity and turn it into useful current?"

* * * * *

IN THE SUMMER OF 2006, Bazerman invited Rogers to join the Consortium of Behavioral Scientists, a secret society formed by University of California, Los Angeles, psychologist Craig Fox to help Democrats apply cutting-edge academic research to liberal politics. Many of the signature discoveries of behavioral science had clear relevance for policymaking, from automatically enrolling workers in retirement plans (and putting on workers the onus to opt out as opposed to opting in) to showing consumers their neighbors' energy-use levels as a form of social pressure. Thaler and a University of Chicago colleague, Cass Sunstein, had begun writing of these "nudges"—the government gently pushing people to make better decisions—comprising the core of an ideology they liked to call "libertarian paternalism." But even so they avoided partisan activity. "I kind of stayed explicitly away from public-policy debates," says Thaler. "I did not want behavioral economics to be viewed as a politically motivated field of study. It was hard just getting taken seriously, and there were some people here who always suspected that behavioral economics was just a sheen for government interference."

But the Bush administration radicalized Thaler and many of his peers, who were liberal in their personal orientation but sympathetic to markets and saw a Republican Party seemingly resistant to the type of empiricism that defined their worldview. In 2004, Fox and his mentor Daniel Kahneman, whose Nobel Prize two years earlier had helped to validate the study of flawed decision making in economics, were lamenting that John Kerry had allowed himself to be defined as a flip-flopper. Fox and Kahneman thought it was typical of what they thought of as ruthless, disciplined Republican messaging, like the famous example of pollster Frank Luntz rebranding the estate tax as a "death tax," and they thought that as psychologists they had insights that could help Democrats respond. Fox started attending Los Angeles fund-raisers in the hopes of meeting prominent Democrats. At one, he encountered Congressman Patrick Kennedy and handed him a brief memo outlining what he thought behavioral science could bring to politics, which in turn found its way to Steve Elmendorf, a deputy campaign manager for Kerry. Fox and Cornell psychologist Tom Gilovich and several peers met with Elmendorf in Washington, where they presented two white papers on the psychology of messaging. "Our style was to be intellectually honest but try to offer advice. If you qualify everything, and put too much jargon in, people aren't going to use it," says Fox. But Kerry's campaign never appeared to adopt any of the advice. "In hindsight it was spectacularly naïve to think we'd have any effect at all six weeks before the election," Fox says. "They had lots of issues they were dealing with at the time."

After the election, Fox kept the group together as the Consortium of Behavioral Scientists, and as the 2006 midterms approached, the group's e-mail list became a lively forum for trading notes on election-year strategy. For many of the participants, who had never before been involved in politics, the group's activity augured new relevance for their once-marginalized work. "Why is it psychology and other behavioral sciences have less of an impact than economics on policymaking?" laments Fox. Because consortium members knew their involvement made them easy targets for critics—who happily ridiculed the approach as highbrow nanny-statism or even ivory-tower-approved government mind control—many adopted a *Fight Club* mentality toward publicity, even refusing to speak the group's name in front of strangers. But when Fox met Senator Hillary Clinton as part of a 2006 fund-raising effort, he told her about his consortium and the science of messaging. Several weeks later, she called back to invite the group to brief the Democratic Senate leadership.

Fox extended the consortium's circle, in essence preparing to lead a high-level delegation from academia for a strategy session with national opposition leaders, and planned a daylong meeting in New York to prepare. As he looked over his ranks, Fox realized he had one Nobelist and multiple members of the National Academy of the Sciences but hardly anyone who had ever seen the inside of a campaign headquarters. "Most of us were amateurs at politics," Thaler recalls. "We knew our stuff, but it was good to have somebody who knew the other side as well." Bazerman proposed that Rogers, the only graduate student on an e-mail list that didn't even include any assistant professors, join the group in Washington. The twenty-nine-year-old had already impressed him with not only a high quality of scholarship (which wasn't unusual among Bazerman's students) but natural political instincts (which were). "There are a lot of people who assume he'll be a congressman or a senator someday—by which path no one knows," says Bazerman.

Less than two weeks later, a small group of consortium leaders took their seats across from Clinton, Senate Minority Leader Harry Reid, and Senators Debbie Stabenow and Byron Dorgan, both members of the party's leadership, in Reid's office suite. Over the course of a campaign year, politicians hear many supporters give them unsolicited advice about lines they should use in their speeches and ads they should run, but these presentations may have had an unusually prestigious patrimony. New York University psychologist Susan Andersen told the senators their messaging could be more emotionally resonant if they stayed away from aspirational themes. People are more sensitive to losses than equivalent gains, Andersen explained, so Democrats should focus their language on restoring what's been lost. Promise to "reverse erosion of our security," she proposed, or a "return to a balanced federal budget." When it was Thaler's turn, he looked at Clinton and employed a pedagogic tool he has honed over three decades of teaching a "Managerial Decision Making" course to cocky students at the University of Chicago's Booth School who arrive in his class believing that they are too smart to make the mistakes that Thaler believes infect markets. He begins the inaugural session of his semester-long course with a rapid-fire series of stunts and quizzes he privately calls "the magic show," which is designed to humble his students into understanding that their brains are as feeble as everyone else's. Now Thaler read the senator a brief excerpt from a speech in which entreaties to vote were paired with statistics warning against low turnout, before citing Rogers's research that argued for the opposite approach. Clinton, sheepishly, recognized the words from one of her own speeches. "I wanted to show her how easy it is to get this wrong," he says. "This is from long experience teaching people about decision making. You first have to show people that they make this mistake."

Rogers had happened upon the nexus of two scholarly minded subcultures lurking in the shadows of the Democratic Party's exile from power: the behavioralists who thought they could direct government to help citizens make better decisions, and the political scientists teaching campaign consultants how to manage field experiments. By the time Democrats won back Congress in November 2006, as many as sixty people were coming to Mike Podhorzer's geek lunches, and participants had begun calling themselves the Analyst Group. The following summer, Rogers, who had not attended any of the sessions, was invited to speak. He gave a presentation called "The Behavioral Science Toolbox," in which he argued for a "psychologically enriched understanding of why people vote."

Any Analyst Group lunch attendees with a preconception of what being lectured by a psychology graduate student would be like were probably surprised once Rogers walked to the front of the room. He maintained an athletic build typically hidden behind billowing dress shirts and pleated khakis, and possessed an intense ebullience that came out as soon as he began talking about his research. Even though he was fully committed to the Gerber-Green experimental method, Rogers was trying to subtly distance himself from one of the conclusions that had emerged from their body of work. In 2004, when they had reviewed the findings from their experiments and those of acolytes, Gerber and Green had concluded that when it comes to GOTV, "the message does not seem to matter much." Instead, they then attributed the tremendous disparity in effects—an average 8-percentage-point boost from in-person canvasses, compared with less than 1 point from paid phone calls or direct mail—to means of delivery. "Face-to-face interaction makes politics come to life and helps voters to establish a personal connection with the electoral process," Gerber and Green had written. "To mobilize voters, you must make them feel wanted at the polls. Mobilizing voters is like inviting them to a social occasion."

Rogers didn't quite disagree with the Rockwellian glow that brightened these sentiments, but he thought that there were other, perhaps darker social dynamics that could mobilize someone to vote. Political scientists who had concluded that message didn't matter had just been testing the wrong ones. Rogers argued that campaigns needed to treat being a voter not as a temporary condition that switched on or off each election day, but as a form of identity crucial to individual self-consciousness. "Changing how people see themselves can change behavior," Rogers said, citing an experiment in which people who had been informed by a survey taker that they were an "above-average citizen" turned out at a higher rate than those told they had an "average likelihood of voting and participating in politics." He summarized the experiment that Grebner had run in

Michigan, which preyed on a similar vulnerability in voters: their desire to conform to what they thought were their peers' expectations for good citizenship. Rogers emphasized that the Grebner test was also important because it considered an individual's mind-set before, during, and after election day. Campaign operatives could no longer think of voter contact as a series of discrete communications, Rogers argued, but needed to consider voting as a "social behavior extended over time."

Rogers described an experiment that he and Gerber had conducted just a few months earlier, in the run-up to Kentucky's gubernatorial primary. The week before election day, 660,000 households in the state received an automated phone call that announced itself with a recording: "This is Voter Roll Call with a two-minute opinion survey about Tuesday's election. If you are registered to vote in Kentucky, press 1." The 68,490 people who did so and stayed on the line were asked how likely they thought they would be to vote. If they signaled an interest, an exchange ensued that, amid the frenzy of political calls that weekend, was notable only for what it did not ask. Unlike pollsters' calls, there was no question about which candidate voters preferred in the Democratic and Republican primaries, or why. And unlike canvassers for either candidate, or the unions backing them, callers did not offer a ride to the polls or last-minute help turning out to vote. The recorded voice could have been asking about any election anywhere.

> *When on Tuesday will you vote? In the morning? At lunchtime? In the afternoon? Or in the evening?*
> *Will you drive to the precinct? Walk? Or take public transportation?*
> *Will you travel to the precinct from your home? Your place of work? Or from someplace else?*

Rogers did not care what voters' answers were to the three questions, only whether they had any. He was testing a psychological concept he referred to as the "plan-making effect," which suggests people are more likely to perform an action if they have already visualized themselves doing it. There was a rich history of testing these "implementation intentions," as Rogers described them, in areas other than politics. One experiment conducted on a college campus involved a set of reading materials that students were told were optional for a course. One set of students was asked to develop a plan for when they would drop by their teaching assistant's office to pick them up: when they would go, the way they would get there, how long it would take. Another set was not asked to formulate a plan for picking up the materials, and eventually did so at a lower rate. Rogers thought he might be able to nudge people to vote by tricking them to rehearse parts of their election-day regimen in advance, inadvertently forcing them to develop a plan.

The presentation before the Analyst Group was something of an audition for Rogers. The lunches' reach had become so broad that their participants needed a structure to coordinate new research projects and share findings, and Podhorzer was scheming to transform the informal Analyst Group into the Analyst Institute. The new entity would operate with the sensibility of a think tank but the closed books of a private consulting firm. As Podhorzer, the institute's chairman, searched for an executive director—reviewing résumés (from the political professionals he talked to for the job) and curricula vitae (from the academics)—he appreciated how much the pick would indirectly determine the nascent group's priorities.

Many of the recent lunchtime presentations had featured microtargeting projects, which had been the source of so much innovation and investment on the left, and had become much easier for many after Catalist developed a common data resource. In his job interviews, Rogers made clear his utter disinterest in building new microtargeting models, which he acknowledged had predictive power but couldn't actually conclude what changes human behavior, and his sole interest in running randomized field experiments. He eventually won over the Analyst Institute's new board by arguing that randomized tests were the area where the new entity could quickly deliver the most value. Rogers liked to describe their purpose as intellectual arbitrage, bridging the gap between the prolific output of academic experimenters like Gerber and Green and their lack of penetration into the world of political practitioners. "The modeling stuff seemed to be pretty quickly fetishized as the answer to all campaigning needs," says Judith Freeman, the executive director of the New Organizing Institute, who interviewed Rogers. "What Todd brought was not just the ability to run experiments or build models but to think critically about what was going to help us. He brought us back to the idea that we need to understand what motivates individual people."

Given his limited background in politics, Rogers initially appeared an unlikely candidate to run the Analyst Institute. But his itching desire to humiliate experts proved him to be a perfect fit. Podhorzer approached Rogers with the executive director post as he was being pursued by Harvard's Kennedy School of Government and Carnegie Mellon University. Rogers summoned Bazerman, who had never before had a student become anything other than a professor, for coffee in Harvard Square to discuss his options. Rogers was drawn to the advantages of doing academic-style work outside the academy: he could commission experiments without nonprofit funding restrictions or the bureaucracy involved in a human-subjects review board. He also realized that if he were to assume a teaching post and see one of his own students take the Analyst Institute job he would feel jealous. "The professor in me was slightly disappointed," says Bazerman, "and the citizen part of me was thrilled."

Rogers's hiring heralded a major shift in the left's research attentions. He ordered boxes of Cialdini's *Influence* and Sunstein and Thaler's *Nudge*, and began handing them out to his new colleagues as a sort of intellectual calling card. He scheduled coffees with representatives of as many liberal groups and party committees as would meet him, to convince them of the value of randomized trials and discuss possible ways to build experiments into their existing programs. Rogers had arrived in Washington with a long list of psychology concepts he hoped to test in the political arena, many of which were altogether foreign to many of those in the Analyst Group's world. Rogers felt that as long as he could demonstrate their effectiveness in the campaign context, they would be an easier sell to consultants and operatives who were pragmatic about vote-winning than they would be to political scientists whose theories of voter behavior were hardened with the stubbornness of philosophy. "We can bring political science theories to these topics, but I'm not sure how valuable those theories are and after eight years we had tried a lot of them," says David Nickerson, a Gerber-Green protégé who went on to teach at Notre Dame and serve as a senior adviser to the Analyst Institute. "Now here comes Todd with a literature in social psychology that we hadn't ever really seen."

* * * * *

THE ORIGINAL POLITICAL EXPERIMENTERS looked on with approval from New Haven as their method snaked from academe through the corridors of power. Gerber and Green were already working on a second edition of *Get Out the Vote!,* which anthologized findings from dozens of electioneering field tests. Many of the studies had been conducted by former students who represented something of an experimental diaspora, with nonacademic collaborators who had emerged after the publication of Gerber and Green's original *American Political Science Review* article. At first the pair had worked on a few small candidate campaigns, including one managed by a former student of Gerber's. Groups promoting turnout among core Democratic constituencies, such as Youth Vote and ACORN, hired Gerber and Green to evaluate their programs. Then, Nickerson, who eventually managed the professors' growing research "shop" at Yale, used municipal elections in Seattle and Boston to test the effectiveness of phone calls bearing a prerecorded message from a local registrar of voters. During a Virginia governor's race, Gerber and two other researchers randomly gifted households in the state's Washington suburbs with free subscriptions to either the *Washington Post* or the *Washington Times,* for a study titled "Does the Media Matter?"

The publication of *Get Out the Vote!* was part of a conscious effort by Gerber and Green to step out of the academy and ensure that lessons from these studies reached a nonscholarly audience. The authors believed they had made this populist mission apparent through the inclusion of an exclamation mark in the book's title. ("This is an unusual thing," Gerber says of the punctuation.) In their introduction, Gerber and Green bluntly declare themselves uninterested in "broad-gauge explanations for why so few Americans vote," like an alienated citizenry and poor civic education. Instead they offer the volume as a "shoppers' guide" for candidates and activists, filled with ratings (up to three stars) of different campaign methods based on the reliability of the academic findings. "Door-to-door canvassing by friends and neighbors is the gold-standard mobilization tactic," they write in one standard passage.

The slim paperback became a vade mecum for organizers working in the ranks of groups who had responded to the era of partisan polarization by shifting their resources from persuasion to mobilization. "If they had published that in 1985 it would have been a blip. In 1985, it was all about TV and media buying," says Kevin Arceneaux, who as a postdoctoral fellow helped run the Gerber-Green lab for two years beginning in 2003. "But there was an explosion of interest in these old methods—shoe-leather politics—and going back to that."

Major Washington institutions began to take notice as well. Green had traveled to the capital during the Republican National Committee's 72-Hour research phase, and Hal Malchow helped get him in front of any lefty crowd that would have him. "I did my rap for every Democratic institution under the sun," says Green, naming the DNC, the Democratic Congressional Campaign Committee, and a gathering of liberal interest groups hosted by EMILY's List. At each stop, Green explained the experimental method and presented some findings from the research he had conducted with Gerber. Even though most assumed that the two Yale political scientists were liberal (and neither rejects the claim), both would always emphasize that they were eager to collaborate with anyone regardless of party or ideology. "I think of myself as being on the science team," says Green. "If Republicans want to do science, I'm happy to jump in. Democrats? Fine."

But by then, Gerber and Green felt they had exhausted most of the questions about the relative effectiveness of individual contact methods. They knew that personal contact was almost always better than mail, and mail usually better than phones. They knew that live calls were better than robocalls. They knew that volunteers were more effective, both at the door and on the phone, than paid workers. They knew that interactive conversations, where the canvasser asked regular questions of a voter, had more impact than a one-sided script. "There is something about canvassing that worked because it was on a personal level," says Arceneaux. "We knew that. We just didn't know why."

Rogers and Grebner were coming from a different set of questions but arriving at a similar understanding of what drove political activity. No one decided to vote in a vacuum, and interpersonal interactions mattered. In fact, their psychologically minded tests and feints were moving toward something that felt very familiar to Gerber. Rogers's project to promote voting as popular and Grebner's threats to expose scofflaws had, if only briefly, reconstructed small corners of late-nineteenth-century America, where voting was a community activity. Since writing his dissertation about the introduction of the secret ballot, Gerber had spent much of his time trying to isolate the slightest ways to increase turnout in the system it had created. In Gerber's eyes, the nineteenth century, where men packed onto courthouse steps to select their leaders with raised hands or words bellowed over the din, represented a kind of Edenic political space of widespread participation.

At one point, Green decided to see if they could bring Gerber's prelapsarian America back to life. Green drove up to Hooksett, New Hampshire, just before the town would host municipal elections, and spent twenty-six thousand dollars to erect a tent on a middle school lawn and hire a DJ to play music beneath it. On the Saturday before, they put a flyer in Manchester's *Union Leader* advertising an "Election Day Poll Party," an alcohol-free, family-friendly version of the festivities that in the nineteenth century were boozy men's-only events. Along with a grad student and a colleague from Tufts, Green put up signs promoting the event, had the town administrator distribute flyers, and recorded phone calls to alert three thousand local households. A coin flip had determined that a demographically similar town, Hanover, would go DJ-free and be used as a control; afterward they could compare turnout and measure whether such festivals had any impact. (State officials advised that, as long as they did not directly reward people for voting, a festival was perfectly legal.) For four hours, families snacked on Yale-subsidized hamburgers and hot dogs as kids played catch under clear skies. Green spun cotton candy for attendees. "One of the things I really would not have anticipated was getting into the nuts and bolts of actual campaign work I don't consider myself particularly good at," he says.

In the crowd was a large man who wore a bemused smile. He was not there for a hot dog or to buy a ticket in the raffle. He was not there to vote, either; in fact, he did not even live in Hooksett. He had already worked for a generation at the highest levels of American politics. Now he was about to take command of a $40 million campaign budget, and he thought the guy spinning cotton candy might be able to help him spend it better.

8

SHOWDOWN AT THE OASIS

t was a two-hour round-trip from Dave Carney's New Hampshire home to the Hooksett election day festival but Carney had ample incentive to make the drive. He was about to become Don Green and Alan Gerber's most beneficent patron. The previous summer, Carney had bought a copy of *Get Out the Vote!* after seeing it promoted in a Brookings Institution catalog as a "practical guide for anyone trying to mobilize voters." The description applied to Carney, a Republican consultant who each year handled only a few campaigns, approaching each with an intensity that often frightened his colleagues as much as his opponents. From his desk in Hancock, he would sit watching an apple orchard bear its fruit while he listened in on conference calls and drafted strategy e-mails for Americans for Job Security. The corporate-funded group offered an independent boost to Republican candidates, usually by running ads that savaged their opponents, and to Carney it represented the kind of low-profile, high-paying mercenary work that sustained his business even as it failed to inspire him. For months, *Get Out the Vote!* had sat untouched, under drifts of polling binders, taking its place on an oddball desktop reading list that included—in roughly ascending order of centrality to Carney's worldview—statistics texts, popular business books, Adam Smith's *The Theory of Moral Sentiments,* and Sun Tzu's *The Art of War.* Then, in November 2004, Carney prepared for a trip to Texas to meet advisers to Governor Rick Perry, his main political client and the one whose campaigns most inspired Carney, so the two could begin formal preparations for Perry's bid for a second full term. Carney tossed the book into his briefcase as in-flight reading material.

In 2002, when he was directing Perry's first gubernatorial campaign, Carney had helped to design a massive turnout operation, spending $4 million to pull voters to the polls, much of it concentrated during Texas's two-week early-vote period. Carney's forces, tapped from temp agencies statewide, indiscriminately knocked on doors in one thousand "fortress precincts," as party operatives referred to the areas where they typically garnered more than 60 percent of the vote. At the same time, Texas Republicans hired Brent Seaborn, a junior staffer at Alex Gage's firm, to draft a primitive microtargeting plan that would help locate conservative-minded independents who resembled potential Perry voters and could be persuaded on specific issues like taxes, education, or tort reform. (Texas voters do not register by party, but those who regularly choose to participate in a party's primary are usually treated by strategists as though they were formally attached to it.)

Perry won the race by 18 points. Carney was pleased with the result, yet eager to find out who should deserve the credit. Had his unprecedented investment in a get-out-the-vote operation mobilized voters who would have otherwise stayed home? Did Seaborn's data find Perry voters that the campaign would have otherwise ignored? Or had Perry just been a great candidate running in a conservative state as the heir to a popular governor now serving as a wartime president? After election day, Carney had asked Mike Baselice, Perry's pollster, to commission a survey in search of answers, but he was unsatisfied with what the numbers told him.

Carney designed his own bootleg experiment for Perry. He took four demographically similar markets that could be isolated in a "bell-jar kind of a way," as one Perry adviser described it, and assigned a treatment to each. In one city, Carney had the campaign buy newspaper ads; another got a blast of robocalls; the third received radio ads and a dusting of mail; the fourth just mail. It was out of an election cycle, so the messages referred to general issues in front of the state legislature rather than campaign themes. He had Baselice poll in each market before and after to measure Perry's support among voters and their awareness of each issue. Carney attributed the differences in how public opinion moved in each market to the delivery mechanism: the radio and mail combination seemed to change minds slightly, while newspaper ads didn't at all. "It wasn't done in the truly academic sense, so you couldn't say it doesn't work," Carney says of the after-action tests. "We just couldn't show much tangible improvement."

Somewhere between Manchester and Austin, it all started to make sense for Carney. As soon as he arrived in Austin, Carney went onto the Yale website and searched for e-mail addresses for Alan Gerber and Don Green. In their book, the political scientists lament that most of their field experiments up till that time had been of the same sort: working with nonpartisan groups on their efforts to turn out voters. The few times that Gerber and Green had been invited into candidate campaigns had been on small-scale local races. The next campaign on Carney's docket was a wholly different affair. Perry had spent $25 million in 2002, and Carney anticipated a much tougher reelection in 2006, when voters were likely to have tired of Republicans and be eager for alternatives. Kay Bailey Hutchison, a popular Republican whom Carney had helped win her first election to the U.S. Senate, was considering a primary challenge, and a formidable Democratic threat likely followed in the fall. Carney had begun planning for a budget of $40 million, the bulk of which—as was typical in statewide races, especially with a geographically far-flung electorate like Texas's—would naturally go to television and radio. "Would you be interested in being in a real campaign?" Carney wrote to Gerber and Green.

It was an audacious offer, inviting a pair of Yale political scientists into a Republican war room, not least because Perry's exuberant anti-elitism was usually quite specific in its disdain for Ivy League credentials. "You don't have to have a Ph.D. from Harvard in political science to understand our economics," he would say. But it was another aspect of Perry's personality—the fact that he was "a cheap bastard"—that made Carney think the governor would take to the idea of using academic researchers to effectively audit the campaign's budget. "The fact that they had done all these studies that show mail and phones don't work—I thought, 'We spend a lot of money on mail and phones,'" says Carney. "If it's not working, let's spend it on things that do work, or don't spend it."

* * * * *

IN AN ERA of increased specialization among consultants, Carney thought his skill was simply politics. He had been enlisted onto his first campaign in 1978, when a Republican lawyer named Judd Gregg came to Carney's high school social studies class and asked students to go door-to-door as volunteers on his campaign for New Hampshire's executive council. In 1980, Carney spent the summer before his junior year at New England College working for John Sununu, a Tufts University engineer running in the Republican primary for U.S. Senate. Sununu tapped Carney to be his field director, responsible for organizing town chairmen and arranging open houses where the candidate could meet local voters and activists. Carney became close to Sununu, sleeping in the candidate's basement on the nights when he wasn't forced to bunk in the walk-in cooler in the Manchester campaign headquarters that had been converted out of a defunct bagel shop. Sununu lost the Senate race but was elected governor two years later and brought Carney to the statehouse with him as a political adviser with responsibility for his biennial reelection campaigns.

Early in the 1988 cycle, Sununu endorsed George H. W. Bush for president and dispatched Carney to work on his New Hampshire primary operation. Every Monday at 7 a.m., Carney would help convene a group of around two dozen volunteers he called Bush's Freedom Fighters to methodically trawl through a list of five thousand party activists and local officials in the state (which may have more elected officeholders per capita than any jurisdiction on earth). The Freedom Fighters would check in with those in their regions and report back on their preferences—this one is for DuPont, that one's with Kemp—and then Carney would use computers to update the list and circulate a new one each week. At the same time, Carney and other staffers had phone banks call all Republican voters and independents who had previously participated in Republican primaries, to identify them, too.

The Friday before the primary, amid a snowstorm that had debilitated the state, bad news came in to Bush's Concord headquarters. Retired general Al Haig was dropping out of the race and planned to endorse Bush's rival Bob Dole. Carney's office TV was fixed on C-SPAN2, whose cameras showed the empty ballroom at a Manchester conference center where Haig and Dole were to appear together to formalize the endorsement. But Carney's Freedom Fighters were hard at work. Over several hours, they were able to call all seven hundred people in the state who had been tagged as Haig supporters and invite them to back Bush. Carney had Sununu call Haig's leadership team to lobby them to switch, too. Many of them were learning the news for the first time when Bush's campaign called: they had yet to hear from Haig or Dole. "To this day I'm convinced we knew more Al Haig supporters in the state than he did because of our canvassing," says Carney. While Dole dominated news coverage, Bush was winning voters to his side. The following Tuesday, Bush won New Hampshire, finding a clear path to the nomination and eventually the presidency.

As something of a reward, Bush named Sununu to be his chief of staff, and Carney followed his mentor to the White House. Carney was a curiosity, a twenty-nine-year-old who became deputy political director to the president even though he had never worked in politics outside his home state. For his part, Carney was not desperate to be taken seriously: the six-foot-four, 325-pound Carney put a plaque on his desk that read THE BIG GUY and a "Buckaroo" pinball machine behind him, with toy airplanes and Happy Meal trinkets scattered elsewhere in his office. (Bush adviser Mary Matalin called Carney "Stud Muffin.") Promoted after eighteen months to head the White House political office, Carney became responsible for managing the limited time the president had available to spend on politics, and he began speaking regularly to consultants working for Republican candidates nationwide, "because they're all trying to get the president to do things for them—or not, depending on the situation."

As Bush prepared for his reelection, Carney moved to the RNC and then to Bush's campaign as political director. His first project was fending off a challenge from conservative commentator Pat Buchanan. After successfully dispatching Buchanan in a series of primaries, Carney found that the campaign had $7 million left in its nominating budget, which legally had to be spent before the party's convention in August. It was by then becoming apparent that Bill Clinton would be the Democratic nominee, even though the Arkansas governor still had to slog through his own primary calendar with a depleted budget.

The Republicans had assembled a rich research dossier on Clinton's weaknesses against Bush and had polls suggesting that public views of him could still be shaped. Carney proposed spending the $7 million to "destroy" Clinton—a plan that pitted Carney against the campaign's lawyers, who told him that as a general-election tactic it couldn't be covered with primary dollars. "It's a totally legitimate expense," Carney protested. "We're going to show delegates to the Republican National Convention that we're the strongest candidate for them to nominate to beat Bill Clinton."

Carney decided he would try to prove the point. He got permission to use one-tenth of the primary budget for a rough test. He picked one suburban county in each of three competitive general-election states— Georgia, Colorado, and New Jersey—and divided them among three mail vendors. The consultants got a poll of their county, the campaign's opposition research binder, and an assignment to design an anti-Clinton mail campaign for the county's independents and Republicans. Each vendor settled on a different issue: voters in Georgia got a military-issues message, New Jerseyans heard about Clinton's environmental record, and in Colorado a Texas consultant named Karl Rove produced a series of mail pieces about taxes. Afterward, Carney went back and polled the counties, finding a huge improvement in each. After the mailings, Bush led Clinton by nearly 20 percent in the Georgia and New Jersey counties. "In Colorado it was off the roof," Carney recalls.

It was not a randomized trial, but Carney thought he had good evidence that if Bush committed the remaining $6.3 million in the primary budget to an early anti-Clinton campaign it could reposition the race in the incumbent's favor. "Just pick four or five must-win states and we can crush them," Carney argued. But the campaign leadership rejected the proposal, afraid it would draw unfavorable coverage for Bush, and refunded the millions to their donors. "From that point on, I realized there is a real benefit for not being a good team player," Carney reflects. "It's better to be a loud, obnoxious person."

From Bush's Washington headquarters, Carney would sit at the center of a constellation of more than fifty consultants and vendors, many of them grouped into regional teams, patching from one conference call to the next. He grew disgusted with the cautious, corporate nature of the reelection—seven people sharing top decision-making duties—and the inert campaign they ran. "There's not much from that campaign I would recommend other campaigns to follow," Carney reflects wryly. The most important lesson Carney took out of 1992 was one he taught himself with the mail test. "After that I realized campaigns were a lot more scientific, they were much more—I didn't know the term *measurable* at the time," he says, trailing off. "There was more to it than doing the same old thing over and over."

* * * * *

AFTER BUSH'S LOSS, Carney went to work briefly for Senate Republicans, and then decided to start his own firm. Inevitably Carney would come to open an office on Pitt Street in Alexandria, Virginia. The port city, just across the Potomac from Washington, had been part of the original capital district and returned to Virginia's control only in 1847, not long before the federal government stripped its principal economic engine by abolishing slavery. More than a century later, Alexandria's Old Town neighborhood of Federal brick houses set on an eighteenth-century grid found its identity as a new-style company town. Just as the rest of Northern Virginia boomed from a growing federal government and its many private contractors, Old Town testified to the expansion of the political business, on house-museum scale. The neighborhood surrounding Carney's office was a postindustrial cluster like the tech business that popped up around MIT in Cambridge, Massachusetts, with the full diversity of the consulting profession on display. There were media agencies, pollsters, direct-mail firms, fund-raisers, phone vendors, and public relations strategists, most selling themselves with a distinct strength or specialty. They had one thing in common: almost all the Old Town firms were Republican, drawn not only to rents and taxes lower than in Washington, but closer to the suburban homes where most of the capital's conservative elite chose to live.

Yet despite working for more than a decade in campaigns, with several years at the highest level of national politics, Carney lacked a specialty. "He had good organizational skills and good political judgment," says Charlie Black, who had been the Bush campaign's chief spokesman. "He wasn't particularly strong in terms of writing—he wouldn't have become an ad guy—but he could have studied and been a pollster. The natural thing, though, was to be in campaign management." The only way to be in campaign management without vagabonding around the country working full-time for candidates was to be a general consultant, a new role that had emerged to broker honestly between all the specialties fighting for shares of a campaign budget. A general consultant was usually the first person on board a campaign and responsible for designing a strategic plan, assembling a team of specialist consultants, and hiring a campaign manager who could oversee the day-to-day affairs of what in statewide races often grew into a decent-sized small business. "It's like a general contractor and a foreman," Carney says of the relationship between a general consultant and a campaign manager. "A general contractor works with the architect, the plumber, and all the contractors. There's a foreman who's on-site every day and makes sure people are banging the nails and getting stuff done and people are working."

But Carney, who had recently married an RNC staffer named Lauren Zanca, thought Washington was a horrible place to raise their new child. In 1994, he returned to New Hampshire, moving into a big white clapboard house in Hancock, down the street from a Christmas tree farm and just one town over from where Carney had been raised. He and Lauren reopened their consulting business in an office above the garage, calling themselves Norway Hill Associates after their street address. Much of the decision to move concerned lifestyle: the couple couldn't imagine paying twenty thousand dollars in private-school tuition annually, and they liked the sight of Mount Monadnock, supposedly the most-hiked peak in the United States, from the window of an office whose walls they had decorated with framed invitations and tickets to various Reagan and Bush inaugurals.

For Carney a rural New Hampshire mailing address was also an announcement of principle. He had intentionally withdrawn from an Old Town consulting scene he thought had become complacent, relying on media exposure to convince gullible candidates that the help were an indispensable part of the campaign. "There's a lot of talent out in the countryside that gets dissed by Washington and is not the name brands," says Carney. "But there are a lot of people who are really creative and are not concerned with what the *Washington Post* is going to write about them and more concerned with results." Campaign managers, he thought, were drawn to brand-name, usually Washington-based consultants for the same reasons corporate executives believe that "if you pick IBM or AT&T you're not going to get fired."

The consultant then builds an impressive roster of past clients, and a high-profile success or two can be enough to convert him into an indispensable man for the next manager who comes along. "The consultant or the staff person is more important than the candidate—'You have to pay a lot of money for us to work for you'—that is crazy talk," says Carney.

In June 1997, Carney was summoned to Austin by then Texas agriculture commissioner Rick Perry, who had begun his career as a Democratic legislator but had emerged as a force in the state's Republican politics under the hand of Karl Rove. Perry was plotting a run the following year for lieutenant governor, a job with a robust set of constitutional powers and a great looming opportunity for promotion. Governor George W. Bush would also be on the 1998 ballot, but everyone knew he was looking ahead at an immediate presidential campaign. If he won, the lieutenant governor would fill half his gubernatorial term and have a big head start on the 2002 season. Bush understood this delicate dynamic and told Rove, whose mail and strategy business served many of the state's Republicans, that he could work for no one else in 1998. Rove dropped Perry as a client and the agriculture commissioner gave Carney a call.

Carney was familiar with Texas politics from U.S. Senate campaigns and his time in the Bush White House, but he was certainly no Texan. He knew that Perry already had a loyal campaign manager and media consultant from past races, so Carney's pitch to Perry was based in large part on the New Englander's value as an outsider. It was important to hire a general consultant before hiring the rest of a campaign team, Carney asserted, because he could negotiate tough contracts with outside advisers. "Vendors like to get to the candidate directly; they like to seduce them, ingratiate themselves with them, and they end up signing these deals that end up being awkward and expensive to break," Carney says. Then as the campaign progressed, Carney told Perry, he could keep those consultants focused on their strategic objectives even as short-term concerns and outside voices threaten to distract them. A general consultant, Carney liked to say, could keep the campaign on tempo and make sure everyone was hitting their notes. "I try to explain the general consultant is kind of like the conductor of an orchestra," he says. "Having a plan holds everyone accountable. The candidate is accountable, the finance people are accountable, the campaign manager is accountable."

In the closing days of a race, other recent statewide Texas races had crescendoed into a dissonant symphony of attack ads and defiant counterattacks, like the time in 1978 that Senator John Tower devoted a full thirty-second spot to explaining why he had been photographed refusing to shake hands with an opponent he accused of lying about Tower's family. "My kind of Texan doesn't shake hands with that kind of man," Tower said. Carney explained to Perry that a general consultant could manage emotions at such moments. "Sometimes overreacting is a killer. Sometimes you want to overreact and destroy your opponent. There's no guarantee what will work," he says. In such situations all the consultants and vendors, Carney anticipated, would argue for their unique remedy: the media consultant with a last-minute ad, the mail vendor insisting that the final dollars fund a blast of brochures adding new facts to the conversation. "Of course a mail vendor is going to advocate for that, and a mail vendor should advocate that, because you think mail works and you wouldn't be in the business if you didn't think mail worked," says Carney. "But you will save a lot of money at the end if you have someone at thirty thousand feet—someone who's a little more objective, someone who is not as personally invested in the campaign."

Carney noticed that this line seemed to appeal to Perry, whom he had never before met but quickly came to appreciate for their common suspicions of the political profession. Carney proposed that he take a smaller monthly retainer in exchange for a "win bonus," to be paid out only if Perry became lieutenant governor. "Everyone has skin in the game," Carney told Perry, explaining that such a pay structure would leave the campaign more money to spend on its own operations before the election. "If we win, we'll raise the money. If we don't win, we don't need to spend the money." Perry hired Carney that day, at a fee of five thousand dollars per month, and the general consultant got to work building his team.

Many of them, based in Austin, already knew Perry well. The campaign manager, Jim Arnold, had first interviewed for a job with Perry in 1990 as the recently converted Republican prepared his first statewide campaign, for agriculture commissioner. The media consultant, David Weeks, met Perry in 1985 at an air force base near Abilene, where Perry flew C-130s and Weeks was involved in community affairs. The two bought a plane together. "Of course he could fly and I couldn't, so it was really his airplane," says Weeks. "But in true Perry fashion I paid for it." Mike Baselice, the pollster, had worked with Weeks on Kay Bailey Hutchison's 1993 special election for Senate.

Consultants outside Perry's inner circle, however, were extended little loyalty. Over the course of the 1998 campaign, Carney fired three consecutive mail vendors out of disappointment with their performance. "Campaigns are very overly cautious about terminating people," Carney says. "It's a lot easier than people think it is: pick up the phone and say, 'Thanks a lot, buddy.'" (Those involved with the campaign suggest Carney's actual words in those situations tended to be less gracious.) When an outside consultant or vendor disappointed him, Carney usually thought it was because they were overextended and not sufficiently invested in any of their races. So Carney made everyone who wasn't on Perry's payroll work for win bonuses, too, adjusting incentives to make sure their interests would align with the candidate's. For professional fund-raisers, who typically earn a share of each check they bring in, Carney created two separate rates of commission: a high one on money raised from new Perry donors, and a much lower one on the presumably easy task of getting an established contributor to give again. "People keep on writing checks every year for a thousand bucks—we should pay the postal service a commission, you didn't do anything," says Carney.

"I'm a bigger believer in it now: as I get older I get more driven by the economics," Carney says. "There's a lot of money in politics and people should not get paid for poor performance. Yet a lot of vendors in politics, on both sides, get paid whether the campaign wins or loses. I'm not sure that's a great incentive to win. So I'd rather pay somebody a lot of money to win, and less money just to put in effort. I don't really care about efforts; I care about results. If a guy can create his TV ads sleeping in his boxer shorts in his mother's basement, I don't give a shit—I just want to win. So I'd rather pay the guy a lot of money for winning than pay him a bunch of money for working for us."

There was something gleeful about the way Carney approached his fiduciary responsibilities. He had none of the accountant's mien, instead guarding a campaign budget with the same competitive spirit that led him to hunker down with a poll and look for a niche of strategic opportunity. He was intently focused on defeating his client's opponent, but first Carney knew he would have to contend with an intrasquad game and outfox the people who were supposed to be his colleagues. The pinball machine that had once brightened a White House office had been replaced in New Hampshire by a calvary sword, resting atop a bookshelf within permanent reach of Carney's desk. He joked it was a defense against the election attorneys whose overlawyering had made campaigns timid and risk-averse.

As they plotted Perry's campaign, Carney's team feared their greatest problem would come from a supposed ally at the top of the Republican ticket. Bush was the type of popular incumbent governor who could sweep in other candidates on his coattails, but Perry advisers knew that Bush's interests diverged from theirs. Bush's reelection was a sure bet, but in preparation for a presidential bid, Rove was ambitiously aiming to win 70 percent of the vote. Such a sweeping victory would immediately validate the young governor as a plausible president, communicating to the national political community that Bush had broad reach and, especially, appeal among Hispanics. To get that share, Bush would have to turn out friendly Democrats. Perry, however, didn't want to see any Democrats at the polls. His opponent, state comptroller John Sharp, was much more formidable than Bush's. Rove's strategy to market Bush as a bipartisan figure would likely trigger a flood of new Bush-Sharp ticket-splitters that would drown Perry at the polls.

When Baselice's polls showed Perry's lead over Sharp shrinking, Baselice repeatedly went to Carney and Perry to suggest it was time to attack Sharp. Perry usually deferred to his advisers' strategic instinct, and agreed that Weeks should begin creating negative ads. But before Weeks could launch the ads, Perry would come back and say he had changed his mind. Someone appeared to be going around Carney and Jim Arnold and getting to the candidate directly, and everyone in Perry's circle assumed it was Rove. One time, after learning that Perry had once again vetoed plans to begin a negative-ad campaign against Sharp, Carney punched a hole in the wall of Arnold's office out of frustration. He suspected that Rove, who liked to present himself as the strategist who had turned Texas red, was sabotaging Perry's campaign.

Bush won his race by more than 37 points, Perry his by less than 2. "Depending on who you talk to, he was either carried on Bush's coattails or there were no Bush coattails," says Arnold. As Perry held a slim lead over Sharp on election night and prepared to declare victory, he stopped on his way to the podium at the Austin Convention Center and pulled Carney, Weeks, and Baselice close. "I'm never going to allow anybody else to dictate the direction of our campaigns again," Perry told his advisers.

*   *   *   *   *

IN 2005, four academics walked into the PlainsCapital Bank building on Congress Street in Austin, two blocks south of the Texas State Capitol and around the corner from the Texans for Rick Perry headquarters. The campaign's conference room could barely fit ten, and so whenever a meeting demanded more attendees, they were left to rent out a restaurant or reserve a conference room in the offices of the bank where campaign chairman James Huffines served as president. After their first e-mail exchange the previous fall, Carney had extended the type of invitation Gerber and Green had hoped to receive since they first hit the New Haven sidewalk but never actually expected to see. The idea that the offer would come with the personal sign-off of "the most conservative governor in the country," as Carney insisted on labeling Perry, was a particular surprise. Green immediately knew that he and Gerber would come under suspicion as "two guys from Yale who wouldn't probably vote for Governor Perry ever," as Carney describes them, and looked for wingmen who might be more ideologically in sync with Perry's circle.

It was not hard to pick out the two Republican professors. They were the ones who didn't look like academics. Daron Shaw, a young San Diegoan with Ken-doll looks and a surfer's frame, had worked on the polling team of George H. W. Bush's 1992 campaign before completing his graduate work in political science. Two years later, Shaw joined the faculty of the University of Texas at Austin, where a colleague introduced him to Karl Rove, who was then advising George W. Bush's second gubernatorial campaign at the same time he worked to complete his undergraduate degree. (In 1971, Rove had dropped out of the University of Utah to become executive director of the College Republican National Committee as the group prepared for Richard Nixon's reelection.) The two started meeting regularly for lunch, and Rove, who had an autodidact's fascination with American history, was eager to learn political science theories he could apply to the campaigns he understood only in anecdotal terms.

In the spring of 1999, Rove hired Shaw to work as director of election studies in the fourteen-member strategy department of Bush's presidential campaign. Early every morning Shaw would arrive at headquarters to sort through the reams of polling that had arrived overnight from around the country, and begin analyzing it so that the campaign could shift its resources accordingly among battleground states. He was called "Dr. Shaw" by younger colleagues, a title intended with deference that couldn't help but sound sarcastic given the nicknames that usually circulate on campaigns. (Early in his career, Bush had dubbed Rove "Turd Blossom.") But the acknowledgment of Shaw's scholarly credentials, and the fact that he was constantly shuttling between Bush's headquarters and his university office blocks away, highlighted the unusual nature of his moonlighting. While academics often advised candidates on policy matters, it was rare for one of them to maintain a staff job as a political operative working on the exact tactics he studied. Shaw's research focused on electoral-college strategies, and his terms for accepting Rove's job offer was that after the election he would have access to all of Bush's internal polling and media-buying data. (Previously he had had to scrounge for files from former campaign strategists, like the battered box of unsorted folders with all of Bob Dole's TV purchases that sat beneath Shaw's desk.)

Green called Shaw about the Perry project in early 2005, at the same time he roped in James Gimpel, another clean-cut young political scientist who had worked for Republicans in the federal legislative and executive branches before beginning a teaching career at the University of Maryland. In 2001, Rove had suggested that Shaw recruit political scientists to an "Academic Advisory Council" to consult with the Republican National Committee on its 72-Hour research as well as broader electoral trends. Could Shaw round up other conservative scholars who would be friendly to Bush's objectives? Rove asked.

"Jeez, Karl, I don't know how many of those are out there," Shaw told him.

"Well," replied Rove, "let's expand the definition to being nonhostile."

Shaw ended up identifying eight academics who met the standard, including Gimpel, and Rove called them his "Team B." (The political professionals were Team A.) When the Academic Advisory Council gathered in Washington in late 2001 to preview the next year's midterm elections, Gimpel arrived with a list of industrial midwestern counties where he said Bush had suffered in 2000 because younger Republicans had turned out at dismal rates. A renewed sense of civic interest after September 11 could offer a window to register and mobilize young conservatives, Gimpel suggested, a project best accomplished by mining his county data to identify precincts with the best combination of young populations and Republican performance. It was in many ways a classic Gimpel subject: his specialty was political geography, with a focus on the spatial dimension of campaigns. His work with the RNC gave Gimpel access to the party's national voter database, making him one of the rare political scientists comfortable with the same tools that campaign operatives used.

None of the four academics who had signed on with Perry expected that they would do much but repeat many of the straightforward voter contact experiments that Gerber and Green had run elsewhere, only this time within a big partisan candidate campaign. Running another test of phones and mail didn't excite them much intellectually but it could help remove the cloud of skepticism that had shadowed Gerber and Green since their first experiment: a persistent critique that lessons learned from a nonpartisan New Haven civics project had little to do with the scrum of real politics. "In some instances, they made conclusions that phones weren't effective based on one call, but they didn't test multiple calls," says Jeff Butzke, Perry's phone vendor. "I'd agree that one call probably wasn't that effective. More calls, especially on election day, are more important."

Carney's doubts about campaign spending extended far beyond phones and mail, however. In 2002, Perry's opponent, a South Texas businessman named Tony Sanchez, spent $76 million, most of it his own money, including what Perry's staff estimated was $40 million in ads attacking their candidate. (Perry had moved into the governor's mansion in January 2001, upon Bush's election as president.) Perry had spent $28 million and still beat Sanchez by almost twenty points. That disconnect between dollars and votes, along with his natural cynicism about the industry that thrived on it all, drew Carney uncomfortably toward the philosophical. "Dave could sit there and get reflective sometimes," says Luis Saenz, who was political director of the 2002 campaign. "'Does any of this fucking matter?'"

That became, to the political scientists' surprise, their research agenda for the 2006 election cycle. What had long been off-limits to experimenters as "real politics" was now on the table: Carney was ready to test anything the academics could figure out how to randomize, from lawn signs to television ads. He liked Gimpel's idea of geocoding fund-raising invitations to learn the optimal radius for drawing people to events. In addition, there were a few things Perry's advisers were itching to learn. Their candidate was pushing for a more manageable travel schedule in 2006 than he'd had in his previous statewide races; Perry told Carney he wanted to sleep in his own bed at night. Could the professors come up with a system for maximizing the effectiveness of Perry's personal visits in a way that would allow him to avoid the long itineraries that kept him away from Austin for days at a time?

Perry's advisers placed only one major restriction on Gerber, Green, Gimpel, and Shaw. They couldn't publicly discuss their work with the campaign until it was over. The outside consultants and vendors feared press coverage that could embarrass them, but Carney wasn't much concerned with their feelings. He didn't want to see leaks that could reveal the campaign's strategic decisions or unmask differences within the leadership. Other advisers worried that the experiments could make it look as though they were trivializing the work in front of them. "I don't think we would want any of this out there—that we were just messing around with professors as though we didn't care about the race," says Saenz, who became campaign manager. "The reason we were doing this is because we were dead serious about the race." In exchange for signing to a nondisclosure agreement, the professors were granted what mattered most in a line of work where "publish or perish" is a vital maxim. After November 2006, they would be free to use any findings from the campaign's work in a journal article or book.

The academics happily agreed to these terms, amazed by their good fortune. They made plans to convene in Chicago to plot specific experiments they wanted to present to the Perry campaign. The four academics sat on the sidelines of the Midwest Political Science Association annual conference, arguing how to exploit an opportunity that had never before been extended to a political scientist. For years, mass media, the dominant form of political communication but the one whose effects were hardest to isolate, had loomed as the holy grail of campaign experiments, and now they were being invited to treat a television advertising budget as their laboratory.

* * * * *

IN THE SPRING OF 2005, Carney stood in an empty Mexican restaurant called the Oasis on Austin's Lake Travis, in front of what amounted to Perry's extended political family, and prepared to introduce a quartet of strangers. A crowd of about thirty people were seated, auditorium-style—a group that included the core campaign staff for 2006; a retinue of outside consultants and vendors; Perry and his wife, Anita; and their kitchen cabinet, many of them former aides.

Those who worked for Perry considered him "a dream client," as Baselice put it: eager to make fund-raising phone calls, willing to defer to his advisers' guidance and stick to a script when put in front of him. He also showed his personal gratitude to those who served him. After 2002, to congratulate them on his victory, Perry invited members of his core team (including Carney and his wife) to join him climbing Guadalupe Peak, the highest point in Texas. A little over a year later, he rounded up many of the same advisers (including Carney again) for a retreat in the Bahamas, an outing that was nominally devoted to school finance policy but was more hands-on in its treatment of scuba-related issues. (The trip triggered an ethics investigation when it was revealed that the expenses had been paid by political supporters. Perry was eventually cleared of wrongdoing.) "The joke is we're like the mafia—you only think you get out," says Deirdre Delisi, who managed Perry's 2002 campaign before becoming his gubernatorial chief of staff. "Perry inspires a lot of loyalty in terms of people who have worked with him and stayed whether they're officially in it or not."

The campaign was preparing for what it expected to be a difficult primary against Carole Keeton Strayhorn, the state comptroller and former Austin mayor. The rivalry was already intense between Perry's world and Strayhorn's, and early in the day Carney had set the tone by claiming,

"We're going to rip her leg off and beat her over the head with it!" The statement jarred Bill Noble, who had expected to be attending more of a planning session than a pep rally, one where there would be an open exchange of ideas about strategy but little need to fire up Perry's loyalists. Then he saw how Carney's bluster was received by four strangers in their midst. "I just looked over at them, and there was this look of shock," says Noble. "It turns out it was for effect."

Carney appeared intent on unsettling everyone at the Oasis restaurant that day: the group of academics he introduced as "our four eggheads" and the political hands they were encountering for the first time. The day-long retreats were a ritual for Perry campaigns—and many in attendance were veterans of past retreats Carney had organized before the 1998 and 2002 races—but this was the first time he had prepared a syllabus. Carney had ordered fifty-five copies of *Get Out the Vote!* and everyone who was to attend the retreat received one with orders to read it.

Perry would likely begin campaigning in the fall and launch his ad campaign in January, setting up before the March 2006 primary a two-month sprint during which the eggheads could run their experiments. There would then be eight months for them to process the results and analyze the findings, leaving Carney enough time to apply their conclusions to Perry's general-election tactics. "When you're spending twenty-five million dollars on an election and you can save two percent, that's a lot of money. You'll have more money to spend on something that works," says Carney, who thought he could boost Perry's summertime fund-raising power by showing off his rigorous experimental regime to "assure donors that we're using their money as best as possible—spend it different, spend less of it."

Don Green began presenting the research that he had done with Alan Gerber over the years, rigorously itemizing all the things that campaigns did that he believed he had proven to be a waste of money. Green did this while facing a room filled with people who had gotten rich off these practices and had been looking ahead to the next Perry campaign as another big payday. Carney likened Green's talk to "going into the Catholic church telling everyone that Mary wasn't a virgin, and Jesus really wasn't her son." Carney delighted in the face-off he had manufactured, the awkward pitting of academics against professionals—with millions of dollars, control of the country's second-largest state, and claims of intellectual supremacy all at stake. "Carney is a very confrontational person. That's how he drags out the best product in people," says Deirdre Delisi. "What he's trying to do is force creative thinking."

There was little evidence of creative thinking at the Oasis that day. In fact, it became apparent pretty quickly to Carney that few of the attendees had read the book closely. Those who might have didn't look any more persuaded by the experimental methods or conclusions Gerber and Green had reached. The consultants replied as Carney expected they would—in what he called "total denial," boasting of pieces of mail or phone campaigns that had proven decisive in past elections. One vendor, making the case for robocalls, recalled a legendary voter registration program that featured a recording of a little girl's voice reminding people to sign up.

"Great," Carney said, wrapping up the presentation. "One of you is right. Either the eggheads are right or you're right. We're going to prove it out, and plan our campaign and allow these guys to develop experiments for everything we do."

Whenever the eggheads walked into Perry's Brazos Street headquarters, Gimpel thought, they were seen as the "internal affairs bureau of the police department," a watchdog monitoring the campaign's outside vendors. "They don't want people looking over their shoulders and checking up on them," he says. When the eggheads were out of earshot, the vendors mused ironically about the prospect that the Yalies were lefty moles. "Let's hope to God there's not an e-mail going out to the DNC," they would joke.

More seriously, randomizing tactics as significant as media buys and candidate travel potentially set Carney up for charges of self-sabotage. Even though the academics had planned their media study in such a way as to make sure it didn't dangerously undermine Perry's prospects, the whole point of randomization was for the campaign to do something that it might not have done for strategic reasons. Nonetheless, research objectives were likely to introduce new inefficiencies into the management of the campaign. What if, as part of a candidate travel experiment, the randomizer assigned Perry to do back-to-back visits the same afternoon in El Paso, in the far west corner of the state, and Shreveport, Louisiana, whose media market straddled Texas's eastern border? "I just wanted to make sure it didn't get in the way of the campaign," says Ted Delisi, who was the campaign's mail vendor (and married to Perry's chief of staff). "Sometimes you've got to get in the car and stomp your foot on the gas and not wonder how the engine works."

* * * * *

ON JANUARY 2, hours before the deadline to file for the primary ballot, Carole Keeton Strayhorn stood at an Austin high school and declared she was leaving the Republican Party and would run as an independent in the fall. The announcement shocked Perry's headquarters, which had begun the new year ready for an eight-week sprint until the March 7 election. Instead, their show of strength had earned them a free trip to the general election, where they would likely be part of a four-way race. (Democrats were far from selecting their nominee, and country singer-songwriter and novelist Kinky Friedman was preparing his own independent candidacy.)

But the news unsettled the eggheads, who had designed their most important experiment—staggering Perry's broadcast advertisements in random waves across the state—to test the effects on the governor's standing in a two-way primary that would no longer take place. Carney huddled with the eggheads and considered their options. Green argued that, if anything, Strayhorn's withdrawal was good news for their experiment and that they should continue as planned. Before her move, the eggheads were unsure of how they would deal with the noise that would come from a lively primary—such as the possibility that Strayhorn could focus her ads in specific markets—noise that could distort their ability to isolate the effects of

Perry's randomized buys. All they would do to adjust is open up the polling to all voters and ask them whether they viewed Perry favorably, then test his performance in a four-way general election. Carney decided to strike the last of the four weeks he had allocated for the experimental buy, to stockpile some money for the fall, but gave the eggheads approval to book ad time.

The morning of January 5, Texans awoke to triumphant coverage of the University of Texas Longhorns' dramatic upset victory in the Rose Bowl's closing seconds to claim the national championship and seal an undefeated season. Television viewers in five media markets across the state were given another new reason to feel good about their state: Perry's first ad of the campaign had slipped into the regular rotation on their local news. "I've never been more proud to call myself a Texan," said the tall, strong-featured man standing before the state capitol, where he kept his office, and fighting for screen time against an immodest parade of Lone Star clichés: waving bluebonnets, the Alamo, cattle patrolling a central business district. The governor recounted his policy successes in education, tort reform, and economic development. "Our people are compassionate. Our vision, bold. Our values, strong. The best is yet to come," he went on. "I'm proud of Texas. How 'bout you?"

The thirty-second ad was standard introductory fare, but the scattered schedule on which it aired looked nothing like the order that David Weeks, who scripted and shot it, would have put in to his media buyer under normal circumstances. Political consultants calculated their buys in terms of gross rating points, or GRPs, the basic unit of measurement for TV exposure; the rule of thumb was that with 1,000 GRPs the average viewer saw each spot ten times in a week. Like most consultants, Weeks—who had begun his career as a campaign spokesman and press secretary—had a set of rules about the size of his ad buys, all grounded in a mix of tradition and instinct. "An ad has to have a certain amount of weight behind it," he says. An attack ad, Weeks believed, needed between 800 and 1,000 GRPs to have an impact; "you can get by" with 500 to 600 points when pushing a positive message. And Weeks adhered to a widely accepted maxim about the importance of keeping a continuous, steady presence on the air for his candidate: "When you go up, you stay up."

The eggheads had designed the experiment to deliver its treatment in three doses: 1,000, 500, and 250 GRPs. Markets were assigned their volume randomly, each one rolled out in a staggered fashion so that at any point different markets would be getting Perry's ads in different volumes, some receiving none at all. (To make the study as unobtrusive to campaign strategy as possible, the eggheads agreed to remove the state's two largest cities, Houston and Dallas–Fort Worth, from the experiment entirely, leaving eighteen media markets. These varied widely in terms of size and demographics and so the academics matched similar ones for balance, reducing the likelihood that the randomizer could end up commanding Perry's media buyer to shrink its presence in all of conservative West Texas at once, for example, or effectively give up on speaking to Latino voters statewide.) Weeks had never bought only 250 points in a market for Perry, as the campaign found itself doing in Odessa-Midland. At such a low volume, the "Proud" ad found its way into the early-morning local news, *Live with Regis and Kelly,* and a pair of early-evening game shows— all prime hours to find older viewers who make up the most loyal voters. In Victoria, which received a 1,000-point buy starting the same day, Perry's declaration of state pride cut a much wider swath through the programming grid, including *Oprah, Law & Order, Extreme Makeover: Home Edition,* and an NFL playoff game.

Green would look at the nightly results of one thousand short polling calls being made statewide to see if the ads were having any effect. During the first week of the experiment, Perry's statewide approval rating was just under 45 percent, and he led the four-way matchup (against Strayhorn, Friedman, and an unnamed Democrat) with 34 percent of the vote. By January 26, every market in the study but one had received Perry ads, although in different volumes, durations, and rhythms. (Abilene had been randomly assigned zero points in each of the three weeks.) Victoria received 1,000 points the whole time, Odessa three weeks at 250, and San

Antonio got nothing the first week but two weeks at 500. At the end of the third week, in which the ad appeared in seventeen markets, the polls registered a significant improvement for Perry: his statewide approval rating had moved up to 47 percent, and a much larger share of these registered as "strongly positive" than they had at the start of January, although he fell slightly in the four-way horse race. When the eggheads took apart these numbers to reflect the broadcasts' distribution and timing, they found that the ads had "sizable effects" on the way voters perceived Perry. His support increased nearly five percentage points per 1,000 GRPs in weeks when his ads aired.

At the end of the third week, the ads stopped. Although Perry did other things befitting a statewide candidate, he ran no more broadcast ads before the primary on March 7. For the final few days before the primary, Green ordered more polling calls. Perry was significantly more popular than he had been just after the new year, with an approval rating over 55 percent. But the eggheads' regression analysis gave the ads no credit for that movement. Even in Victoria, which received the maximum dose of 1,000 GRPs and saw Perry's standing jump by six percentage points over those three weeks, the ads' power had worn off by March. The ads may have delivered sizable effects on the weeks in which they ran, the eggheads concluded, but they decayed rapidly. Much of Weeks's folklore was right: if your goal was to move public opinion, it made sense to wait to go on TV until you would be able to sustain the buy.

Shaw thought that was an important conclusion, but he believed that to reach it Green had made a major trade-off. By staggering the buys for a nuanced understanding of how opinions move over time, the experimenters had decided to be in fewer markets on any given day. As a result, Shaw thought, they had sacrificed the power of the data to illuminate how much advertising moved public opinion at all. Shaw had argued that the campaign should run two different ads as part of the experiment, to be able to measure their relative impact, and lost out to Green. "The real weakness of the study is it's a single ad, and you're extrapolating from that," says

Shaw. "You could make an argument that okay, there's a diminution of effects, but that's just because it's not a very memorable ad."

Much of Shaw's personal research addressed one of the most vexing questions in the study of elections: do campaigns matter? The first postwar studies, like the Michigan scholars who pioneered the National Election Studies, argued that the factors that drove voters' choices—their social networks or party identification—moved more slowly than any individual election season. It suggested that the quadrennial pageant of candidates crisscrossing the country was all but incidental to an outcome that was effectively preordained. In the 1970s, political scientists believed they could explain all presidential elections with the same formulae. The most important inputs were presidential approval ratings and national economic indicators, reduced by statistical models to a neat set of rules: if the economy was growing faster than 1.2 percent annually, the incumbent president would win. It didn't matter how much money he raised, if his ads were any good, or whether his opponent looked presidential. The winner had basically been determined by June.

Shaw's own experience gave him good reason to be skeptical of this thesis that campaigns had "minimal effects." By its standards, Shaw's boss in the 2000 campaign should have been a certain loser. Al Gore entered the nearly two-year election cycle as the tribune of a party with a popular incumbent in the White House, presiding over a very healthy economy. An average of seven academic election-forecasting models (using these criteria and others) presented at the American Political Science Association conference that August predicted that Gore should have carried 56 percent of the popular vote against Bush in a two-way contest. But by November, the Republican had turned the election into nearly a tie. (Gore won 50.2 percent of the two-party vote, leading Bush by a little more than 500,000 votes.) Some of those in the minimal-effects school responded by adjusting the economic indicators that went into the models or arguing that Gore's inability to focus on the economy mitigated the importance of those conditions to voters. But Shaw thought that basically conceded the point. Bush had run a better race than Gore. What they did mattered. Campaigns had effects.

As a graduate student, Shaw had been unsatisfied with previous works that had attempted to answer this question by relying only on survey data or laboratory experiments attempting to measure what types of political communication could shift voters' preferences. "While experiments allow researchers to isolate the influence of particular effects, critics question whether such a controlled environment is comparable to the hurly-burly of an actual campaign," Shaw wrote. Instead, he reconstructed candidates' electoral-college strategies, relying on professional contacts where necessary to understand how past campaigns had selected the states in which they chose to compete and how they allocated resources among them. In the 1980s, presidential candidates largely stopped buying national ads from the three networks and started going to local affiliates in their targeted states. As a result, campaigns began to rigorously divide the country into battleground and nonbattleground states—devoting time and resources to the former and completely avoiding the latter. It created, in effect, a natural (if nonrandomized) experiment that Shaw could test, and he was able to determine that the amount of money a candidate spent in a state did affect the share of the vote he won there, albeit in a minor way.

But TV ads were only one of the "most obvious and visible manifestations of the campaign," as Shaw wrote in his dissertation. The other was the candidate's own travel—the whistle-stop tours and bus trips and swelling rallies that provided the country's dominant political iconography and drove daily news coverage within an election year. What was more of a campaign effect than a visit from the candidate? Major campaigns, especially those covering enough turf that transit time was a consideration, negotiated the candidate's itinerary with more attention than anything else. "At the end of the day there are two finite resources in every campaign: money and time," says Deirdre Delisi, "and the most valuable time is the principal's time." It was possible to put a price on an hour of the candidate's day, whatever he or she could bring making fund-raising calls over that time. But no one knew how to weigh that against the political value of shaking hands in a diner or giving a speech to a neighborhood association.

American history may have been filled with anecdotes of campaigns swayed by the schedule, like how in the last days before the 1960 election, Richard Nixon, holding to a pledge to visit every state, flew to Alaska instead of trying to sway voters in deadlocked Illinois. But in the current era of ubiquitous television and Internet coverage, wondered Shaw, did a politician's physical presence have any impact?

* * * * *

ON JANUARY 10, Rick Perry strode into the Frazier Alumni Pavilion, a shed covered with Spanish-style clay roof tiles and attached to Texas Tech's sixty-thousand-seat football stadium. On autumn Saturdays the pavilion was popular for fancy pregame parties, but on a Tuesday morning in January it housed one hundred supporters, many of them wearing Perry 2006 stickers. "There's been seven times I've stood before the people in this state and asked them to place their trust in me," Perry said, as university flags fluttered from wooden rafters overhead, "and I have never been defeated."

For Texas Tech's daily student newspaper, the *Daily Toreador,* the news the next morning was not about anything specific Perry said but that he had chosen Lubbock as the first stop on his "I'm proud of Texas" tour. "I think people are finally starting to see what's great about Lubbock," the county's newly appointed district attorney, Matt Powell, told the paper. "It speaks volumes that he chose Lubbock to come and kick off his campaign." Congressman Randy Neugebauer noted that "the governor has been a fiscal conservative, and he chose a city that's fiscally conservative to launch in."

None of those factors, however, explains the decision to hold the inaugural stop of Perry's reelection campaign in Lubbock. In fact, it wasn't really a decision at all: the selection had been made by randomization software on Daron Shaw's office computer at Texas Tech's rival, the University of

Texas. The computer had also decided to send Perry by plane from Lubbock to Addison, outside Dallas—where he visited a Texas Instruments
plant under construction—and then later in the day to Tyler and Beau-
mont. It could have just as easily dispatched him to make his debut in
deep-blue McAllen or famously liberal Austin.

Carney had given Shaw the authority to control Perry's travel for a
three-day campaign swing, his first of the election cycle and scheduled to
begin just as Perry's "Proud" ads were completing their first week in rotation. The candidate would do four events a day, each in a different media
market, and Shaw would randomly assign them. Campaign staff would do
the rest, choosing where in each market Perry should appear and what type
of event—a speech? a factory tour? a town-hall meeting?—it would be.

Carney had his own hunch that the candidate's presence mattered, a
lesson he learned the hard way. In 1992, when he had served as George H. W.
Bush's political director, campaign strategists had responded to Bush's
poor performance in a town-hall debate in Richmond, Virginia—he was
seen checking his watch midway through a voter's question—by having
the candidate hunker down in the White House to prepare for the final debate four days later. "It wasn't until that moment that we were able to actually show that in those four days there was a tremendous difference, when
every day Bill Clinton was doing something, even if it was only jogging.
When we didn't campaign, we were off television, off the screen," Carney
said immediately after the election. "It was the fatal flaw: we should have
been doing something to get back in the mix."

But a decade later, Carney still had no idea how those dynamics really
worked. He agreed to give Shaw the nightly polling data from Butzke's calls,
along with the campaign's information on its fund-raising intake and volunteer sign-up. Shaw would be able to segregate it all by day and location. If
going to Lubbock actually made people there more likely to vote for Perry,
volunteer for his campaign, or give money, Shaw would be able to tell.

When Shaw reviewed the local media, he saw that Perry's physical
presence had a remarkable ability to drive coverage. In the twelve media

markets Perry visited, he earned a report on the evening TV news in nine of them and a story in the next morning's newspaper in all twelve. And unlike the stories produced by the Austin bureaus of the big Texas papers, which Perry's aides often felt were unfair to their boss, the local coverage of his trips was almost exclusively positive. When Shaw coded the stories in all twelve markets on a five-point scale of how good they made Perry look, they found that the campaign stop warmed the tone of the coverage in all but one. In the eight control markets that Perry didn't visit, the governor was barely covered in the media during the same period.

Shaw could tell that Perry was boosted by the warm reception he got on the road. Contributions went up in the cities that he visited, along with the number of new volunteers. Across the twelve markets, Perry's approval rating went up from 41 to 46 percent, with his unfavorable number dropping slightly. While Perry gained four points in the four-way horse race, his lead over Chris Bell, the likely Democratic nominee, remained steady, though, each of them appearing to benefit from voters abandoning the two independent candidates. Shaw assumed, sensibly, that this meant that Perry's presence energized not only Republicans but Democrats, too. When Shaw went back the following week, however, Perry's lead hadn't evaporated the way his TV-aided boost had. He held on to four points he had gained.

This was a valuable insight for Carney, who seemed comfortable, even satisfied, when he learned that something that had been a staple of traditional campaign practice wasn't as valuable as everyone had assumed. "You always think technology can make the difference. In a state as big as Texas, if you can sit in a studio and do twelve interviews on the nightly news in six markets in the time it takes you to go out to Lubbock," Carney reflected after the tests, "the actual visits make a bigger, more lasting impact than just being on the news. It makes you realize it's a better use of your time."

Among the eggheads, however, the findings reinvigorated the unsettled debate over campaign effects. They knew that mail and canvassing could have limited incremental effects on voting behavior, enough to influence a race at its margins but not to dramatically alter its structure. Now they had revealed that the dominant political medium was lousy at delivering permanent shifts in public opinion. Campaigns, it seemed, were always going to raise as much money as they could, but political science was running out of useful recommendations on where to spend it. Was there any place a campaign could direct its money in the service of dramatically changing its fortunes? "It says: all these things we've been working on so hard are a waste of time and we probably need to be doing something else," says Gimpel. "Sometimes, the answer to that question—what is the alternative activity?—isn't that clear. Well, what else *should* we be doing?"

9

MODELS AND THE MATRIX

In September 2007, Dan Wagner left the office of his Chicago economic consulting firm for the final time and walked up Michigan Avenue to join a presidential campaign. The twenty-four-year-old had been a consultant for two years. A self-described motorhead who had grown up in the Detroit area fixing cars with his father, Wagner had exulted when he learned one of his clients would be Harley-Davidson, only to later despair when the assignment left him isolated for a year crunching numbers in a small room in the bike maker's Milwaukee headquarters. He thought back to something he once heard from Steven Levitt, who taught in the University of Chicago's economics department while Wagner was studying there as an undergraduate major. Levitt told his students they would be smart to live below their means, so they could always have the flexibility to afford taking a different job if it was lower-paying. Wagner had never worked on a campaign, but like many of his generation who yearned for greater meaning from public life, he was enthralled by his state's junior senator.

When Barack Obama announced his candidacy for president in February 2007, Wagner looked at the eight thousand dollars he had saved from his consulting paychecks and decided he was ready to deplete it in the service of heeding Levitt's advice. Obama's campaign didn't care that Wagner's résumé was devoid of political accomplishments; in fact, it was the experience Wagner described making economic-forecasting models that would help Obama get elected president.

Wagner was dispatched to Des Moines to serve as deputy manager of Obama's Iowa voter file, at a salary of $2,500 per month. He did not know quite what to expect, and some of his first tasks demanded frustratingly little of his expertise. Because the campaign's state office did not yet have any tech staff, responsibility for fixing colleagues' sputtering Outlook software fell to the closest thing there was to a computer guy, which was Wagner. One day, Mitch Stewart, Obama's Iowa caucus director, walked over to his desk and threw a stack of handwritten cards upon it. "Enter these into the VAN!" Stewart said.

Supporter cards, signed pledges to caucus for Obama the following January, were a long-standing feature of political life in Iowa. Perhaps because they would end up literally standing with their preferred candidate at their precinct caucus, Iowans had little expectation of privacy and were generally happy to commit their support in writing. Much of a campaign's canvassing operation would be devoted to collecting the cards and using them to perform triage on the electorate: putting pledged supporters aside as eventual turnout targets (or cultivating them as volunteers) and identifying the undecided as persuasion targets, all while trying to discern which voters were committed to an opponent, so those could be cut out of future efforts. Every day for a month, Wagner would decipher the name and contact details scribbled on the cards, transcribe them into a computer, and try to match it to a record in the Iowa voter file, which contained richer information on the signer's party affiliation and vote history.

The VAN made this easy. The Voter Activation Network was the Web interface that field organizers used to interact with the huge voter databases maintained by the campaign. The software was developed for Iowa Democrats in 2001, shortly before the federal Help America Vote Act had been enacted to reconcile the patchwork of inconsistent local election laws that came to be viewed by many, especially on the left, as a national outrage. The law encouraged states to centralize their electoral data and organize their voter files in standard formats that for the first time made it easy to manipulate records across state lines. By the 2006 elections, Democrats had access to two competing national databases, one controlled by the national party and the other by Catalist, and the VAN emerged from a pack of state-specific interfaces to become the national standard for voter contact across the left.

By the time Wagner familiarized himself with its features, the VAN was nearly a full-fledged digital substitute for the clipboarded voter lists and large wall maps that were the familiar trappings of campaign fieldwork. The software assigned every individual a unique, seven-digit VAN identification code that was supposed to serve in essence as the political equivalent of a Social Security number—a durable marker that would stick with a voter throughout his or her lifetime. In a mobile country, voters would no longer be traceable only as a name at a fixed address but could be followed when they relocated, even across county or state lines, and their political behavior collected throughout. That individual record could be synced instantly across platforms, so that once Wagner entered a supporter's name and address off a card into the VAN, any canvasser who called up the individual's name on a Palm Pilot application would see that they had been marked, for instance, as a GOTV target with no need for further persuasion.

What Wagner didn't know is that those supporter cards were also helping to make similar determinations about voters who had not pledged themselves to Obama and might never communicate with the campaign at all. The data Wagner entered—along with all the records of door knocks and phone calls made by Obama's growing army of staff and volunteers across Iowa—was being fed into a database that linked up nightly with racks of computers that filled a small room in a converted Capitol Hill apartment building just blocks from the United States Senate. Most days, the only noise that competed with the whirring of the fans tempering those computers' processors was the sound of Obama himself asking for money, audible through a thin wall from the political office that the freshman senator used to make his fund-raising phone calls. Both would prove to be essential engines of his rise.

Sandwiched between the heroic presidential candidate who positioned himself as uniquely able to loosen a nation's intellectually sclerotic politics, and the unrivaled hordes of volunteer activists and supporters who believed in him, sat one of the vastest data mining and processing operations that had ever been built in the United States for any purpose. Obama's computers were collecting a staggering volume of information on 100 million Americans and sifting through it to discern patterns and relationships. Along the way, staffers stumbled onto insights about not only political methods but also marketing and race relations, scrubbing clean a landscape that had been defined by nineteenth-century political borders and twentieth-century media institutions and redrawing it according to twenty-first-century analytics that treated every individual voter as a distinct, and meaningful, unit. "It wasn't something they were doing off on the side anymore; it was integral to how they did everything," says Jeff Link, who oversaw Obama's paid-media spending in southern and western battleground states. "That was the first campaign where you had that level of integration."

The 2008 Obama campaign would become, in a sense, the perfect political corporation: a well-funded, data-driven, empirically rigorous institution that drew in unconventional talent ready to question some of the political industry's standard assumptions and practices and emboldened with new tools to challenge them. "It was like the old Bell Labs," Larry Grisolano, a senior Obama strategist, says of the analytics teams assembled at Chicago headquarters. "They had a lot of ability to create and innovate without being concerned what the outcome was. There was a laboratory attitude with those guys. It was the overwhelming culture of the campaign."

* * * * *

THE SECOND-FLOOR CAPITOL HILL OFFICE with the computers, in reality little more than a closet-sized apartment, was the official Washington address of Ken Strasma, whose black-box algorithms had become something of a legend in Democratic data circles but were almost entirely unknown outside them. His appearance made the case for anonymity. Tidy and plain-featured, the Wisconsinite looked like he came out of middle management in the middle of the country in the middle of the last century.

Strasma had worked as research director of the National Committee for an Effective Congress, which started mapping and scoring precincts in the 1970s to give Democrats their first resource for systematically targeting voters. In the late 1990s, Strasma had watched as the precinct was displaced by the individual as the essential unit of targeting, a shift manifest in the form of a personal rivalry between his boss, Mark Gersh, and Hal Malchow, played out in sparring memos that did little to mask the two men's mutual resentment. Strasma may have worked for Gersh, but Malchow's approach won his heart and mind. While working for state legislative candidates in Minnesota in 1996, Strasma conducted large-scale polls in each of the small districts, and used the results to find personal targets, based on voter-file attributes and Census-tract data, much as Malchow had done earlier that year in Oregon. "We were tiptoeing into the individual level," Strasma says. "I was doing microtargeting before we had a name for it."

After 2002, the ability to do that type of individual-level targeting improved significantly. Greater computer speeds made it easier to swiftly churn through millions of records. Perhaps most important, the release of data from the 2000 U.S. Census created a reservoir of free, up-to-date information unavailable elsewhere; tract-level figures that in 1998 were nearly a decade old had been refreshed to account for years of movement and demographic change. "At the time, individual targeting was basically non-existent, so anything we did would be an improvement," says Strasma. But it threatened NCEC's monopoly as a provider of targeting guidance, and Gersh took Strasma's development of the new specialty as something of a betrayal, like a child abandoning his parents' faith to join a cult. "It seemed like the same general field, just going into another niche," says Strasma. "I tried my best to tiptoe very carefully around the politics of it." In 2003, Strasma quit NCEC to open his own firm, Strategic Telemetry, which rightfully evoked a distant scientific frontier inaccessible to the naked eye and traditional tools. His firm's products would be what Strasma called "virtual IDs."

The "hard ID"—a voter who tells a caller or canvasser which candidate he or she supports—remained the truest currency in predicting support, a certain vote as long as the voter could be turned out. But no campaign had ever been able to hard-ID every voter in its universe, or even a majority of them. The costs or volunteer demands were almost always prohibitive, and it was getting much harder: the proliferation of cellphones and caller identification made it simply impossible to get through to a significant share of the population. Except in precincts where they had a strong partisan advantage, campaigns would often be forced to forget about those they couldn't reach and turn out only those whom they had individually identified as supporters.

Strasma believed it would be possible to simulate IDs for the whole electoral universe, regardless of whether the campaign was ever able to talk to voters directly about their preference. By writing statistical algorithms based on known information about a small set of voters, he could extrapolate to find other voters who looked—and presumably thought and acted—like them. If he could identify enough matchable variables from one set to the next, the campaign could treat these virtual IDs as an effective replacement for hard IDs where it couldn't get them.

Strategic Telemetry's first client was John Kerry, and its initial project was to develop a computer model that could virtual-ID participants in the Iowa caucuses. The differences between caucusing and voting were beyond semantics, and a unique information culture had developed around the distinctions. Campaigns approached the caucuses by developing a two-tier system for counting backers: there was the usual system of hard IDs, in which canvassers ranked voters from 1 to 5, the spectrum from a strong commitment to support Kerry to an equally strong commitment to one of his rivals. On top of that, Iowa caucus campaigns had a robust tradition of asking caucus-goers to sign supporter cards vowing their commitment, which were typically treated by both sides as an inviolable pledge. "If they answer on the phone 'I'm supporting Kerry,' that tells us that at the moment they felt they're supporting Kerry," says Strasma, who had first worked in Iowa in 1988, entering Dukakis supporter cards onto computers. "If they sign the card, they've actually done something for us." But voting was not that simple: delegates were awarded proportionally from each of the state's 1,784 precincts, and a candidate had to receive 15 percent at an individual caucus site to emerge from it with any. If a candidate failed to meet that threshold, he was effectively eliminated at that site. His supporters disbanded and were free to walk to another candidate's corner. This complex system meant that campaigns had to build statistical models specifically for the Iowa caucuses. Strasma conducted a brief ten-thousand-person survey, a far bigger statewide sample than typically used by caucus candidates, asking voters how likely they were to turn out the following January and whom they supported.

The voter files that the Iowa Democratic Party sold to candidates are rich with historical information, including allegiances like membership in the party's rural and gay-lesbian caucuses and past hard IDs that the candidates are required to return to the party after each year's voting. In addition, Strasma collected some of his own data, such as a list of those who had applied for a tax benefit that Iowa extends only to military veterans. Instead of a two-sided prediction, Strasma had to develop multidimensional scores that would predict an individual's likelihood of supporting each of the top candidates, including Howard Dean, Dick Gephardt, and John Edwards—to calculate precincts where certain candidates, including Kerry, would fail to meet the 15 percent threshold, or where rivals would do so, allowing Kerry to claim their orphaned supporters before the second round of voting. "The Iowa caucus was the best possible petri dish for this stuff," says Strasma.

He tuned his system to serve as a fulcrum between the campaign's data processing and its field organization. Every evening by midnight, Kerry's field staff was required to input the results of that day's canvass, including supporter cards, into a computer system. Strasma would wake at 4 a.m. to see what his algorithms had done to the numbers. Based on the new predictions, Strasma would update vote totals for every precinct in Iowa, which had been established to keep Kerry on pace to meet the statewide delegate goals necessary for victory. By 8 a.m., that report would be sent to Kerry's Iowa caucus director, Jonathan Epstein, so he could adjust resources daily to make sure they were being committed to precincts where Kerry stood to gain, or protect, the most delegates. Epstein would hassle Strasma if he was fifteen minutes late in delivering what the field staff referred to as their "crack sheet."

Those spreadsheets, based on real and virtual IDs, gave Kerry's campaign hope through the autumn of 2003, when Dean's rise in the polls appeared to eclipse Kerry's standing as front-runner in Iowa and nationally. "At the time, with my friends and family—when I told them I was working for Kerry, they would act like my dog had died or something," Strasma recalls. But he was always far more confident about Kerry's standing. Kerry was hitting his targets, while Dean's support seemed to be slowly buckling in ways that polls, and his own strategists, were unable to pick up. First off, Dean backers seemed to be densely packed into precincts, especially those around college campuses, where they could overwhelm rooms on caucus nights but fail to materialize any extra delegates from it. More surprising to Strasma, Dean canvassers did not appear to be going back to people once they had been ID'd as supporters, banking them as a vote even as the race's dynamics changed. The Kerry campaign watched this phenomenon among its own supporters: they called it a "flake rate," which Strasma quantified and monitored closely. He measured the speed at which voters peeled away from Kerry to support another candidate, and again as onetime supporters of other candidates switched over to Kerry. But Dean's campaign, blinded by encouraging polls and press coverage claiming their candidate's certain victory, didn't seem to notice until too late.

The Dean experience hung over Obama's Chicago high-rise headquarters and every one of the three dozen field offices it eventually opened in Iowa. Shortly after Obama had announced his candidacy, Larry Grisolano and Pete Giangreco had gathered in Chicago to sketch early vote goals for Iowa. Neither man's portfolio gave him specific responsibility for turning out caucus-goers—Grisolano was Obama's paid-media and opinion research director, and Giangreco his lead mail consultant—but the campaign was still hiring its field staff and the two men had both worked in the Iowa caucuses since the 1980s and were familiar with its peculiar practices. They knew that Obama, competing with Hillary Clinton and John Edwards, would have a tough time cracking the insular pool of reliable caucus-goers. If turnout was around 125,000, as it had been in 2004, Obama would have no shot of breaking through. Total turnout, Grisolano and Giangreco concluded, would have to reach 180,000, far more Democrats than had ever before participated, a particular challenge in a year when Republicans had their own wide-open primary fight. (Iowans could participate in either party's caucus, regardless of their registration before caucus day.) Obama would succeed only if he could enlist tens of thousands of new caucus-goers, many of them young people traditionally underrepresented there. This was sensible as a strategy, but it invited a comparison that bedeviled Obama's advisers. They knew that after the 2004 outcome, the world was ready to dismiss the arrival of another antiwar candidate pledging to deliver a caucus coalition of liberal activists and young, first-time caucus-goers. "In the political community, it was 'Obama's got all this buzz but it's just like Dean.' We were hearing that and, to a certain extent, it was true.

Our challenge wasn't how to pretend it wasn't true. It was how to turn that into an advantage," says Strasma. "We had almost the perfect blueprint. What we needed to do was avoid the pitfalls that had befallen Dean."

The supporter cards that Wagner was processing in Des Moines were feeding into the computers at Strategic Telemetry's Capitol Hill office. Those commitments, along with some traditional polling, had already helped to refine Obama's back-of-the-envelope vote goals in Iowa. But the real power of Strasma's black box, like all microtargeting models, was extrapolatory: the names of those who had signed supporter cards went in, and out came the names of other Iowans who looked like them. These algorithms were matched to 800 consumer variables and the results of a survey of 10,000 Iowans. Going a step further than the Kerry campaign, Strasma wanted to create a model that would help Obama's advisers decide which topics they should use when communicating with its targets. Strasma's polls asked voters for opinions on eight issues, and separately, asked for their top two concerns. Obama's pollsters had realized that if they called likely Iowa caucus-goers in the summer of 2007 and asked what issue was most important to them, nearly everyone would say Iraq. When they asked for the top two, it opened a Pandora's box of progressive worry: the environment, health care, civil liberties.

But Strasma was also looking for people who weren't on the Democratic rolls, or even yet voters. Iowa residents who would turn eighteen by November's election day were allowed to participate in caucuses, but no campaigns had ever gone after the population of eligible seventeen-year-olds, in part because no one knew who they were—since they weren't registered and had no political history, they didn't show up in the state voter file. The Obama campaign, desperate to reach its 180,000 target, created a "BarackStars" program to contact Iowa high school students, and it was Strasma's job to help field organizers find them. "I had never before been involved in a campaign where that was such a rich vein to mine," he says. Strasma acquired lists of high school seniors who had taken the ACT college admissions test, names typically marketed to college admissions officers seeking to mail potential applicants. Separately, the campaign had student supporters gather school directories, but—fearing that it would look creepy if it had adult phone banks calling high schoolers—created a system for young backers to call their peers. "A massive program targeting seventeen-year-olds is fraught with peril," says Strasma. His models treated most seventeen-year-olds in the correct birthday range as strong Obama targets, except for those with a Republican for mother and father. "We assumed kids wouldn't necessarily go against both their parents," says Giangreco. As the BarackStars initiative progressed, Obama's Iowa team worked to avoid a mistake Dean had made with college-age supporters. When Strasma's scores identified Iowa college students as targets, a field staffer would call to convince them that it was more useful for them to caucus at their home address than at their school, to disperse them in precincts across the state and not just pack them into those surrounding campuses. Strasma suggested this would also have a beneficial plan-making effect: talking aloud about the details of where they would vote was likely to increase their chances of following through on it.

Strasma's craft was in writing algorithms, and his currency was the scores that emerged from them to predict individual behavior. Each score, calculated out of 100, reflected the percentage likelihood that a person would perform a certain act. For every Iowan in Strasma's database, including Republicans and unregistered seventeen-year-olds, Strasma produced two scores measuring the basic questions every campaign had when it looked out over the electorate. What were the odds someone would vote? And whom was he or she likely to back?

The first of these was known as a turnout score, calculating as a percentage the likelihood someone would participate in the Democratic caucus. The second was called the Obama support score, which indicated the probability that he or she would support Obama, even if it was unlikely he or she would show up in the first place. (For this reason, Strasma saw a lot of Republicans with turnout scores close to zero and Obama support scores near 100: the algorithms determined that they were very unlikely to attend the Democratic caucuses, but if they did so would almost certainly end up in Obama's corner.) Strasma also generated individual support scores for Obama's opponents, which allowed field organizers to change their tactics for each precinct. These scores all ended up on the voter file, so field organizers putting together local walk lists or call sheets could just call up names within certain score ranges for persuasion or GOTV contact. Strasma liked to analogize the scores to precinct averages. If 100 people with 75 percent Obama support scores went to the polls, he would get 75 votes. Among a group of 100 people with 40 percent turnout scores, there would be 40 voters.

Because Strasma had generated predictive scores for every voter, and not only those whom the campaign had directly identified or solicited for supporter cards, Obama's team had remarkably good intelligence on where the opposition's support was located and could plug it into their turnout projections. With that information, Obama strategists knew where it made most sense to call Hillary Clinton backers—in the hopes that converting a small number of them to Obama's side could keep Clinton under a threshold that would grant her campaign an additional delegate—or where John Edwards was uncertain to prove viable and his supporters could be persuaded to consider Obama as a second choice. While Obama's voter file did not initially include support scores for Ohio congressman Dennis Kucinich, a liberal gadfly unlikely to contend for delegates, Strasma added one after seeing in polls that Kucinich's strongly antiwar supporters would almost unanimously default to Obama when they had to make a second choice. Based on that information, the state director, Paul Tewes, lobbied Kucinich to issue a statement endorsing Obama as a fallback, which Obama's campaign was then able to get to everyone whom the scores predicted to be a likely Kucinich supporter.

The arrangement with Kucinich, and a similar deal with New Mexico governor Bill Richardson's campaign to swap second-round backing in cases where one of the two failed to be viable, represented an odd moment for Obama, who often renounced transactional politics as old-guard tactics. His campaign had a conflicted relationship with the things one has to do to win elections. Obama, the former community organizer, believed in a certain purity of grassroots politics, equal at least to the contempt with which he dismissed opponents' political activity as craven or the media's interest in the contest as superficial. At the same time, Obama and his spokespeople bragged incessantly about the campaign's mechanistic accomplishments: how many volunteers they had enlisted, dollars raised, text messages sent. It is little coincidence that these were all numbers. Early on, campaign manager David Plouffe had insisted that the campaign try to measure everything it did as a method of gauging its effectiveness, and that sense of data-intensive empirical rigor quickly moved into all corners of a campaign that would become the largest in history. "We had a lot of money, but we were incredibly efficient with our spending, and that came from Plouffe every single day," says Link. "He just didn't like spending money. For a guy who spent a lot of money in the election, it killed him to authorize a check."

But as money continued to come in, Obama's campaign was able to create increasingly specialized roles around data and technology. Wagner's job as the one-man IT team for the Des Moines headquarters disappeared, its component roles spun off; after a month of processing piles of supporter's cards, Wagner's data entry duties fell to someone else, as did the need to fix the office computers. His schedule freed up, Wagner committed himself to building a software program that could guide tactics for Obama representatives at each caucus location. He went about it by rewriting each of the unusual rules and protocols of the Iowa nominating process—the viability thresholds, the multiple rounds of voting and subsequent realignments, the proportional allocation of delegates—as a series of interlocking game-theory problems. When did it make sense to release some of Obama's supporters to a rival to keep him in play for another round? Or how many of a no-longer-viable candidate's supporters would Obama need to pick up to qualify for an extra delegate? The program Wagner wrote, the Caucus Math Tool, was loaded onto laptops that campaign representatives could bring to their precincts. Its straightforward interface required only entering each candidate's tallies after every round of voting and would deliver practical instructions on how to adjust for the next one. (The broad objective of every move was to block Hillary Clinton from accumulating delegates, regardless of who won them instead.)

At headquarters, campaign officials knew well before results from the first round of votes were typed into Caucus Math how things would go. As voters arrived at precincts across the state for the six-thirty caucus start time, Obama volunteers would call a hotline to report the number who had checked in. The numbers on Wagner's computer were rising faster than anyone had anticipated. By the time local supporters wrapped up their speeches, it was clear to Obama's strategists that they had easily met their goal of delivering 180,000 Iowans at the caucuses. In fact, the final number ended up being 239,000. News reports relied on exit polls to describe who they were: half were participating in a caucus for the first time, and the share of voters under the age of twenty-five had tripled from Kerry's win four years earlier. Very late that night, Wagner went to sleep, barely budged from his bed for two days, and then drove straight east to Chicago.

* * * * *

AS SOON AS he arrived back at Obama's national headquarters, Wagner was pulled aside by Jon Carson, who had been charged with handling the campaign's preparations for February 5. Twenty-four states would vote that day across four time zones, a combination of simultaneous primaries and caucuses heretofore unparalleled in its scope and influence on the nominating contest. Obama had begun paying attention to the delegate count well before Clinton, and starting in the summer of 2007 Chicago had become attuned to the varied and byzantine ways that delegates were awarded around the country. While Clinton appeared to be ignoring those states she was unlikely to win outright, especially those with caucus systems, Carson had developed distinct tactics for each state with the goal of maximizing his delegate haul nationwide. Some campaign departments were well prepared for this shift. Obama had begun in early 2007 to develop a robust volunteer and fund-raising network in all fifty states to exploit his popularity among Democratic activists. But Strasma's microtargeting work during that period was focused almost exclusively on Iowa, with little effort to formalize efforts elsewhere. As a result, the data team's early delegate projections were based on simple demographics: the numbers of African-Americans and Democratic voters under thirty in each district. Analysts tallied them on a whiteboard as "Group A" and "Group B," to keep the simple classifications opaque to reporters tramping through headquarters hoping to pick up hints of campaign strategy.

Obama's data operation was forced to grow quickly to meet the circumstances of a national race. In late 2007, Strasma's scores showed up for the first time on the state voter files maintained in Obama's New Hampshire, South Carolina, and Nevada field offices. In Nevada, the VAN was the province of Ethan Roeder, a graduate of the School of the Art Institute of Chicago who had learned how to use databases while preparing donor reports for Lambda Legal, a gay rights advocacy group. When he won a job with the Obama campaign, that experience was enough to earn him an assignment to Las Vegas as the state voter-file manager. Until Strasma placed microtargeting calls into his state, Roeder had assembled target universes without help from modeling scores. He would look at polls, find population segments that were inclined to support Obama—mostly young whites and African-Americans of all ages—and use geography and basic demographic categories on the voter file to compile walk lists and call sheets for the state's growing crew of field organizers. When Strasma's support and turnout scores showed up in the VAN, Roeder saw how much more finely the electorate could be broken down. "We were dealing with chunks that big, and he comes to us with these small slices," says Roeder.

In campaign offices around the country, a generation of political data experts was being born, forced by exigency to learn how to manipulate voter files and invited by a decentralized campaign to improvise with them. Jim Pugh, who worked in Chicago on online analytics, was still fin-ishing his dissertation on robotics at the École Polytechnique Fédérale de Lausanne, in Switzerland. Matt Lackey had worked on nuclear reactor design for Westinghouse before starting his own comic book business; he ended up managing the Indiana voter file. John Bellows was a graduate student in econometrics at Berkeley and yet another campaign neophyte before he walked into a California field office during the primary season. Because Obama was not aggressively contesting California, Strasma had never built a model for the state. Instead, the campaign decided to open up access to the VAN to anyone who registered as a precinct captain. Bellows used the opening to assemble his own statistical models to identify likely Obama supporters, but the campaign's state director, Buffy Wicks, was at a loss for what to do with them. She put Bellows in touch with Wagner. "I don't know what you two nerds are talking about," she said.

Strasma's national projections were sharpened after Iowa, when he ordered his first calls into the February 5 states. In many of them, self-organized volunteer cells had already been canvassing voters for months. Strasma took their hard IDs and the new results of his large-sample polls and fed them into the algorithms to develop state-specific scores and as-sign them to voters. Carson built a small February 5 team to work through all the new information coming in from around the country and recruited Wagner to be its targeting analyst. In the month before February 5, Wag-ner would arrive at headquarters at seven each night for a twelve-hour shift, processing the numbers that came out of Strasma's computers over-night and assembling them into a daily report that could help Carson move resources among the states. No longer would the campaign rely solely on an outside consultant for an interpretation of the microtargeting models he had developed. "The analyst has to be inside, so that the campaign manager can look to his right and say 'What's going on?'" says Wagner. "He has to be able to answer two questions: Are we going to win or are we going to lose? And what the hell are we going to do about it?"

The answers to those questions shifted regularly, as Strasma's support scores recalibrated to account for a changing race. Previous campaigns that had used microtargeting usually ran their numbers a single time. They conducted the polls, gathered individual-level data, performed the analysis, and gave everyone a score or a segment that stuck with their voter-file record for the whole campaign. It was treated as an inflexible personal attribute, like gender. There were perils in doing a onetime microtargeting project, however. When Bush's team began its large-sample surveys in late 2003, a year before the election, many of the "anger points" questions had been drafted to prepare for an anticipated contest against Dean, who at the time led Kerry considerably in polls. One tested attitudes toward recitation of the Pledge of Allegiance in schools, the subject of a case just accepted by the Supreme Court that Republicans thought could offer a successful wedge issue against Dean.

Primaries presented an even bigger need for fresh microtargeting information. Unlike in a general election, a voter's partisanship was rarely predictive of how he or she would vote, because most of those who cast ballots in a primary were members of the same party. In those cases where it was predictive—in his presidential campaigns John McCain repeatedly did better with non-Republicans who voted in Republican primaries—it was not always intuitive. Because the major fault line of party didn't exist, lots of little ones (demographic, ideological, geographic, issue-based) emerged, intersecting in complex geometries that required nimble analysis of many variables. More than ever, the basic poll subsamples that could handle only three or four overlapping voter characteristics at once were insufficient. Microtargeting solved that problem, but a single-shot approach couldn't keep up with the fluidity of primary-season opinion—voters seemed quicker to change their minds when parties weren't hemming them in. It was possible to have a very good microtargeting algorithm that gave the wrong answer to the most important question of all, just because the which-types-of-people-support-whom data went stale before it could be used.

Indeed, as they talked with voters around the country, Obama's field operatives lost faith in the turnout scores that Strasma's algorithms were sending them. The two major variables that went into them were vote history and the self-reported answer when survey callers asked how likely someone was to vote. Strasma liked to think of the first as measuring if someone was a regular voter, and the second as a gauge of their current enthusiasm. He knew that people always overestimated their chances of voting when asked by a stranger, but now vote history was becoming increasingly problematic for planning turnout. Until Barack Obama won Iowa there had never before been a viable African-American candidate for president, and Strasma's algorithms struggled to measure this historic change. Predictive models were built on established behaviors, and Obama's campaign was now operating in a space without precedent.

The support scores, fed with new IDs from paid call centers and volunteer contacts, moved around in a way that accurately reflected the volatility of the race. They showed that the spine of the Iowa microtargeting model remained intact: voters were unlikely to change their views on issues or their election-year priorities, and the attributes that made someone a likely Obama caucus backer traveled well. Highly educated and upscale voters pulled high Obama-support scores around the country, as did African-Americans and the young. But it was evident from any newspaper poll that voters were moving around among candidates. Edwards was fading from contention, allowing Clinton to solidify her position as the candidate of older, rural white voters.

To the outside world, Obama's campaign had become notable for its digital prowess, which was given much of the credit for his ability to outmaneuver Clinton's establishment support. But in Chicago, the long march through what turned out to be fifty-six primaries and caucuses exposed major weaknesses in a data infrastructure that Carson likened to a Rube Goldberg apparatus. The campaign was gathering an unprecedented volume of information that individual Americans volunteered about themselves. There were the thirteen million people who would sign up for updates from the campaign website, plus those who gave their phone numbers to receive a text-message alert announcing Obama's vice presidential selection. There were the three million donors, many of them contributing small amounts but supplying the campaign with personal data required by federal campaign finance law. Then there were the regular streams of those who put their names on a sign-in sheet at a field office or a clipboard outside a campaign rally.

But the campaign was unable to bring these rivers of data together. Chris Hughes, a founding executive of Facebook who became Obama's director of online organizing, battled often with Blue State Digital, the consulting firm that had grown out of Dean's campaign and built Obama's website. The parts of the online operation facing outward performed brilliantly, engaging supporters in volunteer activity and raising money from them. But the Blue State site was incapable of linking to databases used by other parts of the campaign, leaving different types of personal records—financial contributions, online contacts, field IDs—isolated in their own silos. The campaign didn't know whether a Marjorie Jackson who gave one hundred dollars to attend a concert fund-raiser was the same one who put in two volunteer canvassing shifts the previous weekend—and if she was a married white Republican living in the suburbs, Strasma's algorithms may have predicted her to be a likely McCain voter. If she had written in an online sign-up form that she cared about the environment or a woman's right to choose, that information was unlikely to find its way to someone planning a direct-mail piece addressing one of those issues.

As the primaries wound down, Plouffe decided to reorganize the campaign's data and targeting operations entirely for the general election. He assigned chief of staff Jim Messina to enter surreptitious negotiations with Catalist on a deal to use its voter files rather than rely on those built by the Democratic National Committee, despite the fact that the company was distrusted by many Obama supporters because it had close ties to Hillary Clinton's world and had supplied her campaign with its data. At the same time, Carson convened a group tasked with designing a new targeting structure and invited Wagner and Roeder to be part of it.

Like many junior staffers pushed into roles as targeting analysts, they had chafed throughout the primaries at their inability to know exactly how Strasma made the projections behind his scores. There were active debates about different statistical techniques for finding relationships between variables, and Strasma's black box relied on a complex formula that combined several of them. But none of the campaign staffers who spent their days processing data for Strasma's algorithms was able to see how they actually worked. It was the way business traditionally worked for an outside consultant or vendor like Strasma, who felt he had a unique skill to protect: the campaign ordered a service from him, and he delivered a final product. No one had ever expected a media consultant to publish the f-number to which he set his cameras so that campaign staffers could try to reverse-engineer the distinctive look of his ads. Why should Strasma be expected to explain his algorithms? Yet for the Obama staffers who came from academic backgrounds, where researchers published all their formulae for wider review—or merely tech geeks from a generation with an open-source attitude toward collaborative software development—the opacity of Strasma's shop was particularly frustrating.

Carson believed that the process Obama's campaign had used during the primaries, with Strasma's firm producing models as they became necessary and analysts like Wagner scrambling to interpret them, didn't make sense for the general election. Instead he recommended to Plouffe that the campaign bring its data and targeting operation in-house. Strasma would maintain a consultant's role overseeing it all, and his computers on Capitol Hill would continue to churn out the scores. But data would now be treated as a core internal function with day-to-day needs, like communications and research, and not a boutique service that had to be done by a specialist off-premises. "It was the beginning of the move away from the Wizard of Oz model of microtargeting," says Michael Simon, who had worked with Strasma on Kerry's campaign and joined Obama's.

That shift was soon reflected in the campaign's feng shui. Along an east-facing wall at headquarters, staffers had moved furniture to create a daisy chain of six pods that would be called Team 270. There was one pod per region—the Great Lakes, Midwest, Southwest, West, South, and Northeast—each with seven specialists, covering such basic campaign functions as press and scheduling visits by surrogate campaigners. Regional desks were nothing new in campaigns, but the presence of a specialist each for data and targeting was; in the states, another set of officials would also do nothing else. Each state headquarters would have a data manager, who was charged with managing the voter file and augmenting it with unique sources of information by acquiring lists of veterans collected by local governments or persuading state parties to share their IDs from past campaigns. A separate targeting director would help translate the models for those on the campaign who used the scores for voter contact.

The campaign's obsession with documenting metrics meant that it was generating far more potentially useful data than any of the pods would have time to sift through. Simon, who became Team 270's lead targeting analyst, enlisted a group of Democratic consultants who weren't formally affiliated with the campaign as what he called the targeting desk's "kitchen cabinet," a panel able to take on discrete research questions beyond the purview of his department's daily operations.

Simon introduced the kitchen cabinet to a largely secret stockpile of data known within the Obama campaign as the Matrix. It was a centralized repository that would gather every instance of the campaign "touching" a voter, as field operatives like to put it, including each piece of mail, doorstep visit, and phone call, whether from a volunteer or a paid phone bank. It had its origins in the Iowa Contact Matrix, which compiled each contact that came in through the VAN so field staffers could track their activity. When, two months before the caucuses, Strasma noticed that one woman had been reached 103 times and remained undecided, he considered asking Obama to call her personally.

For the general election, the Matrix was expanded to include non-targeted communication to which an individual was exposed, including broadcast and cable ads and candidate visits to their media market. This created a ready-made data set that could be used to answer questions that campaigns rarely tried to ask, let alone answer, with any methodical rigor. (Obama's campaign never seriously undertook randomized field experiments for individual voter contact. There had been talk, shortly after Obama won the primaries, about sending rounds of general-election persuasion mail and measuring their effects through polls, much as the AFL had done four years before, but campaign officials felt they were too cramped for time to properly build such a system.)

At one point, Simon invited Aaron Strauss, who worked for pollster Mark Mellman's firm, to see if he could identify whether Obama's travel schedule and television buys were moving voters' support scores. "The effects of any campaign activity are ephemeral," Strauss says of his findings. "Just because you touched someone in, let's say, the beginning of October doesn't mean they'll be with you two weeks or even one week later." Strauss's project never changed the campaign's tactics for the sake of research—Obama and his ads still went where Plouffe and his strategists thought they would be most electorally effective—but the massive volume of existing data being automatically collected by Chicago's computers opened up rich new possibilities to measure the campaign's impact. "The presidential campaign was just nothing like anything else that ever exists," says Judith Freeman, Obama's new-media field director. "You could try out things with all the data—it was totally just scale."

* * * * *

ON THE NIGHT OF JUNE 3, Barack Obama strode to a podium at the Xcel Energy Center in St. Paul, Minnesota, unsubtly chosen as the place where Republicans would formally nominate John McCain exactly three months later. McCain had already been campaigning against Obama for three months, having vanquished the last of his primary opponents in March. Obama had continued to battle Hillary Clinton during that time, straight through the final primaries in Montana and South Dakota, where polls had just closed as Obama prepared to speak in Minnesota. The race had been decided on the accumulation of delegates, a reality to which Clinton's team had not adjusted until it was too late. "Because of you," Obama said, "tonight I can stand here and say that I will be the Democratic nominee for the president of the United States of America."

In Portland, Oregon, sixty Obama staffers and volunteers watched the speech on MSNBC, making their way through cases of Pabst Blue Ribbon. Obama's campaign had cleared out of its state headquarters in a former Wild Oats natural foods market after his resounding victory in the Oregon primary two weeks earlier, but the workspace still had its computers plugged in, so it became host to a "data camp." The assembled group represented, by traditional campaign standards, a gang of misfits. The only prerequisites for winning an invitation to Portland—and a subsequent job in the new regime—was being "someone who understood field, and the usefulness of data," as Simon put it. By that measure, many arrived in Portland well prepared, having bounced around among primaries in as many as a half-dozen states, each time refining their procedures and trying new things. "They had been working on the most sophisticated campaign in history for a year," says Mike Moffo, the Nevada caucus field director. "That's real experience even if it's your first campaign."

Over the two-week-long data camp, Strasma and Simon led basic training that gave many in the room their only formal introduction to the world of voter files and models. Simon took them through a voter file, projecting a list of individual records onto the wall as though a simple spreadsheet: in the leftmost column, there was the VAN ID, the unique code that a voter unknowingly ported through life. Then columns rained down from left to right, each an individual attribute: an address, gender, age, race, party registration, vote history. Simon would go through a row, using demographics to sketch a person in profile: the young Hispanic woman or the middle-age white man with a Rural Free Delivery address.

"What is this voter?" Simon asked. "Obama or McCain?"

Most of the time it was comically obvious, something anyone with a basic understanding of American politics would intuit. "The human eye is pretty good at figuring it out," says Simon.

Simon would let another column fill in, the result of hard IDs gleaned by volunteers that showed voters' stated preference between the two candidates. But for the 100 voters in the spreadsheet, the campaign had hard IDs for only 10. The task of the modeler, Simon explained, was to direct computers to solve for X, assigning a candidate preference into each of the 90 empty cells based on the 10 that were full. The algorithms that would make those calculations could simultaneously pull in thousands of variables to test for the weight each of them should have in the equation. Strasma had built the core infrastructure with thousands of individual- and precinct-level variables already attached permanently to each record on the voter file. New information that would come in from paid phone IDs could help hone the predictions to reflect enthusiasm levels and preferences specific to the 2008 race.

Carson knew this would put a lot of pressure on the phone vendors who won Obama's lucrative contracts to identify voters, and he worried about their quality. That corner of the political industry had earned a particular reputation for unscrupulous practices, relying on untrained and unenthusiastic call center personnel who were sloppy about how they recorded voters' answers. Campaign staff had long suspected that operators sometimes just made up responses, especially when a voter hung up midway through a script and faking a few answers to the final questions meant not having to throw out the rest of a completed survey. Carson conceived a scheme that within Obama's headquarters was likened to the reality show competition *Survivor,* and those outside it quickly understood why.

In the early summer, the campaign talked to ten of the party's top phone vendors on a conference call and told them they were each getting 10 percent of the nominee's business. Each firm had a different pricing scheme, but the vendors were not going to be judged on price or reputation, as was typically the case. Instead, they were told, they would be tested against one another in real time. Every Sunday night, the Obama campaign would provide each of them a list of VAN identification codes and attached phone numbers, along with a script for callers to use. By mid-day on Friday, the phone vendors would return a spreadsheet of VAN IDs with the voters' answers to the script questions. Each week, the campaign would send out a report to all the vendors that showed how they and their competitors had fared under a "cost-per-opinion" metric that calculated what Obama was actually paying for each call successfully completed. Any firm that underperformed would see their share split among competitors.

After a month, half of the phone vendors were gone. The decision had not been made entirely on relative costs-per-opinion, as they had been told it would be. Obama's team had included a question at the end of each script, asking voters for their age, and often found that what came back from the vendors for that category didn't match up with the date of birth on the voter file. None of the campaign officials who had privately accused phone vendors of fabricating data had ever thought to audit them in the midst of the campaign. There was no way, short of calling voters back and confirming their answers, to see if a call center had accurately tallied their candidate preference, but date of birth was an independently verifiable fact (and, since it came from government registration records, highly reli-able). "It was something they couldn't make up," says Simon.

At the same time, two hundred headquarters staffers were instructed to devise a fictive alter ego that would be given a VAN record and placed, with the employee's actual mobile number, on the lists given each week to the phone vendors. Luke Peterson, the database manager during the pri-maries, became "Joseph Ratzinger," a pro-life hard-liner and political in-dependent who was entirely undecided about whether to support Obama or McCain. Three or four times a day, Peterson's phone would ring and he would answer as Ratzinger; his answers on abortion and his candidate preference would stay stable, but then he was invited to improvise his re-sponses and have fun with accents. Afterward, Peterson would go online and complete a short Web form rating the caller's performance. Did he or she read the script accurately? Was the caller clear and polite?

Five vendors ended up winning a share of Obama's business, and they already appreciated how much more it would demand of them than the typical campaign account. During the primaries, Strasma had treated these paid ID calls as roughly equal in value to the so-called field IDs that volunteers entered into the VAN; they all entered the algorithm interchangeably as indicators of voter support or enthusiasm. For the general election, the number of field IDs available for their calculations would only grow, as Obama's new-media team was working to make it even easier for those willing to place phone calls to do it from their own homes. The new-media team built a calling tool into a prominent feature of the MyBarackObama website, which would automatically assign a volunteer to voters in the nearest battleground state and produce an appropriate script for them to read. They constantly tweaked the design to reduce the number of clicks necessary to actually dial a call, and enlisted a ten-thousand-member National Call Team of committed volunteers who eventually made three million calls through the interface. But over the course of the summer Obama's analysts realized that their candidate was drawing more support among these contacts than ones reached by paid phone banks; people seemed wary of insulting a volunteer canvasser by announcing they supported another candidate, and often lied to say they were undecided instead. The targeting desk decided that the algorithms would have to weight the paid calls far more heavily than the field IDs.

As Strasma explained in Portland, he had designed a system to turn virtual IDs into a continuous process, where individual probabilities moved in a way that accurately reflected that a person's propensity for picking a certain candidate, or voting at all, was subject to near-constant flux. He imagined doing for microtargeting what tracking polls had for the once-static study of public opinion. Pioneered in the 1970s by Bob Teeter and Fred Steeper, those continuous small-sample polls relied on several hundred calls every single night, with each batch of new opinions rolling over one another like lapping waves, so that the older ones bubbled away as they were replaced. They lacked nuance—the calls focused primarily on candidate support—but they captured movement at a price that major campaigns and media organizations could afford.

Already in the primary season, Strasma had seen a hint of how the aggregation of individual microtargeting scores could offer a substitute for polls as a way of tracking opinion shifts. Instead of merely relying on a small sample of voters to say what they felt now, Strasma could use the algorithm to extrapolate how every voter on the file might be moving, then look for patterns in their movement. In early 2008, in states like Iowa that made it easy for non-Democrats to vote in the Democratic primaries, Republican support scores for Obama were always higher than those of his opponents. But in the run-up to the Ohio primary, those scores quickly flipped, and Clinton started pulling higher support scores among Republicans. It wasn't tough to figure out why. On his radio show, Rush Limbaugh was promoting a plan he called "Operation Chaos," to encourage Republicans to cast votes for Clinton as a way of fomenting further conflict within the opposition. Many Democrats were skeptical the stunt would have much impact, but Strasma's changing scores confirmed that voters actually seemed to be following Limbaugh's orders. After Ohio, Obama's campaign all but abandoned its outreach to Republicans.

Strasma believed his algorithm could help Obama make similar strategic decisions in the general election, as well. Typically a campaign would plan to collect a massive batch of paid IDs in the summer so that they could be used to separate persuadable voters from get-out-the-vote targets with enough time to run an aggressive program making the case to the former. But Strasma pushed Plouffe to take the budget for those IDs and spread them out over the entirety of the campaign; he knew Obama's field team would lose some of the precision that comes from having hard IDs on voters but they could make it up with more refined predictive models. Strasma proposed a two-tiered system of IDs that echoed the way the Census monitored population changes. Every week, the Obama campaign would hire call centers to do between 1,000 and 2,000 of what Strasma called long-form IDs per battleground state, which would be closer to a traditional poll, with questions about issues and campaign dynamics. At the same time, the campaign would be doing between 5,000 and 10,000 short-form IDs in each state, quick calls that through as few as two questions did little more than gauge a voter's candidate preference and likelihood of voting. One-quarter of those would always be re-IDs, voters who had been previously contacted and were called again.

After the algorithms worked through the new round of weekly IDs, they would drop a new set of support and turnout scores on every voter's record in the VAN, each of them represented as a percentage probability. After four weeks, Strasma was able to see which voters were moving between candidates. Eventually they had a large enough sample of those who changed from McCain to Obama, and vice versa, that the campaign was able to create a model of these voters they called "shifters." It allowed the campaign to refine its category of "undecided," a catch-all description that long frustrated political scientists and psychologists because it was applied equally to voters who hadn't made up their minds, weren't paying attention, were trying to weigh competing values, or were simply unwilling to share with a stranger what many considered a private matter. Someone who was undecided in June was probably a very different type of voter than one who was undecided in October. Using algorithms to find other undecided voters who looked like shifters (and determine which direction they were likely to go) would help the Obama campaign know which ones were worth targeting, and when to do so.

By the time of the Republican convention in early September, the Obama campaign was placing well over one hundred thousand paid ID calls a week nationwide, with all the data feeding into Strasma's computers. When McCain picked Alaska governor Sarah Palin as his running mate, Obama's strategists were befuddled: they thought the Republican had been gaining traction by highlighting Obama's thin résumé, and he now seemed to be sacrificing that argument by putting forward their own neophyte. But one week after the Republican convention, Strasma saw the first sign that McCain's move might be paying off when the first round of post-Palin IDs came back from phone banks. People were identifying themselves as pro-McCain at a higher rate than their scores suggested they should have been. Strasma bore down into the numbers and saw that the phenomenon was particularly strong among women. Campaign strategists worried that McCain and Palin, running as "two mavericks," may have been proving themselves successful at seizing Obama's themes of change and reform.

When the next round of IDs came in, two weeks after the Palin nomination, the IDs told a different story. The models had begun to integrate the increased levels of support for McCain's ticket, but now the IDs were heading in the other direction, underperforming the scores, especially among Republican women. The modeling scores hadn't caught up to what voters thought of Palin. The disconnect between the two suggested that Palin's selection had offered little more than a temporary bump, as opposed to the permanent boost that McCain's advisers had anticipated. "She ended up being a sugar high for them," says Giangreco, "and she went away as quickly as she came."

That eventually became conventional wisdom among media and the campaigns themselves, but Strasma saw it well ahead of the curve: his perfectly efficient loop of IDs cycling through the algorithm had proven itself a useful tool in the arsenal of measuring public opinion at a high velocity. "You would see things faster than the polling would come back," says Freeman. Once the campaign had developed its modeling score for the action of shifting, it became possible not only to predict what views a voter had but also individual susceptibility to changing them at a given point in the election year. Strasma believed that this predictive modeling gave Obama's staff the tools of the fortune-teller. "We determined that, down the line, they were going to break for us," he says. "We knew who these people were going to vote for before they decided." Now the campaign had to make sure it knew how to reach them.

10

THE SOUL OF A NEW MACHINE

The buses running along the number 6 line in Akron's Metro Regional Transit Authority system often begin their inbound morning trips completely empty. The line's eastern terminus sits along the southwestern edge of that Ohio city, on the sidewalk in front of a Goodwill store in a forlorn shopping plaza so perfectly placeless that the pollster Peter Hart has maintained a permanent storefront facing the JCPenney to host focus groups monitoring a microcosm of the changing American mind.

The bus pulls out of the parking lot and turns past the Akron Springfield Assembly of God church, whose vast grass lawn can often find itself studded with alternating signs promising such varied civic activities as a local Oktoberfest and a Red Cross blood drive. The 6 bus ascends past the oaks and maples that canopy the single-family homes of middle-class, largely white Ellet, and down less verdant stretches of East Market Street that mark the southern edge of Middlebury, one of the city's oldest and most racially mixed neighborhoods. Farther on, the route passes the world headquarters of Goodyear, the tire maker that once made Akron an industrial boomtown, where salarymen pace the sidewalk as they savor their rationed minutes in nicotine's company.

Along the way, the bus gathers passengers—hospital orderlies in teal scrubs, elderly shoppers, students with backpacks and collapsing eyelids—as it rumbles toward the modest skyline of Ohio's fifth-largest city. Two-thirds of the way along its forty-minute route to the Akron Transit Center, the 6 begins to descend the gentle slope that pulls Akron's downtown toward the Ohio & Erie Canal, on which it was founded. The bus disgorges its commuters at the major institutions that keep Akron alive—the orderlies report for their shifts at the Akron City Hospital, students stumble out at the University of Akron, office workers scurry toward the municipal building and courthouse—even as the factories that once sustained the "Rubber Capital of the World" have relocated elsewhere.

In the fall of 2008, riders who didn't devote their commutes to their newspaper or mobile phone might have noticed Barack Obama traveling with them each day. The Democratic presidential nominee gazed triumphantly from one of the 11-by-28-inch cardboard advertisements that lined the bus's interior overhead, accompanied by a message rendered in his campaign's familiar sans serif typeface: "Don't Wait. Vote Early. Our Moment Is Now." In smaller type were a Ohio-specific phone number and website that could offer directions on early-voting procedures, which allowed state residents to cast a vote at their leisure as early as five weeks before the November election.

Obama was at that moment perhaps the most dynamic brand in the country—as omnipresent and approachable as Starbucks, as much an embodiment of the American now as Apple—but the company he kept in the interior of Akron's buses was far less inspiring. Most of the interior ads on Akron's buses are for the Metro system itself, or public service announcements like "Keep Your Baby Sleeping Safe" and "Schizophrenia? Accepting Research Patients Now." In fact, it is rare these days to find any consumer advertising in buses anywhere; those for private businesses speak to a whole different hierarchy of needs, like mental health services or personal-injury law. And yet Obama was there, and it was far from an accident.

Weeks earlier, a data analyst at Obama's Chicago headquarters was reviewing the hundreds of individual-level variables thrown into microtargeting algorithms and realized that one—mass-transit ridership—played an outsized role in predicting which Wisconsin voters were most likely to support Obama. The analyst knew the campaign would already try to mobilize these turnout targets through mail and phone calls, but he thought his new finding pointed to yet one more medium in which it should be able to reach them where they spent time—provided it could be done as efficiently. The analyst alerted one of the campaign's media planners, who called each of the public transit agencies in Wisconsin to see which of them allowed advertisers to target particular routes, stops, or depots instead of covering the whole system at once. Milwaukee did, and so the media planner called over someone from the campaign's graphics department, and together they made a map showing Milwaukee precincts where individuals with high support scores were clustered, and a series of transparencies for each of the city's bus routes. They laid the transparencies atop the support map until they found lines that intersected their target precincts, and sent an order to GMMB, the campaign's lead advertising agency.

Danny Jester, a GMMB vice president and media director responsible for the Obama account, had never processed a request quite like this. Jester placed many of Obama's ads, as his agency had for John Kerry's campaign four years earlier. For a presidential campaign, this typically meant broadcast or cable television, or sometimes radio. Maybe a candidate for city council or county commission would buy bus ads, because they were easier to produce than television spots and intuitively made sense when thinking about geographically constrained electorates, but no one at this level ever proposed putting outdoor advertising on the schedule. Among those who placed political ads, progress had been treated as effectively synonymous with the introduction of new delivery devices. The half-century-long history of refinements in media targeting were a story of technological innovation: moving from buying national ads to local ones in key markets, and then shifting from broadcast waves to cable television, where narrow audiences could be more easily pinpointed. Internet advertising, with its ability to track users' movements through cookies and interests through search engines, was the latest breakthrough.

Obama aggressively bought ads in all of those media, including $16 million in online advertising, among it deep reaches into mobile devices. With no hoopla, however, the campaign also bought bus ads. Milwaukee didn't have the inventory available on the routes Jester requested, but other cities did, and Jester started writing checks. Soon Obama's ads were rolling through select buses in ten cities nationwide, including Philadelphia, Miami, Denver, Flint, and Akron. The most technologically advanced campaign in history had so thoroughly mastered the politics of individual data and testing that it found new value in electioneering tactics many had abandoned as hopelessly last-century. "There's all this shit we used to say no to in campaigns—bus benches, mass-transit advertising, *PennySaver*s, what's that sock they stick the newspaper in?—because we used to do it before TV got dominant," says Larry Grisolano, who coordinated all of the campaign's public-opinion research and media buys. "Now if I know that there are twenty-seven people I want to reach and they all cluster around this bus bench, I'll buy that bus bench. And if I know these twenty-seven people read the *PennySaver,* I'll buy an ad in the *PennySaver*."

* * * * *

ONE OF THE FIRST THINGS Jeremy Bird was handed when he arrived in Columbus in June to be Obama's Ohio general-election director was a series of pages taken from the book that campaign manager David Plouffe called his "bible." The binder had been the principal project that lead targeting analyst Michael Simon undertook with his new team, a series of simple but profound stories outlining Obama's path to victory for every state he was actively contesting.

Vote goals were a staple of any campaign plan, among the initial documents a general consultant or campaign manager would draft in the early days of a race. They were the basic facts on which a theory of the case could be built, but despite their essentially quantitative nature, the numbers were often plucked more or less from the air. A strategist would usually gather past election results from similar races, jigger them to reflect population changes measured by the Census, and then adjust the targets to reflect where things stood that year.

Simon thought there should be a smarter way to make the calculations that would fill the bible. His team had access to new data, from the IDs and microtargeting scores it had generated during the most engaged primary season in modern history. When he assigned his regional analysts to create vote goals for their states, however, he encouraged them to inform their estimates with human intelligence, such as interviews with county party chairmen and local pollsters. Simultaneously, he hoped that his team could approach the task with more data-driven rigor than was typical, while delivering to his pack of statistically minded political debutants a bracing reminder of the limits of data-driven rigor. They needed to understand that some parts of the process, Simon thought, were still "more art than science."

Simon's targeters came back with an estimate of the total number of votes they expected to be cast in each state in November. He sent them back to mine public and private polls and the campaign's own IDs to tally the number of votes Obama could already count on. Then they had to work out Obama's path to 52 percent, far enough over the halfway mark to offer a safe buffer. "What do we need to do here in order to win?" Simon asked them. "What percentage of this victory is going to be boosting turnout and what percentage of it is going to be convincing independents or other people to come our way?" Simon's team split their state goals into three different categories—new registration targets, persuasion targets, and turnout targets—and developed spreadsheets splitting each of them further into geographical and demographic subgroups. As they put the numbers into spreadsheets, it became clear that the path to victory was distinct in each state. Obama could carry Indiana only if he succeeded in persuading Republicans and independents. In Pennsylvania, he could get there just by successfully mobilizing his turnout targets. Nevada had enough new residents in the state that registering them had to be part of the formula.

The Ohio spreadsheet was the handiwork of Dan Wagner, who had been assigned to the Great Lakes/Ohio River Valley pod, which was charged with monitoring the densest concentration of high-stakes battlegrounds—Pennsylvania, Michigan, Indiana, and Ohio—informally known as the "all the states he lost in the primaries" region. This was the toughest assignment of all; it fell to Wagner because he was, in Simon's words, the "purest hybrid of quant and translator" among the numbers geeks. This was a mix of skills he had been forced to develop as a management consultant who had to present his economic forecasts to corporate decision makers. Nothing Wagner produced might be as closely studied by the Obama campaign leadership as his Ohio vote goals. The midwestern state had voted for the winner of every presidential election since 1960, decided by barely 100,000 votes in 2004. Neither party had a reliable strategy for winning the White House in 2008 without it. Wagner's analysis confirmed what many Democrats suspected about their path to victory in the state. Ohio's Democratic base had been ruthlessly raked over by America Coming Together and other independent groups in 2004, leaving little room for the potential registration gains available in other states. Obama would need a set of tactics tilted almost equally toward persuasion and turnout.

Wagner carried the air of the dispassionate outsider, confronting campaign practices for the first time with fresh eyes and an empiricist's skepticism. After February 5, Wagner had been assigned to Ohio and Indiana, where he managed the voter file, and Puerto Rico, where he aided Obama's media-buying team just because he knew enough Spanish to call a radio station and ask about their ad rates. Along the way, he learned how field organizers did their jobs—and the elaborate multilevel structures of state and county leaders presiding over local organizers and the volunteers who talked to voters—and realized that the campaign needed to do a better job packaging its microtargeting scores for these end users. "It was like I was a floor manager at Walmart and I could see how people shop," says Wagner. "Do they look at the top shelf first or the bottom shelf?"

The gap between a campaign headquarters, with its claustrophobic landscape of wall-to-wall carpeting under a drop-ceiling sky, and the world of voters had never been so far apart. Obama's campaign was run from the eleventh floor of a skyscraper abutting Michigan Avenue, buffered from the electorate by building security. Even a decision to open ubiquitous storefront offices was identified in corporate jargon, as "the Starbucks model." When the campaign's Web team wanted to see how normal people responded to their latest innovations, they set out like anthropologists looking to study how natives would handle unfamiliar tools, descending to their building's basement food court with a laptop equipped with Silverback software that could videotape the user's face and track keyboard hand movements.

In the world of campaigns, all politics conducted outside the stale air of headquarters—or the virtual space of broadcast airwaves and the Internet—was referred to as "field." The primary job of a field organizer was cutting turf, as terrain for canvassing was known. By 2008, it made more sense than ever that the world of interacting personally with voters had become suffused with the imagery of agriculture. Both were recalled as pre-industrial practices that seemed to be on their way out of American life just a decade or two earlier, and now enjoyed a resurgence. Like the fad for small-scale urban farming, the notion of people talking to people carried an almost rebellious quaintness, a moral riposte to the tyranny of mechanized mass communication.

As Ohio field director, Bird brought to his tactics a humanistic approach that belied his young age. No one represented the evangelical side of Obama's advocacy as perfectly as Bird, who had grown up in a Missouri trailer park to conservative Southern Baptist parents. As a student at Harvard Divinity School, he had taken a class called Organizing: People, Power, and Change, which he credited with awakening him to the value of politics. The professor, Marshall Ganz, had dropped out of Harvard to register black voters in Mississippi during the civil rights era and went on to serve as an organizer for César Chávez's United Farm Workers and Robert F. Kennedy's presidential campaign in California. Ganz became known for convening meetings in which he would have activists tell the stories of how they came to the movement, a mobilization device Ganz prized as a counterpoint to what he derided as the transactional "politics as marketing" of modern elections. But as television ads and direct mail started to dominate the attention of campaign managers, Ganz withdrew from electoral politics and eventually settled at Harvard, where he was prized as a curio testifying to a lost trade, like a blacksmith continuing to forge tools at a colonial village. Ganz's "personal narratives" were often likened to the stuff of Alcoholics Anonymous gatherings and tent revivals, and the latter fit naturally with the candidacy of a onetime community organizer who had already written a memoir before first seeking office.

A loyal Ganz disciple, Bird preached his mentor's ideas of "motivational organizing." But he also had a modern appreciation for how data could help build new-style structures to support it, a relationship he described to his field staffers as "the yin and yang of organizing." Bird had earned Chicago's notice by directing Obama's shocking primary victory in South Carolina, where Bird controversially ignored the state's culture of mercenary political professionals and built his own network around African-American community hubs like barbershops and beauty salons. Within Obama's campaign, that tactic (which was repeated elsewhere in the country) was lauded for organizing in unconventional locales, but Bird believed that one of the underappreciated keys to the program's success was in the analytics.

For too long, Bird thought, field organizers had collected data on the volume of contacts their teams had made largely for the purpose of impressing campaign higher-ups in memos or bragging to the media about the fearsomeness of their operations. But the metrics-obsessed Obama campaign realized that these figures were not particularly insightful. Who cared how many calls you placed if most of them went unanswered? Or how many doors you knocked if they belonged to voters outside your target universe? When forced to organize in barbershops and salons, however, Bird's field staffers were able to efficiently deploy volunteers only because they adjusted their voter contact data to account for the fact that canvassers were reaching people not at their homes but at other places where they gathered. "There's a myth that if you're using really smart data for targeting, you're therefore marketing and you're not doing people-focused, relationship-based organizing," says Bird. "It hopefully helps our organizers and volunteers talk to the right people, and gives us a better sense of who we're talking to when we call them."

When a field organizer like Bird touched down in a state, one of his first jobs was to divide his area so it could be manageably canvassed. Typically campaigns did this along familiar lines, the indelible boundaries of counties and legislative districts for which both reliable statistics and established lines of political responsibility already existed. But the Obama targeting desk decided that field staff no longer needed to respect the cartographic primacy of parties and political institutions. Wagner believed that, through individual-level modeling, he had successfully disaggregated Ohio into a roster of people who could be reshuffled around the campaign's needs, like its national objective to have such omnipresent field offices that frequent visits would become a matter of routine for volunteers. (Obama would eventually open nearly one hundred of them in Ohio, including five in Cuyahoga County alone.) Wagner's analysis allowed Bird, who would say things like "You have to let the ground tell you when your targeting is working and when it isn't," the ability to survey his turf with an eye for the clumps of the people Obama needed to reach rather than the terrain itself.

Bird settled into the main office in Columbus with Wagner's vote goals spreadsheet and imagined the way he would want his Ohio to look.

He had helped to develop the Obama campaign's field organizing system, a pyramid structure with volunteer neighborhood teams at the bottom. Already the staff organizers responsible for building and managing teams in their regions would have a new tool supposed to transform volunteer recruitment. The targeting team had developed a model that would predict which voters would be most likely to volunteer: those with high support and turnout scores who contacted the campaign were aggressively pressed to contribute their time. Instead of seeing volunteerism as an act distinct from voting, Obama's data team tried to quantify it on a continuum of political behavior. Once a volunteer was on board, Bird would monitor his or her progress along a series of actions that he thought of as adding up to a "leaders test." Those who earned their way into the volunteer hierarchy joined a neighborhood team, each with a lead person and at least three deputies given specific responsibilities: a phone bank captain, canvass captain, a data coordinator responsible for making sure field contacts promptly reached the VAN. (In some places, Bird added a faith liaison to local church communities.)

The goal was to have these volunteers "own their turf," as Bird explained it to them, and that required the neighborhoods to be drawn the way people thought of them. Relying on a targeting-desk analysis of population density, Bird classified every precinct in the state as either urban, suburban, exurban, or rural, and made sure that neighborhoods did not mix categories so that team leaders could master their area—the best way to canvass the housing projects on one side of Youngstown's freeway might be entirely different from the the way to canvass tract houses on the other.

But even though Bird asked volunteers to help generate "best practices" for canvassing neighborhoods, he would not be relying only on their anecdotes and guesswork about efficient voter contact. In early summer, Wagner had tapped the Matrix to develop yet another set of individual-level modeling scores predicting how easy it would be for volunteers to reach a given voter. One, called a canvassability score, measured the odds that a voter would answer his or her door when knocked; a callability score pegged the likelihood he or she would answer the phone. In Indiana, Matt Lackey would go even further, predicting what time of day a given voter was most likely to respond to a call. If you have volunteers in a field office on Tuesday at noon, who do you put on their call sheet to increase the odds that they will get through to people then?

* * * * *

AS OBAMA'S STATE DIRECTORS settled in to their new offices for the general election, several of them were shocked to find a scary number lurking deep in their summer polls. Voters ages eighteen to thirty-five were splitting between Obama and McCain. These young voters were supposedly the bedrock of the Democratic nominee's coalition, having provided the margin for some of his most important primary-season wins. Splitting them with McCain would effectively guarantee Obama's failure, and worry from state headquarters quickly found a home in Chicago, too. Academic researchers had begun to suspect that changes in telephone culture had made it nearly impossible to successfully locate and reliably sample young, mobile voters, but the political world—with its appetite for rapid, cheap surveys—had made few adjustments to compensate. Grisolano decided it was time to solve that problem. He hired Anna Bennett, a pollster outside the triumvirate of survey takers responsible for Obama's polling operation. They had been using the standard method of randomly calling numbers, screening for those likely to vote, and adjusting the sample to ensure it reflected the expected composition of the electorate. Bennett instead specifically went after a sample of eighteen- to thirty-five-year-olds, dialing only mobile phones, a far more costly method. Grisolano welcomed her findings with mixed feelings: Obama's strategic position was safe—he had an overwhelming lead over McCain among younger voters, after all—but the results also showed that the traditional polling method was useless for this demographic. Only 27 percent of Bennett's respondents possessed a landline.

The campaign leadership sent the Bennett poll out to state directors, and the reassuring top-line number had the intended palliative effect. But Bennett's research highlighted a broader challenge Obama's campaign faced: one of its core constituencies could not be easily reached through traditional campaign methods. The voter-file managers went out and bought mobile numbers from commercial vendors, to help ensure that polls and ID calls came out of a realistic sample of the population. Once those phone numbers went into the database, they became grist for the constantly churning algorithms, which found that just having an available mobile number had a predictive power. Cellphone ownership was a proxy for other demographic groups that were established parts of the Obama coalition—the young, the mobile, minorities—and that made identifying cellphone numbers doubly valuable for members of the data team. They eventually took all the phone numbers they had on file, stripped them of the attached voters' names, and sent them out to a commercial database with a request to flag those numbers that belonged to cellphones. (In part because privacy laws regulate mobile phones differently from landlines, they are coded separately.) The data desk now had another variable to help it predict who would be an Obama supporter even if—as was often a problem with caller-ID-equipped cellphones—the person on the other end never answered a call from a volunteer phone bank or professional call center to confirm that informed hunch. The episode was typical of the empirically minded Obama campaign, which was often so ambitious in its troubleshooting of practical concerns that staffers ended up solving problems they didn't know they had.

But the conundrum of how to reach young voters never went away. After working in four states during the primaries, Mike Moffo had invented his own job in Chicago, overseeing "special projects" for the field department, a portfolio he described as "all this cool stuff you want to do as a field director if you have time." Moffo focused on ways to draw new voters into the process, especially young and minority ones, and became known as a font of slightly bizarre ideas that pushed the bounds of where politicians usually took their messages. He studied guerrilla-marketing techniques used to sell albums and liquor, and pored over Big Ten football schedules to find opportunities when two battleground-state schools were playing and it made sense to charter a plane to fly over the football stadium with a banner listing a phone number to call for early-vote information. When modeling scores showed that the presence of a teenager in the household was a variable that made a swing voter more likely to support Obama, Moffo and Michael Organ, a member of Grisolano's media team, schemed to buy space within video games. Soon the early-vote number appeared as advertising in hockey and NASCAR video games; higher-ups said violent games were off-limits for Obama's image.

Each time Moffo had a new idea, he had to shop it around the different departments and find someone to sponsor it. "If you have the purse strings inside a campaign, you're somebody," he says. While waiting to be somebody himself, Moffo tried to build credibility through self-branding. Moffo was obsessed with giving his projects code names, dubbing a canvassing-list cleanup tool "Houdini" and a pre-election volunteer rush "November Rain." He called his new one-person unit "the Jigsaw" and designed a logo that he put on all the presentations he developed for others in the campaign.

As he looked for patrons for each project, Moffo worried that the campaign's willingness to innovate—and to push the stylistic bounds of politics, especially in the service of defining Obama as the cool candidate—was doomed to clash with Chicago's data-centric culture. This conflict was embodied at the top, in Plouffe, who despite his frugality and insistence on proven outcomes often found his ledger flush with cash he considered "Monopoly money"—ready to be freely dispensed to subsidize a culture of inquiry.

In December 2007, Obama's online team decided to test one of the staple elements of its Web splash page: the button accompanying a small form where visitors were asked to submit an e-mail address and ZIP code to join Obama's mailing list. The site had been using the words "Sign Up" on its buttons, but for the experiment programmers created three variants—"Learn More," "Join Us Now," and "Sign Up Now"—and randomly assigned them so that visitors would each see different designs when they arrived at the site. After more than three hundred thousand visits, analysts were able to see that "Learn More" yielded by far the best results, nearly 20 percent more sign-ups than the standard "Sign Up" button. ("Sign Up Now" did slightly worse than the original.)

From that point onward, nearly every time the campaign reimagined its Web splash page or asked for money via e-mail, designers created several options so they could run a randomized experiment comparing them. These A/B tests, as they are known, were straightforward: whichever treatment received more clicks or brought in more money worked best, and would go out to the wider population and contribute to a new set of best practices about winning attention online. There were even glimmers of insight into human psychology; in Iowa, website buttons that said "confirm your caucus location" drew far more clicks than those that said "find your caucus location." ("If you say 'find,' people say, 'I've been caucusing my whole life,'" says Organ.) "Everyone was just 'metrics, metrics, metrics, metrics,'" says Moffo.

He said that with a little less awe than others in headquarters. Moffo was part of a cadre of Obama staffers who saw metrics having a distorting effect on the campaign's priorities; because digital communication was so easy to randomize and measure on a minute-by-minute basis, those who bought online advertising would always have the upper hand in budget debates. It was simply easier to demonstrate results there than in mail or broadcast ads, and certainly easier than in the nontraditional political media that caught Moffo's attention. "The online department doesn't understand this stuff because they understand opening rates on e-mail and fund-raising rates," says Scott Goodstein, who had bounced between music promotion and political campaigns before mixing the two as cofounder of the advocacy group Punk Voter and its related fund-raising series Rock Against Bush. "That wasn't the world I came out of. I understood how you get people to go to a concert or buy a record because they've heard of the band."

In 2006, Goodstein had been one of four organizers behind a massive antiwar march on the National Mall, the crowd rallied almost entirely with digital methods. The next year he joined Obama's new-media team as its external online director, which made him responsible for Obama's digital presence just about everywhere other than his own website. Goodstein established Obama's presence on social media sites like MySpace and Twitter and produced original content for them. By the general election, Goodstein felt there wasn't much more work for him to do on those sites. "You didn't have to convince people to watch a Barack Obama video on YouTube. My initial job was done," says Goodstein. He began to wonder how he could translate his instinct for word-of-mouth communication to reach those young voters, especially non-college-educated ones, who were not active consumers of online political media. "How do I get the offline people?"

He intensified his focus on mobile phones, which were prevalent among youth across class lines and often served as a substitute for a traditional computer. In early 2007, Goodstein had convinced the campaign to spend one thousand dollars a month to rent Obama's surname as a text-message short code, so people could submit information from their phones by typing just 62262 instead of a longer, area-code-specific number. For far less money, Obama could have shared a nondistinctive code with other customers, as Clinton and Edwards had, where messages were routed to a particular destination by a unique keyword. Goodstein successfully argued to the campaign leadership that having a dedicated code would avoid confusion and hassles with the other (usually nonpolitical) customers who would share it. But he eventually realized that it had another benefit: Obama could segregate incoming messages by their content, like those who wrote JOIN from those who wrote GIVE, and track them separately, at no further cost. When he wanted to expand the campaign's list of mobile numbers, Goodstein invited supporters to text the word *Go* to 62262 to win a sticker that read "Got Hope?" When the campaign bought thirty seconds of Super Bowl time in targeted states it used a different code ("text *Hope*") to measure the response of the unconventional ad placement.

Still, Goodstein was disturbed by how rare it was for the campaign to embrace such novelty in its pursuit of a coveted yet elusive demographic group. In June, Obama's media team developed plans for a $30 million television and radio buy targeting young voters. It struck some of those already skeptical of the campaign's youth-marketing efforts as an old person's idea of a young person's ad buy. Most of the spots would go on MTV and Comedy Central, and the aesthetics seemed too conventional to reach nontraditional voters. "What's the difference?" Moffo asked anyone who would listen. "It's the same old ad but has some kids in it and rock-and-roll music." Field director Jon Carson convinced Grisolano to hold off on the buy as he looked for ways to persuade the campaign's leadership to spend the money differently. He realized that there were no bounds to what the campaign would be willing to fund; Organ was messing around with placing ads in movie theaters and kiosks in shopping malls as part of an effort to expand Obama's reach through what the industry called out-of-home advertising. But Carson also knew that if he was going to help Goodstein and Organ commandeer $30 million (or even a chunk of it) toward heretofore unproven communications techniques, they were going to have to devise new empirical methods to prove their effectiveness.

Goodstein's ability to compare text-message response rates offered the metric they needed to redirect the $30 million in the youth-marketing budget. He and Carson began toying with a proposal: before committing the money to TV and radio, how about spending less than 1 percent of it on a field experiment? Moffo put the details into a Jigsaw-logoed presentation, describing a test that could be conducted in August, before the conventions, so that the findings could dictate how money would be spent in the fall. The campaign would budget thirty thousand dollars each to a series of different treatment groups, assigning every medium its own text-message keyword and unique 800 number. They could measure responses-per-dollar-spent, so that the effectiveness of TV ads could be fairly pitted head-to-head against less traditional media. None of the media would be personally targeted, so there wasn't a way to randomize their assignment individually. Separating the buys geographically and comparing Obama's movement in polls across various areas wouldn't help much, either, since the goal wasn't persuading undecideds but rather mobilizing the type of natural Obama supporters the campaign needed to turn out.

Grisolano signed off on the experiment. Now Moffo and Goodstein needed a place to run it. Moffo turned to Ohio, in part because the campaign was less concerned with registering new voters there but understood the value of turning out Obama's base. But most of the reason was the state's leadership: Bird was known as someone who was eager to try new things, and had earned the loyalty of local field staffers, who would have to be counted on to execute some of the nontraditional parts of the experiment.

Bird helped to isolate two Ohio cities reflecting the two major types of young populations Obama was targeting: Columbus, the state's dominant college town, and Cleveland, with its permanent population of young minorities. In each market, Organ would buy cable TV and hip-hop radio ads, as per Grisolano's original plan, and online and mobile-app ads, which could be restricted by geography and specific categories of digital content. Goodstein placed ads in student newspapers and alt-weeklies, as well as on outdoor billboards in carefully selected neighborhoods, and assigned "street teams" of field volunteers to heavily trafficked areas, where they would blanket available surfaces with posters and the polypropylene sheets known as ClingZ. Every medium featured had a "Get a Free Ohio for Obama Sticker" appeal, redeemable by text-messaging 62262. Unlike most candidates, Obama had only rarely given away basic items like stickers; the campaign preferred to sell them, which allowed them to count purchasers as donors and pad their contributor reports. Even so, the prize for the Ohio experiment was something that the campaign thought was appealing enough to lure passive consumers to turn to their phones and send a text message.

As soon as the test was scheduled, Goodstein contacted Shepard Fairey, the street artist who had previously contributed an instantly iconic portrait of a posterized Obama with the word *Hope*. Goodstein wanted permission to use a lesser-known image Fairey had developed specifically for the campaign, with a serious Obama shown in profile above the word *Change*, on the stickers the campaign would be giving away. After a few tweaks, Fairey signed off on the request, and Goodstein had the stickers printed. (Later in the fall, Moffo would prepare a $1 million poster campaign and, relying on internal opinion research that Obama could have an "angry black man" image problem, conclude that Fairey's "Change" likeness was "too severe for GOTV." It became Goodstein's job to tell the artist that the campaign was retiring his famous portrait; Fairey quickly designed a third Obama "Vote" portrait that showed the candidate smiling.)

As it got under way, the experiment became a bit of a bake-off; Goodstein relayed text-message responses hourly, with staffers rooting for their favored mode of contact. When they found that online ads and street teams did best, just about everyone involved in the project exulted. Grisolano erased the television line-item from the youth-advertising budget altogether. Moffo and Goodstein, for their parts, felt as though they could claim victory in a broad, generational battle. They had faced down what had become an unjustified obligation for presidential candidates to mindlessly spend money on television; they had unmasked the medium's inefficiency with new technology and analytics. Only by discrediting establishment tactics, Moffo thought, could politicians truly liberate themselves from establishment money and institutions. "If you can figure out how to do it better, you don't need progressive interest groups or organized labor," he says. "We all had this sense on the Obama campaign that we're changing how politics is done."

*　＊　＊　＊　＊*

UNLIKE SOME CAMPAIGNS, which held their public-opinion research closely among top advisers, the Obama leadership distributed all of the polls they conducted to state-level staff, a degree of openness that became a point of pride for the entire operation. There was even greater satisfaction that not a single number from any of these internal surveys ever leaked, a testament to the "no drama" camaraderie that kept staffers all focused on their common goal rather than pushing personal agendas through the media. So it was a bit out of institutional character that the campaign leadership signed off on a proposal to share all of its private polling with Nate Silver, the amateur statistician whose startlingly accurate electoral forecasts on the blog *Daily Kos* had won him acclaim during the primaries. When Silver launched his own blog, *FiveThirtyEight*, his sympathies for Obama were no secret to readers—even as he claimed his partisan loyalties had no effect on his statistical forecasts—but it was his data-centric approach and skepticism about the existing polling-media complex that won him an obsessive following in Chicago. (When one of Silver's correspondents reported from an Obama field office in Big Stone Gap, Virginia, that 92 percent of the state's neighborhood team-leader slots had been filled, Bird wrote in to say that in Ohio they had reached 93 percent.) Silver had developed a forecasting model that mixed state-level demographic information and available public polls weighted according to their prior reliability, and Obama's targeters wanted to see what would happen if their internal polls were subjected to his formula, as well. After securing a confidentiality agreement from Silver, the Obama campaign gave him access to hundreds of polls it had conducted. "We wanted a little external validation that what we were seeing is what was actually going on," says Simon.

The Obama campaign was blessed with good fortune that demonstrated itself so quietly that its once improbable cause now looks like a matter of historical inevitability. There were a few down moments—a surprise loss in New Hampshire, the emergence of Obama's provocative pastor, the Reverend Jeremiah Wright—but the bigger indicators, like polls and fund-raising figures, almost always pointed up. The campaign's obsessive reliance on data and metrics usually had a calming effect: reality was demonstrable, and not up for debate. Once the system that created the numbers earned people's loyalty, their faith in what the numbers represented naturally followed. But that almost monomaniacal confidence in the ability to accurately measure the vagaries of a presidential campaign tugged a persistent worry in its wake. If one thing was wrong in the ever-complex math undergirding the Obama enterprise—a shoddy source of information entered into the databases, a misplaced coefficient in the algorithm working through them, or an intellectually faulty assumption about how they fit together—an entire chain of tactical and strategic calculations could be flawed.

Such unease dogged the campaign leadership throughout. On the eve of the Iowa caucuses, Plouffe pulled Strasma aside in Des Moines and asked, "So are we going to win?"

"Yes," Strasma replied. "Unless everyone's lying to us."

There was one obvious area where people could be lying. There had never before been a credible black candidate for the presidency. But past opportunities for white voters to cross the color line had produced evidence that they were bashful about acknowledging their hesitation to do so. Throughout the 1980s, as the first black candidates sought major city and state offices, observers noted that polls showing them with large leads seemed to dissolve into lean victories or losses when election day arrived. This became known as "the Bradley effect," after Los Angeles mayor Tom Bradley, a black Democrat who led his white opponent, George Deukmejian, in polls by as many as 15 points in the 1982 California gubernatorial race, only to be defeated by a small margin. One political scientist's later analysis showed that African-Americans running statewide in the late 1980s and early 1990s performed 2.7 percentage points worse than pre-election polls had predicted they would, and white candidates running against blacks began to count on that buffer of latent support to carry them through. "It's just a fact of life," said Bill Roberts, Deukmejian's campaign manager. "If people are going to vote that way, they are certainly not going to announce it for a survey taker."

Early on, there was no suggestion that voters were misleading either Obama's canvassers or public pollsters. "The white Iowa pig farmers were perfectly willing to vote for the African-American," says Strasma. So were their peers in Idaho, Maine, and Wyoming; in fact, Obama ran up some of his most formidable margins in the country's whitest states. But those wins had come in caucuses, which drew from populations of committed party activists, who could be rightfully expected to be more liberal than the general electorate, including on issues of race. Perhaps more crucially, Iowa caucus-goers announced their support in public, which meant that the disconnect of the Bradley effect—between what someone is willing to say aloud to a stranger and what he or she does behind the voting curtain—wouldn't apply.

But in later primary states with greater assimilation, such as Pennsylvania, Strasma sensed that racial attitudes might be pulling Obama down. Unusual patterns "would just bubble up in the models," says Strasma, allowing him to spot specific variables that were exerting an undue influence in predicting candidate preference. Strasma had noticed that high-income white voters in largely black neighborhoods had very high Obama-support scores, while low-income whites in comparable neighborhoods were far less likely to support the black candidate. "If you're high-income and racist, and your neighborhood changes, you move," Strasma theorizes. "If you're low-income and racist, the neighborhood changes and you can't move, you get more resentful and are less likely to vote for Obama."

During the summer, Obama's campaign also found fresh reason to believe that the Bradley effect might be more than a historical artifact. Mike Podhorzer, then the deputy political director of the AFL, called a colleague at the Obama campaign to relay something that had caught his attention. Obama was consistently performing better on polls the AFL conducted with live callers than those, called robopolls, where respondents were prompted by a recording to submit their multiple-choice answers by pressing touch keys. As a result, Podhorzer began tracking the race of the callers at the phone banks who conducted the AFL's polls, and the race of each respondent, looking for patterns between the two. There was one, and it attained the level of statistical significance: Obama repeatedly did better in polls conducted by black callers than those of other races. The AFL's finding reverberated around Obama's headquarters.

Strasma thought that holding racial prejudice was an individual behavior, just like voting or shifting one's preference, and that he should be able to draw up an algorithm to measure its likelihood for every voter in his file. People had all sorts of reasons for preferring John McCain over Barack Obama; maybe they were concerned about Obama's lack of experience or his health-care proposals or always trusted Republicans to oversee foreign policy during wartime. Strasma did not build his models to account for these reasons, merely to predict whether the sentiment was so strong that Obama stood little chance of changing the voter's mind and, if not, what issues could unstick it. He had added a question about gun control to the microtargeting surveys not because it was a big theme of Obama's campaign—in fact, the candidate was unusually quiet on the issue for a Democrat—but because it could help to flag a certain type of likely shifter. Strasma built a model to find voters who were liberal on guns and abortion; even if they were undecided or showed high McCain-support scores, he thought, Obama's campaign should never give up on winning their vote. "When this person pays attention, unless they're nuts they're going to pick Obama," he says.

But racial prejudice appeared to be a different type of block on a voter's part than any constellation of policy issues. It seemed the type of attitude that was irreconcilable, which no amount of new information about McCain's positions or Obama's background could budge. Obama needed to find these people early so that he could give up on them, and not—like Bradley or Wilder or Dinkins—emerge shocked on election day when they quietly cast ballots for his opponent.

During past campaigns, Strasma had built models to pick out individuals with potentially sensitive personal characteristics that were not a matter of public record. When he had tried to identify military veterans for Kerry, in some places—like Iowa, with its county-level tax benefits—it was easy and straightforward. In others, it was roundabout: Strasma had the campaign buy subscriber lists for military-themed magazines, or records of those who had purchased commemorative license plates connected to military service, and fed those into the algorithms. Each of those was an imperfect net for catching veterans, but Strasma was not too worried. If he was catching nonveterans, they looked demographically a lot like veterans and still cared about military affairs. If they got a brochure describing Kerry's military service and attacking Bush's handling of veterans' hospitals, what was the harm?

Yet Strasma also had experience with cases where that kind of false-positive modeling had significant risk. For years, like many of those who targeted voters for Democrats, he had been trying to find a way to profile gays and lesbians so campaigns could speak to them directly on issues of specific interest. The common method was some version of looking on the voter file for two adults of the same sex but different last names living at the same address with birth dates within a decade of each other, a mix of variables that usually sorted out parent-child or sibling combinations. It could not account, however, for people of close age living together platonically, leading to a legendary (and possibly apocryphal) instance in which a campaign ended up targeting some of its gay-themed mail to pairs of roommates at a military academy. Then in 2000, the Census Bureau began to offer an option on its long-form survey for respondents to identify themselves as part of same-sex couples, which were counted in block-group-level profiles. Strasma added the intensity of gay couples in one's neighborhood to sharpen the algorithms predicting if an individual was gay, but also used it to reduce the damage of a false positive. Heterosexuals who lived in significantly gay neighborhoods, he assumed, were less likely to take umbrage at receiving literature addressing gay issues.

Now, as he tried to quantify racism for the Obama campaign, Strasma was in essence looking for a different kind of false positive. He started by focusing on people whom the algorithms positively identified as someone who should be a likely Obama supporter, on the basis of their demographic and political qualities, but answered ID calls by saying they were backing McCain. To build a model that could predict which voters might be biased against his candidate, Strasma had to identify a variable, or a combination of variables, that explained that gap. At one meeting, one member of the targeting staff with little political background suggested just adding a battery of new questions, including "Are you racist?" and "Does racism affect your vote choice?" Strasma shook his head. (That's one of the problems with hiring campaign staff directly from computer science or statistics backgrounds, he thought.) Already pollsters were wary of even inquiring about respondents' race in polls; when they did it was often the last question, after asking about income, so that if the respondent hung up the whole survey wouldn't be ruined. Strasma knew that any question that successfully uncovered a voter's racist sentiment would have to be more sly. He needed to find a publicly available data point that would be an efficient proxy for asking people one of the most indelicate questions in American life.

Strasma tried adding questions about a few different policy issues considered racially-tinged, like affirmative action, but they didn't yield useful patterns in the modeling. So he started paying close attention to the focus groups that David Binder, a San Francisco–based opinion researcher, conducted all over the country. Each night Binder or one of his deputies would moderate a session, which typically lasted an hour, with undecided voters in a different battleground state. Some days, Binder would read statements from the candidates to hear what voters thought of them. Other times he would show the latest ads, or a series of mock anti-Obama ads that the campaign's media consultants would produce to test voters' reactions and audition countermessages. Sometimes Binder would just ask open-ended questions to guide a conversation.

Each of the focus groups was broadcast via the Internet to a room in Chicago, where members of the campaign's different departments could wander in and watch. For senior staffers who had given their lives over to Obama's quest, the focus groups were nightly prime-time entertainment.

Someone would head off to a local supermarket for snacks and a group would settle in for the session, fortified with peanut M&Ms. One night Binder asked, "Do you think your neighbors would be willing to vote for an African-American for president?" Some of the voters answered no, and Strasma watched them closely. Something in that response—perhaps a feeling of being liberated to publicly share an unpopular opinion—convinced him that the people who acknowledged their neighbors' racism might really be confessing a view of their own.

Strasma added the neighbors question to his survey and saw quickly that it worked. Those who had high Obama-support scores but ended up backing McCain said yes to it, so Strasma made it the core of a new "openness" model: another score, out of 100, that assessed how open a voter would be to casting a ballot for a black candidate. Those voters with low openness scores and mid-range turnout scores could be removed from Obama's contact universe altogether, for fear that contact from Obama could have a backlash effect and make them more likely to turn out for McCain. Those with high turnout scores were fairly likely to be voting already, so Strasma thought it may still be worthwhile to try to make a pitch to them. "We knew it wasn't going to be the same motivation message that was working with African-Americans or young people or antiwar voters," he says. So instead of mail with "Change" themes he thought the campaign could send them something with a very straightforward economic message. "That message made sense on the gut level for those voters," says Strasma, "and based on what we were able to see it worked better."

But the openness score was most useful as yet one more variable being added to the hundreds already on Strasma's computers. When added to the models, a low openness score would pull a voter's overall support score down to account for the likelihood that his or her willingness to ultimately vote for an African-American had been overstated. It worked in much the same way that the pro-choice and gun control scores did, only in the opposite direction: a way of correcting for the inability of voters to be as honest and self-aware as pollsters like to pretend they are.

The targeting desk felt confident that it had identified a statistical fix for what had been the biggest uncertainty hanging over its inability to accurately predict voters' preferences. Still it did not fully calm nerves in Chicago. The models had been early to pick up the jolt Sarah Palin delivered to the race, and after the mid-September collapse of Lehman Brothers and the subsequent financial crisis, they saw her influence subside and the race stabilize. The targeting desk would circulate weekly reports to Plouffe and the campaign leadership, with one chart becoming preeminent: a histogram that showed how the campaign's weekly ID calls matched up against the modeled support scores. By October, the charts were reliably producing the elegant step function that analysts wanted to see—voters were telling callers that they supported Obama at the same rate that the algorithms predicted they would. "I was surprised by how unsurprised I was," says Strasma. They would have to wait for election day to get the only further confirmation possible.

* * * * *

THE ROOM SQUEALED when Barack Obama walked into the Greater Columbus Convention Center, where 750 Ohio volunteers had gathered for a daylong training seminar in October. They had expected an immersion in the art of winning votes Obama-style, but not an encounter with the man himself. "We've been designing and we've been engineering and we've been at the drawing board and we've been tinkering, and we've been— now it's time to just take it for a drive," Obama said, as people mounted chairs for a better look at their candidate. "Let's see how this baby runs."

Election day was less than one month away, but the campaign was already producing votes at full thrust. Obama had put a particular emphasis on early voting, which many states had introduced since 2004 to alleviate pressure on their election day operations. Such a service, which often gave people the freedom to cast their ballots either by mail or in person for as long as a month, was almost perfectly catered to the needs of the Obama electorate. First-time and minority voters who might be overwhelmed or intimidated at a polling place, and those too busy to contend with long lines on election day, could do so at a less harried time. Election officials would produce a daily list of those who had voted early, and Obama's tacticians pored over those rolling returns. Getting likely supporters to cast an early ballot locked in their votes and allowed them to be removed from target universes for future mail, phone calls, and canvassers, so the campaign could expand its energies elsewhere. Then the fact that a person had voted early could be used as one more data point to refine projections of who would actually turn out.

Two weeks before Obama's visit to Columbus, a plane carrying an early-vote appeal had floated over the city's Ohio Stadium during an Ohio State–Minnesota football game—the fruit of one of Moffo's many gambits—and buses had begun to roll through Cleveland, Canton, Youngstown, and Akron with the same message. When the soul singer John Legend offered to perform on Obama's behalf, the campaign made sure one of the stops was a midday concert on a modest amphitheater stage in Legend's hometown of Springfield—because the data team's projections suggested Springfield, midway between Columbus and Dayton, was lagging larger neighbors in early-vote participation rates. "We never would have put John Legend in Springfield if we hadn't seen that," says John Hagner, the Ohio Democratic Party's voter-file manager.

The confidence Obama demonstrated before his troops was grounded in his campaign's success at audaciously remaking the political world. It had redrawn states to reflect a preferred geography, redefined individuals and households through algorithms, put political messages where no one ever thought they had a place—but elections were still conducted in the old world. No matter how much Obama believed that his organization had reinvented the machinery of politics, it still had to contend with the existing infrastructure of elections. Votes needed to be cast on paper or behind a curtain, and the institutions that handled those votes could not handle data as nimbly as the MyBarackObama calling tool or Strasma's algorithms. So the Obama campaign turned that lag into a tactical advantage.

Plouffe's decision in early summer to strike a deal to buy data from Catalist was met with suspicion by many in Chicago, since it meant bypassing free access to a national voter file that had been assembled by the Democratic National Committee at significant cost. But being one client among many in Catalist's portfolio of progressive institutions allowed the campaign to create seamless links across the activist left, including outside groups with whom candidates were legally prohibited from coordinating directly. When Democracia USA collected a new voter's registration form in Florida, Obama's targeting team often knew about it before the local board of elections. Democracia would create a record in its databases, which synced daily with Catalist's servers. When the Obama campaign conducted its daily download from Catalist's database, per its contract with the information vendor, the new record would show up in the VAN. The campaign could start treating the person as a voter—assigning model scores, canvassing her, communicating by mail and phone, or getting her an absentee ballot—even before the registration had been officially processed. Republicans wouldn't have any idea the new voter even existed until she went on the books.

Moffo set out to build a system that would allow Obama's field staff to extend its continuous profiling of the electorate straight through the moment the polls closed. Even the campaigns that were best at tracking their voters usually lost the trail on election day. The Iowa Democratic Party, known for one of the country's most efficient general-election vote-rendering operations, had for a generation relied on multiple stacks of cards printed with the name of every Democratic voter. At the polling place, as the judge of elections marked the name of an arriving voter, the person's card would be thinned from the deck. Seven times a day, a runner would get the cards and deliver them to volunteer door-knockers who, three times over the course of the day, did sweeps of houses. Cards still left in the pile at the end of the day would get passed to callers at a phone bank for one last contact. Other local party organizations had their own versions of Iowa's cards.

Moffo believed that new technology had become possible for the names of those who had voted to instantly disappear from a GOTV walk list or call sheet, and thus was born his new system, Project Houdini. (Four years earlier, campaigns tried to automate the procedure with Palm Pilots, but the devices had to be plugged into wired computers to download the information and move it into databases.) Each voter in a precinct was given a four-digit code, and as soon as he or she cast a vote, an Obama worker assigned to the polling place would punch in an update by phone to automatically tag the voter's name in the VAN. As a result, field directors could continuously hone their election day GOTV programs in real time, ensuring that volunteers were dispatched to rouse only nonvoters. As that process freed capacity throughout the day for more contacts, field directors could move past their list of initial targets to include voters with lower turnout scores who were thought to be more of a reach.

Houdini worked magnificently during the morning rush on the East Coast, and a half million people who voted before 9 a.m. were disappeared from future target universes. Hundreds of thousands of people across the country were helping to turn citizens into voters on Obama's behalf—some walking their neighborhoods, others joining the National Call Team from their home computer and phone—and none of them were wasting their time talking to people who had already cast a ballot. By midmorning, those monitoring turnout operations from Chicago saw Houdini begin to slow: as voters began arriving at West Coast polling places, they overwhelmed new phone lines that had been installed at headquarters to handle the expected heavy volume. By 10 a.m., the whole system had locked up, turning away new callers. Moffo hectored the phone company, which told him it was too late to lay additional cables. Others concocted work-around fixes, like having poll workers call a local field office so voters' records could be updated manually by computer there.

On the other side of headquarters, the campaign's new-media team watched National Call Team volunteers continue to log on to the MyBarackObama site to make GOTV calls. Their numbers barely slowed even as the wave of states going blue moved west across the country. News organizations would not formally call the election before polls closed on the West Coast, but their coverage assumed a foregone conclusion: Obama would be the next president, and would get there by vastly exceeding the necessary 270 electoral votes. The technologists were amazed to see that, even as it became evident that the race had been decided, the number of volunteer callers surged. The minute the last polls closed in the continental United States, all the TV networks simultaneously declared Obama the victor. The eleventh floor echoed the exultations made by the quarter-million people celebrating in Grant Park a mile away.

Eventually Uday Sreekanth, the deputy chief technology officer, looked back at his computer screen and saw that MyBO was still clogged with National Call Team volunteers looking to do their parts. He performed some quick calculations and thought about the number of minutes left for voting in the country's newest states. Hawaii, where Obama had been born, was likely to deliver his largest margin of victory, but onetime target Alaska had fallen off Obama's map when its governor had joined McCain's ticket. "We have the capacity to call every voter in Alaska three times, and really embarrass Sarah Palin," Sreekanth alerted his colleagues. "Should we pull the switch?"

They decided not to, and walked away from their screens filled with data, down the elevator, and out onto Michigan Avenue, where they were captured by a stream of people—each one believed at that very moment to be 100 persuasion, 100 turnout, and 100 openness—all headed in the same direction.

EPILOGUE

PUSHING THE ENVELOPE

Barack Obama's election took place exactly one decade after Alan Gerber and Don Green had taken to the streets of New Haven to run their pioneering electioneering field experiments at Yale, and even forward-thinking Republican operatives found something to cheer in the way his ascendance represented a triumph for new-wave empiricism over the reactionary, clubby old campaign world. Finally an industry that had been chronically unreflective about its failures was obsessed with learning from Obama's success. Naturally this swung all too quickly to its own thoughtless excess: any operative with the most fleeting connection to the Chicago operation was reborn as a political celebrity, and any tactic that could be marketed as "Obama-style" found immediate global demand. Meanwhile, the earliest revolutionaries—the social scientists and statisticians who had laid the intellectual foundation for Obama's victory even as they stood apart from it—continued to work away at a fundamental question the field had not yet fully answered. By digging even deeper into psychology and the behavioral sciences, they hoped to finally crack the code of what can turn a person into a voter.

In the spring of 2007, as the Obama campaign was opening its first Iowa offices, Alan Gerber had written to Hal Malchow to let him know he was coming to Washington, and the two arranged to get dinner. The Yale political scientist arrived at the downtown steakhouse Morton's accompanied by a surprise guest, a Harvard graduate student on whose dissertation committee he had just served. But the presence of Todd Rogers wasn't the only evidence that Gerber's attentions had recently swerved dramatically toward questions of voter psychology. Once they were seated and had specified the temperatures for their steaks, Gerber detailed an experiment he and his collaborator Don Green had just completed with Mark Grebner, the Michigan voter-file manager who had gleefully threatened to out nonvoters. Malchow's eyes opened wide as Gerber described the four different versions of Grebner's postcard, and the staggering result that the "neighbors" approach had delivered—three times better than any other technique in the bulging mental archive Malchow maintained of hundreds of voter contact experiments.

Malchow had been one of the first political consultants to fully embrace the use of randomized field experiments, but his relentless commitment to following their findings had not always been good for his business. Even if Gerber and Green's experiments had shown mail could be effective, their preferred efficiency metric of dollars-per-additional-vote highlighted how costly it could be to get the desired results. (This was supposed to measure the price of mobilizing a marginal voter, calculated by dividing the return from a given get-out-the-vote technique over the cost of delivering it.) When the academics compiled dozens of varied mail experiments, they found that it took 333 pieces of mail to turn out one new vote. Malchow added design, printing, and postal fees and realized that the product his firm marketed to campaigns cost them eighty dollars per new vote.

Instead of masking this unpleasant fact, Malchow loudly chastised employees who persisted in preparing get-out-the-vote mail, even though much of his firm's revenue depended on it.

But the Michigan experiment showed it was possible to improve that math dramatically: you had to show only twenty citizens copies of their neighbors' voting histories to convert a new vote. This arithmetic warmed Malchow, who saw in Grebner's social-pressure breakthrough both redemption and opportunity. Here at last was get-out-the-vote mail that worked, and fabulously so.

"Alan," Malchow said across an expanse of white tablecloth. "I will pay you a hundred thousand dollars if you won't publish the results."

Gerber turned away Malchow's only half-joking proposal, but he agreed to show his dinner companion the experimental materials well before they would become public in the *American Political Science Review*. Malchow rushed to take advantage of the head start he had been given to master social pressure. The next election on his firm's calendar was a Dallas municipal election, working with a gay and lesbian group doing independent advocacy on behalf of a candidate running to be the city's first openly gay mayor. The group refused to embrace the approach of revealing neighbors' vote histories, for fear of inflaming an already delicate contest; the best Malchow could do was persuade them to mimic Grebner's "self" mailing, which includes only voting records for those within the receiving household. Even so, the group braced for an unfavorable response, creating a front group with an anodyne name and a decoy return address. They were right to fear a backlash; a local Fox television affiliate tracked the mysterious letters to a Mail Boxes Etc. location that Malchow's clients had used as their address, and parked a camera crew outside on an ultimately fruitless stakeout. "I don't think anyone went back there for two months," Malchow says.

Malchow knew that the candidates, party committees, and major institutions that made up most of his clientele would not find similar glee in resorting to such stealthy tactics. The social-pressure technique needed refinement if he was going to put it into wider use, and so Malchow turned where he often did when he had an idea he wanted to test. The group Women's Voices Women's Vote had been established by Page Gardner in the wake of the 2000 election, when strategists in both parties began to prioritize turning out their known supporters instead of hunting for swing voters to win over. Gardner had been startled to see exit polls expose what she considered a "marriage gap," a staggering split in voting behavior between married women and unmarried ones. The latter were among the most loyal Democratic blocs but among the least likely to actually vote. Commercial database vendors did not maintain reliable lists of who was married and who was not, and so Gardner hired Malchow to see if he could use statistics to predict whether an individual was single. Malchow liked the puzzles this challenge posed: if two people of similar ages live at the same address, how do you tell if they're married and not roommates or siblings?

With the 2008 campaign looming, Gardner expanded the group's mandate to focus on other parts of what she called the "Rising American Electorate," including not only unmarried white women but Latinos, African-Americans, and young voters of both genders. Together they comprise 53 percent of the voting age population, but they are chronically underrepresented at the polls. The question wasn't whether they would vote Democrat or Republican, but if they could be made to vote at all. (Even though the group was officially nonpartisan, for tax purposes, there was no secret that the goal of all its efforts was to generate new votes for Democrats.)

To placate the Women's Voices donors who would have to back the new social-pressure technique, Malchow set out to find more delicate language that could maintain the implied threat without making the recipient feel like he or she was under investigation. He designed an experiment to take place in the Kentucky governor's race that fall, replicating the original Michigan experiment. Malchow, however, added a new twist that went beyond the one-way communication of Grebner's mail. One group would get phone calls asking if they were planning to vote in the November election. Those who said yes were sent a simple letter restating that commitment followed by a robocall just before election day reminding them that they had pledged to vote as part of a study that would check on their follow-through afterward. It ended up being a small group—only 30 percent of those initially contacted said that they intended to vote—and a complicated technique to execute. But while the sequence of calls and mail was expensive up front, the return was so good that it proved a relative bargain, producing new votes at eighteen dollars each.

Women's Voices donors signed off on this new so-called Promise technique, and Gardner included it in the group's plans for turnout operations in 2008. At the same time, Malchow giddily went to an Analyst Institute lunch with PowerPoint slides documenting the Kentucky test, hoping that his peers at other liberal groups would be as eager to put social pressure to work in their 2008 voter contact programs. The institute later promoted Promise as part of its best practices for improving turnout rates. But even the members who found the experiment fascinating also found it hard to imagine such manipulation finding a place in the political toolbox—they couldn't visualize their name as the return address on a letter that told voters they were subjects in a study, even if it worked.

Malchow knew he had more work to do if he was to find a way of provoking anxiety in people for not voting without antagonizing them. "This is the frontier—thinking about ways to do this that are unoffensive," says Malchow. What if instead of embarrassing people for not casting ballots, he just sent a list of their neighbors who voted all the time? He mentioned this idea to Green, who referred Malchow to Costas Panagopoulos, a former Yale postdoctoral researcher who had collaborated on research with Green at the time of his Michigan experiment with Grebner.

Panagopoulos had already been investigating other forms of social surveillance, such as the increasing affection that law enforcement officials had for publicizing the names and images of sex offenders, johns, and those delinquent on child support payments. Along the way, he learned about two newspapers that had applied a similar logic to citizenship. In 1994, the *Dallas Examiner* published local electoral rolls with an indication of who had voted in a recent election and who hadn't. Before the 2006 elections, the *Tennessee Tribune* ran its own list of nonvoters in selected Nashville city council districts. The papers, both targeted at local African-American communities, claimed that they had boosted turnout when they introduced the disclosure program in their pages.

Panagopoulos decided to put the method to the test. He identified three small midwestern towns that would be conducting nonpartisan municipal elections in November 2007 and randomly selected households in each to receive pre-election postcards. In Monticello, Iowa, and Holland, Michigan, the cards told recipients that a list of those who voted would appear in the local newspaper after the election. "The names of voters who did not vote will *not* be published because only voters deserve special recognition," the cards read. In Ely, Iowa, postcards made the opposite threat: the local paper would publish a roster of deadbeats only. "The names of those who took the time to vote will not appear on this list," Ely voters were told.

Local election officials traced the letters back to Panagopoulos before he could run the post-election ads, and persuaded him not to follow through on his vow to do so. But citizens who received the letters would have had no way of knowing that, and when he was able to look back at the voter file after November he saw, as he expected, that the threat of shaming was far more potent than the promise of praise. Ely residents who received the postcard were nearly 7 points more likely to vote than those in the control group; turnout in Monticello and Holland increased by 4.7 points and 0.9 point, respectively. The impact in Monticello was only half as robust as the strongest of Grebner's Michigan letters but still nearly six times better than the traditional-style GOTV mail that had wanly reminded prospective voters of their civic duty.

Panagopoulos started reading from the expanding portfolio of research being assembled by behaviorally minded economists who had found that expressions of gratitude helped to stimulate what they described as prosocial behavior. (In one field experiment, two psychologists found that restaurant servers whom they directed to write "thank you" on their bills received larger tips from customers.) Panagopoulos, then teaching at

Fordham University, set up an experiment to take place in a New York City Council special election scheduled for February 2009. He identified single-voter households who had participated in the city's last municipal election just over three years earlier, and sent around two thousand of them a postcard thanking them for having done so, and included a reminder about the upcoming special election. Those who received it ended up voting at a rate 2.4 percentage points higher than a control group receiving no contact. (Another group got just a postcard with an election reminder but no expression of gratitude; it had barely any impact on turnout.)

But most amazing to Panagopoulos was the silence. His surveillance hadn't triggered any response—no disgruntled local election officials or righteous local television crews or death threats. When news of this trickled back to East Lansing, Grebner's satisfaction at the influence of his approach was tempered by disappointment that decorum seemed to be winning the day. "We've now found forms that are nearly as effective that don't turn people ballistic," he says. "Although it still turns out that making them ballistic—boy, is that powerful!"

Malchow had had the idea of generating an "honor roll," a roster of voters who never missed an election, and which would be sent to their neighbors. After Malchow learned about Panagopoulos's work, the two partnered to compare their approaches in an experiment in New Jersey before voting there in 2009. Working with a labor-backed group defending Governor Jon Corzine against a challenge from Republican prosecutor Chris Christie, they sent out twenty-three thousand letters. Half contained Malchow's honor roll, and half Panagopoulos's declaration to recipients that "we hope to be able to thank you in the future for being the kind of citizen who makes our democracy work." Both proved effective, with the "Thank You" letter increasing turnout by 2.5 points among recipients, and the Honor Roll by 2 points—the first costing just more than eleven dollars per additional vote. Since it was upbeat and congratulatory and threatened no future surveillance, there seemed to be no downside at all. When Malchow presented the New Jersey experiment at the Analyst Institute, he finally saw his excitement reflected in his audience. "People lit up about that," he says. "Because anyone can send a letter that says 'thank you for voting.'"

Lighting up an Analyst Institute luncheon no longer amounted to impressing a small group of Malchow's geek peers, but was now a method of directly inserting a new idea into the campaign plans of leading national Democrats. Obama's inauguration had ushered in a new Democratic establishment in Washington, its rise bringing the data-driven crowd in from the outside. Hundreds of people were now cycling through the lunches and weekend retreats, an expanded audience that perhaps counterintuitively made participants even more eager to share their private research. Where better to show off? Many of the young staffers who had learned analytics on the Obama campaign had moved into top party jobs and reviewed the Analyst Institute presentations with commensurate authority and budgets.

When Malchow delivered the New Jersey results, it caught the attention of an operative from the Democratic National Committee, the same organization that Malchow had vainly tried to convince of the value of testing pre-election mail since Bill Clinton's first presidential campaign. In the spring of 2010, before a special election for a Pennsylvania U.S. House seat, the Analyst Institute advised the DNC on its own version of the thank-you test. The experiment found that having the state's popular senator Bob Casey tell voters on his letterhead that "our records indicate that you voted in the 2008 election"—and thank them for their "good citizenship"—helped nudge them to the polls this time. Analyst Institute members who had scoffed at harder-edged versions of social pressure were now eager to use it in the field. The approach may have been psychologically manipulative, but it no longer felt that way. "Volunteers were excited to deliver a thank-you message," says Regina Schwartz, the institute's outreach director.

By election day 2010, tens of millions of social-pressure mailers, in slightly different versions, were sent out by campaigns in both parties. Many had no ties to Gerber and Green or the Analyst Institute world, but merely took their core finding that social pressure worked and improvised.

In one case, Utah Republican Mike Lee's Senate campaign e-mailed supporters with a list of other voters in the same precinct who had a record of turning out in presidential elections but not in off years. "These voters do not understand the importance of mid-term elections and the direct impact their vote can have on our state," the e-mail from the Lee campaign read. "We need to inform these voters!"

Suddenly, the use of social pressure as a turnout trick was so widespread that Gardner was describing it as "the hula hoop of American politics." Even though the right did not have anything like the Analyst Institute to distribute such research in the form of simple recommendations, new techniques and tactics still moved from one operative to the next, or outward through the influence of officials at the party campaign committees. Whoever drafted the letter for Mike Lee's campaign would probably pass it on to dozens of other Republicans by 2012, when they could use it to rouse their voters. Any competitive advantage the left had gained would likely fade, and as voters became aware of the letters the psychological impact of receiving one would weaken. The pressure was on Malchow to find something new.

* * * * *

SIX MONTHS LATER, Malchow eased his new Chevy Volt out of the garage of his suburban Virginia home, whose backyard tumbled down onto the banks of the Potomac River, and drove to the Service Employees International Union headquarters near Dupont Circle in Washington. Malchow had purchased the electric car for all the usual lefty reasons, but it was not a sense of social responsibility that most tickled him about being a Volt driver. When the Chevy dealership offered Malchow a chance to participate in a Department of Energy program that would install an advanced recharging station in his home at no cost in exchange for being able to analyze the data it collected about his driving habits, he said yes without hesitation. Malchow has a guileless disinterest in privacy concerns when a trove of new data hangs in the balance, and he was plainly pleased to have stumbled into an experiment, even as a subject.

These days, Malchow's focus was on promoting a young-adult fantasy novel he had coauthored with his dyslexic teenaged son and beginning work on another. The challenge of selling a youth genre book fascinated Malchow, and he gave the impression of being more satisfied by drafting the marketing plan than he had been by the narrative itself, which grew out of the bedtime stories he began concocting with his son, Alex, when the boy was eight. Alex was now a high school football player, and at book readings he evinced a visible discomfort at being continually implicated in this vestigial preadolescent project, wincing as his father volubly declared his plans to pursue a sequel.

It was a Wednesday morning, and Malchow was in the unusual position of not having an office to go to. The previous November, on the eve of the midterm elections, he announced he was disbanding MSHC Partners, which had been one of Washington's most successful consulting operations for two decades and a preferred mail vendor for four consecutive Democratic presidential nominees. (He had worked for Hillary Clinton in the 2008 primaries.) Malchow was accustomed to the rough-and-tumble of the business, but for him it had finally gone too far. He decided he would get out of the day-to-day of campaigns, disturbed that they often consisted of little more than strategizing how "to smear some poor guy with different beliefs."

Many who received Malchow's e-mailed announcement were shocked by it, but they rolled their eyes when they got to the part where he declared that "politics is not what it was when I started 25 years ago." His claims of a conversion were disingenuous, some said, rumoring instead that he was easing out of the business for commercial reasons and grasping for a noble rationale to cloak his desperation. Even as Malchow insisted that 2010 had given the firm among its biggest revenues ever, there were signs that his business model had grown unsustainable. A major problem was the way Malchow's instincts for entrepreneurship and self-promotion could frequently be at odds with each other. He would eagerly run experiments and research projects to develop new techniques, often at significant cost, but then instead of guarding the findings for competitive advantage would rush to present them at Analyst Institute meetings. "The repercussions were that other people copied and sold it," says Joel Rivlin, the director of analytics at Malchow's firm. "Hal made his money. He always wants to push the envelope and bring everyone else with him because he thinks we can always do this stuff better." Meanwhile, the firm's corporate infrastructure grew so large (a five-person HR department, for example) that the roster of clients had to grow every year just to cover the overhead, a demand that employees described as "feeding the beast."

Malchow noted in his announcement that he did intend to maintain one political client "I especially admire." Everyone who knew the contours of Malchow's enthusiasms understood he was referring to Women's Voices Women Vote. The group's limited focus on increasing participation and not persuasion meant it was always working on the easiest thing in politics to cleanly measure—the electoral rolls keep good track of who's registered and who turns out—and so nearly from its outset Gardner decided that Women's Voices would impose a sense of metric accountability on its operations. "We're not big on exhortation," she says. "We're big on proving." The group's annual summits, a parade of academics and consultants showing off their latest research breakthrough on a series of PowerPoint slides, were part of the identity Gardner had worked to build as she fought to engage donors who had many other liberal organizations angling for their dollars. "Some of it is just Page showing off, for the community: here's what we're up to," Malchow said. "Bring people in so they'll do more stuff with you."

But it was that "stuff"—including running more than one hundred field experiments since the group's founding—that won Malchow's heart: Women's Voices had impressed him as perhaps the most empirically minded of all the institutions and candidates for whom he had worked in twenty-five years. "They have the best agenda of everybody out there," said Malchow. When he shut down his firm, Malchow saw no reason to cut his ties to Women's Voices. In fact, its research agenda seemed the best way for Malchow to relieve himself of the corporate hassle while keeping his hand in the one part of politics where he believed he could still make a difference: the semisecret cabal of social science experimenters that he considered the only hope for imposing accountability on the multibillion-dollar industry that helps Americans choose their leaders.

Yet when Malchow arrived at Gardner's 2011 summit, he was quickly bored by what felt like another PowerPoint-intensive reminder of how poorly Democrats had fared in the prior year's midterm elections. Pollster Celinda Lake navigated slides showing that, while the Rising American Electorate represented 46.6 percent of the electorate when Obama was elected in 2008, the share had fallen to 41.9 percent two years later. Women's Voices registered one million people in 2008, but two years later few of them bothered to cast a ballot; only 3 percent of the people Women's Voices contacted during the 2010 elections had ended up turning out. Everyone in the room knew the implication of those numbers: unless Democrats could figure out by 2012 how to reanimate this core part of their coalition, Barack Obama would have a very difficult time winning a second term. "The key fight," says Gardner, "is: who's in the electorate?"

The presentations dragged on, and Malchow perked up only when he heard an old friend describe a novel tool for getting registered voters to turn out to cast ballots. In his presentation, Alan Gerber told of stumbling upon a question in a 2005 Michigan survey in which nearly one-fifth of voters said they believed that their vote choice was not secret. Other national polls showed as many as 27 percent of people shared that view. When they were asked, "How difficult do you think it would be for politicians, union officials, or the people you work for to find out who you voted for, even if you told no one?" only 12 percent said it would be impossible. The finding was consistent across three surveys, and it floored Gerber, who had begun his career by studying the introduction of the secret ballot to American politics in the late nineteenth century. The end of public voting coincided with a dramatic, and not fully understood, drop in turnout rates. (The share of the population voting dropped from nearly 80 percent in 1896 to 65 percent eight years later, and never recovered.) Gerber wondered if nonvoters simply didn't trust, or understand, the idea of confidentiality at the heart of the process. Gerber commissioned his own survey. Among adults who had never voted, 20 percent expected their ballot to be marked so it could be identified as their own, and 12 percent thought that upon arrival at a polling place someone would ask for whom they were voting.

Gerber went on to tell his audience how he had then set up an experiment to measure whether he could bring those skeptics to the polls. Just before election day, he had randomly divided a set of Connecticut voters into five groups. Three of them were sent slightly different letters from the Connecticut secretary of state, each describing how the voting process keeps individual votes secret. A fourth group got a placebo election reminder, and the last control sample got no mail at all. After the election, Gerber saw that his letters had no impact on those who had been to the polls before. But when they reached people who were registered but had never voted, participation spiked: the letters emphasizing ballot secrecy created 2 or 3 new voters for every 100 people who received them.

It was only the latest example of someone using twenty-first-century tools to assimilate lessons from nineteenth-century politics. More and more, those who looked anew at the act of voting were beginning to think of it in altogether different terms. Maybe what stopped people from voting wasn't a lack of information about the candidates or a feeling that the outcomes of races didn't matter or a sense that a trip to the polls was inconvenient. What if voting wasn't only a political act, but a social one that took place in a liminal space between the public and private that had never been well-defined to citizens? What if toying with those expectations was key to turning a person into a voter? What if elections were simply less about shaping people's opinions than changing their behaviors?

* * * * *

MALCHOW HAD SPENT a quarter century living off the mail, but not until his revelatory steakhouse dinner with Gerber did he give much thought to envelopes. After he had overcome his initial awe at the power of the social-pressure tool used in Michigan, Malchow looked closely at the mailers themselves. They were simple copy paper, laser-printed and crudely folded, the result of Grebner scrambling to produce them cheaply in his own office rather than hiring a professional copy shop for the job. They looked appropriately amateurish, unlike anything Malchow had put out in his years of sending political mail to raise money, persuade voters, or turn them out. By the traditional standards articulated by direct-mail vendors, valuing high-impact visuals that "cut through the clutter" of the mailbox, Grebner's bland letters should have been a dud. But, of course, they hadn't been, and now Malchow began to wonder whether their success owed something not only to psychological tricks but to their humble packaging as well.

One of Grebner's letters didn't even try to exercise social pressure, instructing a voter merely, "Remember your rights and responsibilities as a citizen. Remember to vote." Such generic "civic duty" messages rarely made any impact on turnout, starting with the first Gerber-Green experiment in New Haven. In fact, the only reason they had included it in the Michigan test was as a baseline against which they could measure the various social-pressure effects. Yet in Grebner's hands the civic-duty message increased turnout by nearly two points over the control group, and the only reason Malchow could find to explain it was the primitive format. He thought about the other pieces of paper that shared those aesthetics: a jury-duty summons, a letter from the taxman, the homeowner's association announcing a policy change. What if, Malchow wondered, an unstylized simplicity had become a signal at the mailbox that something was to be taken seriously?

So he started testing. He ran experiments pitting letters against glossy brochures, black-and-white against full color, slick against clunky. The evidence piled up, all pointing in the same direction: toward plain, official-looking communications. Others at the Analyst Institute reported experimental findings that seemed to confirm the virtues of simplicity. A group called Our Oregon, which runs state ballot initiative campaigns for progressive causes, found that it could increase its vote tally in select precincts by five points by replacing its glossy mail with a bland, text-heavy voter guide devoid of endorsements from politicians but instead featuring the validating logos of groups like the PTA and the League of Women Voters. Rock the Vote found that e-mail and text messages arriving from unexciting senders like "Election Center" often do better than those with livelier "from" lines, like the names of celebrities. "If you believe this, it says we're doing everything wrong," says Malchow. "There's a principle underneath this. When people see the fingerprint of Madison Avenue, it becomes advertising—and advertising is not important to them."

Throughout 2011, Malchow was eager to press these concepts further, and to deploy new modeling tools that combined microtargeting and experimental methods to predict which individual voters would best respond to a given appeal. He and Page Gardner, along with others at Women's Voices, assembled a list of twenty experiments they wanted to run that year. Malchow conjured a single layered design that would mix and match treatments in different combinations and test their compatibility with proven techniques, such as social pressure. He wanted to tweak Gerber's ballot secrecy reminder the way he had the social-pressure menace, changing the language or the presentation to see if he could squeeze more new votes out of the electorate. He and Gardner planned to administer the experiments in Kentucky, which would be selecting a governor in the last scheduled election before the 2012 election cycle began, affording enough time to analyze the results and deploy the best new tactics nationwide to boost Obama's reelection.

But when Gardner went out to pitch donors on these tests, she couldn't find any willing to sponsor them. This had to do in part with the changing dynamics of the Kentucky race, which for largely local reasons had lost the interest of liberal donors nationally, but more with a changing set of priorities for Democratic strategists. The question of how to most efficiently get large numbers of new voters on the rolls had moved to the top of their list of concerns. "We want to do some research as we go into 2012," says Gardner. "What is the most appealing way to make the process of registration easiest for people most underrepresented in our democracy?"

So Malchow shifted his own focus, too. Through weekly Tuesday strategy calls with Women's Voices staff, Malchow arrived at fourteen variations to the group's standard voter registration package to test. In some cases he and Gardner decided to fiddle with the format (adding a fake Post-it note to direct a recipient to the fields she needed to complete) and in others made more substantive adjustments (would putting an NAACP return address on the envelope make black Mississippians more likely to register to vote?). Malchow produced each of the test mailings, assigned treatment and control universes across twenty states, and in mid-September, a little more than a year before Obama would reappear on a ballot, postmarked just under a half-million registration forms. "What seems to be a very small difference in response rates . . . becomes a difference in cost per net vote," says Gardner. "All these nitty-bitty things have magnified effects."

Registration was the first step in the process of winning a vote, but it rarely earned sustained attention from campaign operatives. The tax code treated it as a civic function rather than a political one, something that was unquestionably good for democracy rather than a tactic to back one candidate. Because outside groups would take on this work, especially on the left, campaigns rarely did it themselves. To the extent there was expertise in the art of registration, it had belonged to groups like ACORN and its many satellites, who specialized in overwhelming minority neighborhoods with unskilled workers who were typically paid for each form they returned. The workers knew their turf, and would often do little but set up a card table outside a well-trafficked grocery store, with a stack of forms handed out indiscriminately to passersby who said they were unregistered. The going rate for each new registrant was about fifteen dollars, covering labor and administrative costs. Often there wasn't a computer in sight, or any way of matching the names to the voluminous databases that could help predict what party that voter was likely to join, or—if it was not a first-time voter but merely someone registering in a new location—document his or her history of political behaviors with great specificity. Groups, parties, or campaigns that had learned to rigorously target their mail and phone communications to maximize votes and lower costs would often mindlessly use their registration programs to put new supporters of their opposition on the electoral rolls at great expense to themselves.

Gardner had long yearned for a more refined approach. Her experience with Women's Voices had taught her that the group could not just adopt a card table strategy, since unmarried women did not segregate in particular neighborhoods. She also fixated on the obvious inefficiencies in the standard process; lowering the cost per registration meant expanding her program's reach. So years ago she and Malchow had turned to new commercial databases that covered the entire adult population, pulled out unregistered women who appeared to be unmarried, and started sending out registration packages by mail. Through those tests, he had found he was able to bring the cost down to around eleven dollars per registration.

In part because of this success, Women's Voices' contributors pushed Gardner to start hunting for other targets, such as African-Americans and Latinos (regardless of gender or marital status). Malchow built a model to predict which members of this expanded target universe would be most likely to register through a mailed appeal. He refined the statistical models each time, increasing the response rate and bringing down the costs. (Malchow even paid the post office for the mailers it returned as undeliverable, and used their common attributes to develop a model that could predict which addresses were likely to be bad so they could be preemptively removed from future lists.) In 2008, Women's Voices had sent out nearly 20 million applications, and registered just under 1 million of them in time for Obama's election. Thanks to Malchow's modeling and experimentation, they had cost around seven dollars each.

Most of this activity took place quietly and deliberately, receiving little attention outside a small circle of liberal foundations and activist groups that shared its objectives. The one time that the group did earn wide notice had come in the spring of 2008, when North Carolina election officials condemned its robocalls targeting black voters with a request to return a forthcoming voter registration packet. The calls had arrived after the deadline for the primary, and many (particularly Obama supporters) accused the group of trying to mislead voters who were already registered into thinking they were not, as part of a scheme to depress the black vote on behalf of Hillary Clinton, to whom Gardner and Malchow both had ties. For bloggers who covered the controversy, Gardner's statement that "these calls were our sincere attempt to encourage voter registration for those not registered for the general election this fall" was treated as a bit of obfuscation. In fact, the whole process grew out of experimental research that showed that, for nonvoters with available phone numbers, an advance alert by robocall increased response rates to a mailed registration form. (The fact that some registered voters were targets marked a modest, if predictable, failure of the data Malchow had run through his statistical models.) Hackles were raised largely because of the tradition of race-based voter suppression, but for a more banal reason, as well. Women's Voices' approach to the largely unscientized process of registering voters was so unusually methodical (*The Economist* called it "Rube Goldberg–ish") that the group regularly garnered suspicion from opponents and local authorities who suspected that its only purpose could be fraud or manipulation.

In November 2011, as Malchow sat in his home in Virginia monitoring his latest round of experiments, those registrations were no longer a sideshow to the project of picking a president. With a year to go until his re-election, Obama's popularity had fallen so precipitously, especially among swing voters, that questions about persuasion no longer seemed as urgent. Turnout would, as ever, remain crucial, but economic disillusionment from some core constituencies made it imprudent to rely on mobilization efforts alone. Indeed, the first maps to line the wall in Obama's new Chicago headquarters reflected how much Democratic plans for holding on to the White House depended on changing the composition of the electorate. Demographic shifts, particularly Latino-population spikes away from the Mexican border, made it conceivable that nontraditional Democratic states like North Carolina and Arizona would be friendlier turf than old battlegrounds like Ohio. Nevada and New Mexico could be moved from battlegrounds to safely Democratic states, giving Obama the ability to devote his time and resources elsewhere. But Democrats and their allies would have to successfully register those potential new voters, certainly hundreds of thousands of them, if not millions. They would also have to do it early enough in the process not only to meet legal deadlines, but so that they could be identified, canvassed, and modeled in such a way that Obama's campaign was able to meaningfully communicate with them throughout the election year.

Malchow tracked the experiments' progress on what were known as PLANET Code reports. They were named for a service that the U.S. Postal Service had introduced years earlier permitting a mailer to place a unique bar code on a piece of mail and record when it entered the postal system. The PLANET codes allowed a person to return a registration form directly to election officials on his or her own terms without denying the original sender the ability to track the response in real time. The codes were a small innovation, unknown to most political consultants and practically useless to all but a sliver of those who work with direct mail. But as with so many other developments Malchow had latched onto during his career, their introduction had taken a discrete campaign activity with latent impact and made it instantly measurable. It was thanks to the codes that Women's Voices and Malchow were able to run the experiments and modeling programs that, in just four years, had cut in half the cost of registering a new voter.

Now Malchow was hunting through the code reports to see whether any of his tests could help bring that cost down even further. He had auditioned one letter that tried to replicate the social pressure Grebner had aimed at nonvoters for use as psychological leverage on nonregistrants, and it seemed to be working, with a response rate about 25 percent above Women's Voices' standard mailer. But an effort to do the same with Gerber's privacy message—by including a reminder that an individual's registration could not legally be used for commercial purposes—looked like a flop, drawing barely half the standard response. Maybe, he assumed, some of those unwilling to register were so detached from political institutions that nothing could win their trust, or perhaps just raising the issue of privacy reinforced their paranoia.

The best performer, to Malchow's surprise, wasn't one of the packages that played devious mind games with its recipient but the type of straightforward, even earnest, entreaty that had fallen out of favor in the Analyst Institute world. This winning package was targeted at African-Americans on their eighteenth birthdays, framing their first election—and their chance to be part of it—as a monumental occasion. Women's Voices already had a robust "birthday" program, which mailed forms to teenagers as they turned eighteen, and it was one of the most effective mechanisms the group had. But emphasizing the historic moment of Obama's presidency brought in even more voters.

There was an unusual sweetness to that finding, especially since Malchow was at a complete loss to explain it. He was comfortable with the honest cynicism about human decision making that informed much of the behavioralist revolution in voter contact, but he couldn't understand why this appeal to civic duty would be succeeding where so many others had failed. Malchow grasped briefly at a few possible causes, but gave up on each quickly. He fell uncharacteristically silent, alone for a minute with the pleasing thought that there might still be a place in political life for innocent uplift.

AFTERWORD

THE SOVEREIGNTY OF NUMBERS

Two years after the election of Barack Obama as president, Democrats suffered their worst defeat in decades. The congressional majorities that had given Obama his legislative successes, reforming health insurance and financial markets, were gone; control of the House flipped; and the Democrats' lead in the Senate shrunk to an ungovernably slim margin. Pundits heralded the rise of the Tea Party, but voter disappointment with the Obama agenda was widespread in the midterm elections, manifest through independents breaking right and Democrats staying home. In 2010, the Democratic National Committee had failed its first test of the Obama era. It had failed to keep the Obama coalition together.

But there was some reassuring news in the dismal outcome: Dan Wagner had seen it all coming. Wagner served as the committee's targeting director, which when he was hired in January 2009 meant that he was responsible for the work of collecting voter information and analyzing it for the purpose of individually targeted contact. But Wagner appreciated that the data he was feeding into his statistical models, and that which was returned to the party's databases by volunteers interacting with voters in the field, amounted to a series of surveys. He had the DNC's technology department develop software that could turn that information into a series of tables that could be read like a poll, and he called it the Survey Manager.

That fall, before a special congressional election to fill an open seat in upstate New York, Wagner had successfully predicted the final margin within 150 votes well before election day. Then, months later, as traditional pollsters projected Democrat Martha Coakley a certain bet to win a Massachusetts special election to replace Senator Ted Kennedy, Wagner's Survey Manager pointed to a more dismal outcome: Republican Scott Brown was likely to prevail in the strongly Democratic state. "It's one thing to be right when you're going to win," says Jeremy Bird, who after 2008 became national deputy director of Organizing for America, the Obama campaign-in-exile housed at the DNC. "It's another thing to be right when you're going to lose."

It is yet another thing to be right five months before you're going to lose. As the 2010 midterms approached, Wagner built statistical models for contested Senate races and the seventy-four congressional districts Democrats had decided to target. Starting in July, he began predicting the election's outcomes, down to improbably accurate forecasting of their margins. But he did not get there with traditional polls. He counted votes one by one, including among those people who weren't even yet registered to vote. His first clue that the party was in trouble came from the thousands of individual calls matched to the rich statistical profiles in the DNC's databases. Core Democratic voters were telling the DNC's callers that they were likely to cast a ballot at a much lower rate than Wagner's statistical models predicted they would. Wagner could also calculate the impact the Democrats' mobilization programs would have on increasing turnout among supporters, and in most key races he knew it wouldn't be enough to close the gap that was revealing itself in the Survey Manager tables. His congressional predictions were off by an average error of only 2.5 percent. "That was a proof point for a lot of people who don't understand the math behind it but understand the value of what that math produces," says Mitch Stewart, Organizing for America's director. "Once that first special happened, his word was the gold standard at the DNC."

Wagner's influence would be felt beyond his ability to declare winners months before election day. His approach amounted to a disruptive break with all the twentieth-century tools for tracking public opinion, by thinking of voters as individuals and aggregating projections about their personal opinions and behavior until it revealed a picture of everyone. It marked a fulfillment of a new way of thinking about the electorate, a decade in the making, in which voters were no longer trapped in old political geographies, tethered to traditional demographic categories based on which of their attributes pollsters decided to ask about, or marked by the classifications of commercial marketers for consumer purposes. Instead, citizens could be seen as a collection of individual units who could each be measured and assessed on his or her own terms. The available data had begun to recognize the sovereignty of the people who participated in politics. Now it was up to a candidate who wanted to lead those people to build a campaign that would interact with them in kind.

Within two years, the Obama campaign would become celebrated for its user-facing technology, the bulk of it developed by an in-house software team that was hired in much the same way one would staff a Silicon Valley startup. Their products redefined how individuals could use the Web, social media, and smartphones to participate in the political process, from the mobile app that allowed a canvasser to download and return walksheets without ever entering a campaign office to a Web platform called Dashboard that gamified volunteer activity by ranking the most active supporters to "Targeted Sharing" protocols that mined Obama backers' Facebook networks in search of friends the campaign wanted to register, mobilize, or persuade.

But underneath the expanded use of screens were the scores, a new political currency that represented an individualized way of predicting human behavior, where a campaign didn't just profile who you were but knew exactly how it could turn you into the type of person it wanted you to be.

*　*　*　*　*

AFTER OBAMA'S 2008 VICTORY, many of his top advisers decamped from Chicago to Washington to make preparations to govern. Wagner, however, was instructed to stay behind and serve on a post-election task force. Its members were being asked to review a campaign that looked, at least to the outside world, technically flawless. From within, however, the shortcomings of the Obama data operation were apparent. The scale of the campaign's ambition had revealed one of the major limitations of political information infrastructure: the ways campaigns were forced to store their knowledge about people and the interactions with them in separate places, largely because the databases built for the purposes had been developed by different consultants, with no interest in making their systems work together.

But the task force knew they weren't stuck with that reality. Obama would run his next campaign not as an insurgent against a party establishment, but as the establishment itself. For four years, the task force's members knew, their team would drive the marketplace. Their report recommended developing a "constituent relationship management system" that would allow staff across the campaign to look up individuals not just as voters or volunteers or donors or website users but as citizens in full. "We realized there was a problem with how our data and infrastructure interacted with the rest of the campaign, and we ought to be able to offer it to all parts of the campaign," says Chris Wegrzyn, the campaign's database applications developer and member of the task force.

Wegrzyn became the DNC's lead targeting developer and oversaw a quiet series of costly acquisitions intended to free the party from its traditional dependence on outside vendors. The committee installed a Siemens Enterprise Communications phone-dialing unit that could put out 1.2 million calls a day to survey voters' opinions (and was set so that when it heard the tri-tone error message it would automatically purge a wrong number from a voter's record). At the same time, party leadership signed off on a $280,000 license to use Vertica software from Hewlett-Packard that allowed its server platform to access not only the party's 180-million-person voter file but all of the data about volunteers, donors, and those who interacted with Obama online. No longer would Democrats' ability to collect and use basic voter data be limited by what political consultants made available.

Many of those who spent 2010 guarding the president's electoral priorities in Washington reunited the following spring, in 2011, to mount his reelection campaign. They had suffered epic losses together at the head of a party organization, a chastening experience that separated them from those who had memories only of the 2008 campaign, where there was little such hardship. "From a character perspective," says Bird, who became the national field director for Obama's reelection, "people who did '08—and didn't do '10 and came back in '11 or '12—they had the hardest culture clash."

But those who had also came to Chicago with a firsthand appreciation for Wagner's methods of atomizing the electorate. It was a way of thinking that almost perfectly aligned with the straightforward theory of what Obama's strategists thought it would take to get him reelected: get everyone who voted for him in 2008 to do it once more. At the same time, Obama's team knew it would need to succeed at registering and mobilizing new voters, especially from some of the fastest-growing demographic categories, to make up for votes lost among those who abandoned the president after a term, all while using their powers of persuasion to hedge against further defections.

Barack Obama's campaign began the year of his reelection fairly confident it knew the names of every one of the 69,456,897 Americans whose votes had put him in the White House. The votes may have been cast via secret ballot, but because Obama's analysts had come up with individual-level predictions, they could look at the Democrat's vote totals in each precinct and identify the people most likely to have backed him. Pundits talked about reassembling Obama's 2008 coalition at the level of abstraction. Within the campaign, it was a daunting but eminently practicable goal. They would reassemble the coalition, one by one, through personal contact.

* * * * *

WHEN MANAGER JIM MESSINA arrived in Chicago and imposed a mandate on his new staff to make decisions that were data-driven and measurable, it meant something different than it had four years earlier. The 2008 campaign had been data-driven, as people liked to say, a reflection both of a principled Obama imperative to challenge the old-guard political establishment with an empirical approach to electioneering, and of manager David Plouffe's affection for spreadsheets. Plouffe's appetite had often been for "metrics," which usually took the form of performance reports: How many of a field office's volunteer shifts had been filled last weekend? How much money did that fund-raising blast bring in?

But for all its reliance on data, the 2008 Obama campaign had remained largely insulated from the most important methodological innovation in twenty-first-century politics. The first Obama campaign integrated the cost-free findings of field tests conducted by Don Green, Alan Gerber, and their acolytes—tweaking their call scripts and canvassing protocols—but never fully embraced the experimental revolution. After Wagner moved to the DNC, the party began working with the Analyst Institute to administer its own experiments. "We inserted ourselves into the world of research, so we could become not only people who do research but a driver of research for the Democratic party," says Wagner.

The new methods for refining registration techniques were of particular interest to party officials, who knew that adding new Democratic voters to the rolls had to be a crucial element in their strategy to change the electorate before 2012. Even if a mail-based registration program was the most easily targetable way to do that, it didn't necessarily satisfy the other imperatives Obama faced—all those volunteers who needed to be reengaged, for whom a visible registration drive would be a first step toward an ongoing presence in their communities. In 2010, the DNC ran experiments to measure whether it was more effective to set up tables in high-traffic areas where volunteers could distribute forms or to dispatch them to preselected doors. In one Virginia test, Democratic officials compared whether it was better to map shopping centers in areas that Census data suggested were likely to have both a high concentration of potential registrants and a politically favorable complexion, or to just let volunteers decide where to install themselves. "Even when we didn't tell people, they went to the right places," says Bird.

Wagner's department kept a record of those new voters who had registered at sites, and later called them: 85 percent were likely to be Obama supporters. Starting in 2011, the campaign ran its own experiments and discovered that outfitting the volunteers who manned registration tables in Obama T-shirts increased their rate of converting supporters. People were so self-selective about the Obama brand, Wagner concluded, that the shirts ended up sorting through prospective registrants as effectively as any microtargeting model could.

The Obama campaign signed on the Analyst Institute as a client for $22,000 per month, embedding its social scientists at headquarters. Already their experimental ambitions had moved beyond merely modifying noncitizens' behavior through registration and mobilization to the most vexing problem in politics: changing voters' minds.

The expansion of individual-level data made such testing possible. Experimenters had typically calculated the average effect of their interventions across the entire treated population. But as campaigns developed deep portraits of the voters in their databases, it became possible to measure what statisticians called "heterogeneous treatment effects": What are the attributes of the people who were actually moved by an experiment's impact? A series of tests in 2006 by EMILY's List had illustrated the potential to rethink tactics by overlaying experimental designs onto microtargeting databases. When the women's group sent direct mail in favor of Democratic gubernatorial candidates, it barely budged those whose scores placed them in the middle of the partisan spectrum. Instead, it had a far greater impact upon those who had been profiled as soft Republicans.

That test, and others that followed, demonstrated the limitations of traditional microtargeting scores. Those individualized predictions were, after all, derived from observed data, mostly demographic attributes, and represented an effort to situate a voter on a series of political spectra. Targeting decisions, however, rested on a series of longstanding, intuitive assumptions—that middle-of-the-roaders were the most persuadable, and that infrequent voters were the ones who would most benefit from a get-out-the-vote drive. Experiments introduced a new uncertainty to these assumptions: those people who were identified as having a 50 percent likelihood of voting for the Democrat might in fact be perfectly cross-pressured between the two parties, or might look like centrists because not enough data was attached to their records to push a partisan prediction in one direction or another. "The scores in the middle are the people we know less about," says Chris Wyant, who served as a field organizer on the 2008 campaign and became Ohio's general-election director for Obama's reelection. "The extent to which we were guessing about persuasion was not lost on any of us."

If Wagner had demonstrated the value of scores to depict an atomized electorate, persuasion experiments were the equivalent of exerting force against the whole universe and then measuring which units of matter responded to the stimulus. To more confidently sift through the electorate in search of the ripest targets, the Obama campaign charged its experimenters with designing two types of persuasion tests. The first would be a series of so-called experiment-informed programs that would measure the relative effectiveness of different types of messages on moving public opinion. The traditional model was to use focus groups to audition themes and language in front of voters and then to put them in polls to see which categories of voters seemed to respond to each. But Obama's leadership came to the early conclusion that "American polling is broken," as Messina put it after the election, thanks in part to the tiny samples for demographic subgroups available through traditional polls. "You're making significant resource decisions based on a hundred and sixty people?" asks Stewart. "Isn't that nuts? And people have been doing that for decades!"

Like-minded Democratic operatives had begun to see experiment-informed programs, which they called EIPs, as a replacement. Campaigns could still use artificial environments like focus groups and polls to develop a range of prospective messages, but then subject them to empirical testing in the real world. Experimenters would randomly assign voters to receive different four-piece flights of persuasion direct mail on the same policy theme, and then use ongoing survey calls to isolate the attributes of those whose opinions moved as a result.

In March, the campaign used this technique to test various ways of promoting the administration's health-care policies, including one series of mailers that described the various components of Obamacare and another that—more closely resembling a letter from an insurance company—advised voters that they were now entitled to a free regular checkup and ought to contact a doctor to schedule theirs. It didn't move Obama's position in the horse race, but it did improve attitudes toward his signature legislation and the question of which candidate did a better job protecting access to health care.

The experiment also revealed the ways in which female voters responded differently by age. Older women's views of the bill improved upon receiving reminders on wellness checkups and free preventive care; younger women's did after being told about contraceptive coverage and new rules that prohibited insurance companies from charging more for women. "It was not about *what,* it was about *who,*" says Terry Walsh, who coordinated the campaign's polling and paid-media spending. "We figured out the *what* in the survey research and the other stuff beforehand. The EIP was almost exclusively about the *who.*"

In July, the campaign ran another EIP, around middle-class economic themes, which vetted broad arguments about the social safety net against direct comparison of Obama's and Romney's tax proposals and critical depictions of the Republican's overseas bank accounts and experience at the Bain Capital private-equity firm. When Congressman Paul Ryan was named to the Republican ticket, Obama advisers rushed together an EIP to compare different lines of attack around Medicare. What they found, when segmenting by age range the voters whose opinions shifted, was that the biggest gains could be found not among those over 65, but among those in the two decades just beneath it. People between 45 and 55, and between 55 and 65, were more likely to change their views about the candidates after being presented Obama's Medicare arguments than those currently on the program. "The electorate was very inelastic," says Walsh. "In fact, when we did the economic and Medicare EIPs, we got positive movement that was very heartening because it was at a time when we were not seeing a lot of movement in the electorate."

That movement came from places where a campaign traditionally would probably have never gone hunting for minds it could change. A July EIP designed to test Obama's messages aimed particularly at women found that those between 20 and 40 support scores showed the greatest response to his arguments about feminine health and equal-pay measures. Their low support index meant that other indicators of their partisanship pointed strongly to likely Republican attitudes; here was one thing (probably the only thing) that could pull them to Obama. As a result, when Obama unveiled a track of his direct-mail program addressing only women's issues, it wasn't to shore up interest among core parts of the Democratic coalition, but to reach over for conservatives who were uniquely cross-pressured on gender concerns. (Separate polling by the campaign found Planned Par-

enthood unexpectedly popular among rural voters; in many remote loca-
tions, it was the most accessible medical provider.) "The whole goal of the
women's track was to pick off votes from Romney," says Walsh. "We were
able to persuade people who fell low on candidate support scores if we
gave them a specific message."

At the same time, Obama's campaign was pursuing an even more audacious adventure in persuasion. Traditionally, campaigns have kept their
persuasion efforts focused in channels like mass media or direct mail, where
they can maintain control of the presentation, language, and targeting. In
most cases, volunteers are used for short survey-style interviews to identify
voter preferences, and to register and mobilize those expected to be supporters. Sending volunteers to do persuasion would, by definition, mean
forcing them to interact with opponents—or voters who are undecided in
part because they consider themselves alienated from political communication—on delicate issues like abortion, where the wrong exchange could
provoke a backlash. Campaigns have typically resisted the risk. "You can
have a negative impact," says Bird. "You can hurt your candidate."

In February, Obama volunteers attempted 500,000 conversations with
the goal of winning over new supporters. The voters had been randomly
selected from a range of voters identified as persuadable, and were polled
after a phone conversation that began with a volunteer reading a script
with a few talking points and general instructions to open up a conversation with the person at the other end of the line. "We definitely find certain
people moved more than other people," says Bird. Analysts identified their
attributes and made them the core of a persuasion model that predicted,
with a range of zero to ten, the likelihood that a voter could be pulled in
Obama's direction after a single volunteer interaction. (A zero designated
a voter likely to be repelled by the interaction, and actually pushed toward
Romney or a third-party candidate; a one projected a minimal possibility of persuasion; and a nine predicted someone who could be easily persuaded.) The experiment also taught Obama's field department about their
supporters. California, which had always had perhaps the most mature

volunteer organization of any nontargeted state, saw that sophistication manifest in skills of persuasion. It didn't matter whether they were calling in to Nevada or Ohio; the voters who spoke with Californians were more likely to become Obama supporters. "It's not about time zone, it wasn't about culture," says Bird. "It was that their volunteers were better."

Obama's strategists grew confident that they were no longer restricted to advertising and direct mail as channels for persuasion efforts. Previously, campaigns had been wary of relinquishing control of ground-level interactions with voters because they didn't know enough about their supporters or volunteers to assess the risk of putting them in potentially combustible situations with one another. "Persuasion calls are a more difficult thing for a volunteer to do because it's a lot easier to hang up on someone than slam a door in their face," says Wisconsin Democratic Party chairman Mike Tate. "You're not just asking someone who they're going to vote for or reminding them to vote—you're going to people who are undecided, who don't want to hear from you, and are often sick of politics." But newly armed with persuasion scores, Obama's field organizers began sending trained volunteers to knock on doors or make phone calls with the objective of changing minds—a quietly dramatic shift in the culture of electioneering in America.

The change may have been felt on the street, but it was possible only because of advances in analytics. Wedged between the campaign's technology and digital departments, Wagner's team had its closest relationship with the field staff, dating back to his 2008 work generating microtargeting models to direct voter contact. Linking previously unconnected databases presented new opportunities to modernize the basic work of turning out votes.

Wegrzyn developed a program code-named Airwolf to take the lists released by county and state officials with names of the people in their jurisdictions who had voted early, or had more requested mail ballots, and match them to the campaign's list of e-mail addresses. Voters who had been modeled as likely Obama supporters would get regular reminders to return their ballots and, once they had, a message thanking them for having voted and proposing other ways for them to be involved in the campaign. A local field organizer would get automated daily lists of the voters on his or her turf with outstanding ballots in their hands to follow up with personal contact by phone or at the doorstep. "It is a fundamental way of tying together the online and offline worlds," says Wagner.

Wagner, however, was turning his attention beyond field. He had begun making the rounds of the other units at headquarters, from fundraising to communications and campaign management, offering to help "solve their problems with data." The former corporate consultant imagined the analytics department—which was growing into a fifty-four-person staff housed in its own windowless office known internally as the Cave—serving as an "in-house consultancy" whose clients would be other parts of the campaign. "There's a process of helping people learn about the tools so they can be a participant in the process," he says. "We essentially built products for each of those various departments that were paired up with a massive database we had."

*   *   *   *   *

AT ROMNEY'S HEADQUARTERS in Boston's North End, his advisers monitored the job notices—seeking specialists in text analytics, computational advertising, and online experiments—coming out of the incumbent's campaign in Chicago with a combination of awe and bewilderment. Throughout the primaries, Romney appeared to be the only Republican running a twenty-first-century campaign. A savvy and disciplined use of individual-level voter data had helped Romney lay the groundwork for a surprise win in the Iowa caucuses (later corrected and awarded, too late, to Rick Santorum) and to methodically bank early votes in states like Florida before his disorganized opponents could establish operations there.

But the Republican had not built much institutional expertise on the way to the nomination. Romney, trying to correct what in his first race for the presidency had been a bloated campaign wracked by internecine consultant battles, kept his second effort small. While Obama's long primary slog against Hillary Clinton in 2008 had served as a massive recruitment and training exercise, for both data analysts and field organizers, Romney shuffled the same small cadre of staffers from state to state. The exceptional competence they demonstrated when compared to other Republican candidates distracted from a dramatic gap between the two parties and their allies when it came to the sophistication of their efforts.

Since his first campaign for governor, in 2002, Romney had maintained a particular reliance on TargetPoint Consulting, the Virginia firm founded by Alexander Gage as he pioneered the practice he called "microtargeting." Such techniques had offered George W. Bush's reelection campaign a major edge in voter-contact operations, but Republicans had done little to institutionalize that advantage in the years since. By 2006, Democrats had not only matched Republicans in adopting commercial marketing techniques, but had moved ahead largely by integrating methods developed in the social sciences. Where Democrats had cultivated a broader culture around those analytical advances—generating new institutions to coordinate and distribute research, and a class of targeting-director and voter-file-manager jobs—the Republican data ecosystem had remained relatively static. "There was a false sense of security, a sense that we figured out how to do this microtargeting—we'd figured out how to do it pretty well—and now there are other things for the party to focus on," says Blaise Hazelwood, who, following Bush's reelection, started her own firm, Grassroots Targeting.

Romney's advisers knew that Obama was building robust data and analytics departments, treating each as a core campaign function, like field or communications. Romney had little choice but to rely on Target-Point, his longtime consultant, to develop his voter segments and then deliver them to the campaign's databases. The campaign began assigning those scores in June, and engineered systems so that new information from Republican field canvasses and phone banks could help to refine the statistical models on an ongoing basis. But even those within Romney's campaign who looked enviously at Obama's ambitious staffing resigned themselves early on to a much more modest conception of what campaign analytics could be. "The Obama team had the luxury of knowing exactly what they'd be doing on July 1, 2012, because they've been planning for six years—definitely three and a half years," digital director Zac Moffatt said over the summer.

Romney's data-science team would end up being less than one-tenth the size of Obama's analytics department. It was headed by Alex Lundry, who took a leave from his post as TargetPoint's vice president and in turn enlisted Tom Wood, a postdoctoral student in political science at the University of Chicago, and Brent McGoldrick, a veteran of Bush's 2004 campaign who had left politics for Financial Dynamics, a firm that works with health-care and energy companies to segment consumers. Instead of trying to refine their handling of the small stuff, Lundry's team fixated on trying to unlock a big question, the subject of a persistent mystery to academics who have studied elections and which political professionals have filled in with hunches and theories and anecdote but little empiricism. "How can we get a sense of whether this advertising is working?" Lundry asks. "You usually get GRPs and tracking polls. There's a very large causal leap you have to make from one to the other."

Lundry decided to insert measurable, intermediate steps that could help make sense of that information flow. His team converted subjects of political communication into discrete units they called "entities." They initially classified two hundred of them, from issues like the auto-industry bailout and controversies like the failure of the federally funded energy company Solyndra to catchphrases like "the war on women." When a new concept or phrase emerged as part of the election-year lexicon (like Obama's July line "you didn't build that"), the analysts added it to the list. They tracked each entity on the National Dialogue Monitor, TargetPoint's contribution to a burgeoning sector of tracking the volume and sentiment of social-media activity. Unlike many of its competitors, however,

TargetPoint also integrated content from professional media, collecting closed-caption transcripts of broadcast programs and scraping newspaper websites. Lundry's team treated these as two separate categories—the informal sphere of social media, especially Twitter, and the journalistic product that campaigns call earned press coverage—to examine how every entity fared in each.

Ultimately, Lundry wanted to assess the impact each type of public attention had on what ultimately mattered for a campaign: Romney's position in the horse race. He turned to vector autoregression models, which equities traders use to isolate the influence of single variables on market movements. In this case, Lundry's team looked for patterns between the Dialogue Monitor's time-series data and Romney's number in Gallup's daily tracking polls. By the end of July, they felt they had identified a three-step media-diffusion process they called Wood's Triangle, in honor of the postdoc who represented one of the rare successes conservatives had pulling academic specialists into the ranks of their campaigns.

Within three or four days of seeing a new entity enter the conversation, either via paid ads or organically through the news cycle, it was possible to have a well-informed hypothesis about whether the new topic was likely to win media attention by tracking whether it was the subject of chatter on Twitter. That informal conversation among political-class elites typically led to traditional print or broadcast press coverage one to two days later, which could then have an impact on the horse race. "We saw this process over and over again," says Lundry. "It was the same pattern every time."

They began to think of ads as a "shock to the system," a way to either introduce a new topic into the flows or to restore focus in an area in which elite interest had faded. If an entity didn't gain its own energy, like a Republican critique of a summertime welfare waiver granted by the White House, Lundry would recommend a "re-shock to the system" with another ad on the subject five to seven days after Romney had first mentioned it. After twelve to fourteen days in the system, Lundry found, an entity had

traveled through the system and exhausted its ability to move public opinion—so he would recommend that the campaign's communications staff
move on to something new. "There are people who say you keep hitting
things as long as you possibly can," says Lundry, but he would cite Wood's
Triangle to argue that "we can't really dwell on something for more than
two weeks."

Those insights offered campaign officials a theory of information
flows, but little specific guidance in how to allocate resources among
states as part of an electoral-college strategy. Assuming that Obama had
superior ground-level data and analytics, Romney's campaign fixated on
trying to leverage their rivals' strategy to shape their own; if Democrats
thought a state or media market was competitive, maybe that was the best
evidence that Republicans should, too. "We were necessarily reactive, because we were putting together the plane as it took off. They had an enor-
mous head start on us," says Lundry. "To only have six months to try to
match that, the best we could do was say, 'What are these guys doing, and
how can we match that?' "

Romney's political department began hosting a weekly meeting to
review how Obama assigned resources—particularly ad dollars and the
president's hours—geographically to try to divine the calculations behind
them. It was in essence the way Microsoft's Bing approached Google: trying to hack the market leader's code by reverse-engineering the visible
outputs. "We watch where the president goes," said Dan Centinello, the
Romney deputy political director who oversaw the meetings. "We're trying to piece together his top ranks."

Obama's media-buying strategy proved particularly hard to decipher,
and in early September, as part of his standard review, Lundry noticed that
Obama had aired sixty-eight ads the week after his convention in Dothan,
Alabama. Dothan was one of the country's smallest media markets, and
Alabama one of the safest Republican states. Even though the market was
known to savvy ad buyers as one of the places a media market crosses
state lines, Dothan stations reached only about nine thousand Florida

voters, and around seven thousand of them had voted for John McCain. "This is a hardcore Republican media market, it's incredibly tiny, but they were advertising there," says Lundry.

Romney's advisers might have formed a theory about the broader media environment, but whatever was sending Obama hunting for a small pocket of votes was beyond their measurement. "We could tell," says McGoldrick, "that there was something in the algorithms that was telling them what to run."

* * * * *

IN DECEMBER 2011, Carol Davidsen received a message from Dan Wagner. Already the Obama campaign was known for its prodigious, even relentless e-mails beseeching supporters to give their money or time, but this one from Chicago offered something that intrigued Davidsen: a job. Wagner had sorted the campaign's list of donors, stretching back to 2008, to find those who described their occupation to the Federal Election Commission with terms like *data* and *analytics* and sent them invitations to apply for a job in his new analytics department. At the same time, Wagner had sent the campaign's chief scientist, Rayid Ghani, a veteran of Accenture Labs, to college campuses and professional meetings to recruit other data-science professionals. "There are a lot of people with political experience," says Wagner. "We tried to figure out who are the most talented people to solve this problem."

Davidsen was working at Navic Networks, a Microsoft-owned company that wrote code for set-top cable boxes to create a record of a user's DVR or tuner history, when she heeded Wagner's call. One year before election day, she started work in the campaign's technology department, serving as product manager for Narwhal. That was the code name, borrowed from a mythical tusked whale, for the ambitious if arcane engineering effort to pull information from previously unconnected databases and match records so that a user's online interactions with the campaign could all be synchronized. With Narwhal, e-mail blasts asking people to volunteer could take into consideration their past donation history, and the algorithms determining how much a supporter would be asked to contribute could be shaped by knowledge about her reaction to prior solicitations. The integration enriched the A/B testing that had been a staple of Obama's 2008 online fund-raising efforts; now analysts could leverage personal data to identify the attributes of those who responded, and use that knowledge to refine subsequent appeals. "You can cite people's other types of engagement," says Amelia Showalter, Obama's director of digital analytics. "We discovered that there were a lot of things that built goodwill, like signing the president's birthday card or getting a free bumper sticker, that led them to become more engaged with the campaign in other ways."

If online communications had been the aspect of the 2008 campaign that was most rigorously scientized—it was easy to randomly assign e-mails in an A/B test and measure response via click-through rates or donation levels—mass-media strategy remained among the least. Television and radio ads had to be purchased by geographic zones, delineated as either media markets or cable systems; the available data on who watches particular channels or shows, collected by research firms like Nielsen and Scarborough, often includes little more than viewer age and gender. That might be good enough to guide buys for Schick or Foot Locker, but is of limited value for advertisers looking to define audiences in political terms. "The process for buying media is antiquated," says Walsh. "The process for targeting media is antiquated."

As Messina prepared to spend as much as half a billion dollars on mass media for Obama's reelection, he set out to reinvent that process. He hired Amy Gershkoff—who had traded a promising academic future, earning her Ph.D. in political science from Princeton, for a career in political targeting—after she won recognition among Democratic operatives for her 2009 success in getting some cable systems to open up their user data just enough that it could be anonymously linked to individual microtargeting profiles. Messina gave her command of a media-planning department

he charged with helping to intelligently allocate resources across broadcast, cable, satellite, and online channels. "If you think about the universe
of possible places for an advertiser, it's almost infinite. There are tens of
millions of opportunities where a campaign can put its next dollar, and you
want to win," says Gershkoff. "You have all this great, robust voter data
that doesn't fit together with the media data. How you have to knit that
together is a challenge not only in the political world but in the corporate
world."

Within months, though, Gershkoff had left the campaign, and her department's responsibilities were assumed by Wagner, who had maintained
the confidence of campaign leaders since his prognosticative successes at
the DNC and had become an increasingly confident practitioner of bureaucratic politics. As he expanded analytics' scope, Wagner defined his purview as "the study and practice of resource optimization for the purpose of
improving the program and earning votes more efficiently." That usually
meant distilling any campaign activity to a calculation of votes gained for
a volume (and, by extension, cost) of contact. "In every case we're trying
to get the same outcome," says Wagner. "The closer you get to that, the
better you're going to be."

But when it came to buying media, such calculations had been simply
impossible, as campaigns were unable to link what they knew about voters to what cable providers knew about their customers. Obama's advisers
decided that political advertisers had long been asking the wrong questions, warped by the data that the private sector made available. "It was
not to get a better understanding of what thirty-five-plus women watch on
TV," Walsh says of the effort to reimagine the media-targeting process. "It
was to find out how many of our persuadable voters were watching those
dayparts."

Wagner brought over Davidsen, whose previous work had left her intimately familiar with the rich datasets that resided on set-top boxes. She
understood that a lot of that data existed, compiled by research firms that
aggregated records of viewers' tuner and DVR histories initially collected

by cable providers—but it was not available at the individual level, for privacy reasons. "The hardest thing in media-buying right now is the lack of information," Davidsen says. "And for these economic systems to work you need information flow."

Davidsen began negotiating with research firms to have them repackage their data in a form that would permit the campaign to access the individual-level histories while still abiding by the cable providers' privacy standards. (A deal she worked out with one of those firms, Rentrak, ended up costing more than $350,000 over the course of the campaign year.) The campaign would provide a list of persuadable voters and their addresses, based on its microtargeting models, and Rentrak would look for them in cable companies' billing files. When a record would match, Rentrak would issue it a unique household ID that allowed the campaign to identify a single set-top box's viewing habits but kept it stripped of personally identifiable information. (Political advertisers were already relying on similar anonymous matches to link voter-registration records to browser cookies to deliver individually targeted online ads.)

The Obama campaign had effectively created its own television ratings system, a Nielsen where the only eyeballs that mattered were connected to a mind not yet fully committed to a presidential candidate. But Davidsen faced a looming deadline: she had to get the information into a practical form by early May, when Obama strategists planned to take advantage of a weakened, underfunded opponent by beginning their anti-Romney ad campaign. Davidsen oversaw the development of a software platform that Obama staff called the Optimizer, which broke the day into ninety-six quarter-hour segments and assessed which time slots across sixty channels offered the greatest number of persuadable targets per dollar. (By October, Davidsen had unlocked an even richer trove of data: a Toledo, Ohio, cable system that tracked viewers' tuner histories at second-by-second increments.) "The revolution of media-buying in this campaign was to effectively turn what was a broadcast medium into something that looks a lot more like a narrowcast medium," says Walsh.

When Obama approached television as a mass medium, it was because the Optimizer had concluded it would be a more efficient way of reaching persuadable targets. Sometimes it was a better bargain to buy a national cable ad than to make local buys of the same spot across a large number of the sixty-six media markets reaching battleground states. In those instances, reverting to a national ad-buying strategy also had other benefits, like a boost to fund-raising and volunteer-motivation activities in states that weren't essential to Obama's electoral-college arithmetic. "Also, it helps hide some of the strategy of your buying," Davidsen adds.

Obama's buys perplexed the Romney analysts in Boston. They had invested in their own media-buying platform, which was called Centraforce and had been developed by former Bush adviser Sarah Taylor Fagen. It used some of the same aggregated data sources that were feeding into the Optimizer, and at times it seemed to send both campaigns to the same unlikely ad blocks, like those within TV Land reruns. But there was a lot more to what Lundry called Obama's "highly variable" media strategy, as when the Democrat's ads were sent into fringe markets, marginal stations, and out-of-the-way times where few political candidates had ever seen value. At the core of the mystery was the fact that Romney's data scientists could never decode Obama's media-buying decisions without the voter models or persuasion experiments that helped Obama pick out individual targets. "We probably were never able to figure out the level of advertising and what they were trying to do, and the level of targeting, how specific they were doing it," says McGoldrick. "It wasn't worth reverse-engineering, because what are you going to do?"

* * * * *

WHEN THE CAVE began producing analytics tables that looked a lot like polls, it was not because the Obama campaign was suffering from a polling shortage. It had a public-opinion team comprising seven outside firms whose productivity shocked new arrivals at the Chicago headquarters for the variegated breadth of the research that arrived on their desks daily. "We believed in combining the qual, which we did more than any campaign ever, with the quant, which we did more than any other campaign, to make sure all communications for every level of the campaign were informed by what they found," says polling director David Simas.

Simas considered himself the "air-traffic controller" of such research, which was guided by a series of diaries Obama's team commissioned as it prepared for the reelection. "We needed to do something almost divorced from politics and get to the way they're seeing their lives," says Simas. The lead pollster, Joel Benenson, had voters write about what they were experiencing, at home and at work, and this fixed the attention of campaign strategists on the frequently occurring word *disappointment*—which helped explain attitudes toward Obama's administration, but also a broader middle-class dissatisfaction with economic conditions. "That became the foundation for our entire research program," says Simas.

Obama's advisers used those diaries to develop a messaging regimen focused heavily on contrasting Obama with Romney as a fighter for the middle class. Benenson's national polls (which called across battleground states and weighted responses by electoral votes) tested specific bits of language to see which moved voters in survey experiments and direct questioning. A quartet of consultants were assigned specific states, where their surveys would track the horse race and feel for which national themes fit best with local concerns. Eventually Obama's media advisers created more than five hundred ads, and before airing any tested them using an online sample selected by focus-group director David Binder.

But the campaign had to play defense, too. When something potentially damaging would pop up in the news, like Democratic consultant Hilary Rosen's declaration that Ann Romney had "never worked a day in her life," Simas checked in with The Community, a private online bulletin board populated by one hundred undecided voters recruited by Binder. (He would cycle participants out, replacing them with new ones, as they made up their minds between candidates.) Simas would monitor Community conversations to see what news penetrated voter consciousness, or would have Binder show them controversial new material—like a video clip of Obama's "you didn't build that" comment—and ask if it changed their views of the candidate. "For me, it was a very quick way to be drawing back and determine whether something was a problem or not a problem," says Simas.

Obama's welfare waivers did look like a problem, since Community members responded to the first reports of the policy change by saying it smacked of unfairness. Binder was running focus groups nearly nightly, rotating among battleground states, and was able to adjust his agenda to chase curiosities emerging from Chicago. Within a day, Binder confirmed that the welfare issue was worthy of the campaign's concern: middle-class voters saw it as part of a pattern of government policy ignoring their hard work and instead rewarding others with, as one campaign adviser summarized it, "bailouts going to people at the top, handouts to ones at the bottom." Then the campaign added welfare questions to polls, to gauge how large a problem the policy could become, and with which category of voters. Within five days, Simas felt, the campaign had identified an issue, diagnosed the underlying sentiment, quantified the scope of the threat, and set to work plotting a response—eventually a statement from Bill Clinton calling Romney's welfare claims misleading. "It's rare we were flying blind," says Simas.

The relentlessly quantitative approach of the analytics department reflected a different approach to measuring public opinion, one with little texture for the ways people talked about politics but the ability, through statistical models, to draw inferences about not only where the entire population stood but also where it would end up. "It was very robust because of other things they were doing in support of field," says Walsh. "They had a very granular view of what the electorate would look like, and a very precise prediction of what the electorate would look like organically and what it would look like after our persuasion and ground activities."

When Wagner started packaging his department's research into something that could be read like a poll, a pattern became apparent. Obama's number in key battleground states was lower in the analytics tables, but Romney's was, too. There were simply many more undecideds— sometimes nearly twice as many as the traditional pollsters found. There was a basic methodological distinction that helped to explain this: micro-targeting models required interviewing a lot of unlikely voters to give shape to a profile of what a nonvoter looked like, while pollsters tracking the horse race wanted to rigorously screen for those likely to cast a ballot. "I spent a lot of time within the campaign explaining to people that the numbers we get from analytics and the numbers we get from external pollsters did not need strictly to be reconciled," says Walsh. "They were different."

But the analytics polls were nonetheless a threat to the pollsters' primacy, and potentially to their business model. The survey calls that fed into the microtargeting models were significantly cheaper to conduct, partly because they relied on databases for information about respondents' demographics instead of asking for it. (Also, because the pollsters were using their calls to test messages, there was more of a concern in their work about how to sequence questions and train operators to get unbiased responses.) When in October a firm responsible for some of Obama's battleground-state polls, Anzalone Liszt, announced it was sponsoring a "Beat the Pollsters" prediction contest, one of its partners joked that he'd like to see Wagner's department compete for the $1,000 prize. "The game is on between Analytics and Pollsters, baby," John Anzalone joked.

But the sheer scope of the analytics research gave it an ability to pick up movement too small for traditional polls to perceive. In mid-October, as part of his standard review of Wagner's analytics tables, Simas was alarmed to see that what had been a steady Obama lead of one to two points in Green Bay had flipped into a Romney advantage of more than seven. Green Bay was the only Wisconsin media market that experienced such a shift, and there was no obvious explanation for it. But it was hard to discount as a statistical fluke. Whereas a standard eight-hundred-person statewide poll may have had only one hundred respondents in the Green Bay area, analytics was placing five thousand calls into Wisconsin in each five-day cycle—and benefiting from tens of thousands of other field contacts—to produce and update microtargeting scores. Analytics was talking to as many people in the Green Bay media market as traditional pollsters questioned across Wisconsin every week. "We could have the confidence level to say 'this isn't noise,' " says Simas. Returning to traditional polls to understand local attitudes, Simas directed media buyers to increase the campaign's presence in Green Bay (with an ad attacking Romney on outsourcing) and beseeched Messina to reroute Clinton and eventually Obama himself for rallies there.

Mostly the analytics tables were a source of calm for Obama's team, a dynamic census that—contrary to the fluctuation of hourly polls from media and academic institutions—offered constant reminders of how stable the electorate was, and how predictable individual voters can be. (Having hundreds of data points contributing to an assessment of whether a person resembled a voter proved more useful than the seven-question battery Gallup used to sort out likely voters.) "When you see this pogo stick happening with the public data—the electorate is just not that volatile," says Stewart.

In states that had early voting, while the public tracked polls, Obama's advisers were already counting ballots. The campaign each day overlaid the lists of early voters released by election authorities with its modeling scores to arrive at a projection of how many votes they could claim as their own. On election day, the analytics tables turned into predictions. Wagner projected that Obama had won 56.4 percent of the votes in Hamilton County, Ohio's third-largest and home to Cincinnati; the final count had Obama at 57. Florida was even closer to the mark: Obama's margin was only two-tenths of a percent off from where Wagner had said it would end up.

A few days after the election, as Florida authorities were still counting provisional ballots, Simas marveled at how intimate Obama's approach to counting votes had been. He had never been so involved in a presidential election, but he had perhaps the most deeply felt sentimentality of anyone at headquarters for the human aspect of campaigning. Before he had become a political operative, Simas had been a politician, serving on the city council and school board in his hometown of Taunton, Massachusetts, running for office by knocking on doors and individually interacting with constituents, or those he hoped would be, and trying to track their moods and expectations.

Analytics had been greeted by the old guard in campaigns as a disruptive force, but in many respects it represented the purest return to the electorate as it is viewed by local candidates: as a collection of people, each of them approachable on his or her own terms, their changing levels of support and interest and enthusiasm open to measurement, and thus to respect. "What that gave us was the ability to run a national presidential campaign the way you'd do a local ward campaign," Simas said. "You know the people on your block, people have relationships with one another and you leverage them so you know the way they talk about issues, what they're discussing at the coffee shop."

Few entities in American life other than a presidential campaign interact on a single day with 180 million adults, or even a significant fraction of that—certainly no corporation, no civic institution, and very few government agencies. Obama had done so by reducing every American to a series of numbers, but it was his or her own series of numbers, and it was not merely a demographic classification (based on the way another behemoth, like Nielsen or the U.S. Census, had cut its categories) but a recognition of individual dynamism. The scores measured the ability of people to change, and be changed by, politics.

POSTSCRIPT

I n the spring of 2015, the Cato Institute identified six hundred Americans who read more than twenty books per year, and made arrangements to send them each one more. The libertarian think tank assigned their potential readers to one of three groups. One group received a free copy of Ayn Rand's *Atlas Shrugged,* one got longtime Cato executive David Boaz's *The Libertarian Mind,* and one received a book that Cato scholars considered a useful placebo to free-market doctrine: the Bible. After three months, six months, and twelve months, members of all three groups would be surveyed to see if the unsolicited books they had received could explain differential response rates to one question: *Do you consider yourself a libertarian?*

A few weeks later, the Cato researcher behind the project explained to other members of a secret gathering known as CSI that the six hundred books were just part of a pilot test. If the design appeared to work properly, the experiment would be ramped up to a much larger scale, with another twelve thousand books ready to be shipped to randomly elected readers nationwide and plans to survey a sample of them to see whether they were any more likely to consider themselves as libertarian afterward. "Political books have never been tested," says David Kirby, who had worked for Cato over the last decade, most recently as a vice president and senior fellow. "Think tanks think that books persuade people. Do they?"

Very few of other members of the CSI circle ever used books as their tools for changing minds. A range of political consultants and vendors, they tended to trade in more ephemeral modes of communication: television ads and robocalls, direct mail, digital ads, and door knocks. But they were there for the same reason that Kirby had been willing to entertain the perfidy of using Cato resources to question whether reading Ayn Rand actually led people to libertarianism—a willingness to take everything they thought they knew about what works in politics and hold it up to empirical investigation.

The mere existence of what is officially known as the Center for Strategic Initiatives field experiments seminar represented the right's most constructive engagement with the continued traumas of 2012—not just the fact that it had lost, but that it didn't know at the time it was losing, and even afterward was at a further loss to understand how or why it had done so. While many Republicans responded by conceding catchphrase-ready deficiencies—a need to do more and better with Big Data or The Ground Game—others were wiling to acknowledge that the underlying problem was the lack of a culture to encourage innovation. For a small but significant share of the party's electioneering class, however, any true reckoning with 2012 invited a deeper epistemological crisis about how to run smarter campaigns in the twenty-first century.

"We should not assume anything. Absolutely every aspect of the campaign, from the best way to knock on doors to the best way to broadcast television, should be tested," says Blaise Hazelwood, the group's founder. "'This is the way I did it on this campaign that won, so this is the way we should do it on all campaigns,'" Hazelwood says, mocking the prevailing sentiment of entrenched political consultants. "The test for them is whether they win or lose on election day. That cannot be a valid test."

The conservative establishment had been famous over the years for its organized gatherings. First there were Paul Weyrich's weekly "coalitions" lunches, held on Wednesdays when Congress was in session. Anti-tax activist Grover Norquist later claimed the breakfast slot that day, his sessions focused more on economic policy than social issues. Donors and journalists in New York started meeting one Monday per month for an hour and a half; after relocating to South Carolina, Monday Meeting founder Mallory Factor took the concept south with him, launching the Charleston Meeting. All these were devoted to ideological cohesion and legislative strategy, the matching of like-minded donors and politicians. They tended to reaffirm certainties rather than challenge them.

The CSI circle never fell into a reliable schedule, and its gatherings, taking place roughly every six weeks or so at Cato's Washington head-quarters, marked a very different mode of collaboration. There was not a politician in sight, nor many brand-name operatives; few attendees appear to be over the age of forty. This newly scientized sphere of political opera-tives and party hacks angling to remake Republican campaigns include strategists and tacticians for many of the party's top presidential candi-dates, along with staffers from the Republican National Committee and consultants attached to various elements of the political network associ-ated with Charles and David Koch.

"I sense it's one of the few places where the warring factions of the conservative side of the aisle play together in the same sandbox," says political scientist Don Green, who has advised the group since its launch. "You have people who are close to the Tea Party and people who are an-tagonistic towards the Tea Party, and they're all trying to learn from the same research method."

* * * * *

A POLARIZING INCUMBENT wins a closely fought but decisive reelec-tion despite mixed public opinion about his first term. His lead was steady and consistent throughout, and he was boosted on election day by strong turnout from core constituencies, despite suggestions that his supporters could suffer from weakened enthusiasm the second time. The lesson was clear: The president won in large part because of superior tactics and improved technique.

To Hazelwood, the 2012 election echoed a story line that eight years earlier she had observed from the winning side. As political director of the Republican National Committee during the 2004 cycle, Hazelwood had taken advantage of the unique circumstances of a presidential reelection to disrupt the cycle of short-term, election-year priorities and invest in the party's own research agenda instead of being forced to follow a consultant-driven marketplace. Over the course of nearly four years between elections, Hazelwood had managed the 72-Hour Task Force's experimental research and implemented a novel microtargeting program, modernizing the electoral mechanics that made Bush's second victory possible.

By 2008, there was evidence that Democrats had neutralized any Republican advantage in the mechanics of voter contact. Major donors like George Soros had decided not to focus their funding on campaigns to win single elections, as they had in the hopes of beating Bush in 2004, but instead to seed institutions committed to learning how to run better campaigns. Liberals, generally in awe of the success that Republicans had during the 1980s and 1990s in assembling a think tank and media infrastructure to disseminate conservative ideas, responded by building a vast left-wing campaign research culture through groups like the Analyst Institute, Catalist, and the New Organizing Institute.

Republican operatives acknowledged that Barack Obama's campaign had been tactically superior and technically more advanced than John McCain's. Afterward they leafed through campaign manager David Plouffe's memoir, *The Audacity to Win,* for clues to his methods much as Democrats looked for signs of Karl Rove's thinking. But the Republican political class could look at so much else working in Obama's favor—that candidate's unique appeal, a broad distaste for Bush, voter anxieties about economic crisis, strategic inconsistencies in McCain's approach—that curiosity never translated into serious self-examination on the right.

But few of those excuses applied in 2012, when a seemingly vulnerable incumbent president's solid victory owed an obvious debt to his tactics. Democrats were clearly running smarter, more sophisticated campaigns than their opponents, and this time they exploited a presidential reelection campaign as an engine of radical innovation. "It is a rude awakening," Hazelwood said the day after Obama's reelection. "There was a false sense of security, a sense that we figured out how to do this microtargeting—we'd figured out how do to it pretty well—and now there are other things for the party to focus on."

Not long after, Hazelwood was approached by Sally Bradshaw, a Tallahassee-based consultant who had been a longtime adviser to former Florida governor Jeb Bush. Bradshaw was one of five party eminences who had been tapped by Republican National Committee chairman Reince Priebus to oversee the Growth and Opportunity Project, the postmortem report its authors were repeatedly instructed not to describe publicly as an "autopsy." There was one question she was eager to put to Hazelwood: What did Republicans need to do to improve their electoral mechanics?

Hazelwood could point to a lot that had gone wrong. The culture that had incubated the 72-Hour Task Force withered away. In 2003, the Republican National Committee wrapped up the task force's work and never again subjected any of its programs to systematic testing. "After 2004 the drive just left," says Hazelwood. Instead, buffeted by the cockiness that came from seeing one's political machine control the White House—as books, with titles like *One Party Country,* proclaimed the dawn of a "permanent Republican majority"—the committee relapsed into the cronyism that left so many political consultants uncurious about the effectiveness of their work.

When one of Green's protégés approached an official on the Indiana Republican Party's 2006 coordinated campaign to see if he could integrate experiments into the party's efforts, there was only one question that mattered. Was the political scientist "in the family"? That described a very specific qualification—having worked on one of the two Bush-Cheney campaigns—and it was not on David Nickerson's CV. Soon, though, there was a Ph.D. from Yale, then an associate professorship at Notre Dame, and then in 2012 a title that had never before existed in the history of presidential politics: director of experiments at Obama for America. That year, when Hazelwood worked as part of Mitt Romney's targeting team, neither the Republican National Committee nor its nominee's campaign ran a single randomized trial. "We no longer did the testing and we ended up where we ended up in 2012. We just kind of stopped."

She made the case to Bradshaw that the party should take the initiative in spurring a return to such experimentation, albeit with a different objective than the one that had inspired the 72-Hour Task Force tests. "Back then we framed it completely differently. It was 'we're getting back to grass roots and showing why grass roots works,'" Hazelwood explains. "Now it's about tests, and getting to test ROI and how you measure efficiency and effectiveness." Hazelwood helped Bradshaw rewrite the Growth and Opportunity Report's section on "campaign mechanics" to offer its imprimatur for what had become her pet project. Republicans should "identify a team of strategists and funders to build a data analytics institute that can capture and distill best practices for communication to and targeting of specific voters," as the report put it. "Using the GOP's data, the data analytics institute would work to develop a specific set of tests for 2013 and 2014—tests on voter registration, persuasion, GOTV, and voter mobilization—that will then be adopted into future programs to ensure that our voter contact and targeting dollars are spent on proven performance."

The report cautiously avoided suggesting that the RNC incubate or host such an institute itself. The national party was a subject of more distrust among conservative activists than it had been during the early Bush years, and after *Citizens United* even more political spending was being driven by groups that were legally forbidden from coordinating with the party or its candidates. Hazelwood found a model for such an independent a "data analytics institute" in the organization that had paved Nickerson's way into Democratic campaigns after he was turned away by Indiana's Republicans. Hazelwood decided also to structure her project as a for-profit consulting firm that could operate with little concern for ever returning a profit, a status that permits work with both parties and campaigns as clients without being subject to disclosure laws itself. Hazelwood was transparent in her debt to the Analyst Institute, down to the unhelpfully abstract name. Hazelwood called hers the Center for Strategic Initiatives.

* * * * *

SHE PITCHED HERSELF to collaborators across the right, eager to take advantage of the oddball calendar of off-year elections to begin running tests. There was one in Massachusetts, where the American Crossroads super PAC agreed to randomly assign its robocalls on behalf of Gabriel Gomez, a first-time candidate challenging Congressman Ed Markey to replace John Kerry in the Senate. In Minneapolis's mayoral campaign that same year, Hazelwood worked with the pro-business Minnesota Jobs Coalition to test what type of messaging works best to boost a conservative candidate in a officially nonpartisan race with a large, fragmented field.

In parallel, Kirby was also digging more deeply into experiments himself. He had spent 2012 working at FreedomWorks, the well-funded conservative grassroots organization that had invested heavily in field activity designed to help elect a Republican president and a more conservative Congress. Kirby emerged from the experience resentful of the confidence political professionals brought to their decisions about tactical approaches. "We were disappointed in 2012 with how much money we spent and how little we had to show for it," Kirby says. "I felt integrity-bound to ask whether we could do any better."

Kirby was drawn to the experimental method as a tool for resolving that curiosity. He signed up for a brief summer course on randomized trials taught by Green, recognized as political science's most prominent evangelist for field experiments as the only tool capable of truly disentangling cause and effect in campaigns. (In 2011, he left Yale, his longtime home, for Columbia University.) Green was inspired by Kirby's enthusiasm and—after years of finding more interest in his methods from labor unions, environmental advocates, and ACORN—the opportunity to see if conservative targets responded differently to political communication than liberal ones. "Almost all the research to date has been on the left or center-left. Very little of it has been on the center-right or right," Green says. "There isn't a base of knowledge about the message, the messenger, and the audience they care about."

Kirby was interested in starting with lawn signs. "It is the most elemental political tactic," he says. "At FreedomWorks we spent probably at least a million dollars on that—hundreds and thousands of yard signs." Yard signs were often held up as an example of wasteful and pointless campaign spending (*yard signs don't vote* is a frequent refrain of the bienpensant political class) although there was little empirical evidence to sustain that skepticism. The limited research literature could be attributed partly to methodological complications—it is not easy to control for the spillover effects of, say, voters who drive past signs in a precinct other than the one in which they vote—but some stemmed from a lack of obvious incentive for political professionals to run an experiment. "In the case of lawn signs, what's odd is if you're dealing with a person who is deeply skeptical they're not interested enough to do a test," says Green. "People working in low-salience races see them as their one and only affordable tactic and don't want to take out a control group."

Working with Green, Kirby ran an experiment in which Virginia precincts were isolated and then randomly assigned to have signs placed at a certain density in road medians, each of them photographed and geotagged so it would be possible to monitor whether they were removed by opponents or vandals. They didn't measure a significant impact on election results in those precincts—"maybe a glimmer of an effect" on both turnout and vote share, according to Green—but given how cheap signs are to print and place, the experimenters thought that they might have demonstrated signs might not be a waste after all.

Kirby became an enthusiastic booster of Hazelwood's project. After he went to work at the Cato Institute in early 2014 he offered one of the think tank's large conference rooms to host the right's version of the "geek lunch." The first "field experiments workshop," in August 2013, drew more than one hundred people from across conservative politics. "It was the right moment," says Kirby. "People were curious." Green led a three-hour introduction to the experimental method and encouraged attendees to think of it as a tool for assessing the effectiveness of their current tactics and auditioning new ones. Many of the experiments that attendees concocted in response—to test direct mail and phone calls around turnout—addressed research questions that some lefty groups felt they had settled through replication as much as a decade earlier. "It wasn't breaking any new ground," Kirby says, "but at least it was getting the muscles flexing."

Other firms formed that specifically marketed themselves as specialists in designing and administering experiments. At the New Analytics Company, Luke Thompson, a Green acolyte who had worked as analytics director of the National Republican Senatorial Committee after receiving his Ph.D. from Yale, cited the left's success with the Analyst Institute as he sought collaborators and backers. He found a crucial one in John H. Sununu, a former New Hampshire governor and White House chief of staff who had served as chairman of his state party in 2012 and emerged afterward convinced that Democrats had taught themselves to compete under an entirely different set of rules. Adam Schaeffer, whose Evolving Strategies had launched in the 2012 cycle to help conservatives refine messages through laboratory-style experiments online, enlisted James Gimpel, the University of Maryland political scientist who had been one of Rick Perry's eggheads, to bring message tests into the real world. (They were involved in a series of experiments for FreedomWorks, including Kirby's signs test, during Virginia's 2013 elections.) Meanwhile, Brian Stobie, who as an official at the Charles Koch Institute had pushed unsuccessfully during the 2012 election to test the Koch network's electioneering operations, struck out on his own. Stobie partnered with data and voter contact specialists Scott Tranter and Chris Faulkner but was not, however, immediately convinced that their Øptimus Consulting would find success in the marketplace. "Testing, whether done on the right or left, tends to show that the majority of what you think 'works' doesn't," Stobie says. "To the majority of operatives and organizations, paying for the opportunity to find out much of what you are doing is ineffective is not an appealing investment."

Within the CSI circle, there was resignation that one cultural problem Republicans face modernizing their campaigns remained beyond their immediate control: limited access to academic social scientists capable of designing, administering, and analyzing field experiments. For his part, Green—with his politically catholic view toward experimentation and promiscuous search for collaborators who will let him test scientific theories in the real world—remained something of a unicorn. "The left enjoys a lot of sympathetic academics and legions of ideologically aligned grad students that we on the right just won't have the same level of access to," says Stobie. (On its website, Evolving Strategies felt obliged to assign each of the analysts in its network a pseudonym, like ES-9 and ES-11, to "protect his independence as an academic researcher.")

Yet over the next few months, CSI vagabonded through the suburban Virginia offices of consulting firms with meeting rooms spacious enough to play host. Eventually the group settled into its routine at the Cato Institute, where Kirby had been able to secure a large conference facility and the ability to wheel out a bar with wine and beer for a postmeeting cocktail hour. Attendance had shrunk since CSI's launch, to maybe half as many as had materialized for the inaugural meeting. It amounted to a meaningful sorting out of the merely intrigued and those who took seriously the tradeoffs involved in a regime of uncompromising experimentation. "There's a growing community of people who have a hunger to see this type of work going on," says David Seawright, the director of analytics and product innovation at Deep Root Analytics, who presented the results of a nonexperimental assessment of his firm's work targeting television ads in 2014 on behalf of Senate Majority Leader Mitch McConnell's reelection. "We need more of this collaborative testing on the Republican side."

The emergence of the CSI circle unmasked a generational divide more fundamental than the one between practitioners of online and offline politicking, which defines most press coverage of the Republicans' technology predicament. There a Web-savvy new guard chafed against the old-line consultants who continue to profit from spending on television, phone, and mail. Their disputes—on the percentage of a budget devoted to Web and mobile advertising, a campaign's willingness to sign on to Periscope or Snapchat, or whether a digital consultant has a proverbial "seat at the table" on strategic decisions—were lost on the CSI crowd. Many there were eager to take on the digital consultants and the grandiose claims some of them made, unchallenged, about their potential impact on elections. Those in the experimental set pronounce themselves agnostic about tactics, interested only in those whose worth have been proven, empirically. What can be measured to deliver votes—rather than just clicks or eyeballs—and at what cost?

* * * * *

UNLIKE MOST CSI agendas, which typically list multiple presentations, the one circulated before the May 29, 2014, meeting had just one, an indication of just how much bolder the study titled "The Abbott Campaign Experiments: Persuasion and Turnout in Texas" was than anything CSI had seen before.

The paper had a patrimony familiar to students of both modern political science methods and the Republican consulting class. The previous December, University of Texas professor Daron Shaw had been summoned to participate in a strategy session with Texas attorney general Greg Abbott's campaign advisers. Shaw had been well-known to the state's Republicans, from his time as a staff analyst at George W. Bush's headquarters during the 2000 election. Five years later, as a member of the team of in-house experimenters that strategist Dave Carney retained for Perry's reelection, Shaw was part of a collaboration that produced more peer-reviewed papers than any other campaign in history.

The paper they published after randomizing Perry's television ads became a scholarly landmark yet had little impact on the political profession. Those who saw the Perry results often pointed first to the unusual conditions under which the research had been conducted, such as the fact that the television experiment had been conducted at a time when Perry did not have a clear opponent. "One of the most common criticisms one hears from practitioners about political science experiments is that the treatment is 'not what we'd do in a real campaign,'" Shaw later reflected. "The obvious solution is to give the professionals the resources and discretion to design and implement their preferred outreach within the context of the experiment."

By 2013, Carney had parted ways with Perry and had begun advising Abbott, the likely Republican nominee to succeed him. Carney once again invited Shaw to make the campaign a laboratory, this time including all the online tactics that had emerged since their 2006 partnership. (YouTube had just launched as the Perry television experiment was being planned.) They settled on February as an experimental window, just before a primary in which Abbott maintained a vast lead. The campaign's consultants were asked to devise plans at a budget that would "allow them to do what they needed to in order to produce an impact." Then Shaw would be given the opportunity to randomize those tactics, so no one could complain afterward that the communication had been artificially devised for the sake of a study. Ultimately, the experimental treatment amounted to $1.6 million worth of campaign communications—across broadcast and cable television, a variety of digital formats, radio, and direct mail—with effects measured at both individual and neighborhood units. Three entire media markets, including El Paso and Amarillo, were assigned to a control group that received no Abbott campaign communication over the course of that month.

When he compared polls conducted before and after the experiment, Shaw found that three weeks of campaigning increased Abbott's popularity by nearly eight points among the voters he was trying to persuade, with targeted broadcast television buys doing so with the greatest force. At the same time voters in zip codes served Facebook and online pre-roll video ads were less likely to support Abbott afterward, and turned out at the same rate as those who lived in areas that never received the ads. (Shaw did find that, in some combinations, Internet advertising did have a modestly positive impact on turnout, according to voter registration records updated after the primary.)

When Shaw was ready to reveal those findings to a CSI meeting, in the midst of Abbott's general election race against state senator Wendy Davis, Carney invited back the consultants and vendors whose services he had audited to be part of the discussion—an equivalent of beauty pageant contestants being forced to stand onstage while judges render a verdict on their presence and poise. Shaw, meanwhile, continued his efforts to translate across the conceptual divide that typically separated such researchers from their subjects. "One thing that has traditionally differentiated consultants from political scientists is attentiveness to the costs of different modes of campaign outreach. Practitioners need to not only understand how different forms of campaign outreach affect voters but also how much money it takes to realize such an impact," Shaw wrote in an article on the experiment and its results that he, as part of his deal with Abbott's campaign, submitted to scholarly journals for publication. "Indeed, they might argue that the relatively modest effects associated with online outreach in our tests still constitute a more cost-effective investment than broadcast television."

* * * * *

ABOUT FIFTY PEOPLE responded to Hazelwood's invitation to gather at Cato in June 2015, and she began by reminding them of CSI's one rule:

what they were about to hear was off-the-record. "Ask questions like you usually do," she said. "Attack our speakers, like sometimes happens."

She should not have had to appeal to the competitive impulses of her attendees. It already looked as though she had summoned representatives of the various warring families of Republican politics; arrayed before her, at long tables in lecture hall formation, sat operatives with ties to all of the candidates then thought to comprise the first tier of contenders for the party's presidential nomination. One of the presenters came from the firm Jeb Bush had hired to help target its television ads, another from a phone vendor that had worked for Wisconsin governor Scott Walker and had close links to his campaign-in-waiting. A pair of analysts from Øptimus, by then advising Florida senator Marco Rubio, sat in the back of the room, not far from where the founders of Targeted Victory, the firm Perry had hired to handle digital advertising and media analytics, found seats after arriving a few minutes late. Hazelwood herself was a longtime advisor to Louisiana governor Bobby Jindal, through her firm Grassroots Consulting, and had since joined his allied super PAC as a consultant.

That diversity of loyalties was its own evidence about how Republicans had matured in their understanding of the role analytics could play in their campaigns. At the same point four years earlier, Mitt Romney had been the only Republican candidate who had even attempted to develop a sophisticated approach to using data. (Romney's strongest rival in the primaries, Rick Santorum, boasted of not even having a pollster in his employ.) In 2016 there did not seem to be enough talent in conservative politics to sustain all the serious investments being made in analytics. One candidate, Texas senator Ted Cruz, even hired a London-based firm to serve as his analytics department, an inversion of the typical outsourcing of American political expertise to other countries. Cambridge Analytica promoted what it called "psychographic" profiling—essentially statistical models that predicted where voters would fall on the Big Five personality traits—supposedly refined through its work as a "psy ops" contractor to governments working in global conflict zones. Cruz's strategists weren't quite sure what it would do with a list of every Iowa caucusgoer likely to be both highly neurotic and conscientious, but they were grateful to have a readymade data-sciences team staffed by University of Cambridge astrophysics postdocs, even if none had ever before worked on a political campaign.

With initially seventeen candidates seeking the Republican nomination, the diaspora across campaigns and super PACs made the distinction within CSI between collaborator and competitor increasingly fluid. "We've actually been surprised by the broad spectrum of folks," says Hazelwood. "There are Koch people there, although they're not as willing to share their experiments, but they're there and participating. We're hoping at some point they do share their experiments with the group, so other people can learn."

* * * * *

A FEW WEEKS later, Hazelwood met RNC chairman Reince Priebus for lunch at the Capitol Hill Club and handed over the results of an experimental study he had commissioned from her firm. Hazelwood's reputation had impressed Priebus long before the first two met, in 2009, back when he was a lawyer who oversaw field offices near his Wisconsin home and had "done every yard-sign job in the party you can imagine." Sharing a ticket with Bush in 2004 during a failed state senate run, Priebus saw how, by "dividing states into turf, and measuring outcomes and metrics," as he put it, Hazelwood's internal reforms had modernized the party's approach to field organizing. "I've known her as the author of that concept," Priebus says. "I really do understand the ground game and what we need to do."

The 72-Hour Task Force had been established to convince local party activists like Priebus that the ground game was not merely something one did or didn't do, but that some tactical approaches to it were better than others. Hazelwood had isolated "precinct organizing" (assigning a full-time field staffer for a month), "GOP flushing" (indiscriminately turning out Republican voters in the last two days before an election), and "volunteer calling" (compared to paid call centers) as three distinct activities, and subjected each to separate tests. As a result of the impact—two to three percentage points' increase in turnout for each—the Task Force prescribed that Republican campaigns assign one person to be individually responsible for every forty to one hundred voters. "Back to People Power," an internal RNC presentation at the time titled the recommendation.

After Bush's reelection, the party let much of that field infrastructure wither, along with the ethos behind and intellectual justification for it. During the years since, experiments have revealed a cognitive logic for understanding what mobilizes voters. Basic interactions immediately became more potent when they were personalized in a way that introduced a sense of individual responsibility around voting. Campaigns now frequently remind citizens of their past history casting a ballot, and recruit them to sign pledges to do so again. The behavioral psychology behind such techniques gave new depth to campaigns' understanding of "people power."

Hazelwood developed a hypothesis that people power could learn something from stalking. Campaigns have long thought of voter contact as part of a narrative progression: a flight of six direct-mail pieces over which a candidate's argument unfurls, or a "layered" approach in which phone calls and door knocks are delivered in a deliberately choreographed sequence. But campaigns rarely share these plans with the voters themselves, often preferring to let the interactions speak for themselves and not draw undue attention to their volume. Instead, Hazelwood thought it was time to mash up the various tactics that the 72-Hour Task Force had segregated into distinct programs. As with the pledges and the vote history techniques, walking voters through the process as it was happening could dissuade them from assuming that get-out-the-vote interactions were isolated encounters.

But even though the RNC had offered an early endorsement of such testing in the abstract, she had trouble getting party officials to commit to a specific one. To test an existing program, a campaign has to agree to isolate a mass of voters it would have otherwise targeted to serve as a control group, and commit to not contracting them altogether or deliver some sort of placebo treatment. To test a fresh hypothesis in an actual election environment, a campaign has to create an entirely new program on top of its existing tactics. "There's been a general openness to it, because there's been a cultural change where now we get it that testing is necessary—but the issue is a willingness to pay for it," says Hazelwood. "It's just like data—campaigns get it, but not the thought that it should cost money."

Hazelwood was anxious that the party not let a busy midterm election year pass without using every opportunity to hone tactics it could deploy in earnest in 2016. After San Diego announced a special mayoral election scheduled for February 2014, Hazelwood convinced a friend managing Republican Kevin Faulconer's campaign to let the Center for Strategic Initiatives get involved. Hazelwood took command of some of the party's field program there, randomly assigning some areas to receive specialized attention from local precinct captains. When after the election she was able to show that her tactics had increased turnout among 8.5 percent among the party's so-called low-propensity voters, the party's chairman took notice.

That finding intersected neatly with what Priebus had identified as his party's strategic challenge, and one of the areas the Growth and Opportunity Project had blamed for the party's inability to win the presidency or the Senate in 2012. "We're a really good midterm party, but for some reason presidential-year-only voters have been trouble for us," Priebus says. "If we put people out in the field—and we have a limited amount of people and limited amount of time—what's the combination of things we can do that have the best effect of turning out people who vote only in presidential years?"

Over the summer, Priebus signed off on Hazelwood's proposal to have the Center for Strategic Initiatives help answer that question. He was insistent that Hazelwood's experiments not interfere with the party's plans to spend $105 million across key races in midterm battlegrounds.

In three states, however, Hazelwood's firm was permitted to layer atop the party's extant organization an additional precinct program that would target the type of low-propensity voters that Republican strategists did not expect to necessarily vote in 2014 but knew they needed to mobilize in 2016. After working with her on how to structure her study, Green directed Hazelwood to enlist Oklahoma State University professor Brandon Lenoir, whom he had guided on another lawn sign experiment, for help implementing it.

In nine counties across Colorado, Iowa, and Arkansas, Hazelwood's team worked with the state parties and the Republican Senate candidate to hire dedicated local organizers it called precinct captains. Each was given a list of voters who had cast a ballot in one or fewer of the past four major elections, with directions to visit each voter in mid-October for an introductory conversation. "I was designated your Precinct Captain for the Republican Party, for the duration of the election," the canvassing script instructed. Then over the next few weeks the precinct captain would make contact four more times, in a specific order: again at the door, by phone, followed by a postcard and a final door visit. If the voter was home each time, it meant a recurring interaction with an increasingly familiar neighborhood figure.

If the voter didn't answer the door or phone, however, the precinct captain was instructed to make the missed encounter just as personally memorable. Each door hanger left behind should have a handwritten Post-it note attached to it, inscribed with a message that the "personalized note instructions" recommended should say: "Hi Mary, sorry I missed you today! . . . I will be back in the neighborhood again next week and try to catch you then." The postcard would pick up the theme: "I have stopped by your house a couple times and tried to call to make sure you have all the information you need to vote." For a voter who wasn't home after two door visits and a phone call, the next note would turn even more ominous: "I will keep checking the list to see if you have voted and if not will drop by your house again to follow up."

Over the course of three weeks, Hazelwood's "stalker test" deployed some of the most potent psychological tricks known to nudge a citizen into the act of voting, along with some new ones, all as part of a borderline-creepy courtship that would be difficult to ignore or forget about. After the election, Green and Lenoir found that it had a considerable impact, increasing turnout among targets by between two and three percentage points. It had not been easy, though, as stalking demanded attention, resources, and planning that campaigns do not always have for their field programs. (The report did not calculate the cost of such contact, and it was certainly conceivable that at a much lower price yard signs could prove more cost-effective—if less targetable—than the elaborate program that required the same field staffer to be available for every interaction with an assigned voter.)

When Hazelwood presented the analysis to Priebus at the Capitol Hill Club, she put the paper that Green and Lenoir had written in a thick, glossy brochure with far more elaborate graphics than typically package academic articles. Priebus says the findings confirm what he had assumed about the value of localized field programs that focus on sustained personal contact, but now, he says, "I can take that information and go sell it to the state parties, and go to into a boardroom to get people to cut a check."

The finding that most excited both Hazelwood and Priebus, however, grew out of an accident. In Colorado, canvassers were mistakenly assigned to go to some of the party's reliable voters, who had cast ballots in all four of the most recent elections. After being hounded by a precinct captain, they voted a lower rate than those who received no contact at all. "We have proven fact now that we should stop calling these people," Hazelwood says, with comic impatience. "Stop wasting time!"

ACKNOWLEDGMENTS

t's my good luck to have learned how to cover campaigns in Philadelphia. Politics in an old, big city has remained a wondrously physical affair. The campaign operatives I talked to tended to brag not about the size of their television ad buys but about how many election day workers they would have on the street and how many vans they had rented to drive voters to the polls. I savored election days not as a twelve-hour lull between the frantic close of a campaign and its result, but as the occasion where electioneering machinations were forced out in the open. I spent those days taking long walks on city streets. For one primary, starting just across the city line in Delaware County when polls opened and winding my way by dusk nearly to the Montgomery County border near Oak Lane, I traveled around twenty-four miles, nearly a proper political marathon—stopping along the way to check in on polling places and union staging areas, and to talk to party committeemen and ward leaders.

Philadelphia offered a real education in political tactics at their most tactile, at what I only years later appreciated had been a transformative moment in the way campaigns counted, targeted, and mobilized votes. Those experiences instilled in me a sense that campaigns were more than a procession of speeches, ads, debates, and press conferences, in a way rarely reflected in political journalism. So I owe a lot to my friends and sources in the Philadelphia political world, particularly Nathaniel Parks and Harry Cook, who gave me my earliest lessons in the rudiments of field and voter contact, even though I wouldn't have had the language to describe what I was learning that way. Others have been generous with their time and wisdom then and since, including Tom Lindenfeld, Mike Roman, Neil Oxman, J. J. Balaban, Doc Sweitzer, Sam Katz, Jim Baumbach, Maurice Floyd, Michael Bronstein, Mark Nevins, Ken Smukler, Maureen Garrity, Al Spivey, Elliott Curson, Eleanor Dezzi, Rebecca Kirszner Katz, Brian Stevenson, Mark Alderman, Micah Mahjoubian, Stephanie Singer, Tracy Hardy, Appollos Baker, John Hawkins, Chris Mottola, Commissioner Josh Shapiro, and Congressman Bob Brady.

The *Boston Globe* allowed me to cover the best presidential campaign I have any right to have lived through, let alone track across thirty-eight states and six countries. I am grateful to Peter Canellos for making me a newspaperman, and to Marty Baron for taking a chance on someone who had never before written a daily story. Great colleagues in both Washington and Boston made it an exceptional place to practice journalism: Matt Viser, Bryan Bender, Farah Stockman, Susan Milligan, Scott Helman, Michael Kranish, Michael Levenson, Marcella Bombardieri, Jim Smith, Foon Rhee, Gareth Cook, and Steve Heuser. Thanks to Christopher Rowland for letting me remain part of the family, and to Stephanie Vallejo for all her help and good humor along the way. I am also in hock to the transatlantic gang at *Monocle* for harboring this refugee from the American newspaper crisis, and their understanding when I felt moved on short notice to write this book: Tyler Brûlé, Andrew Tuck, Aisha Speirs, and Steve Bloomfield.

This book started as an article for *The New York Times Magazine* about the use of behaviorally minded field experiments in politics. I lived with the piece for nearly a year, and on several occasions I worried that I had lost the access and cooperation of subjects I would need to breach the secretive world where the most compelling and influential research was taking place. At one point, fearing that I wouldn't be able to deliver the narrative I had promised, I wrote my editor, Chris Suellentrop, to suggest we just abandon the assignment. "It's too good of a story to give up without a little fight," he wrote back. Chris was right, and I owe him for his commitment to telling that story—along with Gerry Mazorzati for commissioning it, Hugo Lindgren for publishing it, Lia Miller for fact-checking it, and James Ryerson for carrying it across the finish line. Thanks, as well, to David Haskell and David Wallace-Wells at *New York* for further indulging my interest in the science of politics. Since then, I have joined *Slate* to cover that terrain on an ongoing basis, and have been part of the best political team on the Web, including David Plotz, Michael Newman, Will Dobson, John Dickerson, Dave Weigel, and John Swansburg, who edits better than anybody who can edit faster, and edits faster than anybody who can edit better. Immediately after the 2012 election, I wrote a long narrative for *Technology Review* about the use of analytics by the Obama and Romney campaigns, which forms the basis of the afterword added to the paperback edition.

The greatest debt is owed to those whose names fill this text. My subjects and sources are often those who, in an industry propelled by self-promotion, choose to remain in the background. But this book is possible only because they shared my commitment to having the story of the largely underappreciated revolution in American politics be told with the scope and detail the subject demands. Over the course of the year I reported and wrote this book, I conducted hundreds of interviews, and the identities of those who shared their time and candor with me will be apparent to readers. (Nearly all of my interview subjects spoke, to some extent or another, on the record.) I am most appreciative of their patience. I began this project with little grasp of even the most basic technical aspects of randomized experimentation or statistical modeling, and when I think back to some of my earliest interviews I am embarrassed by some of the questions I asked and can only imagine how weary they made my inter-locutors. There are a few whose contributions—unearthing documents, tracking down other sources, making introductions—are out of proportion to whatever place (if any) they have in the narrative: Debra DeShong Reed, Anu Rangappa, Amy Chapman, Brent Colburn, Mark McKinnon, Adrian Gray, and Regina Schwartz.

A salute is due to traveling companions from an epic 2008 campaign and electioneering adventures since: Bret Hovell, Adam Aigner-Treworgy, Bethany Thomas Jordan, Mosheh Oinounou, Kelly O'Donnell, Michael Cooper, Elisabeth Bumiller, Lisa Lerer, Maeve Reston, Katie Connolly, Seema Mehta, Athena Jones, Jonathan Alter, Hans Nichols. Former colleagues RoseMarie Terenzio and Lisa Dallos remain good friends who have offered a useful boost as I've tried to find my footing writing books. I can thank a warm circle of erstwhile Washingtonians for welcoming me to Washington: Mike Madden, Mindy Saraco, Mark Paustenbach, Dan Reilly, Meg Reilly, Scott Mulhauser, Cecily Craighill, Betsy Barnett, Ben Wallace-Wells, Juliet Eilperin, Jill Zuckman, Carrie Budoff Brown, Jose Antonio Vargas, Christina Bellantoni, Brian Weiss and Aimee Agresti, Michael Schaffer, Keltie Hawkins, and Eleanor and Eva Schaffer. Good friends still make Phila-delphia feel in many ways like home: Jason Fagone, Rich Rys, Andy Putz, Michael Karloutsos, Phil Press, Russ Tisinger, Jeff Steinberg, Bridget Mor-ris, Alessandra Bullen, Elliot Bullen.

Some of my best friends happen to be talented writers and editors who offered their time to read and work over my text at various stages: Lisa Wangsness, Benjamin Wallace, Jack Bohrer, Geoff Gagnon, April White. They made essential contributions, as did others. I never had the good sense to study with Rick Valelly when I attended Swarthmore, but I'm glad to have gotten to know him since; he offered sage scholarly counsel on this project, partially by belatedly assigning me the political science syllabus I dodged as an undergraduate. I receive continued inspiration from Jonathan Martin; he is probably the best political reporter of my generation, and I feel fortunate to have the opportunity to watch him up close as he practices his craft. And above all there is my longtime friend and professional co-conspirator, James Burnett, who makes just about all my work better.

A young writer could not have better champions than my agent Larry Weissman and his partner, Sascha Alper. I knew Larry had led me into the right hands for this project when at one of our early meetings my new editor, Zachary Wagman, asked me—more than eighteen months before election day—what I thought of Martin Heinrich's chances in New Mexico's Democratic Senate primary. He was responsible for publishing an ebook preview from this work, *Rick Perry and His Eggheads,* a remarkable midsummer feat of improvisation and nimbleness. For its success I owe thanks to the rest of the team at Crown: Annsley Rosner, Dyana Messina, Rachel Rokicki, Julie Cepler, Michael Gentile, and Molly Stern. I am fortunate to have as talented a journalist as Dan Fromson fact-checking my manuscript (along with timely research assistance from Claire Kim) and as creative a tactician as Mary Krause making sure the final product finds an audience. Thanks to David Fields for once again agreeing to briefly unretire from photography to take my portrait for the book's jacket, to Dan Shepelavy for his aesthetic guardianship, and to Tom Kennedy and Dan Seng at Tom Kennedy Design for their work on the book's website.

My family let me knock on strangers' doors and spend school nights at phone banks as I dabbled in political campaigns beginning at the age of twelve and similarly encouraged me when I settled into another line of work that polls show to be one of the country's least admired. For that support and love I thank my grandmothers, Olga Issenberg and Pola Brodzki; my late grandfathers, David Issenberg and Ludwik Brodzki; my aunt Gayle Brodzki; my sister, Sarina; and my parents, to whom this book is dedicated.

NOTES

PROLOGUE

3 at the time the polls opened: Lisa Rein, "Election 2010: Bennet-Buck Outcome in Colorado a Tossup," *Washington Post,* November 2, 2010, www.washingtonpost.com/wp-dyn/content/article/2010/11/02/AR2010110201571.html.

3 "The Bennet thing was pretty instructive": Axelrod quoted in Ron Brownstein, "In 2012, Obama May Need a New Coalition," *National Journal,* January 7, 2011.

4 $6-billion-per-year: Patricia Zengerle, "U.S. Vote in 2012 Will Be Record, $6 billion Election," Reuters, August 30, 2011, http://www.reuters.com/article/2011/08/30/us-usa-campaign-spending-idUSTRE77T3ZX20110830.

10 Franken's lawyers watched their adversary: Jay Weiner, *This Is Not Florida* (Minneapolis: University of Minnesota Press, 2010), 133.

10 a 477-vote deficit on election day: "Recounting of Minnesota's Senate Race," timeline by *Minneapolis Star Tribune,* ww2.startribune.com/projects/timeline/recount.html.

11 "A campaign rally is three people": Shrum quoted in Frank I. Luntz, *Candidates, Consultants, and Campaigns: The Style and Substance of American Electioneering* (New York: Blackwell, 1988), 22.

11 "The current crop are like": Morris quoted in Susan B. Glasser, "Consultants Pursue Promising Web of New Business," *Washington Post,* May 3, 2000.

① BLINDED BY POLITICAL SCIENCE

17 The university had opened its doors: Richard J. Storr, *Harper's University: The Beginnings, a History of the University of Chicago* (Chicago: University of Chicago Press, 1966), 86.

17 one of the first schools: Martin Bulmer, *The Chicago School of Sociology* (Chicago: University of Chicago Press, 1984), 7.

17 still new to American academia: Lori Thurgood, Mary J. Golladay, and Susan T. Hill, *U.S. Doctorates in the 20th Century: Special Report NSF 06-319* (Arlington, VA: National Science Foundation, 2006), 4.

18 terse memos: Barry D. Karl, *Charles E. Merriam and the Study of Politics* (Chicago: University of Chicago Press, 1974), 46.

20 keeping the Union intact: Ibid., 4.

20 Charles and his brother teased: Ibid., 5.

20 Oregon became the first state: "Direct Election of Senators," U.S. Senate website, www.senate.gov/artandhistory/history/common/briefing/Direct _Election_Senators.htm.

20 sent a questionnaire: Karl, *Charles E. Merriam and the Study of Politics,* 56.

21 hoped to use the university: Charles E. Merriam, "The Present State of the Study of Politics," *American Political Science Review* 15, no. 2 (May 1921): 173–85.

23 twice as many women: Harold F. Gosnell, "The Marriage of Math and Young Poli Sci: Some Early Uses of Quantitative Methods," *Political Methodologist,* newsletter of the Political Methodology section of American Political Science Association, 3, no. 1 (Winter 1990).

23 "general indifference": Charles E. Merriam and Harold F. Gosnell, *Non-Voting: Causes and Methods of Control* (Chicago: University of Chicago Press, 1924).

23 first major political science study: Karl, *Charles E. Merriam and the Study of Politics,* 148.

23 "If scientific methods seem": A. N. Holcombe, review of *Non-Voting: Causes and Methods of Control,* by Charles E. Merriam and Harold F. Gosnell, *American Political Science Review* 19, no. 1 (February 1925): 202–3.

26 likely the first field experiment: Gabriel A. Almond, *Harold Dwight Lasswell, 1902–1978: A Biographical Memoir* (Washington, DC: National Academy of Sciences, 1987).

26 "has the high merit": George E. G. Catlin, "Harold F. Gosnell's Experiments in the Stimulation of Voting," *Methods in Social Science: A Case Book,* ed. Stuart Arthur Rice (Chicago: University of Chicago Press, 1931), 705.

26 "This study is not only a model": Review from August 14, 1927, quoted in unpublished Gosnell autobiography, apparently written in 1981, Harold F. Gosnell Papers, Special Collections Research Center, University of Chicago Library.

26 "Perhaps Mencken is right": Quoted in Douglas Bukowski, *Big Bill Thompson, Chicago, and the Politics of Image* (Urbana: University of Illinois Press, 1998), 3.

27 used new statistical methods: Samuel J. Eldersveld, "Experimental Propaganda Techniques and Voting Behavior," *American Political Science Review* 50, no. 1 (March 1956): 154–65.

27 entire decades would pass: Donald P. Green and Alan S. Gerber, "Underprovision of Experiments in Political Science," *Annals of the American Academy of Political and Social Science* 589 (September 2003): 94–112.

28 One of the pollsters: Clyde H. Coombs, *Angus Campbell, 1910–1980: A Biographical Memoir* (Washington, DC: National Academy of Sciences, 1987), 46.

29 His 1952 survey: From Gosnell's speech to 1959 conference of the American Association for Public Opinion Research, Harold F. Gosnell Papers, Special Collections Research Center, University of Chicago Library.

29 Campbell's questionnaire: American National Election Study, 1952 codebook, University of Michigan, Center for Political Studies, Ann Arbor.

31 In 1972, Popkin had: Joe Klein, *Politics Lost* (New York: Doubleday, 2006), 42.

32 McGovern hadn't lost: Samuel Popkin, John W. Gorman, Charles Phillips, and Jeffrey A. Smith, "Comment: What Have You Done for Me Lately? Toward an Investment Theory of Voting," *American Political Science Review* 70, no. 3 (September 1976): 779–805.

33 "These contests are commonly": Samuel L. Popkin, *The Reasoning Voter* (Chicago: University of Chicago Press, 1991), 8.

② A GAME OF MARGINS

37 Bob Squier had happily abandoned: Bart Barnes, "Robert Squier, Leading Political Consultant, Dies at 65," *Washington Post,* January 25, 2000.

37 Peter Hart launched: "There and Back," *Campaigns & Elections,* June 2009.

38 only full-time employee: Theodore White, *The Making of the President, 1960* (New York: Atheneum, 1961*)*, 60.

39 Reese worked to get the Democratic party: "The Political Campaign Industry: Joe Napolitan, Matt Reese, Brad O'Leary and Tom Edwards Talk About the Ups and Downs, the Highs and Lows, of Being Political Consultants," *Campaigns & Elections,* December–January 1993–1994.

39 He effectively rewrote: Ron Faucheux, "Final Advice from Matt Reese," *Campaigns & Elections,* February 1999.

39 "You go where the cherries is": Quoted in David Lee Rosenbloom, *The Election Men* (New York: Quadrangle Books, 1973), 37.

39 "I wish God gave": David Chagall, *Kingmakers* (New York: Harcourt Brace Jovanovich, 1981), 331.

40 "If the 1964 election": Rosenbloom, *The Election Men,* 77.

40 landing jobs as an administrative assistant: Ibid.

40 "Consultants have become possible": Larry J. Sabato, *The Rise of Political Consultants* (New York: Basic Books, 1981), 267.

45 the AMA struggled to sustain: "Medicine: Sore Throat Attacks," *Time,* August 18, 1975.

47 As part of its post-Watergate reinvention: James M. Perry, "The GOP: Dying for Real?," *National Observer,* November 27, 1976.

50 hard at work trying to modernize: Jere Nash and Andy Taggart, "Education Transforms the Mississippi Legislature, *Journal of Mississippi History,* Fall 2006.

50 When legislators blocked: Jere Nash and Andy Taggart, *Mississippi Politics: The Struggle for Power* (Jackson: University Press of Mississippi, 2009), 138.

52 Even before the election in 1982: Wendell Rawls Jr., "Mississippi Governor Is Big Winner on Education," *New York Times,* December 27, 1982.

53 "To me, a political consultant": Joseph Napolitan, *The Election Game and How to Win It* (Garden City, NY: Doubleday, 1972), 2.

54 candidates spent $100 million: Bill Peterson, "Direct Mail Writes New Chapter in How to Run a Political Campaign," *Washington Post,* November 17, 1982.

54 nearly ten for each person: Michael Barone and Grant Ujifusa, *The Almanac of American Politics 1986* (Washington, DC: National Journal, 1985), 1398.

56 group Census data in twenty-five categories: Dennis W. Johnson, *No Place for Amateurs* (New York: Routledge, 2007), 149.

56 Smith dismissed his Democratic opponent: David Reinhard, "Voters' Guide to Senate-Race Broadsides," *Oregonian,* December 9, 1995.

57 populist DeFazio had attacked Wyden: Benjamin Sheffner, *Roll Call,* December 4, 1995.

57 Wyden carried the Portland metro: Ashbel S. Green and Jeff Mapes, "Hot Topics: Democrat Naito Joins Exodus from House," *Oregonian,* December 10, 1995.

60 The Wyden campaign reached: Hal Malchow, "The Targeting Revolution in Political Direct Contact," *Campaigns & Elections,* June 1997.

63 the Democrat won on January 30: Certified results from Oregon secretary of state, January 30, 1996.

67 late tactical shift from attacks: Ronald D. Elving, *PS: Political Science and Politics* 29, no. 3 (September 1996): 440–46.

69 with whom the vice president enjoyed discussing: Remarks by Bill Clinton, March 9, 1998, http://clinton4.nara.gov/Initiatives/Millennium/19980309 -22774.html.

③ THE NEW HAVEN EXPERIMENTS

73 Running the federal Office of Economic Opportunity: Robert Levine, Harold Watts, Robinson Hollister, Walter Williams, and Alice O'Connor, "A Retrospective on the Negative Income Tax Experiments: Looking Back at the Most Innovative Field Studies in Social Policy," in *The Ethics and Economics of the Basic Income Guarantee,* ed. Karl Widerquist, Michael Anthony Lewis, and Steven Pressman (Aldershot, UK: Ashgate, 2005), 4.

74 Each season, scientists: David Salsburg, *The Lady Tasting Tea* (New York: Henry Holt, 2001), 5.

74 plots of rye, wheat, and potato: Ibid., 40.

74 Even though Rothamsted researchers: D. J. Finney, "The Statistician and the Planning of Field Experiments," *Journal of the Royal Statistical Society, Series A (General)* 119, no. 1 (1956): 1–27.

75 Not far from Fisher: Richard Doll, "Sir Austin Bradford Hill and the Progress of Medical Science," *British Medical Journal* 305, no. 6868 (December 19–26, 1992): 1521–26.

75 "chance was regarded as an enemy": Harry M. Marks, *The Progress of Experiment: Science and Therapeutic Reform in the United States, 1900–1990* (Cambridge, UK: Cambridge University Press, 1997), 141.

75 But Hill thought that: Alan Yoshioka, "Use of Randomisation in the Medical Research Council's Clinical Trial of Streptomycin in Pulmonary Tuberculosis in the 1940s," *British Medical Journal* 317, no. 7167 (October 31, 1998): 1220–23.

75 "It is obvious that no statistician": A. B. Hill, "Principles of Medical Statistics: The Aim of the Statistical Method," *Lancet* 1 (1931): 41–43.

75 In 1943, a New Jersey chemist: Yoshioka, "Use of Randomisation."

76 The "S" cases were to receive: "Streptomycin in Pulmonary Tuberculosis: A Medical Research Council Investigation," *British Medical Journal,* October 30, 1948.

77 When, a few years later, Jonas Salk: Liza Dawson, "The Salk Polio Vaccine Trial of 1954: Risks, Randomization and Public Involvement in Research," *Clinical Trials* 1, no. 1 (February 2004): 122–30.

77 In 1962, the Food and Drug Administration: Marks, *The Progress of Experiment,* 230.

77 "well-controlled investigations": *Code of Federal Regulations,* Food and Drug Administration, title 21, sec. 860.7.

80 They had selected three basic modes: Alan S. Gerber and Donald P. Green, "The Effects of Canvassing, Telephone Calls, and Direct Mail on Voter Turnout: A Field Experiment," *American Political Science Review* 94, no. 3 (September 2000): 653–63.

81 Putnam looked at declining membership: Robert D. Putnam, *Bowling Alone: The Collapse and Revival of American Community* (New York: Simon & Schuster, 2000), 438–44.

82 Party organizations that had once mobilized: Steven J. Rosenstone and John Mark Hansen, *Mobilization, Participation, and Democracy in America* (New York: Longman, 2003), 162.

④ THE TWO PERCENT SOLUTION

90 joined the committee as its research director: Interview with Mark E. Steitz, October 31, 1992, in *1992 Clinton Presidential Campaign Interviews,* Diane D. Blair Papers (MC 1632), University of Arkansas Libraries, Little Rock, Special Collections.

91 That gave analysts a granular unit: "Census Tracts and Block Numbering Areas, U.S. Census, http://www.census.gov/geo/www/cen_tract.html.

91 "He had worked for four years": Quoted in Robin Toner, "Paul Tully Is Dead at 48; Top Democratic Strategist," *New York Times,* September 25, 1992.

92 Party efforts were boosted: Steve Rosenthal, "Building to Win, Building to Last: The AFL-CIO Political Program," in *Not Your Father's Union Movement: Inside the AFL-CIO,* ed. Jo-Ann Mort (London: Verso, 1998), 104.

94 At the White House, an exultant Rove: Joshua Green, "The Rove Presidency," *Atlantic,* September 2007.

94 Rove dubbed him: Karl Rove, *Courage and Consequence: My Life as a Conservative in the Fight* (New York: Threshold, 2010), 196.

⑤ YOU MEAN YOU DON'T DO THIS IN POLITICS?

108 "a kind of black art": Quoted in Maureen Dowd, "Bush's Top Strategists: Smooth Poll-Taker and Hard-Driving Manager," *New York Times,* May 30, 1988.

108 Teeter was barely out of college: Daniel Golden, "The President's Point Man," *Boston Globe Magazine,* April 19, 1992.

108 hired the young Michigander: Biographical summary in finding aid to Robert M. Teeter Papers 1967–2004, Gerald R. Ford Library, Ann Arbor, Michigan.

108 spend more than $1 million: Lawrence R. Jacobs and Robert Y. Shapiro, "The Rise of Presidential Polling: The Nixon White House in Historical Perspective," *Public Opinion Quarterly* 59, no. 2 (Summer 1995): 163–65.

109 "Midwestern barometer": Golden, "The President's Point Man."

109 "I had the best of both worlds": Quoted in Tom Henderson, "The Merchants of Influence," *Corporate Detroit,* June 1993.

111 one of the thirty largest: Randall Rothenberg, "The Boom in Political Consulting," *New York Times,* May 24, 1987.

112 dabbling in election season punditry: Henderson, "The Merchants of Influence."

112 Gage's portfolio had become stocked with corporate clients: Ibid.

112 But in the 1980s: Thomas H. Davenport and Jeanne G. Harris, *Competing on Analytics: The New Science of Winning* (Boston: Harvard Business School Press, 2007), 85.

116 In his 1964 novel: "In Memoriam: Eugene Leonard Burdick, Political Science: Berkeley," University of California (System) Academic Senate, June 1967.

117 "They went through every poll": Eugene Burdick, *The 480* (New York: Dell, 1964), 59.

117 "the underworld of cigar-chewing": Ibid., 5.

117 "The new underworld is": Ibid.

117 "This underworld, made up of psychologists": Ibid., 7.

118 Pool wanted to predict: Ithiel de Sola Pool, Robert P. Abelson, and Samuel Popkin, *Candidates, Issues & Strategies: A Computer Simulation of the 1960 and 1964 Presidential Elections* (Cambridge, MA: MIT Press, 1964), 19.

118 compiling sixty-six pre-election polls: Ibid., 14.

118 "The Presidential election of 1960": Ibid., 15.

119 his interest in how people made consumer decisions: Jean M. Converse, *Survey Research in the US: Roots & Emergence, 1890–1960* (Berkeley: University of California Press, 1987), 136.

119 A major project was panel studies: Peter H. Rossi, "Four Landmarks in Voting Research," in *American Voting Behavior,* ed. Eugene Burdick and Arthur J. Brodbeck (Glencoe, IL: Free Press, 1959), 15.

119 "the psychology of choice": Larry M. Bartels, "The Study of Electoral Behavior," in *The Oxford Handbook of American Elections and Political Behavior,* ed. Jan E. Leighley (New York: Oxford University Press, 2010), 239.

120 "For many voters political preferences": Bernard R. Berelson, Paul F. Lazarsfeld, and William N. McPhee, *Voting: A Study of Opinion Formation in a Presidential Campaign* (Chicago: University of Chicago Press, 1954), 310.

121 "The lifelong Democrat": Pool, Abelson, and Popkin, *Candidates, Issues & Strategies,* 12.

122 "the consequences of embitterment": Thomas B. Morgan, "The People-Machine," *Harper's,* January 1961.

122 each copy numbered: Burdick, *The 480,* 7.

122 Inside was a ranking of thirty-two: Ithiel de Sola Pool and Robert Abelson, "The Simulmatics Project," *Public Opinion Quarterly* 25 (Summer 1961): 169–83.

123 Pool calculated that Simulmatics' state rankings: Pool, Abelson, and Popkin, *Candidates, Issues & Strategies,* 57.

123 "This is the A-bomb of the social sciences": Morgan, "The People-Machine."

123 "We did not use the machine": Quoted in "Top Aides Deny It: 'Brain' Assist Seen in Kennedy Campaign," United Press International, *Los Angeles Times,* December 19, 1960.

124 In 1974, computer scientist Jonathan Robbin: Michael J. Weiss, *The Clustering of America* (New York: Harper & Row, 1988), xii.

124 customer surveys and block-level Census data: "Getting and Sending the Message," *National Journal,* November 14, 1981.

124 Robbin's computers assigned each ZIP code: Weiss, *The Clustering of America,* 4–5.

124 "King of the Zip Codes": Ibid., xii.

124 his clustering system could be used for politics: Ibid., 217.

125 "The campaign was so carefully targeted": Quoted ibid., 218.

126 "In 1987, the conventional labels": Norman Ornstein, Andrew Kohut, and Larry McCarthy, *The People, the Press, & Politics: The Times Mirror Study of the American Electorate* (Reading, MA: Addison-Wesley, 1988).

126 By the end of the 1980s: David Beiler, "Precision Politics; Technology and Circumstance Are Pushing Voter Files into the Driver's Seat of the Campaign Bandwagon, but Who's Got the Keys?," *Campaigns & Elections,* February–March 1990.

127 A two-page summary of Claritas's "Downtown Dixie-Style": Weiss, *The Clustering of America,* 377.

128 In 1969, an Arkansas school bus manufacturer: "About Acxiom: Timeline & History," www.acxiom.com/about_us/overview/milestones/Pages /1969-1979.aspx.

128 Charles Ward had decided: Robert O'Harrow Jr., *No Place to Hide* (New York: Free Press, 2005), 38.

128 took the Acxiom name in 1988: "About Acxiom: Timeline & History."

129 Between 1983 and 2004: O'Harrow, *No Place to Hide,* 43.

131 the state's nearly two million independents: "Elections: Massachusetts Registered Voter Enrollment: 1948–2004," Massachusetts Secretary of State Elections Division, www.sec.state.ma.us/ele/eleenr/enridx.htm.

139 the president's national approval jumped: Eric Dienstfrey, "US: Bush Approval Avg (Gallup 2001–2008)," Pollster.com, www.pollster.com/blogs/us_bush_approval_avg_gallup200.php?nr=1.

141 The front flap featured: "In the 11th Hour, Political Accusations Through the Mail," graphic, *New York Times,* October 30, 2004.

141 When Bush had run an ad in March: Paul Farhi, "Bush Ads Using 9/11 Images Stir Anger," *Washington Post,* March 5, 2004.

142 The story noted: Thomas B. Edsall and James V. Grimaldi, "On Nov. 2, GOP Got More Bang for Its Billion, Analysis Shows," *Washington Post,* December 30, 2004.

⑥ GEEKS VERSUS THE GURUS

144 Podhorzer expected to have an election-year budget: Steven Greenhouse, "A.F.L.-C.I.O. Plans to Spend $44 Million to Unseat Bush," *New York Times,* March 11, 2004.

147 the wealthy neophyte enlisted: Susan B. Glasser, "Winning a Stake in a Losing Race; Ad Commissions Enriched Strategists," *Washington Post,* May 1, 2000.

156 a 1972 CBS News report: *CBS Evening News,* January 18, 1972, www.youtube.com/watch?v=9HPnW4EBed4.

157 In June 2002, a Senate staffer: Elisabeth Bumiller, "Red Faces in White House Over '02 Analysis," *New York Times,* June 14, 2002.

161 A *Washington Post* analysis of the $2.2 billion: Edsall and Grimaldi, "On Nov. 2, GOP Got More Bang for Its Billion."

165 As a junior physics major at Princeton: John Aristotle Phillips and David Michaelis, *Mushroom: The Story of the A-Bomb Kid* (New York: Morrow, 1978), 19.

165 In 1983, their Aristotle Industries released: Scott Barancik, "Corporate Vigilante," *Washington City Paper,* June 7, 1996.

169 In 1956, engineer Bill Fair: Eric Belsky and Allegra Calder, "Credit Matters: Low-Income Asset Building Challenges in a Dual Financial Service System," Joint Center for Housing Studies of Harvard University, BABC 04-1, February 2004.

169 able to cut delinquencies by one-quarter: Hollis Fishelson-Holstine, "The Role of Credit Scoring in Increasing Homeownership for Underserved Populations," Joint Center for Housing Studies of Harvard University, BABC 04-12, February 2004.

170 In 1989, the company introduced: Ibid.

170 "Copernicus took individuals out of the center": Quoted in Yochi J. Dreazen, "Democrats, Playing Catch-up, Tap Database to Woo Potential Voters," *Wall Street Journal,* October 31, 2006.

171 Capital One was the first credit-card company: Thomas H. Davenport and Jeanne G. Harris, *Competing on Analytics: The New Science of Winning* (Boston: Harvard Business School Press, 2007), 41.

177 Throughout 2004, a Democratic consultant: Matt Bai, *The Argument: Billionaires, Bloggers, and the Battle to Remake Democratic Politics* (New York: Penguin Press, 2007), 23.

178 who had each given $20 million: Ibid., 9.

179 Already the company ran nearly fifty thousand experiments: Dan Gross, "What's in Capital One's Wallet?," *Slate,* October 25, 2002, www.slate.com /id/2073179/.

⑦ WHEN SHAME PAYS A HOUSE CALL

183 Bazerman had just published an article: K. M. O'Connor, C. K. W. deDreu, H. Schroth, B. Barry, T. Lituchy, and M. H. Bazerman, "What We Want to Do versus What We Think We Should Do," *Journal of Behavioral Decision Making* 15, no. 5 (August 2002): 403–18.

187 Cialdini had found repeatedly: R. B. Cialdini, R. R. Reno, and C. A. Kallgren, "A Focus Theory of Normative Conduct: Recycling the Concept of Norms to Reduce Littering in Public Places," *Journal of Personality and Social Psychology* 58 (1990): 1015–26.

190 "self-expressive social behavior": Todd Rogers, Alan Gerber, and Craig Fox, "Rethinking Why People Vote: Voting as Dynamic Social Expression," in *The Behavioral Foundations of Policy,* ed. Eldar Shafir (Princeton, NJ: Princeton University, in press).

193 Their work relies on an unusual data set: Raymond E. Wolfinger and Steven J. Rosenstone, *Who Votes?* (New Haven, CT: Yale University Press, 1980), 4.

193 The Census Department's Current Population Survey questions: "Short History of the CPS," Bureau of Labor Statistics and the Bureau of the Census, accessed via www.census.gov/history/www/programs/demographic/current_population_survey.html.

193 a rolling panel of fifty-six thousand households: "Current Population Survey: Design and Methodology," Technical Paper 63RV, U.S. Department of Labor and U.S. Department of Commerce, March 2002.

193 So they started matching respondents: John P. Katosh and Michael W. Traugott, "The Consequences of Validated and Self-Reported Voting Measures," *Public Opinion Quarterly* 45, no. 4 (Winter 1981): 519–35.

196 was designed to gently scold: Donald P. Green and Alan S. Gerber, "Introduction to Social Pressure and Voting: New Experimental Evidence," *Political Behavior* 32, no. 3 (2010): 331–36.

196 "Why do so many people fail to vote?": Alan S. Gerber, Donald P. Green, and Christopher W. Larimer, "Social Pressure and Voter Turnout: Evidence from a Large-Scale Field Experiment," *American Political Science Review* 102 (February 2008): 33–48.

197 the idea of "norm compliance": Cialdini et al., "A Focus Theory of Normative Conduct."

204 "the message does not seem to matter much": Donald P. Green and Alan S. Gerber, *Get Out the Vote! How to Increase Voter Turnout,* 1st ed. (Washington, DC: Brookings Institution, 2004), 36.

204 average 8-percentage-point boost from in-person canvasses: Allison Dale and Aaron Strauss, "Don't Forget to Vote: Text Message Reminders as a Mobilization Tool," *American Journal of Political Science* 53, no. 4 (October 2009): 787–804.

204 "Face-to-face interaction makes politics": Green and Gerber, *Get Out the Vote!,* 41.

204 "To mobilize voters, you must": Ibid., 92.

205 Rogers described an experiment that he and Gerber: Todd T. Rogers, "Experiments in Political Communications: Citizenship Behavior and Political Decision Making," Ph.D. diss., Department of Organizational Behavior and Psychology, Harvard University, 2008.

210 They knew that personal contact was almost always: Summarized in *Young Voter Mobilization Tactics: A Compilation of the Most Recent Research on Traditional & Innovative Voter Turnout Techniques,* Center for Information and

Research on Civic Learning and Engagement (CIRCLE) and Young Voter Strategies, George Washington University Graduate School of Political Management.

210 Green drove up to Hooksett: Donald P. Green and Alan S. Gerber, *Get Out the Vote: How to Increase Voter Turnout,* 2nd ed. (Washington, DC: Brookings Institution, 2008), 111.

211 boozy men's-only events: Elizabeth Addonizio, Donald Green, and James M. Glaser, "Putting the Party Back into Politics: An Experiment Testing Whether Election Day Festivals Increase Voter Turnout," *Political Science & Politics* 40 (2007): 722.

⑧ SHOWDOWN AT THE OASIS

216 While Dole dominated news coverage: Gerald M. Boyd, E. J. Dionne Jr., and Bernard Weinraub, "Bush vs. Dole: Behind the Turnaround," *New York Times,* March 17, 1988.

217 Carney put a plaque: John Aloysius Farrell, "Pomposity Eludes N.H. Aide to Bush," *Boston Globe,* March 20, 1991.

217 Bush adviser Mary Matalin called Carney: "Trio Have Backed Governor for Years," *San Antonio Express-News,* October 23, 2006.

219 The neighborhood surrounding Carney's office: Matea Gold, "Alexandria, Va., Hosts a Quiet Hub of Republican Power," *Los Angeles Times,* January 20, 2011.

226 Rove had dropped out: Nicholas Lemann, "The Controller," *The New Yorker,* May 12, 2003.

230 The trip triggered an ethics investigation: R. G. Ratcliffe, "Perry travel paid for by others," *Texas Politics* blog, *San Antonio Express-News* and *Houston Chronicle,* July 26, 2009, blog.mysanantonio.com/texas-politics/2009/07 /perry-travel-paid-for-by-others.

233 Strayhorn stood at an Austin high school: Gardner Selby, "Strayhorn to Run as Independent," *Austin American-Statesman,* January 3, 2006.

237 political scientists believed they could explain all presidential elections: Daron R. Shaw, *The Race to 270: The Electoral College and the Campaign Strategies of 2000 and 2004* (Chicago: University of Chicago Press, 2006), 22.

237 An average of seven academic election-forecasting models: Christopher Wlezien, "On Forecasting the Presidential Vote," *Political Science and Politics* 34, no. 1 (March 2001): 24–31.

237 responded by adjusting the economic indicators: Larry M. Bartels and John Zaller, "Presidential Vote Models: A Recount," *Political Science and Politics* 34, no. 1 (March 2001): 9–20.

238 "While experiments allow researchers to isolate the influence": Daron R. Shaw, "The Effect of TV Ads and Candidate Appearances on Statewide Presidential Votes, 1988–96," *American Political Science Review* 93, no. 1 (June 1999): 345–61.

239 "I think people are finally starting": Brittany Barrientos, "Perry Begins Campaign Trail in Texas Tech Area," *Daily Toreador,* January 11, 2006.

240 "It wasn't until that moment": Quoted in Charles T. Royer, ed., *Campaign for President: The Managers Look at '92* (Hollis, NH: Hollis, 1994), 266.

⑨ MODELS AND THE MATRIX

251 the three dozen field offices it eventually opened: John McCormick, "No. 37 in Iowa for Obama Offices," *Swamp Politics* blog, *Chicago Tribune,* www .swamppolitics.com/news/politics/blog/2007/11/no_37_in_iowa_for _obama_office.html.

254 the state director, Paul Tewes, lobbied Kucinich: David Plouffe, *The Audacity to Win* (New York: Viking, 2009), 127.

256 the share of voters under the age of twenty-five had tripled: Analysis by CIRCLE (the Center for Information & Research on Civic Learning & Engagement), "Revised Estimates Show Higher Turnout Than Expected; Iowa Youth Turnout Rate More Than Triples; 65,000 Iowans Under the Age of Thirty Participate in the Caucuses," January 4, 2008, www.civicyouth.org /PopUps/PR_08_Iowa_turnout_Jan4.pdf.

258 was still finishing his dissertation on robotics: Rahaf Harfoush, *Yes We Did: An Inside Look at How Social Media Built the Obama Brand* (Berkeley, CA: New Riders, 2009), 162.

260 There were the thirteen million people: Craig McLurg, "Inside WebTrends Engage 2009: Obama Data Crunchers," *Web Analytics World,* April 8, 2009, www.webanalyticsworld.net/2009/04/inside-webtrends-engage-2009 -obama-data.html.

261 There were the three million donors: Michael Luo, "Study: Many Obama Small Donors Really Weren't," *The Caucus* blog, *New York Times,* November 24, 2008, thecaucus.blogs.nytimes.com/2008/11/24/study-obamas -small-donors-really-werent/.

265 "Because of you": Barack Obama's Remarks in St. Paul, as provided by CQ Transcriptions, *New York Times,* June 3, 2008, www.nytimes.com/2008/06/03/us/politics/03text-obama.html?pagewanted=all.

265 headquarters in a former Wild Oats natural foods market: Jeff Mapes, "Obama Opens a Mega-Office in Portland," *Jeff Mapes on Politics* blog, *Oregonian,* March 28, 2008, blog.oregonlive.com/mapesonpolitics/2008/03/obama_opens_a_megaoffice_in_po.html.

⑩ THE SOUL OF A NEW MACHINE

272 middle-class, largely white Ellet: "Ellet," Akron Neighborhood Profiles, Department of Planning & Urban Development, City of Akron, ci.akron.oh.us/planning/cp/neighborhoods/Ellet.pdf.

272 one of the city's oldest and most racially mixed neighborhoods: "Middlebury," Akron Neighborhood Profiles, Department of Planning & Urban Development, City of Akron, ci.akron.oh.us/planning/cp/neighborhoods/Middlebury.pdf.

275 including $16 million in online advertising: Kate Kaye, "Google Grabbed Most of Obama's $16 Million in 2008," *ClickZ,* Jan. 6, 2009, www.clickz.com/clickz/news/1703163/google-grabbed-most-obamas-usd16-million-2008.

278 who had grown up in a Missouri trailer park: Ari Berman, *Herding Donkeys: The Fight to Rebuild the Democratic Party and Reshape American Politics* (New York: Farrar, Straus & Giroux, 2010), 38.

279 The professor, Marshall Ganz, had dropped out: Scott Martelle, "Famed Organizer Sees History in the Making," *Los Angeles Times,* June 15, 2008.

279 "politics as marketing": Quoted in Micah L. Sifry, "Marshall Ganz on the Future of the Obama Movement," *TechPresident,* November 20, 2008.

284 cash he considered "Monopoly money": Plouffe, *The Audacity to Win,* 191.

284 In December 2007, Obama's online team decided to test: Dan Siroker, "How Obama Raised $60 Million by Running a Simple Experiment," *The Optimizely* blog, http://blog.optimizely.com/how-obama-raised-60-million-by-running-an-exp.

290 Bird wrote in to say that: Sean Quinn, "On the Road: Big Stone Gap, Virginia," *FiveThirtyEight,* October 25, 2008, www.fivethirtyeight.com/2008/10/on-road-big-stone-gap-virginia.html.

291 One political scientist's later analysis: Daniel J. Hopkins, "No More Wilder Effect, Never a Whitman Effect: When and Why Polls Mislead about Black and Female Candidates," *Journal of Politics* 71, no. 3 (July 2009): 769–81.

291 "It's just a fact of life": Quoted in Wallace Turner, "California G.O.P. Candidate Dismayed by Aide's Racial Comment," *New York Times*, October 9, 1982.

297 "We've been designing and we've been engineering": Quoted in Robert Barnes, "Obama Encourages Early Voting in Ohio," *The Trail* blog, *Washington Post*, October 10, 2008, voices.washingtonpost.com/44/2008/10/obama -encourages-early-voting.html.

EPILOGUE

306 In 1994, the *Dallas Examiner* published: George E. Curry, "How to Increase Black Voter Turnout: Those That Don't Vote Will Be Put on Blast," *District Chronicles*, August 26, 2004.

306 Before the 2006 elections, the *Tennessee Tribune* ran: Costas Panagopoulos, "Affect, Social Pressure and Prosocial Motivation: Field Experimental Evidence of the Mobilizing Effects of Pride, Shame and Publicizing Voting Behavior," *Political Behavior* 32 (2010): 369–86.

307 Ely residents who received the postcard: Ibid., 377.

307 two psychologists found that restaurant servers: Bruce Rind and Prashant Bordia, "Effect of Server's 'Thank You' and Personalization on Restaurant Tipping," *Journal of Applied Social Psychology* 25, no. 9 (May 1995): 745–51.

310 Utah Republican Mike Lee's Senate campaign: Genelle Pugmire, "E-mail from Mike Lee Campaign Puts Voter Privacy in Question," *Daily Herald*, October 19, 2010.

314 The share of the population voting: "Voter Turnout in Presidential Elections: 1828–2008," American Presidency Project, University of California, Santa Barbara, www.presidency.ucsb.edu/data/turnout.php.

319 "these calls were our sincere attempt": Quoted in Paul Kiel, "Nonprofit Women's Voices Women Vote Stops Suspicious N.C. Robo Calls," *Talking Points Memo*, April 30, 2008.

319 "Rube Goldberg-ish": "Clinton, Nixon; Nixon, Clinton," *Democracy in America* blog, *The Economist*, April 30, 2008.

INDEX

A

Abacus Associates, 181, 183
Abelson, Robert, 118, 121
abortion, 115, 133, 139, 140, 161–62,
    261, 267, 293, 296
ACORN, 208, 317
ACT admissions test, 252–53
Acxiom, 115, 128–34, 174–75
affirmative action, 295
AFL-CIO, 92, 143–56, 167, 176, 178,
    179, 264, 292
African Americans, 23, 26, 30, 37, 46,
    47, 64, 86, 118, 122, 172, 174, 257,
    260, 279, 283, 290–98, 305, 307,
    317–21
AFSCME, 150
Alaska, 239, 301
algorithms, 12, 54–55, 115, 130–31,
    132, 135, 140, 171–74, 176,
    247–53, 258–62, 266–71, 274, 283,
    291, 293, 294–95, 297, 298–99

Alper, Jill, 63
Al Qaeda, 105
America Coming Together (ACT), 145,
    153, 167, 175, 176, 178, 277
American Civil Liberties Union
    (ACLU), 51, 55
American Medical Association (AMA),
    44–45
American National Election Studies,
    28–30, 79, 82, 108, 193, 237
American Political Science Review, 23,
    27, 84, 98, 208, 304
American Voter, The (Campbell, et al.),
    30, 31, 120–21
AMPAC, 44–45
Analyst Group, 178–79, 180, 203–8
Analyst Institute, 7–8, 10–11, 178–79,
    205, 306, 308–9, 310, 311–12,
    315–16, 321
Anderson, Curt, 89, 95, 97
Angle, Sharron, 9–10

approval ratings, 139–40, 235, 236, 237, 241
Arceneaux, Kevin, 209, 210
Aristotle Industries, 165–66
Arnold, Jim, 223, 225
Asian Americans, 47, 62
Axelrod, David, 3, 78–79

Barabba, Vince, 41–45
BarackStars, 252–53
Baselice, Mike, 213, 214, 223, 225, 230
"battleground states," 238–39, 246, 269–70, 272–82, 295–96, 319–20
Bazerman, Max, 183–84, 187, 200, 202, 207
Begala, Paul, 34
behavioral psychology, 133, 166, 169–72, 181–87, 190, 195, 197–98, 200–211, 241–42, 303, 321
"Behavioral Science Toolbox, The" (Rogers), 203–5
Bennet, Michael, 1–3, 4, 6
Bennett, Anna, 282–83
Berelson, Bernard, 119, 120
Binder, David, 295–96
bin Laden, Osama, 140–42
Bird, Jeremy, 275–76, 278–82, 288
Blue State Digital, 167, 261
Bonier, Tom, 93, 127
"Bowling Alone: America's Declining Social Capital" (Putnam), 81–82
Bradley, Bill, 92
Bradley, Phillips, 26
Bradley effect, 291–97
Brazile, Donna, 92
Brown, Ron, 89–90
Buchanan, Pat, 139, 217
Buck, Ken, 1–3
Buckley, Ray, 166
Burdick, Eugene, 116–24
bus ads, 272–75
Bush, George H. W., 111, 139, 215–18, 219, 220, 226, 240
Bush, George W., 4–5, 87–89, 93–97, 100, 101, 111, 113–14, 115, 130–31, 132, 136–42, 143–45, 155–56, 158, 162, 174, 175, 201, 221, 224–28, 232, 237–38, 240, 259, 285, 294
Butzke, Jeff, 228, 240

California, 41, 42–43, 44, 54, 110, 147–48, 258, 291
campaign finance reform, 27, 44–45, 53–54, 86, 145, 153, 164, 167, 176, 260–61
campaigns, political:
    academic research in, 5–9, 17, 19, 20, 27, 31, 33, 70–86, 98, 108–10, 118–19, 153, 181, 183, 193, 196, 198, 200, 202, 206–9, 214–15, 225–32, 235, 237, 262, 264, 282, 302–3, 312
    budgets for, 25–26, 29, 31, 48, 52–53, 60, 66–67, 83, 85, 98–99, 110–11, 128, 133–34, 144, 145, 148, 163–64, 174–75, 211, 217–24, 228, 229–30, 233–39, 248, 265–69, 284–89, 317
    consumer analysis used in, 112–13, 115, 116, 119–20, 124, 125, 127, 160–62, 169–71, 182, 184–85
    corporate campaigns compared with, 4, 6, 112–13, 116, 127, 128–29, 130, 168, 169–71, 174–75
    databases used in, 22–25, 27, 29, 30–31, 42–43, 47–48, 55–56, 59–60, 65, 66, 68–69, 72, 90–91, 98, 99–100, 109–13, 116–24, 129–31, 137–38, 144, 148–49, 150, 156–58, 159, 162, 165–68, 174–75, 179, 194–200, 206–7, 236–39, 243–67, 270, 274–76, 279–84, 290–91, 295, 298–301, 305, 309–11, 317–19
    direct mailings in, 2–3, 6–8, 25–26, 27, 45, 50, 51–54, 55, 58–59, 60, 61, 62–63, 64, 67, 80, 83, 85, 96–97, 98, 99, 102–6, 125, 132, 133, 134, 137, 138, 140–42, 147, 153, 154, 157, 158–59, 166, 174, 188, 195–200, 202, 204, 210–23, 225, 228, 232, 233, 241, 251, 253, 261, 263, 264, 274, 279,

284–85, 294, 296, 297–99, 303–21

marketing techniques in, 2, 4, 5, 8, 11–13, 87, 105–16

media coverage of, 2, 5, 8, 11–13, 26–27, 87, 98–99, 156–57, 199, 229, 251, 257, 319

outside vendors used by, 217–18, 221–24, 229–30, 261–62

paid workers of, 98, 101, 210

phone outreach by, 27, 37, 39, 45, 59, 66, 67, 80, 82–83, 85, 87–88, 91, 98, 102–3, 104, 105–6, 110, 114, 132, 134–35, 136, 137, 153, 154, 174, 176, 186, 196, 198, 204, 205, 208, 210, 211, 215, 216, 219, 223, 228, 230, 232, 245–49, 253, 260, 263, 266–69, 271, 273, 274, 281–88, 292, 298, 299–300, 305–6, 318, 319

polls and surveys analyzed by, 37–38, 58, 60, 79, 87, 88, 108–11, 117, 118, 120–21, 129–31, 143, 144, 151–55, 174, 180, 182, 193–94, 204, 205–6, 213–14, 219, 226–27, 235–36, 240, 241, 247, 250, 252, 258–59, 264, 268–70, 276–77, 282–83, 287–301, 305, 309, 313–14

randomized-control experiments conducted in, 7–10, 12, 22–27, 65, 73–77, 98, 134, 154–55, 171, 187–90, 206–7, 218, 228–29, 232–34, 238, 239–40, 264, 282–85, 287, 303, 307–8, 314, 317, 319

segmentation used by, 116–24, 131–39

statistical analysis used for, 5, 12, 27–28, 54–56, 59–63 72, 108–11, 115, 118–19, 121–33, 135, 138–39, 140, 142, 146, 159–61, 162, 164, 169–74, 175, 176, 180, 189–90, 194–200, 236–39, 247–53, 258–74, 276, 280, 283, 290–99, 302, 305, 318, 319

volunteers used by, 41, 59, 88, 99, 101, 102–4, 132, 136–39, 186–89, 215, 248, 257–58, 262–64, 288–89, 300–301, 309

see also elections, political; elections, U.S.

Campbell, Angus, 28, 29–30, 31, 120–21

Capital One, 170–71, 179

Carnegie Corporation, 85–86

Carney, Dave, 4, 212–34, 240–41

Carson, Jon, 256–57, 258, 260, 262, 287

Carter, Jimmy, 33, 51

Carville, James, 34, 91

Catalist, 174–76, 179, 245, 261, 299

Catholics, 39, 54, 118, 121–22

Caucus Math Tool, 255–56

Census Bureau, U.S., 22–23, 42, 56, 59, 61–62, 90–91, 193, 247–48, 269, 276

Chapman, Amy, 60, 62, 63

Chávez, César, 279

Checchi, Al, 147–48

Cheney, Dick, 73–74

Chicago, 15–27, 28, 46, 123, 243–44, 256, 260

Chi-Square Automatic Interaction Detector (CHAID), 55–57, 60–63, 65, 66–67, 69, 159

Christian fundamentalists, 97–98, 102, 114, 128, 130, 132–33, 259

Christie, Chris, 308

Cialdini, Robert, 182, 185, 186–87, 197, 207

Citizen Action, 149, 150

Civil Rights Act (1964), 30, 47

civil rights movement, 30, 46, 47, 118, 279

Claritas Cluster System, 124–27, 128, 159

Clark, Wesley, 186–89

Clean Skies Initiative, 138

Clinton, Bill, 34, 56, 57, 63, 65, 81, 90–92, 96, 139, 148, 151, 163, 164, 165, 167, 217–18, 240, 309

Clinton, Hillary, 96, 148, 177, 202–3, 251, 254, 256, 260, 261, 264–65, 269, 286, 311, 319

Coleman, Norm, 10–11

College Republican National Committee, 157, 226

Colorado, 1–3, 5, 6, 52–53, 217–18
Columbia University, 119–21
Committee for the Re-Election of the
    President, 156–57
Congress, U.S., 1–3, 4, 6, 9–11, 20,
    43–44, 46, 52, 53, 55, 56–63,
    67–68, 77–78, 89, 90, 96, 97–98,
    100, 108, 149–51, 174, 179,
    196–204, 215, 223, 227, 309
Connecticut, 70–86, 98, 165, 228, 302,
    314, 315
"Conservative Message Machine's
    Money Matrix, The" (Stein),
    177–78
consideration index, 131–32
Consortium of Behavioral Scientists,
    200–203
Constitution, U.S., 82, 164, 191
Copernicus Analytics, 170–74
Corzine, Jon, 308
credit scores, 169–71, 176–77
Cuban Missile Crisis (1962), 117

D

Daily Kos, 290
Daily Toreador, 239
Dallas Examiner, 306
Datamatics, 42–44
Dean, Howard, 143, 167, 177, 178, 186,
    249–52, 253, 259, 261
Dees, Morris, 50–51
DeFazio, Peter, 57, 61
Delisi, Deirdre, 229, 232, 238
Democratic Advisory Council, 119
Democratic Congressional Campaign
    Committee, 209
Democratic National Committee
    (DNC), 40, 41, 48, 55, 63, 65, 69,
    89–91, 96, 114, 118–19, 121–22,
    124, 127, 128, 144–77, 209, 232,
    261, 299, 309
Democratic National Convention:
    of 1960, 121
    of 2004, 189–90
Democratic Party, 1–3, 5, 9–10, 30,
    31–32, 38–40, 41, 43–44, 46–48,
    54, 55, 56–58, 60, 62, 63, 65–69,
    72, 86, 88, 89–93, 94, 95, 96, 102,

114, 118–19, 121–22, 124, 126, 127,
    128, 133, 135, 141–77, 189–92,
    200–204, 209, 232, 233, 235, 252,
    261, 265, 269, 277, 293, 299, 305,
    309, 313, 320
DeShong, Debra, 156–57, 161–62
Detroit News, 199
Deukmejian, George, 291
Dewey, Thomas E., 28–29, 80–81,
    120
Dewey Square Group, 159
Dodd, Chris, 81
Dole, Bob, 216, 227
Dorgan, Byron, 202–3
Dowd, Matthew, 87, 88, 93–99, 105–6,
    113, 115, 119, 131–39
Dukakis, Michael, 249
Dunn, Alex, 116

E

economic issues, 25, 27, 31, 43, 72, 73,
    79, 81, 86, 91, 125, 132, 139,
    155–56, 180, 193, 201, 237–38,
    244, 249, 293–94, 296, 297, 317,
    319
education, 30–31, 50, 52, 61–62, 91,
    102, 132, 140
Edwards, John, 249–50, 251, 254, 260,
    286
"Effects of Canvassing . . . ," (Gerber
    and Green), 84–86
Eisenhower, Dwight D., 30, 31
Eldersveld, Samuel, 27, 119
election day, 46–47, 78, 80, 87–89,
    91–92, 96, 102–3, 188–89,
    193–94, 205–6, 210–11, 228, 291,
    293, 297, 299, 300–301
elections, political:
    absentee ballots in, 10–11, 56,
        299
    base vote in, 91–92, 100–101
    for city council, 25–26
    congressional, 1–3, 4, 6, 9–11, 20,
        43–44, 46, 52, 53, 55, 56–63,
        67–68, 77–78, 89, 90, 96, 97–98,
        100, 108, 149–51, 174, 179,
        196–204, 215, 223, 227, 309
    direct, 20

electoral college in, 34, 91, 118, 122, 131, 227, 238
forecasts and predictions for, 10, 28–29, 41, 48, 74, 80–81, 115, 116, 118, 120, 122, 129–30, 132, 133, 144, 161–62, 169–73, 196, 206, 237, 244, 248–50, 253–54, 258–62, 266, 269–71, 274, 281–83, 289–97, 305, 316–19
gubernatorial, 7–8, 42, 53, 54, 100, 101, 114, 131–32, 147–48, 152–53, 172–74, 189–90, 205–6, 213–15, 221–25, 226, 228–41, 291, 305, 307–8
for House of Representatives, 43–44, 46, 55, 77–78, 89, 90, 97–98, 108, 149–51, 174, 179, 196–204, 227, 309
judicial, 132
legislative, 20, 43, 47, 51–52, 110, 131
mayoral, 18–19
media coverage of, 28, 34, 306–7
municipal, 18–19, 25–26, 208, 210–11, 304, 307–8
popular vote in, 95, 151, 237–38
presidential, 4–5, 16, 30, 31, 36, 37, 38–39, 40, 51, 82, 89–94, 109, 116–24, 154, 158, 217, 218, 219, 226, 237, 240, 244–46, 251–301; *see also specific candidates*
primaries in, 19, 38–39, 56, 57, 89, 92, 131, 148, 159–60, 186–89, 195–205, 217, 231–39, 244–46, 251–65, 282, 290, 311
recounts in, 5, 10–11
referendums in, 9–10, 124
secret ballots in, 78, 210, 313–14, 316, 320–21
for Senate, 1–3, 4, 6, 9–11, 20, 52, 53, 56–63, 67–68, 96, 100, 215, 223
see also voters, voting
elections, U.S.:
of 1840, 40–41
of 1896, 20
of 1901, 18–19
of 1904, 16
of 1907, 20
of 1911, 19
of 1924, 41
of 1948, 28–29
of 1952, 28, 29
of 1957, 53
of 1960, 36, 38–39, 82, 116–24, 239, 277
of 1964, 40, 41, 47, 106, 117
of 1965, 43
of 1966, 42, 43–44
of 1968, 100–101, 109
of 1969, 44
of 1972, 30, 31–32, 37, 108–9, 156–57, 226
of 1974, 47
of 1976, 32–33, 51
of 1978, 215, 222
of 1980, 89, 126, 148, 165
of 1982, 52, 291
of 1984, 58, 89, 94, 126
of 1988, 82, 90, 215–16, 249
of 1992, 34, 90–91, 168, 199, 217–18, 219, 240
of 1993, 223
of 1994, 55, 97–98, 149, 151
of 1996, 56–63, 91–92, 149–51
of 1998, 66, 89, 147–48, 157–58, 177, 221–25, 230, 231
of 2000, 4–5, 87–89, 92–100, 101, 115, 134, 145, 158, 227, 237–38
of 2002, 104–5, 114–16, 131, 153, 157–58, 213–14, 221, 228, 229, 230, 231
of 2003, 132
of 2004, 92–100, 105, 113–14, 115, 136–42, 143, 144, 145–47, 154–56, 157, 158–62, 165, 167, 168, 178, 186–89, 195–96, 248–52, 277, 297
of 2005, 172–74
of 2006, 179, 196–205, 214–15, 228–41, 245, 306–7
of 2008, 10–11, 68, 244–46, 251–301, 306, 309, 311, 313, 318–19
of 2009, 7–8, 9, 307–8
of 2010, 1–3, 5, 6, 9, 47, 309, 311, 313
of 2012, 310, 313, 316–17
Electoral College, 34, 91, 118, 122, 131, 227, 238

EMILY's List, 146, 154, 167, 209
Energy Department, U.S., 310–11
environmental issues, 138, 140, 155,
     180, 184, 185, 218, 261
Experian, 174–75
exurbs, 100, 173, 174, 281

Fail-Safe (Burdick and Wheeler), 117
Fair, Bill, 169–70
Fairey, Shepard, 288–89
Fannie Mae, 170
Federal Bureau of Investigation (FBI),
     165
Federal Democrats, 174
FICO score, 170
Fisher, R. A., 74–75
Florida, 5, 88, 95, 100, 299
focus groups, 151–52, 154–55, 272,
     295–96
Ford, Gerald R., 32–33, 109
480, The (Burdick), 116–24
Fox, Craig, 200, 201, 202
Fox News Channel, 178, 304
Franken, Al, 10–11
Freakonomics (Levitt and Dubner), 78
Freddie Mac, 170
Freeman, Judith, 150–51, 207, 264
Friedman, Kinky, 233, 235
Fusion system, 159

Gage, Alexander, 5, 105–16, 128–35,
     138, 140–42, 158, 159, 160, 161,
     162, 169, 213
Gallup polls, 126
game theory, 71–72, 148–49, 183–84,
     255
Gardner, Page, 304–6, 310, 312–21
gay issues, 142, 249, 257, 294, 304
Gephardt, Dick, 78–79, 249–50
Gerber, Alan, 72, 73–86, 98, 154, 171,
     179–80, 187, 189, 195–98, 200,
     204–15, 226, 228, 229, 231, 232,
     302–4, 309, 313–16, 320–21
Gersh, Mark, 65–66, 247, 248
Get Out the Vote! (Green and Gerber),
     195–96, 208–9, 212–13, 231

get-out-the-vote (GOTV) operations,
     26, 45–48, 59–60, 63, 66, 74, 86,
     87–89, 91, 97, 127–28, 154–55,
     173–74, 188–89, 192–96, 208–9,
     212–13, 231, 244–46, 253–54, 268,
     288–89, 300–301, 303–4, 307
Getting Out the Vote (Gosnell), 26, 74,
     86
Giangreco, Pete, 251, 253, 271
Gimpel, James, 227–28, 229, 232, 242
Gingrich, Newt, 55, 56
global warming, 155, 180, 184
GMMB, 274–75
Goethals, Al, 182–83
Goldwater, Barry, 41
Goldwater, Barry, Jr., 44
Goodstein, Scott, 285–89
Gore, Al, 52, 58, 68–69, 88, 92–93, 96,
     148, 155, 158, 159, 162, 237–38
Gosnell, Harold Foote, 15–27, 74
Gray, Adrian, 5, 97, 133
Grebner, Mark, 6–8, 190–200, 204–5,
     210, 303–8, 315, 320
Green, Don, 70–86, 98, 154, 171, 179,
     187, 195–200, 204–15, 226–36,
     302–3, 306, 309, 315
Gregg, Judd, 215
Grisolano, Larry, 246–47, 251, 275,
     282, 284, 287–88
gross rating points (GRPs), 234–39
gun owners, 102, 114, 129, 162, 172–73,
     293, 296

Haig, Al, 216
Hanna, Mark, 94
Hansen, John Mark, 82, 83
Harrison, William Henry, 40–41
Hart, Gary, 168
Hart, Peter, 37–38, 272
Harvard Business School, 183–85,
     189
Hatfield, Mark, 56, 67–68
Hawking, Stephen, 69
Hawthorne Works, 197, 200
Hazelwood, Blaise, 95–106, 137,
     158
health care, 75–77, 112, 293

Help America Vote Act (2002), 245
Henry, Mike, 172, 174
Hesla, Maren, 146, 161, 178–79
Hill, Austin Bradford, 75–77
Hispanic Americans, 32–33, 47, 94, 97, 140, 158, 161–62, 224, 277, 305, 319–20
Holcombe, A. N., 23–24
Hookset, N.H., 210–11, 212
House of Representatives, U.S., 43–44, 46, 55, 77–78, 89, 90, 97–98, 108, 149–51, 174, 179, 196–204, 227, 309
Huffines, James, 225–26
Hutchison, Kay Bailey, 214, 223

Ickes, Harold, 175–77
InfoUSA, 166, 174–75
Internet, 9–10, 162, 164, 166, 167, 261, 268, 278, 284, 285, 295, 298–99, 301
Iowa, 12, 159–60, 188, 244–45, 249–63, 269, 285, 291–93, 299–300, 303, 307
Iraq War, 252, 286
Isaac, Earl, 169–70

Jackson, Jesse, 90
Jarrett, Ted, 138, 141
Jester, Danny, 264–65
Jewish Americans, 47, 54, 122
Johnson, Lyndon B., 36, 37, 40, 73
Judson, Harry Pratt, 18, 24

Kahneman, Daniel, 33, 201
Kaine, Tim, 172–74
Kennedy, Edward M., 89, 90, 148
Kennedy, John F., 36, 38–39, 116–24
Kennedy, Patrick, 201
Kennedy, Robert F., 117, 121, 122, 279
Kerry, John, 141–42, 143, 144, 145–47, 148, 158, 159–60, 167, 176, 178, 186, 201, 248–52, 256, 259, 262, 274, 293–94

King, Martin Luther, Jr., 64
Kucinich, Dennis, 254

"Labor '96" program, 92, 149–51
labor unions, 43–44, 47, 67, 89–92, 96, 97, 115, 125, 137, 143–56, 162, 163, 167, 176, 205, 279
Lackey, Matt, 258, 282
Lake, Celinda, 91, 146, 313
Larimer, Christopher, 197–98
Lasswell, Harold, 119, 123
Latinos, 32–33, 47, 94, 97, 140, 158, 161–62, 224, 277, 305, 319–20
Lazarsfeld, Paul, 119–20
League of Conservation Voters, 154, 174
League of Women Voters, 26, 81–82, 316
Levitt, Steven, 77–78, 243–44
Lieberman, Joe, 148
Limbaugh, Rush, 178, 269
Lincoln, Abraham, 40–41
Lindenfeld, Tom, 84–85
Link, Jeff, 246, 255
Live with Regis and Kelly, 235
Looper, Kevin, 151–52
Los Angeles, 43, 44

McAuliffe, Terry, 161, 162–67, 177
McCain, John, 115, 259, 261, 264–66, 267, 270–71, 282, 293–96, 301
McCain-Feingold Act (2002), 164
McGovern, George, 31–32, 37
McGreevey, James, 152–53
Mackie, John C., 43–44
Mackinac Republican Leadership Conference, 105–6, 113
McKinley, William, 94
McPhee, William, 118–19, 120
Mahe, Eddie, Jr., 125, 126, 164–65
Maine, 88, 165, 291–92
Malchow, Harold, 2–3, 6, 9, 11, 36–38, 48–69, 146, 154, 159–61, 162, 209, 247, 303–21
Manchester *Union Leader,* 210–11
Mann, Christopher, 64, 85

Market Opinion Research, 107–11
Market Strategies, 111–12
Massachusetts, 115–16, 131–32, 185
Matalin, Mary, 217
Matrix, 263–64, 281
Mayo Clinic, 75–76
Media Matters for America, 178
Mehlman, Ken, 134, 157–58
Mellman, Mark, 9–10, 58, 79, 128, 152, 264
Mencken, H. L., 26
Merriam, Charles E., 18–27, 119
Meyers, Michael, 114, 137–38
Michigan, 6–7, 27, 28, 32, 43–44, 79, 82, 107, 108, 111–14, 115, 120–21, 128, 130, 132, 137–38, 190–200, 204, 237, 277, 304, 305, 306, 307, 313, 315
Michigan State University (MSU), 190–91
microtargeting, 8–10, 11, 131–42, 156–62, 166–67, 174–75, 206, 213, 247–48, 252–53, 257, 258–74, 278, 280–82, 293, 297
Midwest Political Science Association, 229–30
military veterans, 293–94
Miller, Warren, 29, 30
Milwaukee, 47, 274–75
Minnesota, 10–11, 136, 137–39, 144, 247, 265
Mississippi, 36–37, 48–56, 317
Mississippi First, 50–56
Mississippi Freedom Democratic Party, 37
Mississippi Gay Alliance, 50
mobile phones, 260–61, 282–89
Moffo, Mike, 265, 283–85, 288, 298, 299, 300
Mondale, Walter, 89
Morris, Dick, 11
Morris, Nigel, 171, 179
MSHC Partners, 311–12
Murphy, Mike, 110, 115
MyBarackObama, 268, 298–99, 301

Napolitan, Joseph, 53
National Association for the Advancement of Colored People (NAACP), 96, 317
National Call Team, 268–71, 300–301
National Committee for an Effective Congress (NCEC), 45–48, 63, 65, 66, 90, 92, 93, 127, 159, 247–48
National Election Studies, 28–30, 79, 82, 108, 193, 237
National Rifle Association (NRA), 114, 173
negative ads, 140–42, 152, 222, 225
Nelson, Terry, 133, 136
Nevada, 9–10, 257, 277, 320
New Hampshire, 78–79, 92, 165, 186–89, 210–11, 212, 215, 220–21, 257, 290
New Haven, Conn., 70–86, 98, 228, 302, 315
New Jersey, 7–8, 152–53, 189–90, 217–18, 308–9
New Kingmakers, The (Chagall), 11, 51
New Organizing Institute, 178, 207
New Style in Election Campaigns, The (Agranoff), 11
New York City, 18–19, 307–8
New York Herald Tribune, 26
New York State, 16, 21, 54
New York Times, 91
Nickerson, David, 179, 208
Nixon, Richard M., 30, 31–32, 36, 47, 100–101, 108–9, 121, 123, 143–44, 156–57, 226, 239
No Child Left Behind program, 140
Non-Voting: Causes and Methods of Control (Gosnell and Merriam), 23–27
North American Free Trade Agreement (NAFTA), 91–92
Norway Hill Associates, 220–21
November Group, 54

Obama, Barack, 1, 12, 244–46, 251–301, 302, 309, 313, 316–21

O'Brien, Lawrence, 38
"O'Brien Manual," 38–39
Office of Economic Opportunity, U.S., 73–74
Office of Radio Research, 119–20
Ohio, 119–20, 144–45, 154–55, 161, 269, 272–82, 288–89, 290, 297–98, 320
openness score, 295–96
Operation Chaos, 269
Oregon, 20, 56–63, 67–68, 110, 131, 159, 265–71, 315–16
Organ, Michael, 284, 285, 288
Our Oregon, 315–16

Ⓟ

Packwood, Bob, 56
Palin, Sarah, 270–71, 297, 301
Panagopoulos, Costas, 306–8
Pathologies of Rational Choice Theory (Green and Shapiro), 72
PATRIOT Act (2001), 140
Penn, Mark, 63, 64, 65, 147–48
Pennsylvania, 103–4, 132–34, 135, 140, 144, 277, 292, 309
People's Choice (Lazarsfeld, et al.), 119–20
Perry, Rick, 5, 12, 213–15, 221–41
Philadelphia, 46, 103, 138
Phillips, John Aristotle, 165–66
PLANET Code, 320
Plouffe, David, 255, 261, 262, 264, 269, 275–76, 284, 291, 297, 299
Podhorzer, Mike, 143–56, 168, 179, 180, 203, 206, 207, 292
political action committees (PACs), 44–45, 81
political science, 15–35, 37, 70–86, 109–11, 181–211, 237, 241–42
politics:
  advertising in, 2, 5, 8, 11–13, 34, 35, 87, 140–42, 152, 222, 225; *see also specific types*
  caucuses in, 90, 135, 159–60, 249–63, 285, 292
  coalitions in, 70–86, 87, 96–98, 100, 102, 104, 134–35, 255

conservative, 1, 3, 9–10, 36, 50, 56–57, 88, 94–98, 100–103, 109, 114, 115, 126, 128, 130, 131, 132–33, 135, 138–44, 145, 154, 157, 177–78, 209–10, 213, 226–27, 259, 268
conventions in, 20, 41, 108, 121, 189–90, 217, 270–71
in democratic system, 20, 25, 38, 72, 81–82, 116
fund-raising in, 19, 25, 27, 44–45, 51–53, 56, 64, 77–78, 94, 128, 157, 163–67, 175–76, 217–18, 223, 230, 239, 241, 242, 246, 255, 257, 260–61, 316
geography of, 46, 47–48, 66, 97, 102, 126–27, 128, 214, 228, 259, 287–88, 298
grassroots organizations in, 70–86, 87, 97–98, 100, 255
identity-based, 89–90, 96, 120–21
liberal, 1, 9–10, 45, 49, 50–51, 56–57, 91–92, 115, 126, 144–45, 200–204, 209–10, 292, 310, 312, 316
loyalties in, 29–30, 42, 47–48, 59–60
media coverage of, 38, 44, 177–78, 208–9, 239, 240–41, 255
organization in, 40–41, 43, 52–53, 95, 164–67, 229, 254–62, 279–80
parties in, 19–20, 21, 26, 27, 29–30, 31, 40–41, 42, 46–47, 59–60, 82, 108, 120, 121, 189–90, 217, 270–71; *see also specific parties*
in precincts, 42–44, 47–48, 59–60, 63, 65–66, 90–91, 97, 102, 104, 108, 114, 127, 134–35, 160, 172, 173, 193–94, 204–5, 213, 227–28, 244–45, 247, 249–50, 255–56, 258, 310
reform of, 20, 27, 44–45, 49, 52, 53–54, 86, 145, 153, 164, 167, 176, 260–61
urban, 16–17, 25, 46, 92, 272–75
volunteers in, 13, 45–46, 88, 186–89, 192, 210, 244–45, 246, 255, 258, 281–82
see also campaigns, political

Pool, Ithiel de Sola, 118, 121–22
Popkin, Samuel, 31–35, 118, 121
Postal Service, U.S., 124, 320
Practical Political Consulting, 198–99
Precinct Index Priority System (PIPS), 42–44
Project Houdini, 300–301
Project Vote, 86
Promise technique, 305–6
Protestants, 39, 118, 121–22
public transportation, 174, 272–75
Punk Voter, 285
Putnam, Robert, 81–82

Q

questionnaires, 22–23, 28, 29, 115, 139–40, 151–52, 266–69
Quinn, Laura, 68, 156–77, 179

R

racism, 260, 290–97
radio advertising, 35, 46, 54, 64, 77, 78, 96, 102, 120, 135, 163–64, 214, 269, 274, 277, 287, 288
Rather, Dan, 156–57
Reagan, Ron, 160
Reagan, Ronald, 42, 43–44, 47, 50, 62, 94, 96, 110, 126, 143–44, 149
Reagan Democrats, 43–44, 62, 143–44
Reasoning Voter, The (Popkin), 33–35
Reese, Matt, 38–40, 41, 48, 89, 124–25, 126
regression analysis, 27–28, 236
Reid, Harry, 9–10, 202–3
religion, 39, 54, 97–98, 102, 114, 118, 120, 121–22, 128, 130, 132–33, 195, 259, 281
Republican National Committee (RNC), 93–116, 134–39, 162, 163–64, 165, 209, 217, 220, 228
Republican National Convention:
of 1992, 217
of 2008, 270–71
Republican Party, 1–3, 5, 9–10, 19–20, 21, 30, 36, 42, 43–44, 46–47, 54, 61, 87–89, 91, 92, 93–116, 117, 122, 126, 128, 129–31, 134–42, 143, 144–47, 155–56, 162, 163–64,

165, 194, 200, 201, 205, 209–28, 233, 237, 241, 251, 253, 259, 261, 264, 269–71, 277, 293, 299, 302, 305, 308, 310
Richardson, Bill, 254–55
Riegle, Don, 43–44
Rising American Electorate, 305, 313
robocalls, 87–88, 154, 210, 214, 232, 292, 305–6, 319
Rock Against Bush, 285
Rockefeller, Nelson, 41
Rock the Vote, 86, 316
Rogers, Todd, 180, 181–90, 200, 201, 202–8, 210, 303
Romney, George, 108
Romney, Mitt, 12, 115–16, 131–32
Roosevelt, Eleanor, 45
Roosevelt, Franklin D., 28, 30
Roosevelt, Theodore, 16
Roper, Elmo, 28–29
Rosenstone, Steven, 82, 83, 193
Rosenthal, Steve, 4, 149–51, 178
Rothamsted Agricultural Experimentation Station, 74–75
Rove, Karl, 5, 87, 93, 99, 134–35, 156–59, 218, 221, 224–27
Ruml, Beardsley, 24–25
Rumsfeld, Donald, 73–74

S

Saenz, Luis, 228, 229
Salinger, Pierre, 123
Salk, Jonas, 77
Seaborn, Brent, 112, 128–31, 137–38
Senate, U.S., 1–3, 4, 6, 9–11, 20, 52, 53, 56–63, 67–68, 96, 100, 215, 223
September 11th attacks (2001), 105, 139–42, 227
Service Employees International Union (SEIU), 96, 310
72–Hour Task Force, 95–96, 99, 105–6, 113–15, 134, 136–39, 158, 209, 227
Sharp, John, 224–25
Shaw, Daron, 226–27, 229, 236–38, 239, 240–41
Shriver, Sargent, 51
Shrum, Bob, 11, 92, 148
Simon, Michael, 262, 263–66, 275–77

Simon, Paul, 78–79
Simulmatics Corp., 119, 121–22, 123
Smith, Adam, 213
Smith, Gordon, 56–57, 67–68
Social Area Analysis, 42
social conservatives, 88, 100–103,
    132–33
social norms, 5–8, 25, 187–89,
    196–200, 303–21
Social Science Research Council, 21
Social Security, 9–10
"soft money," 163, 177–78
Soros, George, 175–76, 178
Stabenow, Debbie, 202–3
Steeper, Fred, 31, 108–10, 111, 112,
    138–39, 140, 268–69
Stein, Rob, 177–78
Steitz, Mark, 90, 168, 169, 170, 172,
    173–74, 179
Stoltz, Gail, 63
Strasma, Ken, 159–61, 247–71, 291–97,
    299
Strategic Telemetry, 248–50, 252
Strayhorn, Carole Keeton, 229–30,
    233–34, 235
Sunstein, Cass, 200–201, 207
Sun Tzu, 213
Sununu, John, 215, 216
super-segmentation, 116, 131–39
supporter cards, 244–46, 252, 255,
    258–59, 299–300
Supreme Court, U.S., 5, 259

TargetPoint Consulting, 161, 169
Tarrance, Lance, 110
Tarrance Group, 133
taxation, 9, 25, 27, 73, 81, 86, 132, 139,
    180, 201, 249, 293–94, 317
Team 270, 262–64
Teeter, Bob, 31, 108–11, 268–69
television advertising, 2, 11, 12–13, 35,
    37, 39, 41, 43, 46, 53, 54, 57, 64,
    66, 77, 96, 120, 123, 132, 134, 148,
    151–52, 163–64, 209, 214, 224, 227,
    229, 230, 233–39, 240, 241–42,
    275, 287–89, 300, 301
Tennessee Tribune, 306–7

Texas, 11, 135–36, 213–14, 221–41, 304
Thaler, Richard, 33, 182, 200–203, 207
Theory of Moral Sentiments, The (Smith),
    213
Thompson, William Hale "Big Bill,"
    19, 22
Thoreau, Henry David, 182
Tower, John, 222
tracking polls, 110, 268–69
Truman, Harry S., 28–29, 80–81, 118,
    120
Tully, Paul, 65, 89–91, 92

Ugly American, The (Burdick and
    Lederer), 117
unemployment rate, 73, 139, 155–56,
    193
University of California, Los Angeles
    (UCLA), 41–42, 200
University of Chicago, 17–27, 123,
    243–44
University of Michigan, 27, 28–30, 79,
    82, 107, 108, 120–21, 193, 237

Vietnam War, 31, 32, 191
Viguerie, Richard, 50, 51, 52, 96–97
Virginia, 46, 54, 100–104, 172–74, 208,
    219–20
Voter Activation Network (VAN),
    244–50, 257, 263–74, 281, 299,
    300
voters, voting:
    absentee ballots of, 10–11, 56, 299
    age for, 82, 191, 320–21
    base, 91–92, 100–101
    behavior of, 24, 120–21, 133, 166,
        169–72, 181–87, 190, 195, 197–98,
        200–211, 241–42, 303, 321
    black, 23, 26, 86, 122, 172, 174, 257,
        260, 279, 283, 290–98, 305, 307,
        317–21
    blocks of, 59, 122–23, 257
    candidate's visits to, 238–42
    canvassers for, 45–46, 56, 59,
        80–86, 92, 99–100, 132, 174, 176,
        186–89, 205–6, 209, 241–42,

voters, voting:
canvassers for (*continued*)
244–45, 248, 250–51, 258, 261,
262–64, 268–71, 280–82, 298,
299, 300–301, 320
as civic duty, 5–8, 25, 81–82,
180–210, 303–21
class background of, 43–44, 47, 62,
120–21, 143–44
crossover, 48, 101–2, 172–74
demographics of, 4, 22–23, 25, 26,
39, 42–43, 46–48, 58, 59, 61–62,
94, 100, 117, 123–28, 144–45,
151–52, 214, 235, 282–89, 290,
293–94, 319–20
early ballots cast by, 298–99
education of, 30–31, 61–62, 91
exit polls for, 87, 97, 256, 305
files on, 47, 112–13, 115, 129, 134,
160–69, 176–78, 193–95, 244–45,
247, 249, 254, 257, 258–59,
262–74, 283, 294, 307
financial information on, 169–71
identification (ID) of, 105–6,
134–35, 176, 244–50, 257, 258,
260, 261, 263–74, 281, 296–97,
299, 300
immigrant, 22, 26, 62, 94
income levels of, 91
independent, 57–58, 61, 62, 114, 118,
122, 131, 132, 133, 135, 217–18,
234, 241, 276, 277
lists of, 60, 163–67, 245
machines for, 41
minority, 23, 26, 32–33, 46, 47, 86,
90, 92, 94, 122, 127, 144–45, 172,
174, 257, 279, 283, 297–98, 305,
307, 317–21
non-, 22–27, 39–40, 192–200, 303,
306–21
planning by, 205–6, 253
population of, 22–23, 42,
56, 59, 61–62, 90–91, 118–19,
193, 247–48, 269, 276, 305,
313–14
psychology of, 3–8, 12, 24, 25,
31–34, 70–72, 81–82, 119–21, 123,
180–210, 275–76, 303–21

rational choice by, 33–34, 70–72,
182, 190, 193–94, 200–204
registration of, 1–3, 12, 22–27,
39–40, 45–48, 59–60, 99, 103–4,
114, 145, 153, 164–67, 193–200,
213, 227–28, 232, 251, 265, 267,
276–77, 297–300, 306–21
rolls of, 6, 39–40, 81, 193–95, 252,
306–21
self-interest of, 70, 193–94
surveys of, 22–23, 27–28, 29, 30–32,
37–38, 109–10, 115, 120, 139–40,
151–55, 158–59, 193–94, 266–69,
282
swing, 30, 43–44, 72–73, 80–81, 91,
94, 126, 138–42, 144, 145, 152,
199–200, 270–71, 282–89, 293,
305, 319–21
tickets split by, 93–94, 109, 224–25,
282
turnout of, 5, 6–8, 22–27, 38–39,
45–48, 56, 80–86, 92–93, 97, 100,
102–3, 104, 113–15, 133, 145–46,
153, 154, 158, 172–74, 180,
181–210, 211, 213, 244, 251,
253–54, 257, 259–60, 270, 274,
276–77, 281, 296, 300–301,
306–10, 313–15, 319–21
types of, 118–24
undecided, 39–40, 56, 60, 61, 62,
268–71
women, 6, 23, 26, 146, 154, 161,
270–71, 305, 318
younger generation of, 252–53, 257,
282–89
Voting (Berelson, Lazarsfeld, and
McPhee), 120

Ⓦ

Wagner, Dan, 243–45, 252, 255–56,
258, 261–62, 277–78, 280–81
Walden (Thoreau), 182
Warner, Mark, 101–3, 172–73
Washington Post, 11, 34, 49, 51, 142,
148, 161, 208, 220
Watergate scandal, 44–45, 46, 53
Weeks, David, 223, 234, 235, 236
welfare reform, 91–92

"What We Want to Do Versus What We Think We Should Do" (Bazerman), 183–84
Whig Party, 40–41, 126
Whitman, Christie Todd, 153
Whouley, Michael, 92–93
Who Votes? (Wolfinger and Rosenstone), 193
Wilson, Woodrow, 18
Winter, William, 50, 52
Wirth, Tim, 52–53
Women's Voices Women's Vote, 6, 304–6, 312–21
Women Vote!, 146
working class, 43–44, 47, 62, 143–44
Wright, Jeremiah, 290

Wszolek, Fred, 114, 138, 142
Wyden, Ron, 56–63, 159

Yale Human Subjects Committee, 197
Yale University, 70–86, 196–200, 208–9, 215, 231, 302
York, Byron, 145
Youth Vote, 208
Yuhas, Ben, 170–72, 173, 174

Zanca, Lauren, 220
ZIP codes, 55–56, 59, 124–25, 127, 128, 172, 175, 284

Also by Sasha Issenberg

"Eminently readable...anecdote-rich and quirky." —*The Wall Street Journal*

"...the evolution of sushi, from fermented goo to fresh global delicacy." —*The New York Times*

THE

SUSHI
ECONOMY

Globalization and the Making
of a Modern Delicacy

SASHA ISSENBERG

A riveting look at sushi's journey
from Japanese street snack to
global delicacy.

AVERY